John Julius Norwich

John Julius Norwich was born in 1929. After National Service, he took a degree in French and Russian at New College, Oxford. He has written histories of Norman Sicily, Venice, Byzantium, the Mediterranean and the Papacy, travel books on Mount Athos and the Sahara, books on music and architecture and a volume of memoirs. His annual anthology, *A Christmas Cracker*, began in 1970 and has become something of an institution. Lord Norwich is former chairman of the Venice in Peril Fund, co-chairman of the World Monuments Fund and a former member of the Executive Committee of the National Trust. He is a Fellow of the Royal Society of Literature, the Royal Geographical Society and the Society of Antiquaries, and a Commendatore of the Ordine al Merito della Repubblica Italiana. He was made a CVO in 1993.

Praise for *Sicily*

'Norwich returns to Sicily with this whistle-stop historical survey: his love for the island imbues every page'   *Sunday Telegraph*

'The most amiable and freewheeling of guides, Norwich will always find room for the amusing anecdote . . . entertaining on every page'
                                                                          Sunday Times

'[A] riotous, thoughtful journey through the island's rich and varied history . . . an entertaining narrative'   *BBC History*

'Norwich is a perfectly informed guide'   *The Week*

'*Sicily* is illuminated by [Norwich's] eye for the telling detail'
                                                                        Country Living

Sicily

A Short History, from the Greeks to Cosa Nostra

JOHN JULIUS NORWICH

JOHN MURRAY

First published in Great Britain in 2015 by John Murray (Publishers)
An Hachette UK Company

First published in paperback in 2016

I

Map drawn by Rodney Paull

A CIP catalogue record for this title is available from the British Library

ISBN 978-1-84854-897-8
Ebook ISBN 978-1-84854-896-1

Typeset in Bembo MT Pro by Palimpsest Book Production Limited,
Falkirk, Stirlingshire

Printed and bound by Clays Ltd, St Ives plc

John Murray policy is to use papers that are natural, renewable and recyclable products and made from wood grown in sustainable forests. The logging and manufacturing processes are expected to conform to the environmental regulations of the country of origin.

John Murray (Publishers)
Carmelite House
50 Victoria Embankment
London EC4Y ODZ

www.johnmurray.co.uk

To all my children and grandchildren

Contents

Preface

⸻

I DISCOVERED SICILY more than half a century ago, almost by mistake. In June 1961 I happened to be working in the Foreign Office on a Middle Eastern desk when Iraq invaded Kuwait. (*Plus ça change . . .*) This created a crisis; Britain sent in troops, and the result was that I got no leave till mid-October. It followed that if my wife and I wanted any sun and warmth we should have to go fairly far south; and for that reason – and that reason only – we decided on Sicily. It would be the first time for both of us, and neither of us knew anything at all about the island. We drove as far as Naples, then put the car on the night ferry to Palermo. There was a degree of excitement in the early hours when we passed Stromboli, emitting a rich glow every half-minute or so like an ogre puffing on an immense cigar; and a few hours later, in the early morning sunshine, we sailed into the Conca d'Oro, the Golden Shell, in which the city lies. Apart from the beauty of the setting, I remember being instantly struck by a change in atmosphere. The Strait of Messina is only a couple of miles across and the island is politically part of Italy, yet somehow one feels that one has entered a different world.

For the next two weeks we explored that world as comprehensively as we could. To see it all was impossible – the island covers almost exactly 10,000 square miles and most of the roads were still unsurfaced – but we did our best. It was, I think, not only the quality but the extraordinary variety of what we saw that impressed me most: the ancient Greek, then the Roman, the Byzantine, the Arab and finally the baroque; but it was the Normans to whom I lost my heart. I remembered a paragraph in H. A. L. Fisher's *History of Europe* which had given them the briefest of mentions, but I was utterly unprepared for the wonders that awaited me: to mention just two examples, the Palatine Chapel in Palermo, Latin in its ground plan, its walls encrusted with dazzling Byzantine mosaics, its roof purely Arab – a wooden stalactite ceiling of which any mosque would be proud; and, better still, the huge twelfth-century mosaic of Christ Pantocrator at Cefalù, the greatest advertisement for Christianity that I know anywhere on earth.

Once I had seen them, I could not get those Norman monuments out of my mind, and on our return to London I made a beeline for the London Library. To my astonishment, there was practically nothing in English; I did find, however, two volumes entitled *Histoire de la Domination Normande en Italie et en Sicile*, published in Paris in 1907 by M. Ferdinand Chalandon, who described himself as *archiviste-paléographe*. M. Chalandon had done his work with exemplary thoroughness; he had studied every source, trawled through countless monastic libraries, produced footnotes, bibliographies, even – rare indeed in French books of that date – an index. The only thing he had signally failed to do was to see the point of anything he had written. Fact succeeded fact for about 600 pages; never once was there a suggestion that he found anything beautiful, surprising or especially noteworthy. The result was two volumes of quite stultifying boredom. On the other hand, he had done virtually all the spadework; all I had to do was to make it interesting and readable.

Still, it was a challenge – and, as I saw at once, a full-time job. There was nothing for it but to resign from the Foreign Service and take up my pen in earnest. I have not really laid it down since; but it was my own two volumes on the Norman story that gave me the start I needed. While I was working on them, I was regularly asked their subject; only once did I run across someone who had any idea what I was talking about, and fifty years later I still ask myself the same question: how can it be that such a wonderful rags-to-riches story, involving the very brothers and cousins of those Normans who made short work of the English in 1066, is still so little known in England? Nowadays, with so many people going to Sicily for their holidays, the situation is probably a good deal better than it was; but the vast majority of tourists are far more interested in taking photographs than in listening to their guide, so I wouldn't be too sure.

I was still working on the first volume, *The Normans in the South* – it was to be published in 1967 – when I was asked to make a documentary on the subject for BBC Television. Today it seems scarcely believable that it was in black and white; but so it was, and – though not very good – perhaps not too bad for a first effort. Things were not made easy for us. The elderly priest in charge of the Palatine Chapel, Monsignor Pottino, was determined to frustrate us at every turn. First he refused to allow us any lights, on the grounds that they would melt the plaster in which the mosaics were set. We argued that we only needed thirty seconds or so, and the lights would be off again long before the plaster could possibly be affected. Then he looked at our tripod. No no, no tripods in the chapel, they might scratch the floor. We forbore to mention the hundreds of stiletto heels that came in every day, but produced a device called a stretcher into which the tripod legs were set, leaving only a smooth surface to touch the floor. Unimpressed, Monsignor Pottino continued to shake his head; never was there a word of apology, or a suggestion of a smile. At this point our director, who spoke beautiful Italian, lost his head. 'This man,' he said to my acute embarrassment, pointing to me as he spoke, 'is a viscount. He is consequently a member of the House of Lords. When he returns to London he will report to the House on the way in which he has been treated.' Monsignor Pottino looked at him pityingly. '*Io sono marchese*,'* was all he said. It was game, set and match: we knew that we were beaten.

That Monsignor was the only really unpleasant Sicilian I have ever met; but nowhere on the island, it seems to me, does one meet with the sheer unbridled jollity of the mainland. And there is something else immediately noticeable, particularly in the villages: the curious absence of women. They are seldom seen in the cafés; these are entirely dominated by men, who when they are playing cards hurl each card down on the table as if it were the decisive ace of spades and their life depended on it. Laughter is seldom

* 'I am a marquis.'

heard. I sometimes wonder if this might not be partly due to Sicily's Islamic past, but there are many other possible factors to be taken into account: the centuries of appalling poverty, the endless conquests and frequent cruelty of the conquerors, to say nothing of the natural disasters – earthquakes, plagues, even volcanic eruptions. Even in the west of the island, Mount Etna never seems far away.

The writing of this history has been harder than I expected. First, I was surprised and rather shocked to discover the extent of my ignorance. After several visits as a guide lecturer on tours and cruises I had a nodding acquaintance with most of the island; but I thought I knew a good deal more than I did. Guide lecturers, after all, can only skate over the surface of things – they have no time to do anything else – and, outside the tragically short Norman period in the eleventh and twelfth centuries, I could see that I had my work cut out: there was a formidable amount of reading to be done. And I had to face another problem too: from the Middle Ages on, Sicily always belonged to someone else. After the War of the Sicilian Vespers in 1282 it became a colony of Spain, and for the next four centuries or so *virtually nothing happened*. Viceroys came and went, the barons continued to exploit the peasantry, but there were so few important events that a detailed chronological account becomes impossible. Even the great three-volume history by Moses Finley and Denis Mack Smith covers the period in little over one hundred pages; in this book two chapters have proved more than enough.

In the eighteenth century, after the Treaty of Utrecht, things cheered up considerably. There were seven years under Piedmont and fourteen under Austria, and then the Spaniards were back; but this time it was the Spanish Bourbons, who were to grow more and more Italian as time went on and who soon began to detest their cousins in Madrid. Sicily, however, was once again only a province, and the spotlight shifts inexorably to Naples, on which it remains for the best part of the next 130 years. We naturally have to follow it there: the Kings of Naples were the Kings of Sicily as well, and the ever-fascinating story of Nelson and the Hamiltons – which could on no account be omitted – begins in one kingdom and ends in the other. During the Napoleonic Wars, the Bourbons are briefly replaced by the Emperor's brother-in-law, the mildly ridiculous Joachim Murat; they then return for another half-century, after which the Risorgimento disposes of them for ever.

The history of Sicily – as I have remarked more than once – is a sad one, because Sicily is a sad island. Visitors coming, as most of them do, for a week or a fortnight will not, I think, notice this. The sun will shine, the sea will be unbelievably blue, the monuments will evoke wonder and amazement. If those visitors are wise enough to go to Cefalù, they will find themselves face to face with one of the world's most powerful works of art.* But the sadness is there all right, and every Sicilian knows it. This book is, among other things, an attempt to analyse its causes. If it fails, that is because those causes are so many and varied – and also, perhaps, because I am not a Sicilian, and to non-Sicilians this lovely island will always remain an enigma.

Today is my eighty-fifth birthday, and it may well be that I shall never return to Sicily. This book is therefore a valediction. Sad as the island may be, it has given me great happiness, and has provided the beginning – and, quite possibly, the end – of my literary career. The pages that follow are inadequate indeed; but they have been written with deep gratitude, and with love.

John Julius Norwich
London, September 2014

* If they take the ferry across the strait to Reggio and a taxi to the archaeological museum of Magna Grecia, they will encounter two more – that magical pair of Greek statues of naked warriors known as the Riace Bronzes.

SICILY

TYRRHENIAN SEA

Egadi Islands

Trapani • Erice

Castellammare del Golfo

Monreale • **Palermo** •• Monte Pellegrino

• Bagheria

Partinico • Misilmeri

Termini Imerese

•• Segesta

• Calatafimi

Salemi

•• Motya

Caccamo • Himera

Marsala

• Corleone

Castelvetrano

R. Belice

• Bisacquino

• Lercara Friddi

Mazara del Vallo

Selinunte

• Caltabellotta

Casteltermini • • Mussomeli

Sciacca

R. Platani

• Racalmuto

Eraclea Minoa

Agrigento

Porto Empedocle

• Naro

Licata

MEDITERRANEAN SEA

0   10   20   30   40   50 miles

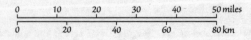
0   20   40   60   80 km

'We are old, Chevalley, very old. For over twenty-five centuries we've been bearing the weight of superb and heterogeneous civilizations, all from outside, none made by ourselves, none that we could call our own. We're as white as you are, Chevalley, and as the Queen of England; and yet for two thousand five hundred years we've been a colony. I don't say that in complaint; it's our own fault. But even so we're worn out and exhausted . . .

'This violence of landscape, this cruelty of climate, this continual tension in everything, and even these monuments of the past, magnificent yet incomprehensible because not built by us and yet standing round us like lovely mute ghosts; all those rulers who landed by main force from every direction, who were at once obeyed, soon detested and always misunderstood. Their only expressions were works of art we couldn't understand and taxes which we understood only too well and which they spent elsewhere. All these things have formed our character, which is thus conditioned by events outside our control as well as by a terrifying insularity of mind.'

Giuseppe Tomasi di Lampedusa
(trans. Archibald Colquhoun), The Leopard

Introduction

'SICILY,' SAID GOETHE, 'is the key to everything.' It is, first of all, the largest island in the Mediterranean. It has also proved, over the centuries, to be the most unhappy. The stepping stone between Europe and Africa, the gateway between the East and the West, the link between the Latin world and the Greek, at once a stronghold, clearing-house and observation point, it has been fought over and occupied in turn by all the great powers that have striven over the centuries to extend their dominion across the Middle Sea. It has belonged to them all – and yet has properly been part of none; for the number and variety of its conquerors, while preventing the development of any strong national individuality of its own, have endowed it with a kaleidoscopic heritage of experience which can never allow it to become completely assimilated. Even today, despite the beauty of its landscape, the fertility of its fields and the perpetual benediction of its climate, there lingers everywhere some dark, brooding quality – some underlying sorrow of which poverty, the Church, the Mafia and all the other popular modern scapegoats may be manifestations but are certainly not the cause. It is the sorrow of long, unhappy experience, of opportunity lost and promise unfulfilled – the sorrow, perhaps, of a beautiful woman who has been betrayed too often and is no longer fit for love or marriage. Phoenicians and Greeks, Carthaginians and Romans, Goths and Byzantines, Arabs and Normans, Germans, Spaniards and French, all have left their mark on her. Today, a century and a half after being received into her Italian home, Sicily is probably less unhappy than she has been for many centuries; but though no longer lost she still seems lonely, seeking always an identity which she can never entirely find.

Even the origin of the name is a mystery. If, as has been suggested, it derives from the Greek *sik*, which is applied to plants and fruits that grow quickly, it might mean 'fertility island', but no one really knows. The old name was Trinacria, referring to Sicily's vaguely triangular shape; this was also used for its ancient symbol, the *triskelion*, of three concentric legs – curiously like the equivalent emblem of the Isle of Man, except that the Sicilian legs are naked while the Manx ones are armoured, booted and spurred. The *triskelion* also has in the centre a head of Medusa, complete with snakes. She is surprisingly popular in Sicily, despite the fact that it was not her home or even the place where Perseus cut off her head. (In the admirable archaeological museum of Syracuse there is a large and rather crude antique sculpture, with huge fangs and lolling tongue, which the guides identify with Medusa, but I feel sure they are wrong – no snakes.) The island is also the scene of several tales of Greek mythology, including the abduction of Persephone by Hades, king of the underworld, which is believed to have occurred on the shore of Lake Pergusa* near Enna. Enna itself – perhaps the most spectacular town in Sicily, built on a towering and precipitous crag and visible for miles on every side – was the site of a magnificent temple to Persephone's mother, the goddess Demeter (or Ceres), erected by Gelon, the tyrant of Syracuse, whom we shall meet again in the following pages. She, it will be remembered, searched in vain for her daughter and, on finally learning the truth, furiously condemned Sicily to total sterility. Fortunately Zeus intervened and decreed that Persephone should spend eight months a year with her mother, during which all vegetation should flourish. With the coming of autumn, however, she was obliged to return to the underworld.

Polyphemus the Cyclops was also a Sicilian. (Perhaps, as a massive giant with a single eye, he was Mount Etna itself.) He was in love with Galatea, a Nereid sea goddess, and so angry was he when she preferred Acis, an ordinary mortal, that he killed Acis on the slopes of the volcano (where the god Hephaestus had his forge), crushing

---

* Visitors are recommended to avoid Lake Pergusa like the plague. It is now surrounded by a motor-racing track and is deeply uncharismatic.

2

him with a rock. Galatea could not revive her lover, so instead turned him into a river running down from Etna to the sea, where the two could be reunited. Acis is still commemorated in the names of Acireale and no fewer than eight other small towns and villages in the neighbourhood. Outside Aci Trezza and Aci Castello a group of three huge rocks emerges from the sea; these, known as the *scogli dei Ciclopi*, are the rocks that Polyphemus on another occasion hurled at Odysseus and his men, who had made their escape by trickery from his cave. Odysseus never had much luck in Sicily: there was another narrow escape shortly afterwards, when he passed through the Strait of Messina and Poseidon's daughter Charybdis played her favourite trick of sucking all the water up into an enormous whirlpool. (Her neighbour, the six-headed sea monster Scylla, lived opposite her on the mainland side of the Strait.)

But this is not a treatise on Greek mythology. It is time to return to the more prosaic world of today. The celebrated words from *The Leopard*, by Giuseppe di Lampedusa, that form the epigraph to this book – words spoken by Prince Don Fabrizio Salina to a Piedmontese officer in 1860, some months after the capture of Sicily by Garibaldi – encapsulate the island's history to perfection and explain the countless differences that distinguish the Sicilians from the Italians, despite the almost infinitesimal distance that separates them. The two differ linguistically, speaking as they do what is essentially another language rather than a dialect, a language in which the normal final *o* is replaced by *u* and which nearly all Italians find incomprehensible. In their place names, they have a passion for five-syllable words with a tum-ti-ti-tum-ti rhythm – Caltanissetta, Acireale, Calascibetta, Castelvetrano, Misterbianco, Castellammare, Caltagirone, Roccavaldina – the list is almost endless.* (Lampedusa gives Don Fabrizio's country estate the wonderful name Donnafugata.) They differ ethnically, a surprising number having bright red hair and blue eyes – characteristics traditionally attributed to their Norman forebears, though it seems likelier that the credit should be given

---

* I once composed a verse for Don Giovanni's 'Champagne Aria', *Fin ch'han dal vino, calda la testa* . . . consisting almost entirely of five-syllable Sicilian place names, but it is – perhaps fortunately – long since lost.

first to the British during the Napoleonic Wars and more recently to the British and Americans in 1943. They even differ gastronomically, with their immense respect for bread – of which they have seventy-two separate kinds – and their passion for ice cream, which they even demand for breakfast.

Wine is also a speciality; Sicily is now one of the most important wine-producing areas in all Italy. It is a well-known fact that the very first grapevine sprang from under the feet of Dionysus as he danced among the foothills of Etna. This slowly developed into the famous Mamertino, the favourite wine of Julius Caesar. In 1100 Roger de Hauteville established the winery at the Abbazia S. Anastasia near Cefalù; it is still in business. Nearly seven hundred years later, in 1773, John Woodhouse landed at Marsala and discovered that the local wine, which was aged in wooden casks, tasted remarkably like the Spanish and Portuguese fortified wines that were then extremely popular in England. He therefore took some home, where it was enthusiastically received, then returned to Sicily, where by the end of the century he was producing it on a massive scale. He was followed a few years later by members of the Whitaker family, whose descendants I well remember and whose somewhat oppressive Villa Malfitano in Palermo can be visited on weekday mornings. So too can the nearby Villino Florio, a riot of art nouveau and much – in my opinion, at least – to be preferred.

Any conversation about Sicily is bound to produce a question about the Mafia; and questions about the Mafia are notoriously difficult to answer, largely because it contrives to be everywhere and nowhere at the same time. We shall look at it rather more closely in chapter 16; here, the important thing to be said is that it is not a bunch of bandits – the average foreign visitor will be as safe in Sicily as anywhere in western Europe.* Indeed, he is extremely unlikely to come into contact with the organization at all. It is only if he decides to settle on the island and starts negotiating for

---

* Travellers still in need of reassurance may take comfort from a certain Miss E. Lowe, who published in 1855 a work entitled *Unprotected Females in Sicily, Calabria and on the Top of Mount Aetna*. She personally climbed the volcano, removing her petticoats one by one as she did so. Her mother, who was with her, wore gutta-percha galoshes, but they let in the snow and were not a success.

a property that he may receive a visit from an extremely polite and well-dressed gentleman – he could well be a qualified lawyer – who will explain why the situation might not be quite as straightforward as it first appeared.

Finally, a word or two about Sicily's writers. Two Sicilians have won the Nobel Prize for Literature, Luigi Pirandello and Salvatore Quasimodo (the pen name of Salvatore Ragusa). Pirandello's play *Six Characters in Search of an Author* was an early example of the Theatre of the Absurd and provoked such an outcry at its premiere in Rome in 1921 that he was forced to escape through a side entrance; since then, however, it has become a classic and is now performed the world over. Pirandello himself became an ardent Fascist and enjoyed the enthusiastic support of Mussolini. Quasimodo's poems are hugely popular in Italy and have been translated into over forty languages. But if you want the true feel of Sicily, you should go not to these giants but to Leonardo Sciascia (pronounced Shasha) and Giuseppe Tomasi di Lampedusa. Sciascia was born in 1921 in the little town of Racalmuto, between Agrigento and Caltanissetta, and lived there for most of his life. His best novels – *The Day of the Owl*, *To Each His Own*, *Sicilian Uncles* – are first-rate detective stories with a distinctive Sicilian flavour; but they also analyse the tragic ills that beset his island, such as political corruption and – as always – the Mafia. Lighter, but still irresistibly Sicilian, are the crime novels of Andrea Camilleri, which have recently been adapted to make a superb television series about his hero, Detective Inspector Salvo Montalbano, chief of police in the fictional city of Vigata. So popular has the series been that Porto Empedocle, Camilleri's birthplace, has recently had its name formally changed to Porto Empedocle Vigata.

As for Giuseppe Tomasi di Lampedusa, he is for me in a class by himself. *The Leopard* is certainly the greatest book about Sicily that I have ever read; indeed, I would rank it with any of the great novels of the twentieth century. To anyone interested, I would also enthusiastically recommend David Gilmour's admirable biography, *The Last Leopard*. Several other works of interest are listed in the bibliography.

But books can never tell us everything. No non-Sicilian, I suspect, will ever be able to penetrate the island's mysteries altogether; the rest of us must simply do the best we can, and I can only hope that this short history may make its own very modest contribution.

I

Greeks

—◆—

NOT SURPRISINGLY FOR an island set virtually in the dead centre of the Mediterranean, Sicily possesses prehistoric sites aplenty. There is, for example, on the island of Levanzo, off Trapani, a vast cave known unaccountably as the Grotta del Genovese, covered with neolithic wall paintings of bison, deer and even fish; these were discovered as recently as 1950. Others, a good deal earlier but somewhat less spectacular, were found a few years later on Monte Pellegrino, that great golden headland that rises only a kilometre or two outside Palermo on the Mondello road. Those interested will find all the information they require – and probably rather more – in the archaeological museum. For those of us, however, who are prepared to leave prehistory to the prehistorians, the first true culture we encounter is the Mycenaean, which extended from about 1600 BC. It was probably around 1400 that Sicily was absorbed into an extensive mesh of trade routes, centred on Mycenae in the northeastern Peloponnese and reaching out as far as Cyprus and even beyond. But it was all too good to last. Mycenae perished – no one knows exactly why or how – around 1200 BC, trade rapidly declined and the Sicilians reverted to their old ways.

Who were they exactly? It is hard to say. Historians talk of the Sicans, the Sicels, the Ausonians and the Elymians, who Thucydides – writing in the fifth century BC – tells us were refugees from Troy (as were, traditionally, the Romans themselves). But little of them is known. For us, the all-important people are the Greeks, who reached Sicily in the middle of the eighth century before Christ. With them at last the island enters the historical age. Their earliest settlements were on the southern coast, where there are virtually no natural harbours, but they had no need of such things. Their

7

custom in those early days was to beach their ships; what they looked for were long flat stretches of sand, and they found them – notably at Naxos, where settlers from Chalcis in Euboea landed as early as 734 BC, at Acragas (the modern Agrigento) and at Gela, where the first permanent Greek-Sicilian settlement was founded in 688 BC. In the years following they gradually dislodged – without actually eliminating – the indigenous inhabitants, together with a number of Phoenician trading posts; they introduced the olive and the vine, and rapidly built up a flourishing community. This soon became one of the major cultural centres of the civilized world, the home of poets such as Stesichorus of Himera – he whom the gods struck blind for composing invectives against Helen of Troy – and philosophers such as the great Empedocles of Acragas, who did much valuable work on the transmigration of souls and, having already served a long and tedious apprenticeship as a shrub, suddenly relinquished his mortal clay for higher things one morning in 440 BC, when another branch of scientific enquiry led him too far into the crater of Mount Etna.

By this time the Greeks had colonized most of the eastern Mediterranean. They had civilized it too, with their art and architecture, their literature and philosophy, their science and mathematics and their manufacturing skills. But – and this is a point that cannot be overemphasized – Magna Graecia, as it was called, was never a nation or an empire in the sense that Rome was to be. Politically, it was simply composed of a number of small city-states; by 500 BC there were some 1,500 of them, extending from the Black Sea to the coast of Catalonia. Intensely proud of being Greek, they supported all manifestations of panhellenism, in particular the Olympic Games; despite this, they were often at war among themselves, occasionally forming temporary leagues and alliances but all essentially independent. Athens in those days was in no sense a capital, any more than, for example, Halicarnassus in Asia Minor, where Herodotus was born, or the Corinthian colony of Syracuse in Sicily, which was the birthplace of Archimedes, or the island of Samos, home of Pythagoras. St Paul was to boast that he was a Roman citizen; such a thing could never have been said about Greece, which – not unlike the Arab world today – was a concept

8

rather than a nationality. There was no precise definition: if you felt Greek and spoke the Greek language, then Greek is what you were.

One consequence of this broad diaspora is that there are as many superb Greek sites in Italy, Sicily and Asia Minor as there are in the area we now know as Greece. The greater part, inevitably, has been lost; and yet, in Sicily alone, at Selinunte – formerly Selinus – there are at least seven temples of the sixth and fifth centuries BC in tolerable states of preservation, though most of those still standing do so only thanks to a long and ambitious programme of reconstruction in the past half-century. Of the nine at Agrigento, five are more impressive still and, particularly around sunset, quite astonishingly beautiful. Loveliest of all is Segesta, set in a fold of hills an easy drive from Palermo (but just out of sight, thank God, of the motorway). It is actually unfinished – the projecting bosses used for shifting the blocks of stone were never filed away – but the general impression is one of quiet perfection, everything a late fifth-century BC Doric monument ought to be. There is also, high on the opposite hillside, a beautifully preserved third-century theatre, from which one can look down on the temple and marvel that such a sublime building should have survived virtually intact after two and a half thousand years.

Finally, the cathedral of Syracuse, one of the only cathedrals to have been built five centuries before the birth of Christ. Its splendid baroque façade gives no hint of what lies within, but the interior tells a very different story. The columns that support the building are those of the original Doric temple of Athena, erected by the tyrant Gelon to celebrate his victory over Carthage in 480 BC and famous for its magnificence all over the ancient world. Under the Romans, its greatest treasures were stolen by the unspeakably corrupt Governor Verres, against whom Cicero so famously thundered. The Byzantines converted it for the first time into a Christian church; the Arabs turned it into a mosque. Normans and Spaniards both made their own contributions; a series of earthquakes did their worst; and there was a major reconstruction in 1693 after the collapse of the Norman façade. Those ancient columns, however, survived all their tribulations, and still stand to prove once again that most curious of historical-religious phenomena: that once a place is recognized as holy, then, regardless of all changes in the prevailing faith, holy it remains.

But who, you may ask, was this tyrant Gelon, who started the whole thing? Of all the tyrants – those men who ruled their cities as virtual dictators and who played all too large a part in Greek-Sicilian history – Gelon could boast the most distinguished parentage. Herodotus claims that his ancestors had founded the city of Gela. The prototypes of these tyrants first make their appearance in the early sixth century BC – Panaetius in Leontini, Phalaris in Acragas and one or two others. About Panaetius we know next to nothing, and of Phalaris very little except that he greatly enjoyed eating babies and small children, and that he possessed a huge, hollow bull of bronze in which he tended to roast those who displeased him. We are a good deal better informed about Pantares of Gela, whose four-horse chariot was victorious in the Olympic Games of 512 or 508, and whose sons Cleander and Hippocrates ruled successively after him. It was on the death of Hippocrates in 491 – killed in battle with the Sicels on the slopes of Mount Etna – that Gelon, his former cavalry commander, seized power. He ruled in his native city for six years, then in 485 moved to Syracuse, taking more than half its population with him. The move was sensible, if not inevitable. Gela, as we have seen, had no harbour; but no one beached ships any more if they could avoid it, and in all the Greek world there were few harbours more magnificent than that of Syracuse.

But Syracuse was more than its harbour. It also possessed an island, separated from it by no more than a hundred yards, which could serve as a huge, self-contained fortress. It was here that the first Greek colonists founded their city, which they called Ortygia after one of the epithets of Artemis. Almost miraculously, the island possessed a seemingly inexhaustible spring of fresh water* at the

---

* So fresh and copious was the water that in June 1798 Nelson used it to provision his fleet of fourteen ships. He wrote to Sir William Hamilton that in view of its source he felt assured of a coming victory. Two months later he defeated the French at Aboukir Bay.

very edge of the sea; this they dedicated to Arethusa, one of the
goddess's attendant nymphs.

Over the next few years Gelon transformed his new conquest
into a powerful and prosperous city. In this he was greatly aided
by an idiotic attack on Syracuse by another Greek city, Megara
Hyblaea, some ten or twelve miles up the coast. Herodotus tells us
the story:

> [Gelon] brought to Syracuse the men of substance, who had insti-
> gated the war and therefore expected to be put to death, and he
> made them citizens. The common people, who had no share in the
> responsibility for the war and therefore expected to suffer no evil,
> he also took to Syracuse and there he sold them into slavery for
> export outside Sicily . . . He did this because he thought the commons
> were the most unpleasant to live with.

It was not long before Gelon, with his ally, the immensely rich
Theron of Acragas, had extended his power across the greater part
of Greek Sicily. Selinus and Messina alone managed to preserve
their independence; and it was Anaxilas of Messina who took what
appeared to be the only course open to him if he and his people
were to escape absorption. He appealed to Carthage.

At this point – and before we go any further – it might be a
good idea to say something about Carthage. It was originally
Phoenician, and the Phoenicians – the Canaanites of the Old
Testament – were a very curious people indeed. Unlike their contemporaries in Egypt, they seem to have made little or no attempt to
found a single, coherent state. The Old Testament refers to the
people of Tyre and Sidon, and we read in the First Book of Kings
how Hiram, King of Tyre, sent King Solomon timber and skilled
craftsmen for the building of the Temple in Jerusalem. His people
had developed one memorable home industry: gathering the shells
of the murex – a form of mollusc which secreted a rich purple
dye, worth far more than its weight in gold.* But their principal
interest lay always in the lands to the west – with whom, however,

---

* Purple was to remain an imperial colour until the fall of Byzantium in 1453.
The principal drawback of the murex industry was the appalling smell that it
created; the piles of broken shells were always sited downwind of the town.

they traded more as a loose confederation of merchant communities than as anything resembling a nation. Today we remember them above all as seafarers, a people who sailed to every corner of the Mediterranean and quite often beyond, setting up trading colonies not only in Sicily but in the Balearic Islands and along the shores of North Africa. Beyond the Strait of Gibraltar they had important settlements on the Atlantic coast of Morocco and on the promontory of Cádiz; they probably even crossed the English Channel in search of Cornish tin.

As for Carthage, it had gained its independence around 650 BC, and by the fifth century it had developed into a formidable city-state, by far the most important and influential of all the Phoenician settlements in the Mediterranean, occupying the site of what is now Tunis. People are always surprised when they look on the map to find that Tunisia is not south of Sicily but due west of it, and that the distance between the two is barely a hundred miles. Carthage was highly centralized and efficiently governed. It was not, in short, a presence that could be taken for granted. It responded to Messina's appeal – and on a scale far beyond anyone's expectation or, indeed, understanding. The response was not immediate, but that was simply because the Carthaginians meant business. They were not interested in just helping out small-time tyrants in distress; they were aiming at something a good deal more ambitious. They spent the next three years amassing a huge army, not only from North Africa but from Spain, Corsica and Sardinia, while building up an equally massive fleet; and in 480, under the command of their Chief Magistrate Hamilcar, they landed at Palermo. From there they advanced eastward along the coast to Himera, and attacked.

What happened next is almost as incomprehensible as the size and scale of the expedition itself. Theron – Gelon's principal ally – who had been carefully following the passage of the Carthaginian fleet and was now standing ready to resist the invaders, at first found himself hopelessly outnumbered; but he was able to hold the situation until the arrival of Gelon from Syracuse, with an army comparable in size to that of Hamilcar but infinitely better equipped and trained. Meanwhile, to their bewilderment, the Carthaginians found themselves entirely alone. Of Anaxilas and his Messinans – who had invited them in the first place – there was not a sign; nor was there any help from Selinus. In the desperate encounter that followed Hamilcar was killed – or, as some say, took his own life by leaping into a blazing fire; his ships, drawn up defenceless on the beach, were burnt to cinders. Vast numbers of prisoners were enslaved, and Carthage was obliged to pay an immense indemnity, of which Gelon made excellent use, building not only his great temple of Athena but two lesser temples in a developing quarter of Syracuse, dedicated to Demeter and Persephone – the goddess of fertility and the harvest, and her daughter, queen of the dead.

After the Battle of Himera – which, Herodotus tells us, was fought on the very same day as the great Athenian victory against the Persians at Salamis – it was as if the Carthaginian expedition had never been. Carthage retired to lick her wounds; she made no attempt to take her revenge or resume hostilities, remaining quiet for the next seventy years. Anaxilas was allowed to continue in Messina as before; indeed, he felt secure enough to travel to Olympia, where he won a not very exciting race for mule-carts at the Games. He seems gradually to have reconciled himself to Syracusan hegemony; a year or two later he married his daughter to Hiero, Gelon's younger brother and successor. As for Gelon himself, he died in 478 BC. For many years he had been the most powerful figure in the entire Greek world – perhaps in all Europe. Despite Herodotus's nasty little story above he had shown himself, for a tyrant, unusually just and merciful; we are told that, as one of the conditions of the peace treaty, he insisted that the Carthaginians should give up their traditional practice of human sacrifice – which they somewhat regretfully did. It was not only in Syracuse, but in many other cities of Magna Graecia, that Gelon was deeply and genuinely mourned.

The immense popularity and respect in which Gelon was held should have rubbed off on Hiero, but it somehow failed to do so. Hiero meant well enough, but he possessed little of his brother's ability and intelligence. Some basic insecurity led him to establish a formidable secret police, which had little effect other than to make him more unpopular still. Like Gelon, he was a great mover of populations, transporting the people of Naxos* and Catania to Leontini, and actually refounding Catania under a new name – Etna – and populating it with immigrants from the Peloponnese. He was ambitious too: in 474 BC, in response to an appeal from Cumae, he sent a fleet across to the Bay of Naples, where it inflicted a crushing defeat on the Etruscans.

Perhaps his most attractive feature was his love of the arts: Pindar and Simonides, together with many other lesser poets and philosophers, were welcomed to his court at Syracuse, as was the tragedian Aeschylus,† but somehow the old magic was gone. It is the inherent weakness of autocracies that their success depends entirely on the character and strength of the autocrat. Hereditary monarchy can take the occasional weak ruler in its stride; tyranny collapses. Hiero, alas, was found wanting. He survived long enough to win an Olympic chariot race in 468 BC, but died in the following year. He was briefly and ingloriously succeeded by two more of his brothers, who were thrown out one after the other.

At this point it was certainly on the cards that some new, unrelated adventurer might have seen his chance and staged a *coup d'état*; for some reason, however, tyranny suddenly dropped out of fashion. It was not only Syracuse – by far the most important city in Sicily – that reverted to a form of democracy, but almost all the petty tyrannies (whose fortunes we have no time, space or reason to follow here) across the island. This change of heart raised its own problems: so many local populations had been uprooted and transported to other cities that it was almost impossible to determine who deserved a vote and who did not, and the result was half a century of considerable confusion. It was this, perhaps, which in 415 BC emboldened the Athenians to launch against Syracuse what Thucydides described as the most splendid and costly fleet ever to have sailed

---

* Not of course to be confused with the Aegean island. Now known as Giardini-Naxos, it lies on the coast a few kilometres south of Taormina.

† It was while he was Hiero's guest in Gela that Aeschylus is said to have suffered a unique accident when an eagle, flying above him, mistook his bald head for a stone and dropped a tortoise on it in an attempt to break its shell. The bird scored a direct hit, and Aeschylus was killed. The fate of the tortoise is unknown.

from a single Greek city – more than 250 ships and some 40,000 men.

For reasons not entirely clear, Athens had been showing a faintly sinister interest in Sicily since the 450s, when she had most improbably signed a treaty of friendship with Segesta – a diplomatic coup comparable, perhaps, to a pact today between China and Paraguay. A number of similar treaties followed, and when in 427 Leontini appealed for help in resisting an attack by Syracuse, the Athenians immediately sent twenty ships. This might have seemed generous enough at any time; during the fourth year of the Peloponnesian War, when Athens was fighting for her very existence, it was little short of astonishing. Thucydides claims, not very convincingly, that their object was to prevent the despatch of corn to their enemies.

The Peloponnesian War – which was basically a struggle between Athens and Sparta – had had little effect on Sicily until 415; in the previous year, however, hostilities had flared up – not for the first time – between the two western cities of Segesta and Selinus. Segesta, being by far the weaker of the two, having appealed in vain for help to Acragas, Syracuse and Carthage, finally in despair sent an embassy to Athens. Athens was still technically at war, but warfare had given way to a period of uneasy truce and she had large numbers of bored fighting men who needed employment. She also had a dazzling young senator named Alcibiades – a former ward of the great Pericles – who enthusiastically championed the idea of a large-scale expedition to Sicily. He had no very high opinion of the Sicilians; and in a long speech to the Senate, he explained why:

> Although the Sicilian cities are populous, their inhabitants are a mixed multitude, and they readily give up old forms of government and receive new ones from outside. No one really feels that he has a city of his own . . . They are a motley crew, who are never of one mind in counsel and are incapable of any concerted action.*

The Athenians believed him, and launched their expedition.

Almost immediately, the plight of Segesta seems to have been forgotten; the Athenians had bigger fish to fry. They may well have

---

* Thucydides, VI.17.

had in mind the subjection of all Sicily, but it was clear that their first objective must be the island's most important city, Syracuse. To Syracuse, therefore, they sailed; but the army had hardly landed before its commanders began to quarrel. Alcibiades, who was by far the ablest of them, was recalled to Athens almost at once to answer charges of profanation, and played no further part in the fighting; had he done so the expedition might have had ended very differently. None of his fellow generals seems to have had any overall plan of attack; for weeks they shilly-shallied, giving Syracuse plenty of time to prepare a firm resistance – and to appeal for help. Sparta with its superbly trained army and Corinth with its magnificent navy were swift to respond, and the Athenians soon found that the conquest of Sicily, or even only of Syracuse, was by no means to be the walkover that they had expected.

Moreover, unlike Athens, Syracuse possessed a superb commander. His name was Hermocrates. He is described by Thucydides as highly intelligent, experienced in war and of conspicuous courage, and by Xenophon as thorough, diligent and, as a general, unusually accessible to his men. In 415 he had been among the first to warn his countrymen of the Athenian danger, and had made a determined attempt to unite all Sicily – together with Carthage – against Athens while there was still time. In this he had failed, being by some written off as an alarmist, by others reviled as a warmonger; and more than a vestige of these suspicions seems to have remained, as the Syracusans absolutely refused to entrust him with supreme command, electing him instead as merely one of three generals who would share the executive authority between them. This asinine arrangement meant that, to a very considerable extent, his hands were tied.

The fighting continued for two full years, and on at least two occasions the Athenians had the city almost within their grasp. In 414 a major slave revolt was narrowly averted, and later the same year Hermocrates was obliged to open peace negotiations; only the timely arrival, with substantial reinforcements, of the Spartan general Gylippus saved the situation. Gylippus was not initially popular in Syracuse, but he soon showed himself a thoroughgoing professional and Hermocrates, swallowing his pride, accepted him as his superior officer. It was these two men together who were ultimately responsible for the Athenian defeat – a defeat which Athens was to take a long time to live down.

But there were other causes as well. As time went by the Athenian soldiers became ever more homesick and demoralized, and thus increasingly vulnerable to epidemics, particularly of malaria – unknown in Athens but rampant in Sicily. At last the Athenian commanders accepted that they had failed and gave the order to withdraw. But they were too late. The Syracusans and their allies launched a sudden last-minute attack; the Athenian fleet was trapped inside the harbour and annihilated. What followed was little short of a massacre. After it, the two principal Athenian generals, Nicias – despite being seriously ill – and Demosthenes, were executed, while some 7,000 of their men were captured and forced to work in those fearsome limestone quarries that can be visited just outside the city. The marks of their pickaxes can still be seen. In the next few months many of them were to die of cold and exposure. Countless others were branded on the forehead with the mark of a horse and then sold into slavery. (Plutarch's claim that a few lucky ones were set free because they could recite a chorus or two of Euripides can, alas, be discounted.) Thucydides summed it up: 'the victors earned the most brilliant of successes, the vanquished the most calamitous of defeats.'

Sicily was victorious and, for the moment, safe from foreign invaders; but the Peloponnesian War was by no means over and Hermocrates, now unemployed, assumed command of a fleet of twenty triremes to fight for Sparta in the Aegean. For two years all went well; but in 410 fate turned against him. Perhaps he was less gifted as an admiral than he was as a general; at any rate, in the course of a grim battle off Cyzicus on the Sea of Marmara every one of his ships was destroyed by an Athenian fleet. He returned to Sicily, only to find the gates of Syracuse firmly closed against him – perhaps because, despite his excellent past record, the citizens mistrusted his obvious ambition and feared that he might make himself a tyrant. Their fears were probably well justified, but we shall never know: in 407, while making a determined bid to force his way into the city, he was surrounded and killed.

★

Among those at Hermocrates's side on that fatal day was a tall, red-haired young man of twenty-four named Dionysius. A recent biographer assumes him to have been 'of well-to-do but undistinguished stock'; he is said to have recognized his destiny one day when a swarm of bees attached itself to his horse's mane.*

In fact we know next to nothing of his family or his origins – only that he was destined to achieve all the glory his former leader had sought, and much more beside. If Dionysius had looked back over recent events, it would surely have been plain to him that both the failure of the Athenian expedition and the narrow escape of his own city had had the same cause: the real or enforced incapacity of their leaders. The Athenian generals had all had their own ideas about how the operation should be conducted, while the senior of them, Nicias, had been far too ill to be capable of high command. Syracuse, on the other hand, had possessed in Hermocrates an outstanding military talent, but had then cravenly refused to give him his head. How had all this been allowed to happen? The fault lay, the young man would have reasoned, in the democratic system. Democracy meant disunity; only if he enjoyed absolute power could a great leader work at full capacity and achieve his highest ambitions.

It would have been pleasant to record that the ignominious departure of the Athenians restored peace to Sicily. Alas, it did nothing of the sort. The old hostilities between Selinus and Segesta were resumed, and in 410 BC a desperate Segesta once again appealed for aid, this time to Carthage. The Carthaginians responded – their catastrophic intervention of seventy years before had presumably been forgotten. In that first year they could manage only a small, hastily gathered force; but 409 saw the despatch of a considerable army under their general Hannibal,† which in little over a week reduced Selinus to a pile of smoking rubble. Those of the city's inhabitants who had not fled for safety were slaughtered. Hannibal

---

* Bees and honey have always had a special significance in Sicily – ever since Daedalus, father of the ill-fated Icarus, dedicated to Artemis a golden honeycomb.
† Not to be confused with the great Hannibal Barca, who commanded the Carthaginian army in the Second Punic War.

then advanced to Himera, where his men perpetrated a further massacre before returning for the winter to North Africa.

By now Carthaginian blood was up; they were not finished with Sicily yet. In the spring of 406 they were back, with a still larger army and a new objective – Acragas, perennially prosperous thanks to the neutrality it had been careful to maintain during previous hostilities. The Syracusans rallied to its defence; but, much to their disgust and despite their furious recriminations, the men of Acragas lifted scarcely a finger. Their life had been too easy for too long; perhaps they had grown too fond of the luxury for which they were famous, and of the supremely comfortable beds and cushions which they exported to every corner of the Greek world. A contemporary military decree forbade soldiers to have more than three blankets or two pillows while on watch; in the circumstances, they were unlikely to put up much of a fight. As a result, their city was abandoned – its inhabitants transferred to Leontini – and then sacked and plundered by the victorious Carthaginians. Among the countless works of art with which they returned home is said to have been the bronze bull in which the tyrant Phalaris had roasted his victims.

The events in Acragas could not fail to have their effect in Syracuse, where an already uneasy political situation became still more confused; and it was now that Dionysius saw his chance. Without much difficulty – for he was already one of the rising stars of the administration – he had himself elected to the city's board of generals, from which it was only a short step to the supreme command. This, it need hardly be said, he had no hesitation in assuming. Carthage was still on the warpath – in the next few months Gela was to suffer a similar fate to that of Acragas – and it was more than likely that Syracuse would be next on the list. And so indeed it was; but suddenly the Carthaginians changed their minds and returned home. Why they did so we cannot tell. The ancient chronicler Diodorus speaks darkly of an outbreak of plague; but it may well be that Dionysius himself had something to do with it. He seems already to have been a remarkably impressive figure. He is unlikely to have been able to intimidate the Carthaginians, let alone to infect them; but his diplomatic skills may perhaps have been sufficient to persuade them that an attack on his city would simply be not worth their while.

Whatever the truth may be, a peace treaty was duly signed; and this treaty marked the first recognition by Syracuse of a Carthaginian province in Sicily. The Carthaginian settlements, all in the far west of the island, were to be the absolute property of Carthage. The conquered peoples were allowed to return to their homes on condition that they left their cities unfortified and paid an annual tribute. In Syracuse, by contrast, Carthage was powerless; Dionysius already had the city under his control. The second age of Sicilian tyrants had arrived.

*

Unwilling to trust his head to a barber, he taught his own daughters to shave him. Royal virgins were thus reduced to the servile trade of female barber, cutting their father's hair and beard. He went still further: when they grew up he took away the cutting instruments and decided that they should singe his beard and hair with heated walnut-shells. He had two wives, Aristomache of his own city and Doris of Locri, and before he came to them at night he had everything examined and searched. Around the bed he had a broad trench dug, traversed by a little wooden footbridge; after he closed the door of the chamber, he himself removed the bridge.

This passage, from Cicero's *Tusculan Disputations* – written, it must be pointed out, some four centuries after the death of its subject – should probably be taken not so much as a historical anecdote than as an example of the wildly extravagant tales that grow up around larger-than-life rulers, particularly if they remain so long in power as to acquire semi-iconic status. Dionysius I of Syracuse ruled for no fewer than thirty-eight years, a period of tyranny that Diodorus describes as 'the strongest and longest of any in recorded history'. How did he do it? Certainly, he possessed all the obvious characteristics necessary for leadership – courage, self-confidence, high intelligence, determination and powers of oratory, this last always of immense importance in the Greek-speaking world. But there was clearly something else as well, later to be evident in a few – a very few – others: men like Alexander the Great, Julius

Caesar and Napoleon. We may call it charisma, or star quality, or what we will. It is in fact impossible to define; all that can safely be said is that we know it when we see it, and that Dionysius of Syracuse had it in spades.

It is fascinating to see how delicately – there is no other word – Dionysius moved into the seat of power. He had allied himself neither with the aristocracy (to which he in no way belonged) nor with the people; never did he allow himself to be seen as a rebel, far less a revolutionary. His claims were principally based on the security of the city and all who lived in it. The enemy was still virtually at the gates; another attack could be expected at any time, and after the poor showing at Acragas and Gela of the other Syracusan generals – several of whom, it was put about by his agents, were in secret negotiations with Carthage – he modestly suggested that he and he alone deserved the supreme command. To strengthen his position still further, he had taken to wife the daughter of Hermocrates,* to whose brother-in-law he had married off his own sister. Only when he was firmly established did he move against his potential enemies.

Dionysius's next step was to appropriate the entire island of Ortygia – which extends over very nearly a square kilometre and was always the most select area of Syracuse, containing as it did the relatively recent Temple of Athena – into his own personal fortress, including the houses of his closest friends and associates, together with extensive barracks for his standing army of mercenaries and part of his fleet.† It had the additional advantage that it was connected to the mainland by a bridge, which – just like the reputed one in his bedroom – could be rendered useless if the need arose.

He had one overriding purpose – to extend his dominions, acquiring as much power and wealth as possible on the way. Just

---

* The two ladies mentioned by Cicero in the passage quoted above were later acquisitions, married simultaneously in 399 or 398. Both marriages, we are told, were consummated in a single night. The resultant daughters were named Prudence, Virtue and Justice (Sophrosyne, Arete and Dikaiosyne) – perhaps to compensate for a mother named Doris.

† On Via XX Settembre the remains of Dionysius's main gateway, the Porta Urbica, may still be seen.

what those dominions were is not easy to define: he was certainly tyrant of a good deal more than Syracuse. His rule extended all over Sicily except for the far western corner (which remained in Carthaginian hands), much of southern Calabria (the toe) and the Basilicata (the instep) of Italy, together with lands around the mouth of the Po and even one or two enclaves across the Adriatic on the Dalmatian coast. A treaty which he made with Athens in 367 BC promised Athenian help in the event of any war against Dionysius or his descendants, 'or any place where Dionysius rules' – one of the few international agreements in history concluded with a head of state personally rather than with the state itself.

His principal enemy was of course Carthage. After a few years consolidating his position in Sicily he began serious preparations for war, bringing to Sicily numbers of specialist shipbuilders, craftsmen and military engineers who provided him with siege engines and catapults, now seen on the island for the first time; and by the end of 398 he was ready. Even before the formal declaration of war, he attacked and plundered the small Carthaginian merchant colony in Syracuse, destroying such of their ships as chanced to be in the harbour; and most of the other Greek cities on the island quickly followed his example. His first main objective was Motya,* a small island off the west coast which sheltered the largest and most populous Carthaginian settlement in Sicily. The causeway linking it to the mainland was cut by the defenders, as a result of which the island somehow held out until the late summer of 397; finally, however, it could resist no longer – and it paid the price of its resistance. Most of its population was massacred, while all Greeks who had remained loyal to Carthage were crucified.

During the following year the fighting spread all over Sicily. A large army and a sizable navy arrived from Carthage, and a few cities made their peace; the majority, however, fought with all their strength. Messina was flattened, and it looked as though Syracuse

---

* Now Mozia. The island was owned by the Whitaker family (see the introduction), whose villa is now an excellent archaeological museum. It contains the celebrated *Giovane di Mozia*, a fifth-century statue of a young man which has been tentatively attributed to Pheidias.

was next on the list; but the city was saved, once again, by plague in the invading army. Dionysius took the initiative with an immediate attack, and the Carthaginians surrendered. They were allowed to return home unmolested on payment of three hundred talents, which was all the money they had. Their allies, who included several contingents of mercenaries from North Africa and Spain, were left high and dry to fend for themselves.

The victory of Syracuse did not mark the end of the Carthaginian wars. There were further invasions in 393 and 392, which came to nothing: in the years following 383, on the other hand, Carthage got its own back. No one now knows the precise site of Cronion, where Dionysius suffered his first major defeat, losing much of his army – which included his brother Leptines. He was obliged to pay an indemnity of 1,000 talents and to accept several new frontiers, depriving him of Selinus and much of Acragas. In 368 he tried to get his revenge, and indeed managed to regain Selinus; but that winter he died, his work unfinished. There are different theories regarding his death. According to one account, he was poisoned by his doctors at the instigation of his son and successor; according to another, he died after too enthusiastically celebrating the news that a play of his, *The Ransom of Hector*, had won first prize at a not very distinguished dramatic festival in Athens.

He had always fancied himself as a man of letters; in 388 his court was honoured by a visit from the great Plato himself, while the historian Philistus and the poet Philoxenus were regular attenders – though Philoxenus had once been despatched to the quarries for being rude about his master's poetry. Shortly afterwards, at the request of several friends, he was released – but alas, just in time for another poetry reading. This he suffered in silence, until the despot asked once again for his opinion. 'Back to the quarries,' he murmured.

Dante consigns Dionysius – somewhat unfairly – to the seventh circle of hell, where he is immersed in the Phlegethon, a river of boiling blood and fire. In fact, the first or second circles would have been more than enough. He was ambitious, charismatic, flamboyant – cruel, perhaps, but no crueller than most of his contemporary rulers and, one suspects, a good deal more intelligent. He never succeeded in his primary objective, which was to drive the Carthaginians out of Sicily for good; had he done so, it has been suggested that he might have conquered the larger part of Italy itself and even put a stop to the growing power of Rome. By the time of his death, however, he was certainly controlling most of the island, to say nothing of his extensive dominions on the mainland. His greatest surviving monument is what remains of the line of fortifications around his city, which he completed in the four years between 401 and 397 and which culminates in the still vastly impressive Castello Eurialo; and his name is preserved for tourists by what the painter Caravaggio was the first to describe as 'Dionysius's Ear', a curious rock formation thanks to which he is said to have been able to overhear his slaves as they worked in the quarries. There is, it need hardly be said, no conceivable way in which he could have done so.

2

Carthaginians

$\thicksim$

IT IS THE misfortune of nearly all despots and dictators that they hardly ever pass on their strength to their successors. Hieron had been a failure after Gelon; similarly, Dionysius II proved only a feeble reflection of his father. All the old energy was gone; the new ruler, though not yet thirty, was a pleasure-loving drunk who spent much of his time in his mother's home town of Locris* in Calabria and was inclined to leave affairs of state – together with the command and management of the large body of mercenaries, now forming a separate caste of their own – in the hands of others. The old despot had, however, been exceptionally lucky in his son-in-law Dion, the husband of his daughter Arete, an excellent administrator with a strong philosophical bent who had served him loyally and might well have done the same for his son had he not been disgusted by the young man's dissolute ways. In an attempt to reform him Dion even invited his old master Plato – now over sixty – to Syracuse, but it was no use: young Dionysius resented all attempts to reform him and soon afterwards sent Dion into exile.

The exile, which he spent in Athens, was not uncomfortable; Dion was a wealthy man, and asked nothing better than to spend his life in quiet philosophical discussion. All would have been well, in fact, if only Plato had kept his mouth shut. Unfortunately he saw fit to appeal for his disciple's return; Dionysius flew into a fury, sent Plato back to Athens and instantly confiscated all his son-in-law's

---

* Plato called Locris 'the flower of Italy'; alas, it remains so no longer. Modern Locri is a hotbed of the 'Ndrangheta, the Calabrian criminal society closely linked to the Sicilian Mafia. It was there, during the primary elections on 16 October 2005, that the vice president of the Calabrian regional assembly, Francesco Fortugno, was publicly gunned down as he cast his vote.

Sicilian property. This was too much; there and then Dion began to prepare his downfall. In 357 he sailed for Sicily with a thousand mercenaries, heading in the first instance not, as might have been expected, for Syracuse but for Minoa on the southwest coast. This was a dependency of Carthage; he was presumably anxious to assure himself, if not of wholehearted Carthaginian support, at least of the city's benevolent neutrality. Only then did he march on Syracuse, a good two hundred miles to the east. There was no opposition on the way – indeed, he found a number of supporters only too keen to shake off Syracusan domination – and surprisingly little when he reached the city itself. Dionysius was predictably away with Mummy in Calabria, and the mercenary garrison lifted not a finger to stop the invaders. Finally a fleet arrived from the mainland, under the command of Dionysius's septuagenarian commander-in-chief Philistus – there was still no sign of the despot himself – which managed to do a certain amount of damage; but soon afterwards this fleet was followed by twenty triremes under Dion's friend and ally Heracleides. In the furious sea battle that ensued Philistus was defeated. Some sources report that he committed suicide; according to others, he was tortured to death. All agree that his body was later dragged through the streets of the city and then hurled out unburied, to the mercy of the wild dogs outside the walls.

But the fighting continued. Dionysius returned briefly from Italy, but realizing that the situation was hopeless returned to Locris, where he set himself up as the local tyrant. Dion did his best to restore order in Syracuse, setting up a government on Platonic lines with himself ruling as a sort of philosopher-king. But it was no use: he was obliged to watch powerless while one adventurer after another strove to establish his authority, the hordes of mercenaries now selling their swords indiscriminately to the highest bidder. The confusion quickly spread to other cities and towns, and as it did so, the whole Dionysian empire began to crumble away. Heracleides quarrelled with Dion; Dion had him killed, and then in 354 BC was assassinated himself. Once again it was open season for the adventurers, and the chaos continued until 346, when Dionysius II at last left Italy and briefly re-established himself on his father's throne.

Not, however, for long. One of those adventurers, a certain Hicetas, who had set himself up as tyrant of Leontini, sought help from Corinth. Some four hundred years before, the first Greek settlers in Syracuse had been Corinthians; Corinth was thus theoretically her mother city, but she had never before interfered in Syracusan affairs. Nor is there any reason why she should have done so now. Exhausted after some fifty years of warfare with various neighbours and desperately short of funds, she had nothing to gain from a new adventure. Nevertheless she responded, sending an extremely modest force – probably fewer than 3,000 men – under an obscure and elderly general called Timoleon. It was a curious choice. Timoleon was known principally as a fratricide, although a relatively honourable one. Diodorus maintains that he had personally wielded the sword to prevent his brother Timophanes's attempt to make himself tyrant; Plutarch rather more charitably reports that he stood by in tears while two others did the deed. In any event, his compatriots seem thereafter to have looked at him somewhat askance, and his appointment was greeted with general surprise.

Nor did Timoleon receive a hero's welcome when in 344 BC he landed with his men on the beach below Taormina; but fortune smiled on him. He marched on to Syracuse, where Dionysius II, walled up in Ortygia, instantly surrendered, on condition only that he was given safe passage to Corinth. (His family, which he had left in Locris, was less fortunate: the locals rose up against them and murdered the lot.) To neighbouring adventurer-tyrants, Timoleon showed no mercy; over the next two or three years they were all seized and, in one way or another, executed. Mamercus, who had taken over Catania, was crucified; the unfortunate Hippo, who had appropriated Messina, was tortured to death in the local theatre, to the vast entertainment of scores of children who had been released from school especially for the occasion. Not even Hicetas, who had been responsible for the initial appeal, was spared; he and his entire family went the way of the rest.

But Corinth was not the only recipient of an appeal to settle Sicily's tumultuous affairs. Another, somehow inevitably, had been addressed to Carthage. The first Carthaginian army to arrive unaccountably refused to fight and returned home unblooded; the second – which Plutarch estimates at 70,000 – was commanded by Carthage's senior general, Hasdrubal, but was none the less destroyed in torrential rain on the river Crimissus (almost certainly the present Belice Destro) in 340. The survivors retreated to their old settlement in the extreme west of the island, and Timoleon was the undisputed master of Sicily.

It was a remarkable achievement, the more so in that Timoleon had no conceivable claim to his power – in Syracuse or anywhere else. He had seized it just as cruelly, just as unscrupulously, as all those others whom he had overcome and subsequently liquidated. The difference lay in what he did with it. Nowhere in his extraordinary story is there any indication that he was prompted by personal ambition or self-interest. Once he was satisfied that his authority was unquestioned, he introduced several radical reforms. He had already done away with all the petty tyrants; he now destroyed Dionysius I's palace-fortress in Ortygia as an unwanted symbol of the old regime, summoned a body of legists from Corinth to change the existing constitution – which remained an oligarchy, but which now provided for a council membership of six hundred, giving it a far broader base than before – and, finally, imported very considerable numbers of foreign immigrants – Plutarch suggests 60,000 – not only from Italy but from all over Magna Graecia, making them generous grants of land and so vastly increasing the areas under cultivation. It was very largely thanks to Timoleon that Sicily was ultimately so productive of corn as to become the principal granary of Rome. Then – perhaps most surprising of all – in 338 or 337 he retired, quietly and without fuss, pleading old age and increasing blindness. On his death he was buried at public expense, and further commemorated not only by a monument in the agora but by a gymnasium known as the Timoleoneum.

The twenty years that followed Timoleon's death were marked by a new prosperity, due in a very large part to the dramatically increased agricultural production that he had initiated. Temples, theatres and public buildings sprang up all over the island; so, however, did fortifications. Sicily was not yet united, nor would she be for a long time to come. Gradually, dissension began once again to grow; once again Carthage and Corinth made their presence felt. It was not so much that another strong man was needed – before long, he was inevitable. And so the scene was set for the last, and some would say the most monstrous, tyrant of Greek Sicily.

Agathocles the Sicilian, not only from the status of a private citizen but from the lowest, most abject condition of life, rose to become King of Syracuse. At every stage of his career this man, the son of a potter, behaved like a criminal; none the less he accompanied his crimes with so much audacity and physical courage that when he joined the militia he rose through the ranks to become *praetor* of Syracuse. After he had been appointed to this position, he determined to make himself prince . . .

One morning he assembled the people and senate of Syracuse, as if he meant to raise matters which affected the republic; and at a prearranged signal he had all the senators, along with the richest citizens, killed by his soldiers; and when they were dead he seized and held the government of that city, without encountering any internal opposition. Although he was twice routed and finally besieged by the Carthaginians, not only did he successfully defend the city but, leaving some of his troops to defend it, he invaded Africa with the rest, and in a short time lifted the siege and reduced the Carthaginians to severe straits. They were compelled to make a pact with him, contenting themselves with the possession of Africa and leaving Sicily to Agathocles . . .

Yet it cannot be called prowess to kill fellow-citizens, to betray friends, to be treacherous, pitiless, irreligious. These ways can win a prince power, but not glory. One can draw attention to the prowess of Agathocles in confronting and surviving danger, and to his courageous spirit in enduring and overcoming adversity, and it appears that he should not be judged inferior to any eminent commander; none the less, his brutal cruelty and inhumanity, his countless crimes, forbid his being honoured among eminent men.

Niccolò Macchiavelli, who wrote these lines, was not an easy man to shock; but even he agrees that Agathocles went too far. He made no secret of the fact that his father was an immigrant potter, who had brought him up in the same trade. It may well have been so; in the later fourth century eastern Sicily was a major producer of red-figure ware, and many of those involved might well have been classed as artists rather than craftsmen. But professional potters, however distinguished, did not normally become army officers, and it is perhaps rather more probable that the father was cast more in the Josiah Wedgwood mould – a well-to-do entrepreneur running a successful slave-operated factory. Born in 361 BC, at the age of twenty-eight Agathocles married a rich widow and for the next fifteen years led the life of what would later be known as a *condottiere*, a soldier of fortune; it was only in 317, at the age of forty-four, that he appeared with an army of mercenaries at the gates of Syracuse. His arrival coincided with a carefully timed popular insurrection in the city, during and after which – according to Diodorus – some 10,000 were killed or exiled. He then summoned the assembly – or what was left of it – which duly conferred on him the supreme authority.

Timoleon had been an oligarch; Agathocles was a man of the people. Even after the massacre in Syracuse they seem to have seen him as one of themselves; we are even told that he needed no bodyguards, such was his popularity in the city. Elsewhere in Sicily, however, he was hated and feared as he gradually spread his power over the island. War with Carthage became inevitable, and in 311 Acragas escaped destruction only when the Carthaginian general Hamilcar inflicted a serious defeat on the Syracusans at the battle of the river Himera*; but the reaction of Agathocles was as courageous as it was unexpected. Leaving Syracuse under the command of his brother Antander, on 14 August 310 he sailed out of the harbour with a fleet of sixty ships carrying 14,000 men, landing at Cape Bon – the extreme northeastern extremity of Tunisia – six days later. He was the first European to invade North Africa with a military force.

The situation was thus a curious one. Now Syracuse and Carthage each had a hostile army at its gates. Hamilcar was obliged to send many of his own forces back to defend their mother city, leaving himself dangerously vulnerable. Antander launched a sudden attack

---

* Not to be confused with Himera on the north coast, site of a previous war with Carthage in 480 BC (see pp. 12–13). The river Himera has its mouth on the southwest coast near Licata.

and took him prisoner; the luckless general was then tortured to death, his severed head being sent to Agathocles in Africa. Agathocles, on the other hand, was doing remarkably well, laying waste and plundering the rich and virtually undefended land lying between Cape Bon and Carthage; but he was aware that he would never be able to capture the great city with the forces at present at his disposal, and looked around for a means of increasing them.

Alexander the Great, who had died aged thirty-three just thirteen years before, had left his immense empire to be shared out among his generals; and one of these, Ophellas by name, was now Governor of Cyrenaica, some thousand miles along the coast (of what is now Libya) to the east. Despite this distance Agathocles made contact with him, suggesting that the two should join forces and together declare war on Carthage. Then, he proposed, after a victory that was virtually certain, Ophellas could keep all North Africa for himself, leaving Sicily to the Syracusans. The Governor leapt at the idea, mustered his army – 10,000 infantry, together with an unknown number of cavalry and chariots – and set off.

Anyone who has ever travelled by land from Benghazi to Tunis will know that, at least until the road turns to the north along the Tunisian coast, those thousand miles are the most featureless and boring that can be found anywhere around the Mediterranean. Ophellas, when he finally reached his destination, would have been physically exhausted and, most probably, not in the best of tempers. But this hardly mattered to Agathocles, who almost immediately had him assassinated, presumably so that he could seize the newly arrived army for himself. His campaign began well enough, with the capture of the small Phoenician colony of Utica together with Hippo Acra (the modern Bizerta); but Carthage, to his fury, remained as impregnable as ever, and he was still pondering his next steps when, early in 307, a general rising of the Greek towns in Sicily led by Acragas called him urgently back to Syracuse. He put down the rebellion with his usual brutality and returned to Africa, only to find his army unpaid and on the point of mutiny. The African adventure was over. There was nothing for it but to make peace with Carthage – which he most reluctantly did in 306 – return to Sicily and put his own house in order.

Two years later Agathocles did something that no previous tyrant had done; he took the title of King. There is little doubt that to many of his older subjects the action would have seemed shocking; but times had changed. In the new Hellenistic world that had sprung up after the death of Alexander, at least two of his old generals – Ptolemy in Egypt and Seleucus in Asia Minor and Mesopotamia – now styled themselves kings; if Agathocles was to deal with these monarchs on an equal footing he had little choice but to follow their example.

Agathocles died in 289 BC. There were those who believed it to have been a natural death, but it is a good deal more probable that he was poisoned by his grandson Archagathus in an attempt to succeed him. The attempt failed; and anarchy followed, as it nearly always did. Sicily was once again pulled apart by its petty tyrants – one of them, Phintias of Acragas, destroyed Gela in 282, wiping it completely off the map for some fifteen hundred years.* He then marched on Syracuse, but was defeated; the Syracusans unwisely pursued him back into the west of the island, whereupon the Carthaginians, fearing to lose their Sicilian territory, sent over an army – and the fighting broke out again.

But now there came a new invader – another adventurer, perhaps, but a man unlike any that the Sicilians had seen before. King Pyrrhus was the hugely ambitious ruler of Epirus. Claiming descent from both Achilles and Hercules, in 280 BC he turned his attention to Italy, most of which was already under the domination of Rome; the city of Tarentum, however – the modern Taranto, on the instep of the Italian boot – was putting up a stiff resistance and appealed to Pyrrhus for help. Pyrrhus asked nothing better. He brought with him an army of 20,000, meeting the Romans at nearby Heraclea and defeating them – but by only a narrow margin, his own losses being very nearly as great as theirs. Plutarch tells the story:

> The armies separated; and, it is said, Pyrrhus replied to one that gave him joy of his victory that *one more such victory would utterly*

---

* It was re-established by Frederick II in 1230 under the name of Terranova. It reverted to its old name in 1927.

undo him. For he had lost a great part of the forces he brought with him, and almost all his particular friends and principal commanders . . . On the other hand, as from a fountain continually flowing out of the city, the Roman camp was quickly and plentifully filled up with fresh men, not at all abating in courage for the loss they sustained, but even from their very anger gaining new force and resolution to go on with the war.

No longer able to face the Romans, Pyrrhus accepted a less challenging invitation to intervene in Sicily. His army had now been reduced to 10,000, but he landed it successfully at Taormina – where he found a very different situation.

Why the Sicilians took Pyrrhus so immediately to their hearts remains something of a mystery. He was new, he was different, he was charismatic; but it still comes as something of a surprise to read that this instant popularity enabled him to treble his forces and increase his fleet to two hundred vessels. With these he had no difficulty in defeating a large and unruly body of unemployed Italian mercenaries known as the Mamertines, and in clearing the Carthaginians out of the island everywhere except in their stronghold at Lilybaeum (now Marsala). He besieged it for two months and then gave up the struggle as impossible – as indeed it was, since Carthage still controlled the sea passage between the two cities and could send in provisions at will. His coins in both gold and silver make it clear that with this exception he was effectively ruler of the whole island; but all too soon he became bored and in 276 returned to the mainland, only to suffer severe defeat by the Romans at Benevento the following year. The subsequent triumphal procession in the capital featured Pyrrhus's captured elephants – the first to make their appearance in Italy.*

In 272 the Romans captured Tarentum. The once obscure republic was now master of the whole Italian peninsula and well on the way to becoming the greatest power in the civilized world. This was

---

* One would love to know how and where Pyrrhus acquired them. At all events, they – and Hannibal's after them – were presumably African; and African elephants, unlike the Indian variety, are always said to be impossible to train. Did Pyrrhus and Hannibal know something that we don't?

not quite the end of Greek Sicily; a certain Hieron – we must, I suppose, call him Hieron II – seized power in Syracuse and retained it, with the title of King, for the next fifty-four years, dying in 215 BC at the age of ninety-two. This fact alone suggests a radical difference from his predecessors. He ruled in eastern Sicily only, making no attempt to increase his dominions, concentrating instead on enriching his existing kingdom – and of course himself – by encouraging agriculture and developing export markets for his produce, especially in Egypt and, later, in Rome.

He was also a builder. Perhaps his most impressive achievement was an immense altar – at well over two hundred yards long, the largest in the world – dedicated to Zeus. It was used principally for the sacrifice of bulls, some 450 of which, we are informed, could be – and were – sacrificed in a single day. Nowadays only the foundations remain, the superstructure having been destroyed in 1526 by the Spaniards, who needed the stone for a new harbour. Until that time the altar is believed to have stood some fifty feet high; but even the foundations are impressive enough.

No one, however, understood better than Hieron the delicacy of the position in which Sicily now found herself, trapped as she was between Carthage and Rome. Clearly he had no choice but to declare himself for one or the other; and in 263 BC he signed a treaty with Rome whereby he gained a Roman guarantee of his authority. This treaty he faithfully observed for the remaining forty-eight years of his life, steadily increasing his exports of corn until Sicily was well on the way to achieving its later status as the granary of Rome. As for Rome itself, one obstacle only remained to its total domination of the western Mediterranean, and with it all the old Magna Graecia. That obstacle was Carthage, which was to remain a thorn in the Roman flesh for well over a hundred years, from 264 to 146, during which the Romans were obliged to fight two separate Punic* Wars before they were able to eliminate it as a threat. It was these two wars that brought Rome to the centre of the Mediterranean stage and – since it soon became clear that

---

* 'Punic' – the term by which these two wars are always known – has the same root as 'Phoenicia'.

Carthage could never be defeated on land alone – made her a leading sea power.

The First Punic War, which continued until 241, was won by Rome, though at enormous cost – 500 ships and at least 100,000 men. It also inflicted terrible suffering on western and southern Sicily, which proved the principal battleground. (Hieron's territory in the east, having declared categorically for Rome, remained unscathed, continuing to supply the Romans with grain just as it always had.) After the siege of Acragas in 261 the Romans sold 25,000 of its inhabitants into slavery. Kamarina, some fifty miles further down the coast, lost almost as many. At Panormus (Palermo) 13,000 were sold, another 14,000 being allowed their freedom only after payment of a stiff ransom. Carthage too did its bit: it completely destroyed Selinus and transferred all the inhabitants to Lilybaeum – although that strategically invaluable promontory was surrendered to Rome in 241, when the Carthaginians finally undertook to withdraw all their forces from the island. The First Punic War was over. All Sicily, excepting only Syracuse, was in Roman hands.

The Second – which began in 218 – was more important, and a lot more interesting. The Romans were also victorious, but not before the Carthaginian general, Hannibal, had proved himself to be the greatest military leader the world had seen since Alexander – perhaps one of the greatest of all time. Hannibal never set foot in Sicily; but he so dominated the last years of the third century BC that he deserves more than a mention here. According to tradition, his father, Hamilcar – who had almost single-handedly laid the infrastructure of a prosperous Carthaginian colony in Spain, with its capital at the modern Cartagena – had made him swear eternal hatred of Rome. He was determined, from the moment of his accession to the leadership in 221, to avenge his country's defeat of twenty years before and was confident that the new Spanish dominion, with all its vast resources of wealth and manpower, would enable him to do so. He left Spain in the spring of 218 with an army of some 40,000 men, taking the land route along the south coast of France, up the Rhône valley, then east to Briançon and the Alpine pass at Mont-Genèvre. His infantry was mostly Spanish, though officered by Carthaginians, his cavalry drawn from Spain and North Africa; it included thirty-seven elephants. The famous crossing of the Alps took place in the early autumn and was followed by two victorious battles in quick succession; by the end of the year Hannibal controlled virtually the whole of northern Italy. A third victory, in April 217, saw the Roman army destroyed after being trapped in a defile between Lake Trasimene and the surrounding hills.

It was no use marching on Rome; the city possessed formidable defensive walls, and Hannibal had no siege engines worth speaking of. He therefore moved on down the peninsula to Apulia and Calabria, where the largely Greek populations had no love for the Romans and might well, he thought, defect to his side. But he was disappointed. Instead of the sympathetic allies for whom he had hoped, he soon found himself faced by yet another Roman army, far larger and better equipped than his own, which had followed him southward; and on 3 August 216 BC, at Cannae beside the Ofanto River – some ten miles southwest of the modern Barletta – battle was joined. The result was yet another victory for Hannibal, perhaps the greatest of his life, and for the Romans the most devastating defeat in their history. Thanks to his superb generalship, the legionaries were surrounded and cut to pieces where they stood. By the end of the day over 50,000 of them lay dead on the field. The Carthaginian casualties amounted to 5,700.

Hannibal had now destroyed all Rome's fighting forces apart from those kept in the capital for its defence; but he was no nearer his ultimate goal, the destruction of the Republic. His strongest weapon, that magnificent Spanish and North African cavalry – by now exclusively equine, the unfortunate elephants having all succumbed to the cold and damp – was powerless against the city walls. He was encouraged, on the other hand, by the hope that his brother – another Hasdrubal – might be raising a second army, this time with proper siege engines, and joining him as soon as it was ready. Marching his army across the mountains to Capua – at that time Italy's second largest city, and surprisingly friendly – he established his headquarters there and settled down to wait.

He waited a very long time, for Hasdrubal had problems of his own. The Romans, swift to take advantage of Hannibal's absence, had within months of his departure invaded Spain, with an army of two legions and some 15,000 troops under a young general called Gnaeus Cornelius Scipio, who was soon joined by his brother Publius. The immediate consequence of this invasion was a long struggle between Roman and Carthaginian forces; the eventual result was a Roman presence in Spain which was to last over six centuries. After the death of the two Scipios in 211 they were replaced by a kinsman, also called Publius, who took Cartagena after a short siege. With the capture of their Spanish capital the Carthaginians swiftly lost heart, and by 206 BC the last of them had left the peninsula.

While he had been thus occupied by the Romans in Spain, Hasdrubal had had no chance of organizing a relief expedition to help his brother. Not until 206, when he knew he was beaten, could he begin to consider such an enterprise, and when in 205 he in turn led his men through southern France and across the Alps he marched to disaster: on the Metaurus River, just outside Ancona, he encountered a Roman army which cut his army to pieces. Hannibal learned the news only when his brother's severed head was delivered to his camp at Capua. He remained in Italy for another four years, but he would have been wiser to return; elsewhere in the Mediterranean, young Publius Scipio had by now taken the offensive.

In 204 Scipio and his army landed on the North African coast at Utica, less than twenty miles west of Carthage, where they routed 20,000 local troops and established a position on the Bay of Tunis, threatening the city itself. In the spring of 203 Hannibal, now seriously alarmed, hurried back to Carthage and in the following year led an army of 37,000 men and eighty elephants against the invaders. The two sides eventually met near the village of Zama where, after a long and hard-fought battle, Hannibal suffered the only major defeat of his extraordinary career. The Roman victory was complete. The prize was Spain: it remained only for Carthage formally to cede the Iberian peninsula to her conquerors. Hannibal himself – who had narrowly escaped death at Zama – lived on until 183 BC, when he took poison to avoid being captured by the enemy he so hated. As for the victorious Scipio, he was rewarded with the title of Africanus, which he richly deserved. He, more than any other of his compatriots, had ensured that it was Rome, not Carthage, which would be mistress of the Mediterranean in the centuries that followed.

In this Second Punic War, Roman-held Sicily constituted an all-important barrier between Hannibal in Italy and his home base in Carthage. It was also the perfect springboard, from which the Romans could launch raids on Africa from Lilybaeum and on Italy from Messina. There were no problems for them for as long as Hieron was alive; but after his death in 215 BC everything was changed. The old man's grandson and successor, Hieronymus, concluded a treaty with Carthage, and although he was almost immediately assassinated Syracuse remained firmly on the Carthaginian side. The Romans sent an army under their leading general Marcellus and put the city under siege; but after two years they were still unable to capture it, or even to blockade it successfully against the Carthaginian supply ships. The reason for their lack of success seems largely to have been a single man, the mathematician and physicist Archimedes, who, having spent most of his life under the pro-Roman Hieron, was now devoting all his ingenuity and genius to the Carthaginian cause. Among his inventions was 'Archimedes's claw', a cranelike arm at the end of which a huge metal hook was suspended. This would be dropped over an enemy ship, and would then swing upwards again, dragging the ship clean out of the water. Another – for which we have only the authority of the Roman writer Lucian, who lived in the second century AD – was an array of bronze or copper burning-glasses, designed to focus the rays of the sun on to attacking ships.★ But not even Archimedes could perform miracles, and at last in 212 Syracuse fell to Rome. Marcellus is said to have immediately summoned the great man, but when the soldier arrived to fetch him he asked to be allowed to finish the problem on which he was working. Perhaps the soldier misunderstood, and killed him on the spot. All we know is that Syracuse was sacked and plundered, and that Archimedes was not among the survivors.

★ Recent experiments have proved both these inventions feasible.

His tomb, which according to his own instructions bore small representations of a sphere and a cylinder, was left untended and soon disappeared among the surrounding vegetation. One hundred and thirty-seven years later, however, it was rediscovered – by Cicero himself. 'When I was *quaestor* in Sicily,' he wrote,

> I managed to track down his grave. The Syracusans knew nothing about it, and indeed denied that any such thing existed. But there it was, completely surrounded and hidden by bushes of brambles and thorns . . . I took a good look round all the numerous tombs beside the Agrigentine Gate. Finally I discerned a small column just visible above the scrub; it was surmounted by a sphere and a cylinder. I immediately said to the Syracusans, some of whose leading citizens were with me at the time, that I believed that this was the very object that I had been seeking. Men were sent in with sickles to clear the site, and when a path to the monument had been opened we walked right up to it. And the verses were still visible, though roughly the second half of each line had been worn away.*

If Marcellus had indeed intervened, successfully or not, in favour of Archimedes, his action was to say the least uncharacteristic. A degree of looting after the capture of a city was normal and expected; he, on the other hand, took virtually everything there was in Syracuse of any artistic value whatever. Statues and busts were torn from temple walls, paintings seized from public and private buildings alike. This was, according to Livy, the moment when Roman eyes were first opened to the splendour of Greek art. It may well have been; but the people of Syracuse were furious, to the point where in 210 – the same year, incidentally, as the Roman consul Marcus Valerian told the Senate that 'no Carthaginian remains in Sicily' – they succeeded in persuading the Romans to replace Marcellus. The Senate, it seems, was only too happy to do so; Marcellus was no more popular in Rome than he was in Sicily. He was still smarting over the denial of the triumph that he had been expecting after his capture of Syracuse; he had had to be content with a mere 'ovation', which he considered almost an insult. His career was over, and he knew it.

The Punic Wars had a traumatic effect. They had brought the

---

* The site is now thought to lie immediately under the I Papiri shopping mall.

Roman Republic several times to the brink of disaster and had in all claimed the lives of perhaps 200–300,000 of her men. And yet there, across the narrow sea, the city of Carthage still stood – its population of some three-quarters of a million recovering from its recent defeat with almost frightening speed: to every patriotic Roman a reminder, a reproach and a warning. How then could its continued survival be tolerated? *'Delenda est Carthago'* – 'Carthage is to be deleted': these words were spoken by the elder Cato at the end of every speech he made in the Senate until they eventually became a watchword. The only question was how the job was to be done. At last, in 151 BC, a pretext was found when the Carthaginians presumed to defend their city from the depredations of a local chieftain. Rome decided to treat this perfectly natural reaction as a *casus belli*, and in 149 once again sent out an invading army. This time the Carthaginians surrendered unconditionally – until they heard the Roman peace terms: that their city would be utterly destroyed and that its inhabitants should not be permitted to rebuild their homes anywhere within ten miles of the sea. Appalled, they resolved after all to resist. The result was a terrible two-year siege after which, in 146, the threatened destruction took place, not one stone being left on another. Cato was obeyed: Carthage had been deleted.

And Sicily was, to all intents and purposes, a Roman province.

3

Romans, Barbarians, Byzantines, Arabs

A FTER THE PAINFULLY complicated story of Sicily's Greek tyrants
and of the Punic Wars which followed them, that of Sicily
under Roman rule is relatively uneventful. There was no question
of the Sicilians being 'allies' or 'half-citizens', as the Romans used
on occasion to call their semi-subject peoples on the mainland.
The all-important fact was that they spoke Greek, not Latin; their
island was thus not just a province but a foreign province, its people
second-class citizens who paid their taxes and did as they were told.
These taxes were severe but not swingeing. They were based on
the principle of the tithe: one tenth of the annual crop of grain,
to be shipped direct to Rome, and similar levies on fruit, vegetables,
olives and wine. There were, of course, plenty of other demands,
made when necessary or when considered necessary – not always
the same thing – by the republican government or the local administration; but on the whole and for most of the time life for the
Sicilians was tolerable enough. The obvious exception was the
iniquitous governorship of Gaius Verres which, thanks to the advo-
cacy of Cicero, used to be well known to every English schoolboy.
We shall be coming to that in due course, but it is perhaps worth
pointing out here that the date was 73–71 BC, some 140 years after
the end of the Punic Wars. What, it may be asked, had happened
in the interim?

There is not a lot to report, but then our knowledge of Sicily
in the second century BC is thin indeed. Contemporary chroniclers
are few, and not particularly informative; and the very fact that
they concentrate largely on questions of administration and taxation
suggests that there were not many major political upheavals to
record. One thing is certain: that the Romans treated Sicily with

little respect. That monstrous inferiority complex to which they always gave way when confronted with Greek culture led to exploitation on a colossal scale. A few Greek cities managed to retain a measure of independence, but much of the island was taken over by the *latifundia*: those vast landed estates, owned by absentee Roman landlords, setting a pattern of land tenure which was to ruin Sicilian agriculture for the next two thousand years. Liberty, meanwhile, was almost extinguished as the slave gangs toiled naked in the fields, sowing and harvesting the corn for Rome.

It was thus hardly surprising that the second half of the century should have seen two great slave revolts. Tens of thousands of men, women and children had been sold into slavery during the third-century Sicilian wars, tens of thousands more as a result of warfare on the mainland in the century following. Meanwhile, the Hellenistic east was in a state of turmoil. The tidy distribution of territories among Alexander's generals was a thing of the past; Asia Minor, Egypt and Syria were now torn apart by dynastic struggles. This meant prisoners, both military and political, a vast proportion of whom, with their families, were swept up by the slave traders and never heard of again. And in Sicily, still steadily developing its agriculture, a strong and healthy worker would fetch a more than reasonable price.

The slave population was in consequence dangerously large, but it gave the authorities little cause for alarm. After all, mass revolts were rare indeed. Almost by definition, slaves – branded, beaten and frequently chained together – were permanently demoralized by the life they led, while the conditions under which they were kept normally made any consultation and planning between them impossible. On the other hand, it should be remembered that many of those who had landed up in Sicily were intelligent and educated, and nearly all of them spoke Greek. And just sometimes, out of sheer desperation, they were driven to action.

The first revolt began, so far as we can gather,* in 139 BC on the estates of a certain Damophilus of Enna, 'who surpassed the

---

* These and other words of caution are necessary. The relevant books of Diodorus are lost; all we have to go on is a number of tenth-century excerpts.

Persians in the sumptuousness and costliness of his feasts' and whose slaves most understandably resolved to kill him. Before doing so, however, they consulted another slave, a Syrian named Eunus, who was generally believed to possess magic, or at least oracular, powers. Would the gods, they asked him, give their blessing to such a plan? Eunus's reply was as categorical as any of them could have wished. He personally marched into Enna with a following of some four hundred fellow slaves; the murder, rape and plunder lasted for several hours. Damophilus and his termagant wife, Megallis, were away in their country villa, but were quickly brought back to the city; he was killed at once, she was handed over to her own female slaves, who tortured her and then flung her from the roof. Eunus had meanwhile been proclaimed king, making his mistress (and former fellow-slave) queen at his side.

Once started, the revolt spread like wildfire. A certain Cleon, a Cilician herdsman working near Agrigento, joined Eunus with 5,000 men of his own; soon they were at Morgantina, then at Taormina. By this time their numbers probably approached the 100,000 mark, though we shall never know for sure. Another mystery is why, in contrast to the speed and efficiency they showed in dealing with similar but much smaller uprisings in Italy, the Romans were so unconscionably slow in sending troops to restore order. Admittedly they had other preoccupations at home and abroad, but the truth is that all through their history the Romans consistently underestimated Sicily; the fact that it was not part of the Italian peninsula but technically an offshore island seemed to lower it in their estimation. Had they properly considered the scale and importance of what was going on, had they sent an adequate force of trained soldiers to the island as soon as the first reports arrived, Eunus and his followers would hardly have stood a chance. As things turned out, it was not until 132 BC – seven years after its beginning – that the revolt was finally crushed. The prisoners taken at Taormina were tortured; their bodies, living or dead, were flung from the battlements of the citadel. Their leader, after wandering for some time at liberty, was finally captured and thrown into prison, where he died soon afterwards. The vast majority of the rebels, however, were released. They no longer constituted a danger – and, after all, if life were to go on as it always had, slaves were a vital commodity.

Unlike the first, the second slave revolt had a specific cause other than general dissatisfaction. It began in 104 BC, when Rome was once again under severe pressure, this time from Germanic tribes to the north. In order to deal more efficiently with these, she appealed for military assistance from Nicomedes III, King of Bithynia in Asia Minor.★ Nicomedes replied that he unfortunately had no young men to spare, thanks to the activities of the slave traders who were seizing so many of them and who were actually protected by the Roman authorities. At this the horrified Senate ordered that all those of Rome's 'allies' who had been enslaved should be released at once. The effect of this decree when it reached Sicily may well be imagined. Huge crowds of slaves assembled before the Governor in Syracuse, demanding immediate emancipation. He granted freedom to some eight hundred, then realized that, if he continued, he would be destroying the entire base of the Sicilian economy. Laying down his pen, he ordered that the still-growing crowds should disperse and return to their homes. Not surprisingly, they refused – and the second slave revolt was under way.

Since the Roman decree – and the Governor's refusal to enforce it – affected the slaves all over Sicily, the whole island was soon in an uproar. The first leader was another Cilician, a certain Athenion, who raised a force of some two hundred from the region between Segesta and Lilybaeum; but he found himself outpaced and outclassed by one Salvius, whose origins are unknown – he may not even have been a slave – but who possessed not only considerable military skill but also vaulting political ambition. For Salvius, to lead a major insurrection was not enough; he had to crown himself king under the Greek name of Tryphon, after which he wore a purple toga and built himself a moated palace (of which not a trace remains). Relations between himself and Athenion varied – at one moment the latter was actually imprisoned – but when Salvius was killed in battle it was Athenion who succeeded him on the throne.

★ Was there not, one wonders, somewhere nearer from which such help could have been obtained?

The Romans had learnt their lesson. This time they moved quickly, and although they were poorly commanded at the start, after the arrival of a certain Manlius Aquilius in 100 BC – he had been Rome's Second Consul during the previous year – the revolt soon collapsed, the rebels having failed to capture a single one of the principal cities. The last few hundred to surrender did so, we are told, only after receiving an undertaking that their lives would be spared. Predictably enough, the Romans broke their promise: the captives were sent to Rome, and were there sentenced to be torn apart by wild animals in the circus. One last gesture of defiance could they make: rather than provide entertainment for the crowd, they all committed suicide or killed one another before the show began.

Most of the rebels had died in the fighting. For the rest no further punishment was necessary; a return to slave labour was more than enough. Only a quarter of a century after the end of the second revolt, Sicily received its new Governor, Gaius Licinius Verres.* From the outset of his career, Verres had been a crook. In 80 BC – after he had already narrowly avoided charges of embezzlement – he was sent to Cilicia where he and his immediate superior, the Governor Dolabella, plundered the province for all it was worth. Two years later they were both summoned back to Rome, where Dolabella stood trial. He was convicted, largely on the evidence of Verres, who thereby secured his own pardon and who, in 74 BC, having bribed his way to the Praetorship – a senior magistracy – thoroughly abused his high office for a year before being appointed Governor of Sicily. Here he found himself virtual dictator of a rich and prosperous island, a superb fruit ripe for the plucking.

In just three years, Sicily suffered greater depredations from Verres than she had from the Punic Wars and the slave revolts combined. He taxed, he impounded, he confiscated, he seduced, he raped, he tortured, he imprisoned, he robbed, he looted – not only from temples, but from private houses as well, of Roman citizens and Sicilians alike. A special ship had to be built, capacious enough to

---

* The middle name is probable, but uncertain.

transport his collection back to Rome. His term of office coincided with another slave revolt, that of Spartacus on the mainland. Sicily was not directly affected, but Verres would single out some important slave of a wealthy landowner, accuse him of sedition or plotting to join Spartacus and sentence him to crucifixion, making it known to the owner that a hefty bribe would ensure his deliverance. Another trick was to invent a purely imaginary slave, to accuse him of subversion and then to accuse some rich man of deliberately hiding him. Once again, the victim could escape imprisonment only by bribery.

Not surprisingly, the Sicilians protested; and so vehement were their protestations that in 70 BC Verres was recalled to Rome and put on trial. To prosecute him the Sicilians engaged the great Marcus Tullius Cicero. Cicero had served as *quaestor* * in western Sicily five years before, and had impressed everyone by his honesty and integrity. He took his task seriously, spending many weeks on the island collecting evidence and talking to witnesses. Then he returned to Rome, where he won the case hands down. His speeches for the prosecution have become celebrated; they show, however, how drastically different was Roman court procedure from modern practice. Only the first speech was relatively short, though it would seem quite long enough today. The second would have taken several hours to deliver, and one pities the miserable jurors who were forced to sit through it. Still, Cicero did not mince his words:

> Some [citizens] he has delivered to the executioner, others he has put to death in prison, others he has crucified . . . The reverence due to, and the holy ceremonies practised in, every shrine and every temple – all were violated by him . . .
>
> The insults offered to the religion of the immortal gods must be expiated, and the tortures of Roman citizens, and the blood of many innocent men, must be atoned for by this man's punishment. For we have brought before your tribunal not only a thief, but a wholesale robber; not only an adulterer, but a ravisher of chastity; not only a sacrilegious man, but an open enemy to all sacred things and

* Financial supervisor.

all religion; not only an assassin, but a most barbarous murderer of both citizens and allies. There is in my opinion no more atrocious criminal in the memory of man.

Fortunately, of the seven orations only two were actually delivered. The effect of the first alone was so overwhelming that the advocate for the defence, Quintus Hortensius, had only one piece of advice for his client: immediate flight. A day or two later, while the trial was still technically in progress, Verres was on his way to Massilia (the modern Marseille). There he lived in exile for a further quarter of a century. He never returned to Rome.

The following few pages may be seen as something of a digression, relating as they do to Roman history – and indeed, its best-known chapter – rather than to Sicilian. The story is worth retelling, however, since it had a profound impact on the events that followed, which in turn affected the whole development of the Mediterranean.

It begins with the three military men who together dominated republican Rome. They were Gnaeus Pompeius Magnus (better known to us as Pompey), Marcus Licinius Crassus and Gaius Julius Caesar. Pompey was a soldier through and through, and a highly ambitious one; Crassus was a rich man, a first-rate general when he wanted to be, but one who usually preferred to remain in Rome, quietly intriguing for his own political and financial ends. His one major military achievement was the suppression of the slave revolt led by Spartacus in 73 BC. When he finally ran Spartacus to earth in Apulia he executed him on the spot; 6,000 rebel slaves were subsequently crucified, their crosses lining the Appian Way.

In that year Julius Caesar was twenty-seven years old. His reputation in Rome was already that of a cultivated intellectual and a formidable orator in the Senate, a provider of lavish entertainments who was consequently always in debt, and a sexual profligate, whose affairs – with men as well as women – were legion, but who had nevertheless been elected Pontifex Maximus, chief of the Roman priesthood. In short he was talented, fascinating, but basically unreliable. When in 59 BC he was elected Consul, he sought out Pompey and Crassus and proposed a coalition. They both willingly accepted, and three years later, at Lucca, the three of them met and decided to divide the Roman world into three spheres of influence. The east would go to Crassus, who would lead an expedition across the Euphrates against the Parthian Empire of Persia; the west was allotted to Pompey, who would take over a five-year responsibility for Spain – governing it, however, largely through subordinates, so that he could remain in Rome as effective head of the administration; and the centre went to Caesar, who would return to Gaul – where he had been fighting since the end of his consulship – to extend and consolidate his conquests.

Of course it couldn't last. Crassus was heavily defeated by the Parthian mounted archers and subsequently killed, together with well over 5,000 of his legionaries. Meanwhile Pompey and Caesar were both becoming more and more aware of the fact that Rome was not big enough for both of them. Pompey, however, had the distinct advantage: he was in Rome, and when the news was brought to Caesar – who was in Ravenna – that his rival had assumed command of all the forces in the Republic, he knew that (in his own words) the die was cast. On the night of 10 January 49 BC he and the single legion he had taken with him crossed the little river Rubicon* which constituted the southeastern border of Cisalpine Gaul. Henceforth it would be a trial of strength: a civil war.

Caesar encountered little opposition. Town after town opened its gates to him without a struggle; when he was called upon to fight, his battle-hardened troops were more than a match for any that might be ranged against them. Soon Pompey was obliged to flee to Dalmatia. Caesar did not pursue him; instead he set off by land to Spain, the heartland of his rival's power in the west, crossing the Pyrenees with an army of 40,000 men. Against him were 70,000, commanded by three of Pompey's leading generals, but he continued effortlessly to outmanoeuvre them until they capitulated.

With his enemies effectively scattered, Caesar had no difficulty in having himself re-elected Consul in 48 BC. He then went after Pompey, who had by now moved on to Greece; and it was there,

---

* Surprisingly, this stream has never been convincingly identified. The modern river Pisciatello is the most likely candidate.

on 9 August, on the sweltering plain of Pharsalus in Thessaly, that the two armies met at last. Caesar – aided by the young tribune Mark Antony, who commanded his left wing – once again won an easy victory. Pompey, we are told, was one of the first to retreat. He escaped to the coast and thence to Egypt, where he was shortly afterwards assassinated. Caesar was now supreme. He had packed the Senate with his own creatures; through them he controlled the state, through the state the civilized world. A cult of personality rapidly grew up around him. Portrait busts were distributed throughout Italy and beyond; his image even appeared on coins, an unheard-of innovation in Rome. But none of this added to his popularity. With all the power now gathered into Caesar's hands, the way was blocked to ambitious young politicians, who grew more and more to resent his arrogance, his capriciousness and, not least, his immense wealth. They also resented his frequent long absences on campaign, which they considered unnecessary and irresponsible. He was after all fifty-six years old and known to be epileptic; future wars should surely be left to his generals. Caesar himself, however, did not share this view. At the beginning of 44 BC he announced a new expedition to the east, to avenge the death of Crassus and to teach the Parthians a lesson. He would be commanding in person, and would leave on 18 March.

For the Roman patricians, to be ruled by a dictator was bad enough; the prospect of being ordered about by his secretaries for the next two years or more was intolerable. And so the great conspiracy took shape. It was conceived and led by Gaius Cassius Longinus, who had originally supported Pompey but whom Caesar had subsequently pardoned. With Cassius was his brother-in-law Marcus Brutus, whom Caesar had made Governor of Cisalpine Gaul. Together, he and Cassius collected some sixty fellow conspirators, and on 15 March they were ready.

On that day, just three days before he was due to leave for the east, Caesar attended a meeting of the Senate in the large hall adjoining the Theatre of Pompey. The conspirators had ensured that his principal lieutenant, Mark Antony, should be detained in conversation by one of their number. Publius Casca seems to have been the first to attack, his dagger striking the dictator in the throat;

within moments Caesar was surrounded by his assailants, all of them frenziedly stabbing, pushing their fellows aside the better to plunge their own blades into whatever part of his body they could reach. Their victim defended himself as best he could, but he had no chance. Covering his bleeding head with his toga, he fell against the plinth of Pompey's statue.

Seeing him dead, those present were seized by a sudden panic. They fled from the building, leaving the body alone where it lay. It was some time before three slaves arrived with a litter and carried it back to his home – one of the arms, we are told, dragging along the ground. Later, when doctors examined it, they counted twenty-three separate wounds – only one of which, however, they believed to have been fatal.

Just six months before his death, Julius Caesar had formally adopted his great-nephew, Gaius Octavius, as his son. Although still only nineteen, Octavian – as he is generally known in his pre-imperial years – had long been groomed for stardom. Already three years before, he had been appointed Pontifex Maximus; since then he had fought courageously with Caesar in Spain. Thus, despite his youth, on the death of his great-uncle he might have expected to assume power; but Mark Antony, Caesar's chief lieutenant, moved fast and – not hesitating to falsify certain of his dead master's papers – seized control of the state. Octavian fought back, and thanks largely to the championing of Cicero – who loathed autocrats in general and Antony in particular, and made a series of bitter speeches against him – gradually won a majority in the Senate. Rome was once again polarized and on the brink of civil war; but by November 43 BC the two had effected an uneasy reconciliation and, with another of Caesar's generals, Marcus Aemilius Lepidus, formed an official five-year triumvirate with two principal objects: first to avenge Caesar, and then to set the government back on its feet.

So far, in this battle of the Titans, there had been fighting in Transalpine and Cisalpine Gaul, in Spain and in Greece. There had even been a brief campaign in North Africa, where Pompey's ally, King Juba of Numidia, had scored a major victory over Caesar's general Curio on the Bagradas River. Sicily, however, had been left mercifully alone. It was to enjoy its isolation no longer. The man who was to turn it back into a battlefield was Sextus, the youngest son of Pompey the Great. Sextus had joined Pompey after his defeat at Pharsalus and had travelled with him to Egypt, where he had personally witnessed his father's assassination in 48 BC. He had then joined the resistance against Caesar. He had fought in North Africa, and with his brother Gnaeus in Spain. There Caesar – after one of his whirlwind expeditions, in which the 1,500-mile journey had taken him less than a month – had defeated them in 45 BC at the Battle of Munda. After this engagement Gnaeus had been captured and executed; Sextus, however, remained at liberty. He was still in Spain when the news came of Caesar's death. In the confusion that followed, having little idea of what the future held in store, he raised an army and a small fleet and shortly afterwards sailed for Sicily.

There was little doubt that the Triumvirate, determined as it was to suppress all opposition, would sooner or later move against him. Its first priority, on the other hand, was to deal with Caesar's murderers – Brutus, Cassius and their followers. Sextus was therefore in no hurry; there was, he knew, plenty of time to prepare for the encounter. Beginning in the northeast corner of the island, he was soon master of Messina, after which the other coastal cities – including Syracuse – seem to have accepted him without a struggle. By the summer of 44 BC his authority was accepted over most of Sicily; by this time too his numbers had increased dramatically. They included several highly distinguished Romans from the senatorial and equestrian orders, men such as Tiberius Claudius Nero, his wife Livia – who was to divorce him and marry Octavian in 39 BC – and their son, the future Emperor Tiberius. Apart from these there were former followers of Pompey, plus all those who had fallen foul of the Triumvirate, vast quantities of fugitive slaves and, inevitably, the usual riffraff of adventurers who were not averse to a little profitable piracy. For piracy there was. Not only did Sextus put a stop to all shipments of corn to Rome; he established a virtual blockade of southern Italy and posted ships along the Adriatic to prevent supplies reaching the army pursuing Brutus and Cassius in the Balkans.

It was not until October 42 BC, after the twin battles of Philippi, that the two arch-conspirators fell on their swords. The triumvirs should then have been free to turn their attention to the rebel who was now their principal enemy. In fact they gave Sextus little trouble – so little, in fact, that in 40 BC he was able to capture Sardinia. In the following year, powerful as ever, he agreed to sign a peace treaty with them at Misenum on the Bay of Naples. The reason they gave was that they needed their hands free for another campaign against the Parthians, to be led this time by Antony; the true reason was the dissatisfaction of the people of Rome, whom a five-year blockade had reduced to near-starvation. The terms of the treaty were all that Sextus could have wished. The triumvirs agreed to recognize his authority over Sicily, Corsica and Sardinia; in return he agreed to lift the blockade, to resume the regular shipments of corn and to accept no more fugitive slaves.

Perhaps it was all too good to be true; at any rate, it did not endure. Fighting soon broke out again, and in 38 BC Octavian attempted a full-scale invasion of Sicily, which was frustrated by the weather. The following year he tried again, but with no greater success. This time he met defeat in a naval battle off Messina and was once again forced to retire. Then, in 36 BC, victory came at last. It was won by Rome's most distinguished admiral, Marcus Vipsanius Agrippa, who led two separate fleets – one of them Octavian's, the other provided by Antony – to Sicily, while yet another, raised by the third triumvir, Lepidus, sailed from North Africa. There were several desperate battles; in August Agrippa defeated Sextus near Milazzo, while Octavian was defeated – and seriously wounded – off Taormina. But the decisive encounter took place on 3 September near the neighbouring port of Naulochus. Agrippa's ships were newer and larger than those of Sextus and also carried a secret weapon, the *harpax*, a catapult-shot grapnel which harpooned an enemy vessel and then winched it alongside for boarding. By the end of the battle, of the two hundred-odd ships with which Sextus had entered the fray, just seventeen remained. He himself took to his heels and escaped to Asia Minor, only to be captured in Miletus the following year. There he was executed without trial. Since he was a Roman citizen, this was strictly illegal – but then he himself had defied the law for much of his life. Rome had had enough of him.

The raising of an African fleet against Sextus Pompey was the last major contribution made by the triumvir Lepidus. By mutual agreement, he was now firmly relegated to a back seat. The remaining two divided up the Roman world between them, Antony taking the eastern half, Octavian the west.

The little town of Tarsus in Cilicia is perhaps best known today for having been the birthplace of St Paul. Some forty years before his birth, however, it was the scene of another event, which had a still greater effect on the world as we know it. It was at Tarsus, sometime in the summer of 41 BC, that Mark Antony first clapped eyes on Queen Cleopatra VII. Six years before, Julius Caesar had first made her his mistress and then established her on the throne of Egypt, together with the man who was both her brother and her brother-in-law, Ptolemy XIV. Before long, according to the wildly incestuous tradition of the Ptolemies, he also became her husband; but even this triple relationship failed to endear him to her and in 44 BC she had him murdered. She now reigned alone; but she needed another Roman protector and had come to Tarsus knowing that it was there that she would find him.

Despite the testimony of Shakespeare – and Pascal's famous remark that if her nose had been a little shorter the whole history of the world would have been changed – Cleopatra seems to have been attractive rather than classically beautiful. Plutarch, in his life of Antony, admits that 'her beauty, as we are told, was in itself neither altogether incomparable, nor such as to impress those who saw her'. She possessed, however, a peculiar 'sweetness in the tones of her voice'. In any case she had little difficulty in ensnaring Antony just as she had Caesar himself, even persuading him to arrange for the death of her sister Arsinoë, whom she had never forgiven for having once established a rival regime in Alexandria. (Arsinoë was the last of her five siblings to die a violent death, at least two of them having perished on Cleopatra's personal initiative.) Antony was delighted to oblige, and as a reward was invited to Alexandria for the winter; the result was twins. After that the two did not see each other again for three years, but in 37 BC he invited her to join him in his eastern capital of Antioch and there they formed a permanent liaison, another son being born the following year.

In Rome Octavian – whose sister Octavia Antony had recently married – was naturally outraged by his brother-in-law's behaviour, and grew more and more resentful of Cleopatra's obvious power over him; and in 32 BC, after Antony had formally divorced Octavia, her brother declared war. On 2 September 31 BC the two fleets met at Actium, just off the northern tip of the island of Leucas. Octavian scored a decisive victory, pursuing the defeated couple back to Alexandria; it was almost another year, however, before the final scene of the drama was enacted. Not until 1 August 30 BC did the victor enter the city, where he gave orders that Egypt should thenceforth be a province of Rome, remaining under his direct personal control. Cleopatra barricaded herself in her private mausoleum and gave it out that she had committed suicide; hearing the news, Antony fell on his sword; but immediately afterwards, learning that the report was false, had himself carried into her presence. Plutarch tells us that the two had a last conversation together before he died.

The manner of Cleopatra's death is less certain. She very probably poisoned herself, but how? Plutarch tells the story of the asp much as Shakespeare wrote it, but adds that 'the real truth nobody knows'. None the less, the arguments for the snakebite theory are strong. The Egyptian cobra – which represented Amon-Ra, the sun god – had been a royal symbol since the days of the earliest pharaohs, who wore its image as a diadem on their crowns; a more regal manner of death could scarcely be imagined. More conclusive still, Suetonius tells us that Octavian later let it be known that the moment he heard of Cleopatra's suicide he had summoned the snake-charmers and had ordered them to suck the poison from the wound. If they came at all, however, they came too late.

The Battle of Actium had two tremendous results. First of all, it ensured that the political spotlight remained firmly focused on Italy and the west. According to the agreement that he had reached with Octavian after Philippi, the largely Greek-speaking lands of the eastern Mediterranean had been the territory of Mark Antony; and if Antony had been victorious he would almost certainly have continued to favour them in any way he could. Under Octavian, however, Rome was still supreme, and would remain so for the next three centuries until Constantine the Great deserted it in 330 for his new capital of Constantinople.

The second consequence of the battle was that it established Octavian, at the age of thirty-two, as the most powerful man who had ever lived, the undisputed master of the known world. The problem for him now was how best to consolidate his position. The Republic was effectively dead, so much was plain; but Julius Caesar's open autocracy had proved fatal to him, and his great-nephew was determined not to make the same mistake. For some time yet, at least in appearance, the old republican forms had to be observed. Every year from 31 to 23 BC Octavian held the consul-ship, using it as the constitutional basis of his power; but his assump-tion, on 16 January 27 BC, of the new title of Augustus was a clear enough indication of the way things were going.

It is thus impossible to put a definite date to the establishment of the Roman Empire. It was a gradual process – but perhaps it was better that way. In his youth Augustus – as we must now call him – was certainly hungry for power; once he had gained it, however, he mellowed and became a statesman. His other achieve-ments are harder to assess. He reorganized the administration and the army; he established permanent naval bases around the Mediterranean, of which Rome was now the unchallenged mistress: between 200 BC and 200 AD there was a greater density of commer-cial traffic than at any time in the next thousand years.* Above all he moulded the old Republic into the new shape that its vast expansion had made necessary, and somehow reconciled to it all classes of Roman society, rallying them to the support of his new regime. It was said of him that he found Rome a city of brick and left it a city of marble, but he did more: he found it a republic and

---

* It is hardly surprising that the most common Latin name for the Mediterranean was *mare nostrum*, 'our sea'. No previous power had ever been in a position to make such a claim; nor has any been able to do so since.

left it an empire – an empire of which Sicily would henceforth be an integral part.

With Sextus Pompey safely out of the way, Augustus took his revenge. Perhaps the personal injuries he had suffered in the sea battle off Taormina increased his vindictiveness; he seems in any case to have been determined to make the Sicilians pay for their support of the unspeakable Sextus. He levied a vast fine on the whole island, and the cities which had resisted him had ample cause to regret their presumption. The entire population of Taormina was deported; 6,000 slaves whose owners had been killed or had disappeared during the fighting were impaled.

As always, Sicily recovered; but it was no longer quite the same. There was, first of all, a much larger Roman element than before. Countless acres around Catania were bestowed in gratitude on the admiral Agrippa, who had been more responsible than anyone for Sextus's defeat; on his death they were all returned to the Emperor. Other senior officers and veterans of the legions were similarly rewarded according to their seniority, often with lands to the north and east of Mount Etna, the centre of trouble in the past. Their loyalty could be relied on; and they also made their own contribution to the slow but steady Romanization of the island. By an imperial decree, all Italians now enjoyed full Roman citizenship; the Sicilians did not. After the Emperor's official visit in 22 or 21 BC, he did however award six cities – Taormina (now presumably forgiven), Catania, Syracuse, Tindari,* Termini and Palermo – the status of *colonia*, making all their citizens effectively Roman. (The fact that the vast majority of these populations were in fact Greeks who spoke not a word of Latin must have created something of a problem; how it was dealt with we have no means of knowing.)

In the remains of ancient Ostia, the port of Rome, you may still see a large floor mosaic of the first century AD, celebrating the four principal provinces from which Rome received her corn. Sicily is of course there, together with Spain, Africa and Egypt. This suggests as clearly as anything could that the island was no longer the only

---

* Now a small and relatively unimportant archaeological site on the coast between Patti and Milazzo.

granary; major advances in the agrarian economy of North Africa, together with Augustus's recent acquisition of Egypt, had seen to that. But it remained, almost certainly, the principal source of grain – it was also by far the nearest – and this was enough to guarantee prosperity, so long as the political situation permitted.

Which, for about four centuries, it did – or, at least, it seems to have. The truth is that we know virtually nothing of Sicilian history for most of the first half-millennium of the Christian era. Writers of the first and second centuries like Tacitus and Suetonius hardly give it a mention. There appears to have been an outbreak of minor banditry in the 260s, but apart from that the island must have been quite astonishingly well behaved. It was also prosperous – just how prosperous can be seen from a visit to the remains of the great villa at Casale, some four miles from the modern town of Piazza Armerina. Built in the first quarter of the fourth century, few of its walls remain; what takes the breath away is the quality and quantity of the superb floor mosaics, which cover some 3,500 square metres. The owner of this extraordinary property has never been identified; he was clearly a man of enormous wealth and distinction, who built it, perhaps, as a hunting lodge. There are countless scenes of hunting and fishing, of animal and marine life, of dancing and feasting and the cultivation of the vine. We even have several scenes from Greek mythology, including Orpheus with his lute, the labours of Hercules and Ulysses in the cave of Polyphemus. Anyone who knows the Bardo Museum in Tunis will be aware of the astonishing wealth of floor mosaics in Roman North Africa. Those of the Villa Casale are almost certainly the work of African craftsmen; the surprising thing is that there is nothing remotely comparable to them elsewhere on the island.

During these early centuries occasional visitors, including the Emperor Caligula, came down from Rome to enjoy the beauties of Syracuse – which, despite its many depredations, had kept something of its reputation as a cultural centre – or to gape at the horrors of Mount Etna; the only other emperors known to have set foot in Sicily were Hadrian (who went everywhere) and Septimius Severus, who had been Governor in his youth. Even the historic decision of Constantine the Great in 330 to move the Empire's capital to Constantinople seems to have left the Sicilians unmoved, and when in 395 the Empire split again and a series of puppet emperors reigned in Italy – mostly from Ravenna – they seem hardly to have noticed.

Constantine's other great achievement, to have effectively made Christianity the official religion of the Roman Empire, had its impact on Sicily as elsewhere, the new religion advancing in ever greater strides. At the time of Christ the old Greek religion had prevailed, though there were also shrines to such eastern divinities as Cybele and the Egyptian Serapis. In Taormina there was actually a temple of Isis.* But from the beginning of the fourth century Christianity spread rapidly across the island; no visitor to Syracuse should fail to visit the ancient and immense catacombs of S. Lucia and S. Giovanni, which were in use between the third and sixth centuries and are second only to those of Rome itself. Meanwhile, the conversion of pagan buildings to churches had begun in earnest – the old temple of Athena in Syracuse was consecrated well before 600 – and church organization kept pace. A bishop Chrestus of Syracuse attended the Council of Arles as early as 314, and bishop Paschasinus of Lilybaeum was at the Ecumenical Council of Chalcedon in 451. (Interestingly enough, the latter delivered his oration in Latin, while demanding during the rest of the proceedings the services of a Greek interpreter.) In 447 Pope Leo I addressed a letter 'to the bishops of Sicily', and by the time of Gregory the Great at the end of the sixth century there were at least twelve, one of them on the island of Lipari.

Gregory was clearly interested in Sicily. He founded no less than six monasteries on the island, but his letters show that he was also deeply disturbed by the marked reluctance of the lower clergy to embrace the rule of celibacy. This is not hard to understand. The majority of Sicilians still spoke Greek, and although spiritually subordinate to the Pope in Rome they probably observed the Greek rite, in which ordinary priests are *required* to marry – unlike monks

* Later it was converted into a Christian church dedicated to, of all people, St Pancras.

and bishops, who are forbidden to do so. After the Byzantine conquest, it was only natural that the Greek influence should increase in strength – although, strangely enough, the Sicilians continued to build nearly all their churches on the basilican plan – with nave, possibly aisles, steps up to the chancel and probably a semicircular apse at the east end. The Greek cross-in-square churches are relatively rare.

Around this time, too, there seems to have been a substantial Jewish immigration. At the end of the sixth century we find Gregory instructing his local representative to try to convert these Jews by offering them lower rents and taxes; on the other hand, we also find him sternly ordering the Bishop of Palermo to replace the synagogues that he had forcibly converted into churches, and to restore all their furniture. Oddly enough, the Sicilian Jews dispensed with their own burial grounds, of the kind regularly found in Rome. They were clearly quite happy to share Christian cemeteries, and often a crudely carved menorah is the only distinguishing feature on the gravestone.

In the fifth century AD, the barbarians arrived. Of their many and various tribes, three only are of interest to us: the Goths, the Huns and the Vandals. All three, at different times, posed major threats to the Empire, though only one showed an interest in Sicily. The three could hardly have been more different. By the end of the fourth century the Goths had become a relatively civilized people, the majority of them Arian* Christians. Although the western branch, that of the Visigoths, was still ruled by local chieftains, the eastern branch, known as the Ostrogoths, had already evolved into a prosperous central European kingdom. The Huns, on the other hand, were savages: an undisciplined, heathen horde, Mongolian in origin, which had swept down from the central Asian steppe, laying waste everything in its path. As for the Vandals – the last of the great barbarian peoples to have cast their shadow over the unhappy

---

* Followers of Arius, a presbyter of Alexandria, who held that Jesus Christ was not coeternal and of one substance with God the Father, but had been created by Him for the salvation of the world. Thus, although a perfect man, the Son must always be subordinate to the Father, his nature being human rather than divine.

fifth century – they had relatively little direct influence on the Roman Empire; but their effect on the Mediterranean was greater than that of the other two put together.

It was the Goths who struck first. Three times between 408 and 410 the Visigothic chieftain Alaric besieged Rome. The first siege starved it out; the Romans were obliged to pay an enormous ransom. The second ended when they agreed to depose the Emperor; the third resulted in the sack of the city. Then came the Huns. They had first smashed their way into Europe in 376; their first contact with the civilized world, however, had had little effect on them. The vast majority still lived and slept in the open, disdaining all agriculture and even cooked food – though they liked to soften raw meat by putting it between their horse's flanks and their own thighs as they rode. For clothing they favoured tunics made from the skins of field mice crudely stitched together. These they wore continuously, without ever removing them, until they dropped off of their own accord. Their home was the saddle; they seldom dismounted, not even to eat or sleep. Their leader Attila was typical of his race: short, swarthy and snub-nosed, with beady eyes set in a head too big for his body and a thin, straggling beard. Within a few years of his accession he had become known throughout Europe as 'the scourge of God': more feared, perhaps, than any other single man – with the possible exception of Napoleon – before or since.

Not until 452 did he launch his army upon Italy. All the great cities of the Veneto were put to the torch; Pavia and Milan were ruthlessly sacked. Then he turned south towards Rome – and suddenly stopped. Why he did so remains a mystery. Traditionally, the credit has always been given to Pope Leo the Great, who is said to have travelled north to meet him and persuaded him to advance no further;* but it seems hardly likely. In any event, Rome was spared. A year later, during the night following his marriage to yet another of his already innumerable wives, his exertions brought on a sudden haemorrhage. As his lifeblood flowed away, all Europe breathed again – although not, as it soon became clear, for long.

---

* The scene is most enjoyably enacted in Verdi's *Attila*, despite the fact that Pope Leo is disguised – as was required by the censor – as 'an old Roman'.

And so to the Vandals, who were the only barbarians to take to the sea. These Germanic tribesmen, their creed fanatically Arian, had fled westwards from the Huns some half a century before and in 409, after invading and laying waste a large area of Gaul, had settled in Spain. There they had remained until 428, when their newly crowned King Gaiseric had led his entire people across the Mediterranean to North Africa. Just eleven years later he captured Carthage,★ the last imperial stronghold on the coast, which he turned into a sort of pirate stronghold. Things looked bad indeed for Sicily. Gaiseric raided it in 440 and again in 456, but it was not until 468 – when he was in his late seventies – that he established full control over the island. He held it, however, for only about eight years, doing little appreciable good or harm.

Which brings us to the year 476. The Roman Empire of the West was now sick unto death, and it was in this year that it breathed its last. The abdication of its last Emperor, the pathetic child Romulus Augustulus – his very name a double diminutive – need cause us no surprise. He was toppled by another Germanic barbarian called Odoacer who refused to accept the old plurality of emperors, recognizing only the authority of the Byzantine Emperor Zeno in Constantinople. All he asked of Zeno was the title of Patrician, in which capacity he proposed to rule Italy in the Emperor's name. One of his first moves was to buy Sicily back from Gaiseric in return for an annual payment of tribute.

Five years before, in 471, a boy of seventeen named Theodoric had succeeded his father as paramount leader of the eastern Goths. Although he had received little or no formal education during the ten years of his childhood spent as a hostage in Constantinople – he is said to have signed his name all his life by stencilling it through a perforated gold plate – he had acquired an instinctive understanding of the Byzantines and their ways which was to serve him in good stead in the years to come. His main objective on his accession, like that of so many barbarian leaders before him, was to find and

---

★ After its destruction in 146 BC Carthage had remained virtually deserted for over a century, until in 29 BC Augustus had made it the capital of his Roman province of Africa.

secure a permanent home for his people. To this end he was to devote the better part of the next twenty years, fighting sometimes for and sometimes against the Empire, arguing, bargaining, threatening and cajoling by turns, until, some time in 487, he and Zeno came to an agreement. Theodoric would lead his entire people into Italy, overthrow Odoacer and rule the land as an Ostrogothic kingdom under imperial sovereignty. And so, early in 488, the great exodus took place: men, women and children, with their horses and their pack animals, their cattle and their sheep, lumbering slowly across the central European plains in search of greener and more peaceful pastures.

Odoacer fought back, but his army was no match for that of the Goths. He withdrew to Ravenna, where Theodoric blockaded him until the local bishop arranged an armistice. It was then agreed that Italy was to be ruled by the two of them jointly, sharing the imperial palace. This solution seemed remarkably generous on the part of Theodoric; but it soon became clear that he had not the faintest intention of keeping his word. On 15 March 493 he invited Odoacer with his brother, his son and his senior officers to a banquet. There, as his guest took his place in the seat of honour, Theodoric stepped forward and with one tremendous stroke of his sword sliced through the body of Odoacer from collarbone to thigh. The other guests were similarly dealt with by the surrounding guards. Odoacer's wife was thrown into prison, where she died of starvation; his son, whom he had surrendered to the Ostrogoths as a hostage, was executed. Finally Theodoric laid aside the skins and furs that were the traditional clothing of his race, robed himself – as Odoacer never had – in the imperial purple and settled down to rule in Italy.

After this violent beginning, he was to do so, quietly and efficiently, for the next thirty-three years, and the extraordinary mausoleum which he built for himself – and which still stands in the northeastern suburbs of Ravenna – perfectly symbolizes, in its half-classical, half-barbaric architectural strength, the colossus who himself bestrode the two civilizations. No other Germanic ruler, setting up his throne on the ruins of the Western Empire, possessed a fraction of Theodoric's statesmanship and political vision. When he died, on 30 August 526, Italy lost the greatest of her early medieval rulers, unequalled until the days of Charlemagne.

In the year 533, the Emperor Justinian launched his great campaign to recover the Empire of the West. To him it was clear that a Roman Empire without Rome was an absurdity; and he was fortunate indeed in having as his instrument the most brilliant general in all Byzantine history, a Romanized Thracian like himself named Belisarius. Belisarius arrived in Sicily in 535, where he was almost universally welcomed. The exception was Palermo, still a small port of only very secondary importance.* Here the local governor attempted a stand; but Belisarius ordered his fleet to sail into the harbour so close inshore that the masts of the ships rose above the town walls. He then had boats full of soldiers hoisted to the yard-arms, whence they were able to shoot down on the defenders.

Sicily was once again an imperial province, ruled by Byzantine governors normally sent out from Constantinople. At one moment, indeed, it almost became a great deal more. In the middle of the seventh century the Byzantine Emperor Constans II the Bearded, understandably concerned for the future of his western provinces under the whirlwind surge of Islam, took the immense decision to shift the balance of the Empire westwards and to transfer his capital accordingly. Rome was the obvious choice; but after a depressing twelve-day visit there in 663 – he was the first Emperor for nearly three hundred years to set foot in the mother city – he gave up the idea and settled instead in the infinitely more congenial Greek atmosphere of Syracuse.

For the Sicilians, the next five years were one protracted nightmare. The honour, such as it was, of finding their island selected for the capital of the Roman Empire was as nothing in comparison with the extortions of the Roman tax-gatherers – for the satisfaction of whom, we are told, husbands were sold into slavery, wives

---

* Despite its superb geographical position, Palermo became a metropolis only under Arab occupation. This explains why the city possesses virtually no classical antiquities – temples, theatres, even ruins – on the scale of those to be found elsewhere on the island.

forced into prostitution, children separated from their parents. Nor can we tell how long these depredations might have continued had not the Emperor unexpectedly come to a sudden, violent and mildly humiliating end. There was, so far as we know, no preconceived plan to assassinate him, far less any deeply hatched conspiracy; but on 15 September 668, while he was innocently lathering himself in his bath, one of his attendants – in what we can only assume to have been a fit of uncontrollable nostalgia – attacked him from behind and felled him with the soapdish. By now the Arabs were directing their main offensive towards Asia Minor and Constantinople itself, and so Constans's son and successor, Constantine IV, had no choice but to return at once to the Bosphorus. Sicily was left in peace again.

This peace continued, generally speaking, throughout the eighth century, during which Sicily, like neighbouring Calabria, became a haven for refugees from the iconoclast movement in the Empire;* but in the ninth it was shattered. The Arabs had waited long enough. They had by now occupied the entire length of the North African coast, and had already been harassing the island with sporadic raiding. Then in 827 they saw their chance of achieving permanent occupation. The local Byzantine governor, Euphemius by name, had recently been dismissed from his post and recalled to Constantinople after an unseemly elopement with a local nun. His reply was to rise in revolt and proclaim himself Emperor, appealing to the Arabs for aid. They landed in strength, rapidly entrenched themselves, took little notice of Euphemius – who soon came to a violent end – and three years later stormed Palermo, making it their capital. Subsequent progress was slow. Messina fell in 843; Syracuse suffered a long and terrible siege, during which the defenders were finally reduced to cannibalism. The city surrendered only in 878. After this the Byzantines seem to have admitted defeat. A few isolated outposts in the eastern part of the island held out a little longer

---

* In 726 the Emperor Leo III had decreed the destruction of all icons on the grounds that they were idolatrous. This caused consternation – particularly in the monasteries – and many people fled, with as many icons as they could carry, rather than destroy them. The decree remained in force – with one short intermission – until 842.

– the last, Rometta, even into the middle of the tenth century – but on that June day when the banner of the Prophet was raised over Syracuse, Sicily became, to all intents and purposes, a part of the Muslim world.

Once the wars of conquest were over and the country had settled again, life continued pleasantly enough for most of the Greek Christian communities. Although they had to endure a degree of discrimination as second-class citizens, they were normally allowed to keep their freedom, on payment of an annual tribute which many must have preferred to the heavy taxation and compulsory military service imposed by the Roman Empire. Meanwhile the Saracens displayed, as so often throughout their history, a degree of religious toleration which permitted the churches and monasteries and the long tradition of Hellenistic scholarship to flourish as much as ever they had done. In other ways too the island benefited from its conquerors. They brought with them a whole new system of agriculture, based on such innovations as terracing and siphon aqueducts for irrigation. They introduced cotton and papyrus, melon and pistachio, citrus and date palm and enough sugar cane to make possible, within a very few years, a substantial export trade. Under the Byzantines Sicily had never played an important part in European commerce, but with the Saracen conquest it soon became one of the major trading centres of the Mediterranean, with Christian, Muslim and Jewish merchants all thronging the bazaars of Palermo.

And yet, among the many blessings conferred upon Sicily by her Arab conquerors, that of stability was conspicuously absent. As the links of loyalty which bound the Emir of Palermo and his fellow chieftains to the North African caliphate grew ever more tenuous, the emirs themselves lost their cohesive force; they became increasingly divided against one another, and so the island found itself once again a battleground of warring factions. It was this steady political decline that was to bring the Greeks in strength back to Sicily – together with their Norman allies.

4

Normans

B Y THE BEGINNING of the eleventh century the Normans had virtually completed the process by which, in barely a hundred years, they had transformed themselves from a crowd of barely literate heathen barbarians into a civilized, semi-independent Christian state. It was a stupendous achievement. Men were still alive whose fathers remembered Rollo, the fair-haired Viking who had led his longboats up the Seine and who in 911 was enfeoffed with most of the eastern half of modern Normandy by the French King Charles the Simple. Already in the following year a consider-able number of his subjects, led by Rollo himself, had received Christian baptism. Within a generation or two, Christianity was universal. And the same was true of language. Before the end of the tenth century the old Norse tongue had died out altogether, leaving hardly a trace behind.

Quick-witted, adaptable and still blessed with the inexhaustible energy of their Viking forebears, the early Norman adventurers were admirably equipped for the role they were to play in European history. They also possessed another quality without which their great southern kingdom could never have been born: they were enormously prolific, which resulted in a continually exploding popu-lation and increasing numbers of footloose younger sons wandering south in the search of *Lebensraum*. And what better excuse to leave on such a search than a pilgrimage? It was hardly surprising, at the dawn of the second millennium, when the world had not after all come to an end as had been predicted and a wave of relief was still sweeping across Europe, that the great pilgrim roads should have been thronged – and that whole parties of pilgrims should have been composed entirely of Normans.

Some pilgrims made their way to Rome, others to the great church of St James at Compostela; but the greatest pull of all was naturally exerted by Jerusalem – which, to all Normans, had an additional appeal: it meant that on the outward or the return journey – or indeed on both – they could visit the cave of the archangel Michael who, since he was the patron of their own great shrine of Mont-Saint-Michel, was always especially dear to Norman hearts. Ships bound for Palestine were normally to be found at Brindisi or Bari, and from either of these ports it was only a short way up the Adriatic coast to give thanks at this other shrine, hidden deep under the rock of the peninsula of Monte Gargano. Centuries before the birth of Christ, this was already a holy place; it had therefore had some thousand years of uninterrupted sanctity behind it when, in 493 AD, the archangel had appeared to a local farmer, leaving behind his great iron spur. Thus it was that Monte Sant'Angelo, as it was generally called, had become in its turn one of the great pilgrimage centres of Europe. And it was there, in the summer of 1016, that a group of Norman pilgrims was accosted by a curiously dressed stranger who introduced himself as Melus, a Lombard nobleman. His people, he told them, had been in south Italy for five hundred years, but a considerable territory that had once been Lombard was now under Byzantine occupation. His whole life was devoted to the cause of Lombard independence, which – with the help of perhaps a couple of hundred stalwart young Normans like themselves – could easily be achieved. Against a combined Norman–Lombard army those Greeks would not stand a chance; and the Lombards for their part would not forget their allies.

Of course the proposal was accepted; how could it not have been? Here was the perfect opportunity – a rich, fertile land which these young men were being invited, implored almost, to enter, which offered endless possibilities for proving their worth and making their fortune. They explained to Melus that they had come to Apulia as unarmed pilgrims and were hardly equipped to embark immediately on a campaign. They must first return to Normandy, but only for so long as was necessary to make the proper preparations and to recruit companions-in-arms. In the following year they would be back, in greater numbers, to join their new Lombard friends, and the grand adventure would begin.

South Italy was a cauldron, never altogether off the boil. Surrounded and pervaded by the constant clashing of two empires, three religions – for the Muslims of Sicily were making constant inroads – and an ever-varying collection of independent, semi-independent or rebellious cities, a strong arm and a sharp sword could never lack employment. And, since the Normans saw themselves as mercenaries, out for what they could get, and the Byzantine Governor knew a good fighter when he saw one, there may have been not too much surprise when, within some five years of their arrival, a well-equipped force of Normans rode off to Apulia to defend the lawful dominions of Byzantium against the continued dastardly attacks of Lombard troublemakers.

So it came about that, some forty years after their conversation in the cave of the archangel, the Normans made themselves the most powerful force in south Italy, thanks in considerable measure to the family of an obscure Norman baron, living in the Cotentin peninsula, named Tancred de Hauteville. Tancred himself was notable only for his determined and persistent fecundity. His two successive wives bore him at least three daughters and no fewer than twelve sons, of whom five made their way to Italy and three became leaders of the first rank. One of them, Robert Guiscard,* was to prove himself the most dazzling military adventurer between Julius Caesar and Napoleon.

For the first generation of Norman immigrants, Sicily was of little or no interest. There were far too many opportunities nearer at hand. In 1035, however, the civil war that had been threatening there for some years suddenly became a reality. The Emir al-Akhal of Palermo found himself confronted with an insurgent army, led by his brother Abu Hafs and stiffened by 6,000 warriors from Africa under the command of Abdullah, son of the Zirid Caliph of Kairouan. Desperate for help, he appealed to the Emperor Michael IV in Constantinople. Michael saw his chance. Constant raids in the eastern

* 'The Crafty'.

Mediterranean by Arab pirates based in Sicily were doing serious damage to the Byzantine economy. Nor was it only the coastal towns that were suffering from their depredations; the city merchants complained that the pirates were everywhere: prices of imports were rising dangerously and foreign trade was beginning to suffer. And the Emperor had another reason too. To all Greeks, Sicily was part of the Byzantine birthright; the island still possessed a considerable Greek-speaking population. That it should still be occupied by the heathen was an affront not only to imperial security but to national pride. The Arabs must go.

Before the Emperor could send more than a token force, word came that al-Akhal had been assassinated; but revolt was now spreading rapidly through Sicily and the Muslims, more and more hopelessly divided, seemed unlikely to be able to offer much resistance to a concerted Byzantine attack. Preparations therefore went ahead; and in the early summer of 1038 the expedition sailed. It had been entrusted to the greatest of living Byzantine generals, a giant named George Maniakes. He was, in character as well as in appearance, well over life-size. The contemporary historian Michael Psellus wrote:

> I myself saw the man, and marvelled at him . . . To look at him, his men would tilt back their heads as if towards the top of a hill or a high mountain. His countenance was neither gentle nor pleasing, but put one in mind of a tempest; his voice was like thunder and his hands seemed made for tearing down walls or for smashing doors of bronze. He could spring like a lion and his frown was terrible.

The expedition did not go at once to Sicily, but first headed round to Salerno to collect more soldiers from the Lombard prince Gaimar. He was only too pleased to help: the steadily increasing numbers of idle Norman adventurers, bored, predatory and utterly unprincipled, looking for trouble and constrained to live off the land, were proving a grave embarrassment to him. Three hundred of the youngest and most headstrong were given their marching orders and, with a number of Italians and Lombards, boarded the Byzantine ships. They included, inevitably, the Hautevilles.

Sometime during the late summer of 1038 George Maniakes

landed his army on Sicilian soil. At first he carried all before him. Messina fell almost at once, to be followed by Rometta, the key fortress commanding the northern coastal road to Palermo. For the next two years the chroniclers are silent; but it seems clear that Syracuse fell in 1040 after a heavy siege. The Normans had certainly played their part: William, the oldest of the Hauteville brothers, had personally unhorsed the city's Emir and left him dead on the ground, thus earning the sobriquet of *Bras-de-Fer*, 'the Iron-Arm'. But the main credit for the Byzantine successes must go to Maniakes himself, for the effectiveness of his intelligence and the speed and energy of his generalship. It was all the more tragic that at this of all moments he should have been summoned back to Constantinople.

The fault was largely his own. He had never bothered to hide his contempt for Stephen, the commander of the fleet, a former caulker of ships who, thanks to a fortunate marriage many years before, had woken up one morning to find himself the Emperor's brother-in-law. The many rows between the two of them had all been one-sided, since the admiral was terrified of the general and less than half his size; some days after the capture of Syracuse, Maniakes actually lost his temper with Stephen and shook him till his teeth rattled. This, however was a disastrous mistake. Stephen sent an urgent message to his imperial brother-in-law denouncing his colleague for treasonable activity. Maniakes was called back to Constantinople, where he was cast unceremoniously into prison. His successor, a eunuch called Basil, proved as incapable as Stephen; the Greeks lost their momentum and the retreat began – without, however, the Normans. A dispute had arisen over division of the spoils, of which the Hautevilles and their friends claimed – probably rightly – that they had received less than their fair share. They had left the Greek army forthwith and had returned to the mainland.

There, their power continued to grow; and it was not surprising, in the circumstances, that by mid-century the Papacy had become seriously concerned. The Normans were now effectively on its very doorstep; there was nothing to prevent their marching into the Holy City itself. Pope Leo IX resolved to move first. He raised an army, and led it in person against them. The two forces met on

17 June 1053 near Civitate, on the bank of the Fortore River, and the Pope was defeated. The Normans treated him with every courtesy and conducted him to Benevento, where they kept him for almost a year while a modus vivendi for the future was worked out. Its details need not concern us here; suffice it to say that just six years later, in the little town of Melfi, Pope Nicholas II invested Robert Guiscard with the dukedoms of Apulia, Calabria – and Sicily.

By just what title the Pope so munificently bestowed on the Normans territories which had never before been claimed by him or his predecessors is open to doubt. Apulia and Calabria were questionable enough, but with regard to Sicily Nicholas was on still shakier ground, since the island had never been subject to papal control. It was unlikely, however, that such considerations bothered the Normans overmuch. By that third investiture, the Pope had issued Robert with an open invitation. Sicily, lying green and fertile little more than a stone's throw from the mainland, was the obvious objective, the natural completion of that great southward sweep that had brought the Normans down the peninsula. It was also the lair of Saracen pirates, still a perennial menace to the Italian coastal towns of the south and west. While Sicily remained in the hands of the heathen, how could the Duke of Calabria and Apulia ever ensure the security of his newly legalized dominions?

To the local populations, the progeny of old Tancred de Hauteville must have seemed almost infinite. Already no fewer than seven of his sons had made their mark in Italy; and still this remarkable source showed no sign of exhaustion, for there now appeared on the scene an eighth brother, Roger. He was the youngest of the Hautevilles, at this time some twenty-six years old; but as a fighter he was a match for any, while as a statesman he was the greatest of them all. His brother Robert quickly recognized his qualities. As a recent arrival, Roger had not yet acquired any territorial responsibilities; he would clearly be the perfect second-in-command for the coming Sicilian expedition.

In the early spring of 1060 Robert and Roger together forced the surrender of the Byzantine garrison in Reggio, the Calabrian town that faces Sicily across the Strait of Messina. Now the only Italian city still in Greek hands was Bari, too far away on the Adriatic to cause any trouble; the way was clear. The Pope had given his blessing, the Western Empire was as powerless as the Eastern to intervene. Even in Sicily itself the situation seemed relatively favourable. In many areas the local population was still Christian – though of the Orthodox persuasion – and likely to welcome the invaders as liberators. As for the Muslims, they were certainly brave fighters, but they were now more than ever divided among themselves. It did not look as though the Norman conquest of Sicily would take very long.

In fact, from first to last it took thirty-one years – in notable contrast to the Norman conquest of England just six years later, which mopped up the Saxon opposition in a matter of months. This cannot all be attributed to the valour of the Saracen armies; it was due principally to the rebellious barons in Apulia, who divided Robert's energies and resources at a time when he desperately needed all he had for Sicily. And yet, paradoxically, it was these Apulian preoccupations that made Sicily the brilliant and superbly organized kingdom that it later became. As Robert was obliged to spend more and more time on the mainland, so the campaign in Sicily fell increasingly under the control of his brother, until Roger could finally assume effective supremacy. This was to lead to the division of Robert's domains and so allowed Roger, finally freed of Apulian responsibilities, to devote to the island the attention it deserved.

On 10 January 1072 the brothers made their formal entry into Palermo. Subjection of the island was still by no means complete. Independent emirates struggled on in Syracuse and Trapani, but henceforth final pacification could be only a matter of time. Robert Guiscard as Duke of Sicily claimed suzerainty over the island, but with his two mainland dukedoms to look after could never remain there long; Roger would be the effective ruler, with the title of Great Count. Sicily was to be effectively transformed. Since the first half of the ninth century it had been wholly or largely in Muslim hands, constituting a forward outpost of Islam from which raiders, pirates and the occasional expeditionary force had maintained an unremitting pressure against the southern bastions of Christendom.

For some 250 years, separately and in combination, the two great empires had striven in vain to subdue them; Robert and Roger, with a handful of followers, had succeeded in barely a decade. Moreover, the Norman conquest of Sicily was, together with the contemporary beginnings of the Reconquista in Spain, the first step in the immense Christian reaction against the Muslim-held lands of the southern Mediterranean – that reaction which was shortly to develop into the colossal, if ultimately empty, epic of the Crusades.

Robert Guiscard never returned to Sicily. Roger, for his part, was only too happy to be left in sole authority. He saw the island with eyes quite different from his brother's. For Robert, it was simply a bright new jewel in his crown, a territorial extension of the Italian peninsula, inconveniently divided by a strip of water from his other dominions. It was Roger who saw that that narrow strait, protecting it from the eternal squabbles of south Italy, offered possibilities of greatness far beyond anything that could be hoped for on the mainland. His first task, however, was to establish and consolidate Norman rule; and with only a few hundred knights under his command he knew that this could be done only by persuading the Muslims voluntarily to accept the new dispensations. This would need, above all, tolerance and understanding. The mosques – apart from the converted Christian churches, which were reconsecrated – remained open, as they always had been, for the prayers of the faithful. Islamic law was still dispensed by the local courts. Arabic was declared an official language, on equal footing with Latin, Greek and Norman French. In local government, many provincial emirs were retained at their posts. Nowhere did the Normans show any of that brutality which was so unpleasant a feature of their conquest of England. Thus, over most of the island, the sullen resentment of the conquered people gradually faded as Roger won their confidence; and many of those who had fled to Africa or Spain came back within a year or two to Sicily and resumed their former lives.

His new Christian subjects presented the Great Count with a more difficult problem. The enthusiasm with which the Sicilian Greeks had first welcomed their liberators soon wore thin. These Frankish knights might emblazon the Cross of Christ on their banners, but most of them seemed a good deal more uncivilized than the Muslims. Now, too, Sicily suffered a hideous influx of Latin priests and monks, schismatics to a man. Did these newcomers not follow the despised Latin liturgy? Did they not maintain that the Holy Ghost proceeded from the Father and the Son, rather than from the Father alone? Did they not cross themselves with four fingers, and from left to right rather than right to left? Worst of all, were they not even appropriating some of the Greek churches for their own use?

The Greeks had already been given full guarantees that their language, culture and traditions would be respected, but this was clearly not enough. Roger saw that he must now give them material help with the reconstitution of their Church. He put funds at the disposal of the Orthodox community for the rebuilding of their churches and monasteries, and before long he had personally endowed a brand-new Basilian* foundation – the first of fourteen that he was to establish or restore during the remainder of his life. And so, from those earliest days in Palermo, the Great Count began to lay the foundations of a multiracial and polyglot state in which Norman, Greek and Arab would, under a firmly centralized government, follow their own cultural traditions in freedom and concord. Inevitably, it took time. Pockets of resistance remained. It was a good seven years after the fall of Palermo before that part of Sicily north of the Agrigento–Catania line accepted the Normans as its overlords – and even then the great fortress of Enna continued to hold out.

And there still remained Syracuse. On 25 May 1085, in the course of a naval battle fought just outside the harbour – precisely where the Syracusan ships had destroyed the Athenian fleet almost exactly fifteen centuries before – the local emir attempted to board Roger's flagship. Already wounded, he jumped short and was drowned by the weight of his armour. Far from surrendering, however, the city held out for another five months (five months, incidentally, during which Robert Guiscard died of typhoid, off Cephalonia, while leading an expedition against Constantinople). Not till October was

* Greek monasteries all follow the Order of St Basil.

the Saracen resistance finally broken. Then in July 1086 Agrigento fell after a four-month siege, leaving only Enna.

A few weeks later Roger arrived beneath the fortress walls and invited the Lord of Enna, the Emir Ibn Hamud, down for a parley. As he had been led to expect, he found the Emir perfectly prepared to capitulate, exercised only by the problem of how to do so without losing face. The Great Count had by this time lived too long among Muslims to underestimate the importance of such a question, and a solution was soon found. A few days later the Emir left the castle at the head of his troops and led them through a narrow defile; the moment they entered it they were set upon by a vastly superior Norman force and quickly surrounded. Strangely enough, however, no lives were lost. Their captors then moved on to Enna itself, which, deprived of its Emir and its army, gave in at once. Presumably in gratitude, Ibn Hamud then had himself baptized and settled in Calabria where, on an estate provided by Roger, he lived out his remaining years, happily and in the style to which he was accustomed, like any other Christian gentleman.

Thus it was that Roger of Sicily had become, by the last decade of the eleventh century, the greatest prince of the south, more powerful than any ruler on the Italian mainland, the Pope included. About his personality and private life we know infuriatingly little – save that he seems to have possessed in full measure the fertility of the Hautevilles. Existing records testify to at least thirteen and probably seventeen children by various mothers, to three of whom he was successively married; but the list may not be exhaustive. Be that as it may, when he died on 22 June 1101 he left only two legitimate male offspring – both born to his third wife, Adelaide of Savona, when he was well over sixty. The elder of these, Simon, died three months after his father at the age of twelve; and it was young Roger, then only seven or eight years old, who succeeded his father as Great Count of Sicily. Seven years later, during which time his mother proved an extremely effective Regent, he took control.

By this time the island was no longer the backwater it had been half a century before. Its economic explosion had been spectacular. The Strait was, for the first time in centuries, safe for Christian shipping; Messina and Syracuse were boom towns; and merchants from every corner of the Mediterranean thronged the streets and bazaars of Palermo. Suddenly Sicily had come into its own as the central island of the Middle Sea. Roger was determined that his own political influence should grow in proportion; and that he himself, like Robert Guiscard before him, should make his power and presence felt among the princes of Europe – and those of Africa and Asia too.

In 1128 he achieved the first part of his grand design: the acquisition of the two Norman duchies on the mainland, conferred on him by Pope Honorius II at Benevento. Now at last, as in the Guiscard's day, Apulia, Calabria and Sicily were all united under a single Duke. And that Duke was still only thirty-two. The second step, however, was more difficult; he desperately needed a royal crown. This was nothing to do with personal vanity. Roger's task was to weld together all the Norman dominions of the south into one nation. To maintain the identities of three separate duchies would have been to invite disintegration; once they were united, the resulting state could be nothing less than a kingdom. Moreover, if he were not a king, how would he be able to treat on equal terms with the other rulers of Europe and the east? Domestic considerations pointed in the same direction. He must have a title that would set him above his senior vassals, the Princes of Capua and Bari, one that would bind all his feudatories with a loyalty deeper than that which a mere duke could command. But the Pope remained and would always remain his suzerain, and he knew that he could not simply assume a crown without papal blessing.

He might never have been able to do so had there not now occurred what must have appeared to him a godsend: a disputed papal succession. By the beginning of February 1130 Pope Honorius II was clearly dying. His obvious successor was Cardinal Pietro Pierleoni. Although of Jewish origins, Pierleoni had an irreproachable background as a monk at Cluny before serving as Papal Legate both in France and in England, where he had appeared with a particularly splendid retinue at the court of King Henry I. But he also had enemies, led by the Chancellor of the Curia, Cardinal Aimeri, who now – by dint of extremely sharp practice, even before

Honorius's body was cold – dragged another Cardinal, one Gregory Papareschi, to the Lateran and there proclaimed him Pope Innocent II. Almost simultaneously, some two dozen cardinals declared those proceedings uncanonical – which they certainly were – and acclaimed Cardinal Pierleoni as Supreme Pontiff under the name of Anacletus II. At dawn on St Valentine's Day 1130 there had been no Pope in Rome. By noon there were two.

In the city itself, the popularity of Anacletus was overwhelming; by April Innocent had been forced to flee. In northern Europe, however, he proved resoundingly popular – the more so since he had at his side the most powerful of all advocates and the outstanding spiritual force of the twelfth century, St Bernard of Clairvaux. With such a champion Innocent could afford to be patient; the same, however, could not be said for Anacletus, who took the only course open to him. Like more than one desperate Pope in the past, he appealed to the Normans. In September he met Roger at Avellino, where the necessary negotiations were soon completed. The Duke promised to give Anacletus his full support: in return, he required a royal crown. For Anacletus, the advantages were obvious. If, as now seemed likely, the Duke was to be his only ally, it was plainly desirable that his position should be strengthened to the utmost. On 27 September 1130, at Benevento, he issued a bull granting to Roger and his heirs the royal crown of Sicily, Calabria and Apulia.

And so King Roger II of Sicily – there was no King Roger I – was duly crowned on Christmas Day 1130, in Palermo Cathedral. Sicily had entered upon her golden age.

The new nation – it was the third largest kingdom in Europe – could not have had a better ruler. Born in the south of an Italian mother, educated during his long minority by Greek and Arab tutors, Roger had grown up in the cosmopolitan atmosphere of tolerance and mutual respect created by his father, and he instinctively understood the complex system of checks and balances on which the internal stability of the country depended. There was little of the Norman knight about him. He possessed none of the warlike attributes which had brought glory to his father and his uncles and, in a single generation, had made the name of an obscure

Norman baron famous throughout the continent. But of all those Hauteville brothers only one, his father, had developed into a statesman. The rest were fighters and men of action to the end. Roger II was different. Although – or perhaps because – he spent most of his first decade as King campaigning with great courage on the mainland and suffering more than his share of disappointments, betrayals and defeats, he hated war and avoided it whenever possible. In appearance a southerner, in temperament an oriental, he had inherited from his Norman forebears nothing but their energy and their ambition, which he combined with a gift for diplomacy entirely his own; and it was these qualities, far more than his prowess on the battlefield, that had enabled him to reunite the south in a single dominion.

The Norman barons in Apulia and Calabria would cause him and his successors continuing trouble. They were products of the old feudal system; they saw no reason to bow down before the upstart Hautevilles. The court was anyway far distant, and they continued to do much as they wished. Roger hated them, above all for the amount of time and effort that was required to keep them in some sort of order. Things were so much easier in Sicily. There, by contrast, feudalism had never existed; everything depended on religious and ethnic tolerance and respect. Each race was allotted tasks consistent with its strengths and weaknesses. Before very long a tradition had come about whereby the navy was always commanded by a Greek, the Greeks being by far the best seamen.* Similarly, the state finances were entrusted to the Arabs, whose mathematics were always better than anyone else's.

And, most miraculously, these political principles were reflected in the art and architecture for which the Normans were responsible. The most obvious and extraordinary features are, perhaps, the clearly Moorish orange and vermilion domes that crown several of the churches, notably S. Giovanni degli Eremiti and S. Cataldo in Palermo; but these are only the beginning. Drive eastwards along the north coast to Cefalù, to the exquisite cathedral which Roger

---

* The English word 'admiral' is a corruption of the Arabic *emir al-bahr*, 'commander of the sea', and comes to us through Norman Sicily.

Byzantine mosaic of Christ Pantocrator in the apse of the cathedral at Cefalù, *c.*1150.
For many, the greatest portrait of Christ in all Christian art.

Greek theatre at Taormina, originally seventh century BC but rebuilt in Roman times.
Mount Etna can be seen in the distance.

Doric temple at Segesta, 420–30 BC. Although never quite finished,
perhaps – in its setting – the most perfect Greek temple in existence.

Mosaic in the church of the Martorana, Palermo, showing Roger II being crowned by Christ, *c.*1150. The King wears the crown and robes of a Byzantine emperor; Christ's feet are off the ground. Note too the words 'ROGERIUS REX' in Greek lettering.

Antique Greek columns supporting the nave of the cathedral at Syracuse. The columns are those of the original Doric temple of Athena, illustrating the curious fact that though religions may change, the sacred places remain the same.

The cathedral at Cefalù, c.1140, founded by Roger II in gratitude after a shipwreck. It was his favourite building, where he had hoped to be buried.

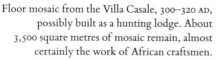

Floor mosaic from the Villa Casale, 300–320 AD, possibly built as a hunting lodge. About 3,500 square metres of mosaic remain, almost certainly the work of African craftsmen.

The Palatine chapel in Palermo perfectly reflects the religions of Norman Sicily: Western ground plan, Byzantine mosaics and a purely Islamic stalactite roof.

Monreale Cathedral: William II presents his building to the Virgin, *c.*1185.

A detail from a capital of the cloister at Monreale representing Norman knights, *c.*1185.

The cloister at Monreale, *c.*1185.

Antonello da Messina, *Portrait of a Man* (possibly a self-portrait), *c.*1460.

The Triumph of Death, *c.*1440: fresco from the Regional Gallery of Sicily, the Palazzo Abatellis, Palermo.

The baroque church of S. Giorgio, Modica. Architect almost certainly Rossario Gagliardi (1698–1762).

The ultimate baroque tour de force. Stucco work by Giacomo Serpotta (1652–1732) in the Oratorio del Rosario di S. Cita, Palermo. The Battle of Lepanto is depicted above the door.

King Charles III of Spain, a passionate hunter, painted by Francisco de Goya, *c.*1786.

Fleet of King Charles III in the port of Naples, 6 October 1759, returning the King to rule in Spain.

began in 1131 and finished seventeen years later. There, high in the conch of the eastern apse, is an immense mosaic of Christ Pantocrator, the Ruler of All – for many of us the most sublime representation of the Redeemer in all Christian art. The style is Byzantine through and through; such a miracle can only have been wrought by the most brilliant of Greek craftsmen, surely imported by Roger from Constantinople.

There are wonderful Greek mosaics, too, in the church of the Martorana (S. Maria dell'Ammiraglio) in Palermo. This was built by the greatest of the Sicilian admirals, George of Antioch, who endowed it in 1143. It is not, alas, as it was: the main apse, with all its mosaics, was demolished in 1683, and replaced by a frescoed *capellone*, the hideousness of which all the efforts of nineteenth-century restorers have been powerless to diminish; the deeply undistinguished western bays were also added – quite unnecessarily – in the seventeenth century. Between the two, however, George's old church has remained, preserving its cross-in-square ground plan and still looking much as it did when it was first consecrated. The mosaics are quietly beautiful – the Annunciation, the Nativity, the Presentation in the Temple and the Dormition of the Virgin are the best.

Above all these, running along the base of the dome beneath the feet of the adoring archangels, you may just discern a narrow wooden frieze. After centuries in darkness, it was only during the restoration work at the end of the nineteenth century that it was rediscovered and found to carry the remains of an inscription, an old Byzantine hymn to the Virgin. Since the Martorana is a Greek church, there is nothing surprising about that, but for one fact – the inscription is in Arabic. Could it be, one wonders, that this hymn was a particular favourite of George of Antioch himself, and that he loved it best in the language in which he had heard it first, half a century before, in his Syrian boyhood?

In the Martorana are two portraits, both taken from life. The first, on a west-facing wall on the north side of the nave near the entrance, is that of its founder, George of Antioch. In its present state it is not a success. The admiral, looking old beyond his years and distinctly oriental, is prostrating himself before the Virgin. The head is the original work, and nearly all the entire, exquisite figure of the Virgin has come down to us unscathed; but alas, the admiral's body has clearly been damaged at some period and a ham-fisted restoration has given him the appearance of nothing so much as a tortoise. More rewarding by far is the corresponding space on the southern wall, in which you will find King Roger himself being symbolically crowned by Christ. There he stands, bending slightly forward, a purely Byzantine figure in his long dalmatic and stole, his crown and jewelled pendants in the manner of Constantinople; even his arms are raised from the elbows in the Greek attitude of prayer. Above his head, great black letters stride across the gold to proclaim him: ΡΟΓΕΡΙΟΣ ΡΗΞ, they read, *Rogerios Rex*. This uncompromising use of the Greek alphabet for a Latin word is less curious than it might seem; by Roger's time the normal Greek word for King, *basileus*, was so identified with the Byzantine Emperor that it would have been unthinkable in this context. And yet the simple transliteration makes an impact of its own and – particularly after one has spotted an Arabic inscription on a nearby pillar – seems to diffuse the whole spirit of Norman Sicily.

This too is a portrait from life – the only surviving likeness of the King which we can safely assume to be authentic. It shows a dark, swarthy man on the threshold of middle age, with a full beard and long thick hair flowing to his shoulders. The face itself might be Greek, or it might be Italian; it even has a faintly Semitic cast about it. Anything less like the traditional idea of a Norman knight could scarcely be imagined. It is always dangerous to read too much into a portrait; but even in something so hieratic and formalized as the Martorana mosaic there are certain inspired touches, certain infinitesimal adjustments and gradations of the tesserae, that bring King Roger to life again before us. Here, surely, is the southerner and oriental, the ruler of subtle mind and limitless flexibility; the statesman to whom diplomacy, however tortuous, is a more natural weapon than the sword – and to whom gold, however corrupting, is a more effective currency than blood. Here is the patron of the sciences, the lover of the arts; here, finally, is the intellectual who has thought deeply about the science of government, who rules with the head and not the heart; the idealist without delusions; the despot, by nature just and merciful, who has learned, sadly, that even mercy must sometimes be tempered in the interests of justice.

There are countless other monuments of Roger's day that could be mentioned; but this is a history, not a guidebook. We must confine ourselves to those which have a historical relevance, and here the Palatine Chapel stands supreme. When Robert Guiscard and his brother had first smashed their way into Arab Palermo, they had established their administrative centre in an old Saracen fortress, which they repaired and strengthened and which became in due course not only the seat of government but the royal palace. As early as 1129, even before he became King, Roger had begun to build his own personal chapel on the upper level, overlooking the inner courtyard. Work on it had been slow, but on Palm Sunday, 28 April 1140, it was consecrated, dedicated to St Peter and formally granted the privileges appropriate to its palatine status.

It is in this building, with more stunning effect than anywhere else in Sicily, that we see the Sicilian-Norman political miracle given visual expression – a seemingly effortless fusion of all that is most brilliant in the Latin, Byzantine and Islamic traditions into a single, harmonious masterpiece. Its form is in essence that of a western basilica, with a central nave and two side aisles separated by rows of antique granite columns, all with richly gilded Corinthian capitals, drawing the eye along to the five steps that lead up to the choir. Western too, though whispering of the south, are the richly ornamented pavements and the coruscating Cosmatesque inlays of the steps, balustrades and lower walls – to say nothing of the immense pulpit, studded with gold and malachite and porphyry and flanked by a gigantic paschal candlestick, a fifteen-foot-high bestiary in white marble.

But if we look up now to the mosaics with which the whole chapel glows gold, we are brought once again face to face with Byzantium. Some of these mosaics have, alas, disappeared; others have been drastically – and in some cases, as in the lower part of the central apse and the two side apses, disastrously – restored. The best, however – the Pantocrator gazing in benediction from the dome, the circle of angels garlanding him with their wings, the four evangelists studious in their squinches – all these are the finest, purest

Byzantine, of which any church in Constantinople would have been proud. Over the choir nearly all bear Greek inscriptions, sure testimony of their date and workmanship; by contrast, the Virgin in the north transept, the scenes from the Old Testament in the nave and those from the lives of St Peter and St Paul in the side aisles were probably added by William I some twenty years later, after his father's death. Here and elsewhere the Latin inscriptions and the preference for Latin saints suggest that William was employing native artists, presumably the Italian pupils of the original Greek masters. Other Italians, in the later thirteenth century, were responsible for the enthroned Christ on the west wall and the two figures of St Gregory and St Sylvester inside the sanctuary arch, unpardonably introduced in the Angevin period to replace an earlier likeness of Roger himself.

These almost antiphonal responses of Latin and Byzantine, set in so lavish a frame, would alone have earned for the Palatine Chapel a unique place among the religious buildings of the world; but for Roger they were still not enough. Two of the great cultural traditions of his country had been dazzlingly reflected in his new creation, but what of the third? What of the Saracens, the most populous group of all his island subjects, whose loyalty had been unwavering – in marked contrast to that of his Norman compatriots – for more than half a century, whose administrative efficiency was largely responsible for the prosperity of his kingdom, and whose craftsmen and artisans were renowned through three continents? And so the chapel was further embellished with what is, quite literally, its crowning glory, surely the most unexpected covering to any Christian church on earth – a stalactite ceiling of wood in the classical Islamic style, as fine as anything to be found in Cairo or Damascus, intricately decorated with the earliest datable group of Arabic paintings in existence – and figurative paintings at that.

Finally, as you wander through this astonishing building, remind yourself of one of its most important aspects – its date. The middle of the twelfth century was just a hundred years after the Great Schism between the Eastern and the Western Churches, which everywhere else were still at daggers drawn. The Crusades, on the other hand, were at their height: while Roger's Arab carpenters were putting together that wonderful ceiling, Christian and Muslim were slaughtering each other the length and breadth of the Levant. Only here, in this one island in the centre of the Mediterranean, did its three great civilizations come together and work together in harmony and concord, as never before or since. Norman Sicily remains a lesson to us all.

As for the court of King Roger, it was by far the most brilliant of twelfth-century Europe. The King himself was famous for his insatiable intellectual curiosity and a respect for learning unique among his fellow princes. By the 1140s he had given a permanent home in Palermo to many of the foremost scholars and scientists, doctors and philosophers, geographers and mathematicians of Europe and the Arab world; and as the years went by he would spend more and more of his time in their company, well able to hold his own in their discussions, whether in French or Latin, Greek or Arabic.

> In mathematics as in the political sphere, the extent of his learning cannot be described. Nor is there any limit to his knowledge of the sciences, so deeply and wisely has he studied them in every particular. He is responsible for singular innovations and for marvellous inventions, such as no prince has ever before realized.

These words were written by Abu Abdullah Mohammed al-Edrisi, Roger's close friend and, of all the palace scholars, the one whom he most admired. Edrisi had arrived in Palermo in 1139; he was to remain there during much of his life, for fifteen years heading a commission established by the King to gather geographical information from all quarters, to correlate it, to record it in orderly form and so ultimately to produce one compendious work which would contain the sum total of all contemporary knowledge of the physical world. Sicily, lying at the crossroads of three continents, her ports as busy and as cosmopolitan as any in Europe, made an ideal centre from which such a work could be undertaken, and for all those fifteen years scarcely a ship put in at Palermo or Messina, Catania or Syracuse, without captain and crew being examined as to every place they had ever visited: its physical features, its climate and its people.

The results of this work, completed in January 1154 barely a month before the King's death, were twofold. The first was a huge planisphere of silver weighing no less than 450 Roman pounds, on which was engraved 'the configuration of the seven climates with that of the regions, countries, sea-coasts both near and distant, gulfs, seas and watercourses; the location of deserts and cultivated lands, and their respective distances by normal routes in miles or other known measures; and the designation of ports'. Alas, it was to be destroyed during the riots of the following reign, within a few years of its completion.

But the second, and perhaps ultimately the more valuable, fruit of Edrisi's labours has come down to us in its entirety.* It is a book, properly entitled *The Avocation of a Man Desirous of a Full Knowledge of the Different Countries of the World* but more generally known as *The Book of Roger*; and it is the greatest geographical work of the Middle Ages. On the very first page we read the words:

> The earth is round like a sphere, and the waters adhere to it and are maintained on it through natural equilibrium which suffers no variation.

As might be expected, *The Book of Roger* emerges as a combination of hard topographical facts – many of them astonishingly accurate for a work produced three and a half centuries before Columbus – and travellers' tales; but even the latter suggest that they have been subjected to stern critical appraisal. Of England we read:

> England is set in the Ocean of Darkness. It is a considerable island, whose shape is that of the head of an ostrich, and where there are flourishing towns, high mountains, great rivers and plains. This country is most fertile; its inhabitants are brave, active and enterprising, but all is in the grip of perpetual winter.

Though Roger's court circle was by no means entirely composed of Muslims like Edrisi, they probably constituted the largest single group; while among Europeans there were many who had been

---

* It too was destroyed during the riots, but ten manuscript copies survive. Two are in the Bibliothèque Nationale in Paris, one is in the Bodleian Library in Oxford.

attracted to Palermo by very reason of its Arab flavour. Unlike Christianity, Islam had never drawn a distinction between sacred and profane knowledge. During the Dark Ages, when the Church of Rome feared and even actively discouraged secular studies, good Muslims remembered how the Prophet himself had reminded them that 'he who travels in search of learning travels along Allah's path to Paradise'. Muslim civilization had long been recognized in the west as superior to anything that Christian Europe could boast. Especially in the field of mathematics and the physical sciences, Arabic had become the scientific language par excellence.

Yet it was a diabolically difficult language to learn and, in northern Europe at any rate, competent teachers were few. Thus, for half a century and more, men like Adelard of Bath – pioneer of Arab studies in England and the greatest name in English science between Robert Grosseteste and Roger Bacon – had been travelling to Spain and Sicily, there to unlock, as they hoped, the secrets of the Muslim world. Many preferred Muslim Spain; for others, however, Sicily possessed one overwhelming advantage: while culturally still very much a part of the Arab world, it also remained in perpetual contact with the Greek east. In the libraries of Palermo, to say nothing of the Basilian monasteries on the island and in Calabria, scholars could find the Greek originals of works known in Spain only in extracts or in translations of doubtful accuracy. Nowadays we tend to forget that, until the thirteenth or even the fourteenth centuries, western Europe was virtually ignorant of Greek; and Roger's Sicily now became the foremost centre of Hellenic studies outside Byzantium itself. But in Byzantium Arabic culture was unknown and mistrusted. Only in Sicily could both civilizations be studied at first hand.

Of King Roger's death we know little, save the day on which it occurred – 26 February 1154. As to its cause, Hugo Falcandus – the greatest of all the chroniclers of Norman Sicily – who begins his history with the new reign, speaks only of 'exhaustion from his immense labours, and the onset of a premature senility through his addiction to the pleasures of the flesh, which he pursued to a point beyond that which physical health requires'. Despite his expressed wish to be buried at Cefalù, his huge porphyry tomb stands in

Palermo Cathedral. It has been opened more than once, to reveal the King's body still clothed in the royal mantle and dalmatic, on its head the tiara with pearl pendants such as we see in the Martorana portrait. It was Roger's last gesture towards Byzantium, the empire he hated but whose concept of monarchy he adopted as his own.

When he died he was only fifty-eight. Had he been granted another fifteen years, his country might have found that national identity that he had laboured so hard to create, and the whole history of southern Europe might have been changed. For a few more years yet Norman Sicily was to increase its influence and prestige from London to Constantinople, while the cultural brilliance of the court of Palermo was to continue undimmed and unparalleled in Europe. But already the internal fabric of the state was showing signs of decay, and with the reign of William the Bad the Kingdom, though still golden in its splendour, embarks on its last sad decline.

5

The End of the Kingdom

━ ━

THE NEW KING William the Bad did not altogether deserve his nickname. It was not even given to him until some two hundred years after his death – and was principally due to two misfortunes which he never managed to overcome. The first was his father, Roger II, by whom he was outshone; the second was the principal chronicler of his reign, Falcandus, who hated him and vilified him at every opportunity. William's appearance, too, was against him. Alas, we have no portrait; but a contemporary chronicle describes him as a huge man, 'whose thick black beard lent him a savage and terrible aspect and filled many people with fear'. Such characteristics, combined with a Herculean physical strength – he could separate two linked horseshoes with his bare hands – cannot have increased his popularity.

Born with three elder brothers between himself and the throne, he had never been groomed for greatness; and when their premature deaths thrust greatness upon him at the age of thirty, it took him by surprise. Lazy and pleasure-loving, he was to devote the greater part of his time to those pursuits which Roger had followed only in his rare hours of relaxation – discussing art and science with the intellectuals with whom he surrounded himself, or dallying with his women in the palaces which ringed Palermo like a necklace. Married in early youth to Margaret, daughter of King Garcia IV Ramirez of Navarre, he appeared after his succession to take little interest in her, or in the four sons she bore him. Even more than his father, he was an oriental through and through. His life was more like a sultan's than a king's, and his character embodied that same combination of sensuality and fatalism that has stamped so many eastern rulers. He never took a decision if he could avoid it, never tackled a problem if there was the faintest chance that, given long enough, it might solve itself. Once goaded into action, however, he would pursue his objectives with ferocious, even demonic, energy.

For ten years before his coronation, the country had enjoyed internal peace; but many of the Norman barons, especially in Apulia, were still unreconciled to the Kingdom. Others, who had decided to throw in their lot with the King, had gravitated to the capital in hopes of obtaining power or preferment, but had been disappointed. Roger's mistrust of his compatriots had lasted to the end of his life. Arrogant, barely literate, self-seeking, speaking no language but their own, they were hopelessly unqualified for positions of responsibility in a highly centralized state; and their record as vassals was not such as to encourage the granting to them of any large fiefs on the island. Thus they had been obliged to watch while Greeks, Italians and Saracens – men often of humble birth, and of races which they considered vastly inferior to their own – rose to eminence and distinction; and as they watched, so their dissatisfaction grew. Roger, after years of struggle, had ultimately earned their grudging respect; but now that his iron hand was no more, the threat of further trouble could not be far distant.

Nor was it. The barons had found themselves a new leader. Robert of Loritello was the King's first cousin, the very prototype of the disaffected aristocrat; and when in 1155 he was approached by an emissary from Constantinople, a certain Michael Palaeologus, with a proposal to join forces and drive King William from Apulia – if not the whole of south Italy – he accepted at once. Their first objective was Bari; and though the small Sicilian garrison fought bravely it was soon obliged to surrender. News of the city's fall, coupled with a spate of rumours of William's death – he was indeed seriously ill – shattered the morale of the coastal towns, which surrendered one after the other. In September a royalist army entered the field, consisting of 2,000 knights and a considerable force of infantry; a pitched battle followed, but ended in a further defeat. By the beginning of the winter rains, all Apulia seemed on the point of collapse.

The Pope at this time was Hadrian IV, born Nicholas Breakspear, the only Englishman ever to occupy the throne of St Peter. Though he had no love for the Greeks, he vastly preferred them to the Sicilians; when, therefore, he received a letter from Palaeologus offering him military help against William together with a subsidy of 5,000 gold pounds in return for the grant of three coastal towns in Apulia he accepted at once. Here was an opportunity that might never recur. He was encouraged, too, by the enthusiasm with which many exiled Apulian vassals, faced with the possibility of regaining their old fiefs, agreed to recognize the Pope as their lawful suzerain in return for his support.

As 1156 began, all Campania and most of northern Apulia was in Byzantine or papalist hands; Michael Palaeologus, mopping up the few pockets of resistance that remained, could congratulate himself on a success greater than he could have dared to hope. In barely six months he had restored Greek power in the peninsula to a point almost equal to that of a century and a half previously, before the Normans had set about the Byzantine theme* of Langobardia and seized it for themselves. On the mainland the King's enemies were in control everywhere except Calabria; and Calabria probably remained loyal only because it had not yet been attacked. At this rate it would not be long before all south Italy acknowledged the dominion of Constantinople. William of Sicily would be crushed, his odious kingdom liquidated.

But overconfidence is always dangerous. With the coming of spring William recovered from his illness and suddenly realized the gravity of the situation. He was, as Falcandus reminds us, 'a man who found it hard ever to leave his palace; but once he was obliged to go forth, then – however disinclined to action he had been in the past – he would fling himself, not so much with courage as in a headstrong, even foolhardy spirit, in the face of all dangers'. As ever, the chronicler's malice shows through; but it is still possible to detect a tinge of admiration in his words. William gave his orders. Army and navy would meet at Messina; this was to be a combined operation in which the Greeks and their allies would be attacked simultaneously from land and sea. In the last days of April, the

---

* The Byzantine Empire was divided into a number of themes, or provinces.

army crossed to the mainland and set off through Calabria, while the fleet sailed down through the Strait and then turned northeast towards Brindisi.

When the news was brought to the Byzantine headquarters that the Sicilians, led by the King himself, were advancing in formidable numbers and strength, the Greeks saw their fellow fighters fall away. The mercenaries chose, as mercenaries will, the moment of supreme crisis to demand impossible increases in their pay; meeting with a refusal, they disappeared en masse. Robert of Loritello deserted, followed by his own men and most of his compatriots. The Sicilian fleet arrived first; then, a day or two later, the army appeared in the west. The battle that followed was short and bloody; the Greek defeat was total. The Sicilian ships effectively prevented any possibility of escape by sea. On that one day, 28 May 1156, all that the Byzantines had achieved in Italy over the past year was wiped out as completely as if they had never come.

William treated his Greek prisoners according to the recognized canons of war; but to his own rebellious subjects he was pitiless. This was a lesson he had learnt from his father. Treason, particularly in Apulia where it was endemic, was the one crime that could never be forgiven. Of those erstwhile insurgents who fell into his hands, only the luckiest were imprisoned. The rest were hanged, blinded or tied about with heavy weights and hurled into the sea. From Brindisi he moved to Bari. Less than a year before, the Bariots had readily thrown in their lot with the Byzantines; now they too were to pay the price for their disloyalty. As they prostrated themselves before their King to implore his mercy, William pointed to the pile of rubble where until recently the citadel had stood. 'Just as you had no pity on my house,' he said, 'so now I shall have no pity on yours.' He gave them two clear days in which to salvage their belongings; on the third day Bari was destroyed. Only the cathedral, the great church of St Nicholas and a few smaller religious buildings were left intact.

One lonely figure remained to face the coming storm. All Pope Hadrian's allies were gone. Michael Palaeologus was dead and his army annihilated; the Norman barons were either in prison or in hiding. Hadrian himself was all too well aware that, if he were to save anything from the disaster, he would have to come to terms with the King of Sicily. The two met in the papal city of Benevento, and on 18 June 1156 an agreement was concluded. In return for an annual tribute, the Pope agreed to recognize William's kingship not only over Sicily, Apulia, Calabria and the former principality of Capua, together with Naples, Salerno, Amalfi and all that pertained to them; it was now formally extended across the whole region of the northern Abruzzi and the Marches. William, negotiating as he was from a position of strength, obtained more than had ever been granted to his father or grandfather. He was now one of the most powerful princes of Europe.

Thus, in the three years separating the Treaty of Benevento from the death of Pope Hadrian on 1 September 1159, a curious change occurs in the relative positions of the three principal protagonists. Alignments were shifting. The Papacy, brought to its knees at Benevento, rediscovered a fact that its history over the past hundred years should have made self-evident – that its only hope of survival as a potent political force lay in close alliance with its neighbour, Norman Sicily. The German Emperor Frederick Barbarossa, impressed despite himself by the speed and completeness of William's victories over the Byzantines in Apulia, looked upon him with undiminished hatred but a new respect, and decided on the indefinite postponement of the punitive expedition to the south that he had long been planning. Instead, he resolved on a campaign against the Lombard towns and cities of north Italy which, though technically part of his imperial dominions, had recently been showing a quite unacceptable tendency towards republicanism and independence. The result was the supreme paradox: the Lombard towns began to see the Sicilian monarchy – more absolutist by far than any other state in western Europe – as the stalwart defender of their republican ideals, hailing its King as a champion of civic liberty almost before the dust had settled on the ruins of Bari. And in the end they were victorious: on 29 May 1176 Frederick's German knights were routed at Legnano by the forces of the Lombard League. It was the end of his ambitions in Lombardy. In Venice in the following year he publicly kissed Pope Alexander's foot before the central door of St Mark's, and six years later, at

Constance, the truce became a treaty. Though imperial suzerainty was technically preserved, the cities of Lombardy (and to some extent Tuscany also) were henceforth free to manage their own affairs.

William returned to Sicily with his international standing higher than it had ever been; but the last years of his reign were anything but happy. His Emir of Emirs – the title given to the chief minister of the Kingdom – a certain Maio of Bari, was assassinated in 1160; and the following year saw a palace revolution in which the King's young son and heir, Roger, was killed and William himself was lucky to escape with his life. The disorder spread through much of Sicily and into Apulia and Calabria, the King as always leading his army in person, captured rebels being punished with hideous brutality. Worst of all, when he returned to Sicily in 1162, he found Christians and Muslims at each other's throats; the interreligious harmony which the two Rogers had worked so hard to achieve had been destroyed for ever.

Four years later, on 7 May 1166, William died at the age of forty-six. He had not been a good king. To be sure, Roger II was a hard act to follow, and it is perhaps hardly surprising that William should have tried to conceal his natural insecurity beneath that fearsome exterior, and to pass off his shortcomings as an administrator with elaborate demonstrations of indifference. In one respect, however, he excelled: he was a far better soldier than ever his father had been, and he knew it. When he was besieged in his own palace, bereft of friends or counsellors, he revealed himself as what he so often was – a hesitant, frightened man; but once he was in the field, his army behind him, he was transformed. And when the crisis came, it was his courage and military skill that saved his kingdom.

This very contrast, however, is typical of him. Throughout his life he remained unsteady and mercurial – perhaps, indeed, what we might nowadays describe as bipolar. Long periods of the profoundest lethargy would be interrupted by bursts of frantic, almost hysterical activity. He could at one moment be cruel to the point of savagery, almost unbelievably merciful the next. Lacking any real equilibrium himself, he proved incapable of maintaining all those delicate political balances on which the safety of his realm depended – between himself and his subjects, nobility and bourgeoisie, Christian and Muslim.

And yet – William the Bad? The epithet still rings false. There was nothing evil about him. He was, one suspects, simply a profoundly unhappy man who saw in every new palace he built and every new pleasure he enjoyed merely another temporary refuge for his troubled spirit. Perhaps William the Sad might have been a better description. We shall never know.

Legally, there was no problem over the succession. The dying King had made it clear that he wished the crown to pass to his surviving son, William; since, however, the boy was only twelve years old his mother, Queen Margaret, was to act as Regent. It all seemed straightforward enough.

On the day appointed for his coronation, young William immediately won all hearts. Unlike his father, he was quite exceptionally good-looking. When, in Palermo Cathedral, the crown of Sicily was laid upon his head, and when, later, he rode in state to the royal palace, the golden circlet still gleaming on the long fair hair inherited from his Viking forebears, his subjects, we are told, could not contain their joy. None the less, Queen Margaret knew that she would be hard put to maintain her position. For one thing, her present advisers were all irremediably identified with the previous regime. All were powerful men. The chief minister was a Muslim eunuch, Caïd Peter. He was an uninspiring character, a civil servant rather than a statesman; but his administrative efficiency and his devotion to the King and his family were both beyond question – as was that of the Grand Protonotary, Matthew of Ajello. Then there was the Queen's cousin, Gilbert of Gravina, a compulsive intriguer who detested Peter and was forever pressing Margaret to appoint him in Peter's place; and finally, two deeply unpleasant Englishmen. The first of these was Richard Palmer, Bishop of Syracuse, by far the ablest of them all but universally disliked for his arrogance and haughtiness; the other was his bitter rival, whose various orthographical disguises – Ophamilus and Offamiglio, to name but two – represent nothing more than desperate Sicilian attempts to deal phonetically with his perfectly ordinary English name, Walter of the Mill. First brought to Sicily as tutor to the royal children, he was now one of the canons of the Palatine Chapel, where he was proving himself even more unscrupulous and ambitious than Palmer. He was soon to occupy the highest political and ecclesiastical posts in the realm, building the present cathedral and becoming certainly the only Englishman in history regularly to sign himself 'Emir and Archbishop'.

None of these men, clearly, would be remotely acceptable as the Queen's chief counsellor. All were self-seeking, determined on their own advancement rather than the good of the realm; they would have been insufferably patronizing, forever attempting to bully or browbeat her into adopting their own policies. What she needed was a compatriot, one who thought like she did and spoke her language; and her choice finally fell upon a young cousin – on her Norman mother's side – named Stephen du Perche. When he landed in Palermo in the late summer of 1166 it was as a pilgrim, on his way to the Holy Land; but Margaret had little difficulty in persuading him, with promises of power, honours and riches, to postpone his pilgrimage indefinitely and to share with her the government of the Kingdom. From the outset he showed himself to be able and energetic; just as important – and in Sicily even rarer – he proved personally incorruptible. Margaret was delighted with him. Scarcely two months after his arrival, she appointed him Chancellor.

The news of the appointment, as might have been expected, called forth a storm of protest. Stephen had arrived with an entourage of thirty-seven; in the following months many more of his friends came out from France to join him; and before long the court and many sections of the administration seemed more French than Sicilian. On the other hand, he was an idealist, determined to make Sicily a better place and pushing through the reforms he believed necessary regardless of public opinion or his own personal popularity. It is hard, therefore, to avoid the conclusion that Queen Margaret was right to bring in an outsider to govern her kingdom. Reforms were obviously overdue; and in the prevailing atmosphere of discord and mistrust it would have been virtually impossible for any Sicilian – whether by birth or long-term adoption – to bring them about. Stephen, impartial and uncommitted, was in a position to do so, and because he did not lack moral courage he succeeded. But in the process, however much favour he gained with the masses, it was inevitable that he should have made himself hated by his senior subordinates. That hatred grew still more bitter in the autumn of 1167 when the Queen, while retaining him as her Chancellor, had him hurriedly ordained a priest and then immediately afterwards elected by the complaisant canons of Palermo Cathedral to the vacant archbishopric of the city.

It was so obviously an unwise move that one wonders why Stephen agreed to it – particularly since by this time new rumours were circulating around Palermo: that relations between himself and Margaret went far beyond those normally expected between a queen and her chancellor, let alone her archbishop. Whether there was any foundation for these rumours we cannot tell. Falcandus speaks elsewhere of how the Queen would be seen 'devouring the Chancellor with her eyes'. Margaret was still under forty and is said to have been attractive; she had been largely ignored by her late husband, and it would perhaps have been surprising if she had not formed some sort of attachment to a young and handsome man of high birth, intelligence and marked ability who was, incidentally, one of the few people in Sicily whom she could trust. Even had there been no such attachment, gossip on the subject would have been unavoidable.

In the autumn of 1167 the whole court moved for the winter to Messina, where Stephen, well-meaning as always, made a conscious effort to endear himself to the local inhabitants; but try as he might, he could never hold their affection for long. Within a month, the arrogance and the high-handedness of his entourage had made the French hated throughout the largely Greek population of the city. The court returned to the capital in March, but in Messina discontent continued to simmer; and it was there, at Easter 1168, that serious rebellion finally broke out. By the end of April, there was not a Frenchman in the city left alive. Nor was that the end; messengers were now arriving in Palermo with reports that grew daily more ominous. The rebels had taken Rometta, an important town commanding the Palermo–Messina road; they had swept down the coast to Taormina; in Cefalù the Bishop had declared openly in their favour. They were now marching on Palermo.

At the first sign of disturbance Stephen had been joined by a number of his followers in the archbishop's palace. The building was ill-equipped to withstand a siege; it had, however, one advantage – a narrow corridor linking it directly with the cathedral, where the party took refuge in the bell tower. The spiral staircase was narrow; they had brought enough provisions for several days; here at least they would be safe for a time, though their long-term future still looked bleak. But salvation was nearer than they knew. By this time the protonotary Matthew of Ajello had put himself at the head of the rebels, and Matthew was growing anxious. Stephen and his friends, he believed, might be able to hold out for a week or more – a good deal longer, probably, than the mob's enthusiasm. The King also presented a problem. He was showing signs of unexpected spirit. Already he had demanded to be allowed to ride out and face his subjects, calling upon them to lay down their arms and to return to their homes; Matthew had had a hard time restraining him. The boy's popularity in the city was as great as ever; once he managed to make his true sympathies known, support for the rebellion could be expected to dwindle rapidly.

And so Matthew and his associates decided to offer the Chancellor terms. Stephen and all those of his compatriots who wished to accompany him would be sent on to Palestine; the rest would be given free passage back to France. As for those Sicilians who had supported him, there would be no reprisals taken against their persons or their property. Stephen accepted; after all, the terms he was offered could hardly have been more generous – or so, at least, it seemed. But his troubles were not quite over. The first galley put at his disposal leaked like a sieve; by the time it reached Licata, half-way along the southwest coast, it could go no further. It was in another vessel, bought at his own expense from some Genoese merchants he met in the harbour, that he finally reached the Holy Land.

Into the two years since he had left France, Stephen du Perche had packed a lifetime of experience. He had attained the highest ranks, both civil and ecclesiastical, in one of the three greatest kingdoms of Europe; he had risen from layman to metropolitan archbishop; he had won the respect of some, the detestation of many – and, probably, the love of a queen. He had learnt much – about power and the abuses of power; about the art of government; about loyalty, friendship and fear. But about Sicily he had learnt nothing. He never understood that the nation's strength, if not its very survival, depended upon the maintenance of its unity; and that since it was by nature heterogeneous and fissile, that unity must be imposed from above. Because of this incomprehension, he failed; and the fact that in the end he accidentally and involuntarily united his enemies against him in no way diminishes his failure.

With the departure of Stephen and his compatriots, Queen Margaret must have been near despair. She had staked everything on these Frenchmen, and she had lost. With her son William still only fifteen, her Regency had another three years to run; but her reputation, both political and moral, was ruined. The last sad champion of the departed order, 'the Spanish woman' was now neither feared nor resented; she was simply ignored. She continued, however, to give continued proof of her total unfitness to govern. Had she collaborated with the self-styled and self-constituted council that was now running the country, she might have regained some at least of her lost influence; instead, she sought to obstruct it at every turn. Stephen's departure, for example, had left the archbishopric vacant, and the cathedral canons had chosen Walter of the Mill as his successor. From Margaret's point of view it would not have been a bad appointment; he had, after all, served as her son's tutor for several years. But he was not Stephen; and so she turned her face against him, protesting that her cousin was still the rightful archbishop and even sending an appeal to the Pope, persuasively backed with seven hundred ounces of gold, that he should refuse to ratify Walter's election. More than ever one suspects that between the Queen and her former Chancellor there had existed something more than a working partnership and a family tie.

Her efforts were in any case in vain. On 28 September 1168, in the presence of the King and his entire court, Walter was consecrated in Palermo Cathedral. After this Margaret seems to have lost heart, and when her son finally came of age she retired, one suspects with considerable relief, into obscurity. She lived on until 1183, when she died at the age of fifty-five; but she never saw Stephen du Perche again.

Queen Margaret's relief at laying down the burdens of state was fully shared by her subjects. Though her Regency had lasted only five years, it must have seemed to them like a lifetime; and they looked gratefully and hopefully towards the tall, fair-haired youth who, sometime during the summer of 1171, formally took the government of Sicily into his hands.

Not that they knew much about him. His good looks, to be sure, were famous; he had preserved them intact through his adolescence, and the boy who had seemed like an angel on the day of his coronation now at eighteen reminded people more of a young god. He was said to be a studious lad, who read and spoke all the languages of his kingdom, including Arabic; gentle and mild-mannered, given neither to those brooding silences nor to those sudden outbursts of rage that had rendered his father so alarming. His statecraft and political judgement were still untried, but this was more an advantage than anything else; having heretofore been kept well away from public affairs, he was safe from blame for any of the disasters that his mother had brought upon the Kingdom.

It was his good fortune that there should have now begun a period of peace and security which was soon to become identified with his reign. It was not of his making; though he was never himself to lead an army in the field, he had a disastrous predilection for foreign military adventures and ultimately proved more bellicose than either his father or grandfather before him. But these adventures, costly as they might be in lives and money, scarcely even ruffled the surface of domestic life in his own realm. Thus it was he who took the credit for this new tranquillity; thus, too, in later years, men looked back on the Indian summer − for such it turned out to be − of the Sicilian Kingdom, thought of their last legitimate Norman King who looked so glorious and who died so young, and gave him in gratitude the name by which he is still known, William the Good.

Nothing bears more persuasive testimony to this change of atmosphere than the fact that, for the first five years of William's majority, the greater part of Sicilian diplomatic activity was taken up with the relatively pleasant task of finding him a bride; and there was not a ruler in Europe who would not have been proud to have the young King as a son-in-law. First in the field had been the Byzantine Emperor, Manuel Comnenus; since his daughter would probably have brought the whole Empire of the East as her dowry, Queen Margaret and her advisers might well have accepted the proposal on the spot. But they had refused to be hurried, and the field was still open when, sometime in 1168, King Henry II of England suggested his third and youngest daughter, Joanna.

Links between the two kingdoms had been forming ever since Roger's day. English scholars, churchmen and administrators had continued to flock to Sicily, and by the 1160s there were few important Norman families in either country who could not claim members in the other. King Henry himself, whose French dominions alone covered considerably more territory than those of his contemporary Louis VII, was beyond question the most powerful prince in Europe. Moreover, though Joanna was still little more than a baby – she had been born in 1165 – he seemed genuinely keen for the match.

But then, on 29 December 1170, came the murder of Archbishop Thomas Becket. A dark pall hung over England. Henry's continental subjects were placed under an interdict; the King himself was forbidden to enter any church until the Pope saw fit to absolve him. All Europe was horror-stricken; to the Sicilians, little Joanna suddenly seemed a less desirable bride. Negotiations were abruptly broken off and, once again, the hunt for a queen began.

In March 1171, the Emperor Manuel offered William his daughter Maria for the second time. She no longer possessed quite the attraction of five years before; in the interim her stepmother had given birth to a son, and the succession to the Byzantine throne was once again assured. But she was still an Emperor's daughter, her dowry would be worthy of her rank and the marriage would, with any luck, put a stop to her father's eternal meddling in Italian affairs. The offer was accepted, and it was agreed that Maria should arrive in Apulia the following spring.

On the appointed day William, his brother Prince Henry of Capua, Matthew of Ajello and Walter of the Mill were at Taranto, waiting to greet the royal bride. Alas, she failed to turn up. After a week, William decided to make a short pilgrimage to the shrine of the archangel Michael on Monte Gargano; but on his return there was still no news. The Greeks had deceived him; clearly, the girl was not coming. Why had Manuel changed his mind at the last moment? He never, so far as we know, apologized or explained, and his motives remain a mystery. But his conduct caused a resentment against Constantinople that smouldered in William's heart for the rest of his life – and that was to cost both Sicily and Byzantium dear in the years to come.

It was, surprisingly enough, Pope Alexander III who proposed that negotiations should be reopened between England and Sicily for William's marriage to Joanna; and at Easter 1176 three specially accredited Sicilian ambassadors presented themselves before the King in London. Henry received them warmly; but before the betrothal could be announced there remained one further – and potentially embarrassing – preliminary; William had sensibly stipulated that he would enter into no formal commitment without some assurance as to the physical attractions of his bride. The ambassadors therefore proceeded to Winchester, where Joanna was living with her mother, Eleanor – held captive by the King since her involvement in her sons' rebellion three years before – 'to see,' in the words of a contemporary chronicler, 'whether she would be pleasing to them'. Fortunately, she was. 'When they looked upon her beauty,' he continues, 'they were delighted beyond measure.'

Though she was still only ten years old, Henry was determined that his daughter should travel in a state appropriate to her rank and the occasion. He ordered seven ships to be made ready to carry her and her suite safely across the Channel. On 26 August, accompanied by her uncle, Henry's natural brother Hameline Plantagenet, the Archbishops of Canterbury and Rouen and the Bishop of Evreux, she set sail from Southampton. Her eldest brother, Henry, escorted her as far as Poitiers, where her second brother, Richard, took over, conducting her safely through his own Duchy of Aquitaine to the port of Saint-Gilles. There Joanna was greeted in King

William's name by Richard Palmer and the Archbishop of Capua. Twenty-five of the King's ships were waiting in the harbour; but it was already the second week of November and the winter gales had begun in earnest. It was decided not to risk the open sea, but to sail along the coast, keeping as close inshore as possible. Even this seems to have been uncomfortable enough; six weeks later the fleet was still no further than Naples, and poor Joanna was suffering so severely from seasickness that it was agreed to remain there over Christmas, giving her a chance to recover her strength – and, perhaps, her looks. She would then complete her journey overland.

She reached Palermo at last on the evening of 2 February 1177. William was waiting at the gates to welcome his bride. She was mounted on one of his royal palfreys and escorted to the palace which had been prepared for her, through streets so brightly illuminated that, in the words of a contemporary chronicler, 'it might have been thought that the city itself was on fire'. Eleven days later, on St Valentine's Eve, the two were married and garlanded with flowers; and immediately afterwards Joanna, her long hair flowing down over her shoulders, knelt in the Palatine Chapel before her countryman Walter of the Mill, now Archbishop of Palermo, as he anointed and crowned her Queen of Sicily.

At the time of her coronation the young queen was barely eleven, her husband twenty-three. Yet despite the difference in age the marriage was, so far as we can tell, an ideally happy one. There was no language problem: Joanna, born in France and educated largely in the abbey of Fontevrault, was by her upbringing far more French than English, and Norman French was still the everyday language of the Sicilian court. Her new subjects, too, welcomed her as they had her husband and took her to their hearts.

*Murriali, città senza cunfortu, o chiavi o mina ventu o sona a mortu.** So runs an old Sicilian proverb; it can only be said that few people react to Monreale in such a way today. As a city – and it is now virtually a suburb of Palermo – it may have its disadvantages; but

---

* 'Monreale, a city without comfort – either it rains, or the wind blows, or bells toll for the dead.'

it also has its cathedral, and its cathedral makes up for everything. It is for this, rather than for his physical beauty or for his English marriage, that William the Good is nowadays remembered. He began building in 1174, lavishing vast sums annually on what is by any account the most spectacular monument in Sicily. Yet it was not built exclusively to the glory of God; there were political reasons as well. From the moment the young King assumed power he had been suspicious – and Matthew of Ajello had constantly reminded him – of the growing influence of Walter of the Mill. As Archbishop of Palermo Walter had by now managed to unite nearly all the leading barons and prelates behind him in a reactionary, feudalist party that, if it were allowed to continue unchecked, boded ill for the Kingdom. Even in ecclesiastical affairs he was pursuing a dangerous course. The upheavals of the Regency had given the Sicilian Church the opportunity to assert itself independently, not just of the Pope – there was nothing new in that – but of the King as well, and this tendency Walter was doing all he could to encourage. His power in the land was already second only to William's own; and William knew that he must curb it while there was still time.

But how could he do so? Only by creating a new archbishopric as near as possible to Palermo, whose incumbent would be equal in rank to Walter himself and who could serve as a direct link between crown and Papacy. The problem was that archbishops were normally elected by the Church hierarchy, and the hierarchy was under Walter's control. Thus it was that William decided on a further refinement to his plan. The new foundation must be a Benedictine abbey, run on strictly Cluniac lines, whose abbot would automatically receive archiepiscopal rank and could be consecrated by any other prelate he might choose, subject only to the King's approval. Walter was furious, but there was nothing he could do. He was forced to stand by while several churches and parishes were removed from his archdiocese and transferred to that of Monreale; and in the spring of 1176 he watched in impotent rage while a hundred monks from the great abbey of La Cava arrived in Palermo on their way to colonize the new foundation.

No one can fail to be impressed by Monreale, ablaze as it is with over an acre and a half of superb mosaics, all completed within five or six years, between 1183 and the end of the decade. It lacks the gemlike perfection of the Palatine Chapel, the Byzantine mystery of the Martorana, or the sheer magic that streams down from the great Pantocrator at Cefalù. Its impact is chiefly due to its size and its splendour. But this impact, like the cathedral itself, is colossal. Wandering slowly through the vast length of the building, one might be forgiven for thinking that virtually every Bible story is here illustrated. Nor would one be very far wrong; but there is one particular mosaic – and not a narrative one either – that should on no account be missed. Look now to the second figure to the right of the central east window. There is no problem of identification: in conformity with the usual canons of the time, the name runs down the side of the halo for all to read: SCS. THOMAS CANTUR. Whether or not it bears any resemblance to the martyred archbishop we have no idea;* it remains, however, the earliest certain representation of St Thomas Becket known to us, dating from only a few years after his death. And there can be little doubt that his presence here is due to Queen Joanna, thus making her own personal atonement for her father's conduct.

Finally, the cloister. Here is the only touch of Saracen influence to be found at Monreale: the slim, Arabizing arches, a hundred and four of them, supported by pairs of slender columns, some carved, some inlaid with the same glorious Cosmati-work that is such a feature of the interior. In the southwest corner they have been extended to make a fountain, Arabic again, but in a form unique to the island. Meanwhile the capitals of the columns, each one an individual triumph of design and invention, constitute a tour de force of Romanesque stone-carving unequalled in all the south. On one of them – the eighth on the west side – King William presents his new cathedral to the Mother of God. The last and greatest religious foundation of Norman Sicily is offered and accepted.

A kingdom in the sun, prosperous and peaceful; youth, good looks and limitless wealth; the love of his subjects and a beautiful young

---

* Unfortunately Queen Joanna would not have been able to give much of a description. At the time of his murder she was only five years old.

queen; with such gifts as these, William II must have appeared to his contemporaries as a man upon whom the gods had always smiled. And so, up to a point, they had. Three blessings only they withheld from him: first, a long life; second, a son and heir; third, a modicum of political wisdom. Had he been granted any one of these, his kingdom might have been spared the sadness that lay in store for it. As he lacked all three, Sicily was doomed.

Sometime during the winter of 1183–84, imperial ambassadors from Frederick Barbarossa arrived in Palermo with a proposal – nothing less than the marriage of his son and heir, Henry, with Princess Constance of Sicily. It seems incredible that William and his advisers should have contemplated the idea for a moment. Constance, the posthumous daughter of Roger II – she was in fact a year younger than her nephew the King – was heiress-presumptive to the realm. If she were to marry Henry and William were to remain childless, Sicily would fall into the Emperor's lap, its separate existence at an end. Admittedly, there was plenty of time yet for Joanna to bear children. In 1184 she was still only eighteen, her husband thirty. But life in the twelfth century was a good deal less certain than it is today, infant mortality was high, and to take such a risk before the succession was properly assured would be an act of almost criminal folly.

Few Sicilians relished the prospect of surrendering their independence to a distant and in their eyes barbarous empire that had always been the traditional enemy of their country. Walter of the Mill, however, took the opposite view. His reasons are not altogether clear. Perhaps, as an Englishman, he considered imperial domination a lesser evil than the civil war which in his eyes might have been the only alternative. But was it? Could not Constance have married any other husband, reigned in her own right, then passed the crown in the fullness of time to a legitimate son? Yet whatever may have been the Archbishop's motives, there was a further consideration in William's own mind when he came to make his decision – a single, overriding reason why, in the next few years, he needed to be sure of the goodwill of the Western Empire; and why, in the summer of 1184, to the horrified dismay of the large majority of his subjects, he gave his consent to the betrothal. He was preparing to march against Byzantium.

He had a moderately acceptable pretext for doing so. The Emperor Manuel I had died in 1180, leaving only one legitimate successor, a peculiarly unattractive boy of eleven. Manuel's widow, the ravishingly beautiful Mary of Antioch, governed as Regent; but owing to her shameless pro-western sympathies dissatisfaction in the capital steadily grew, and two years later the throne was seized by a cousin of the Emperor, Andronicus Comnenus. At first he was welcomed; he could hardly have failed to be, since he was by far the most glamorous Emperor in all Byzantine history. Although already sixty-four, he looked nearer forty. Over six feet tall and in superb physical condition, he had preserved the good looks, the intellect, the conversational charm and wit, the elegance and sheer panache that, together with the fame of his almost legendary exploits in bed and battlefield, had won him an unrivalled reputation as a Don Juan.

As Andronicus advanced on Constantinople, people flocked from their houses to cheer him on his way. Even before he crossed the strait, rebellion had broken out in the capital, and with it exploded all that pent-up hatred of the Latins that the past two years had done so much to increase. What followed was a massacre – the massacre of virtually all the Latins in the city – women, children, even the sick from the hospitals, as the whole quarter in which they lived was burnt and pillaged. And now it was seen that Andronicus's triumph had brought out another side of his character, a degree of cruelty and brutality that few had even suspected. He liquidated first all those who came between himself and the throne; the Regent Mary was strangled, her son garrotted by the bowstring.

Before long the last shreds of his popularity were gone; he had revealed himself a monster. The air was once again thick with sedition and revolt. Conspirators who fell into the Emperor's clutches were tortured to death, often by his own hand; but many others fled to the west, where the massacre of 1182 had not been forgotten and they could be sure of a ready welcome. It was even rumoured that a young man claiming to be the rightful Emperor had presented himself to William in Palermo. We know for a fact that one of the Emperor Manuel's nephews had recently escaped to Sicily and had been received at court, since when he had been urgently pressing the King to march on Constantinople and overthrow the usurper.

But this, to William, would have been only an excuse. Though he admitted it to no one, his ultimate objective was nothing less than to gain for himself the crown of Byzantium; and he was determined that the force he sent out to attain it should be worthy of such a prize – stronger, both on land and sea, than any other ever to have sailed from Sicilian shores. And so it was. By the time it was ready to start, the fleet – commanded by his cousin, Tancred of Lecce – is said to have comprised between two and three hundred vessels and to have carried some 80,000 men, including 5,000 knights and a special detachment of mounted archers. It sailed from Messina on 11 June 1185 and headed straight for Durazzo,* the Empire's largest Adriatic port. From here the old Roman Via Egnatia ran eastward across Macedonia and Thrace to Constantinople. By 6 August the entire land force, commanded by a certain Baldwin of whom practically nothing is known, was encamped outside Thessalonica; nine days later the fleet, having sailed around the Peloponnese, took up its position in the roadstead and the siege began.

Even had it been adequately prepared and defended, it is unlikely that Thessalonica could have held out very long against an attack so furious and many-sided as the Sicilians now launched upon it. The garrison resisted bravely enough, but soon the defences began to crumble. On 24 August, the Sicilian troops poured into the second city of the Byzantine Empire, where they gave themselves up to an orgy of savagery and violence unparalleled since Theodosius the Great massacred 7,000 of its citizens in the Hippodrome eight centuries before. It was a week before order was restored; but the situation in the city remained explosive and it must have been a relief to Greek and Sicilian alike when the army drew itself up once more in line of battle and headed off to the east.

By this time Andronicus had despatched no fewer than five separate armies to block the Sicilian advance. Had they been united under a single able commander they might have been successful; as it was, all five retreated to the hills to the north of the road, from the safety of which they watched it, apparently hypnotized.

* Now Dürres, in Albania.

The vanguard had therefore pressed onward as far as Mosynopolis, nearly half-way to the capital, when there occurred an event that changed the entire situation – completely and, as far as Sicily was concerned, disastrously. The people of the capital rose up against Andronicus Comnenus and murdered him.

It was another cousin of the Emperor's, a certain Isaac Angelus, who, with understandable reluctance, finally accepted the Byzantine crown. He inherited a desperate situation. The invaders' advance column was less than two hundred miles from Constantinople; their fleet was already in the Sea of Marmara, awaiting the army's arrival. Immediately on his accession, Isaac made the Sicilians an offer of peace; when it was refused, he did what should have been done months before: he appointed the ablest of his generals, Alexius Branas, to the overall command of the five armies, sending him the most massive reinforcements the Empire could provide. The effect was instantaneous: the Greeks were suddenly infused with a new spirit. They saw too that their enemy, grown overconfident, had dropped its guard and relaxed its discipline. Carefully selecting his place and moment, Branas swooped down upon the Sicilians, routed them completely and pursued them all the way back to their main camp at Amphipolis.

Now at last Baldwin consented to discuss peace. Winter was approaching, and the autumn rains in Thrace fall heavy and chill. To an army that had counted on spending Christmas in Constantinople, the defeat at Mosynopolis probably proved more demoralizing than its strategic importance warranted, but the Greeks were taking no chances. Fearing that their enemy intended to take advantage of the peace negotiations to catch them unprepared, they decided to strike first. It was the Sicilians who were taken unawares; they turned and fled. Some were cut down as they ran; many more were drowned as they tried to cross the Strymon River, now swift and swollen from the rains; yet others, including Baldwin himself, were taken prisoner. Many of those who escaped found their way back to Thessalonica, where some managed to pick up ships in which to return to Sicily. Since, however, the bulk of the Sicilian fleet was still lying off Constantinople, the majority were not so lucky. The Thessalonians rose up against them, taking a full and bloody revenge for all that they had suffered three months before. Of the titanic army which had set out so confidently in the summer, it was a poor shadow that now dragged itself back through the icy mountain passes to Durazzo. Only the fleet returned unscathed.

And it was just as well. Two years later, that same fleet was ordered to sail to Palestine. William had at last forgotten his differences with Byzantium; there were graver matters on hand. On Friday, 2 October 1187, the Muslim armies under Saladin had retaken Jerusalem. The whole future of Christianity in the Holy Land hung in the balance.

The story of the hopelessly unsuccessful Third Crusade is fortunately not ours; suffice it to say that the Sicilian fleet, under its brilliant young admiral Margaritus of Brindisi, performed magnificently, saving Tripoli and Tyre, at least temporarily, for the Christian cause. Margaritus – 'the new Neptune' – quickly acquired a legendary reputation throughout Christendom; he might have become yet more renowned, and his command even further extended, had the Sicilians ever been able to raise the mighty army of which their King had dreamed; but suddenly his hopes of crusading glory were dashed. On 18 November 1189 William the Good died, aged thirty-six, in Palermo.

Of all the Hauteville rulers of Sicily, William is the most elusive. We know nothing of his death, except that it occurred peacefully, in his bed; about his life, short as it was, we are scarcely better informed. It is sometimes hard to remember that he ruled over Sicily for eighteen years and occupied the throne for almost a quarter of a century; we are conscious only of a dim if faintly resplendent shadow that passes fleetingly over a few pages of history and is gone. For all that, he was regretted as few European princes have ever been – far, far beyond his deserts. His reign did nothing to strengthen his country; instead, it marked a return to the most irresponsible foreign policy that any state can pursue – that of land-grabbing for its own sake, without consideration for political consequences. Nor was it even successful. One might have had a little more sympathy had he led his troops in person; but he never ventured beyond the point of departure. Finally, he must bear the blame for the most disastrous decision of the whole Sicilian epic: his agreement to Constance's marriage. He knew that if he died childless the throne would be hers; and he had been married long enough to understand that Joanna might well fail to bear him a son. True, he could always put her away and take another wife, but who was to say that his second marriage would be any more fruitful than his first? Meanwhile, Constance *was* the Kingdom; and by giving her to Henry of Hohenstaufen he sealed the death warrant of Norman Sicily.

It was not quite the end. After a bitter struggle with a rival claimant, the crown was assumed by William's cousin, Tancred of Lecce. An illegitimate grandson of Roger II, Tancred was described by a contemporary chronicler as *semi-vir*, *embryo infelix* and *detestabile monstrum* – a translation seems unnecessary – but he was determined, if humanly possible, to keep it out of Henry's hands. He fought hard and courageously to do so – against the Empire above all, but also against his fellow Sicilians, Christian and Muslim alike, who were too egotistical or too blind to understand the enormity of the crisis that faced them. Had he lived, he might even have succeeded; but early in 1194 he died in his turn. His son, William, was still a child; his widow, Queen Sibylla, became Regent; but she knew as well as anyone that her task was impossible.

Henry – now the Emperor Henry VI, his father, Frederick Barbarossa, having been drowned on his way to the Third Crusade – failed in his first attempt to reach Sicily in 1191. He ran into unexpected opposition at Naples, and was still besieging it when the Sicilians' only completely trustworthy ally, the southern summer, brought to his army malaria, dysentery and wholesale defections. He was obliged to return across the Alps, what was left of his army shambling behind. But three years later he was back, and on Christmas Day 1194 he was crowned King of Sicily in Palermo Cathedral. Queen Sibylla and her children occupied places of honour; but just four days later they were charged with complicity in a plot to assassinate him and carried off to captivity in Germany. The Queen ended her days in an Alsatian convent; the fate of little William remains a mystery. One story has it that he was blinded and castrated in a German prison; another – which does not necessarily contradict the first – that he was freed and sent to a monastery. Captive or cloistered, however, he did not long survive. By the turn of the century, hardly out of his boyhood, he was dead.

And what, finally, of Constance? She, after all, was the true monarch of Sicily; Henry was merely her consort. Why, many of her subjects must have wondered, was she not at her husband's side, leaving him to kneel alone at the altar for his coronation? She had a reason, and a good one. At the age of forty, and after nearly nine years of marriage, Constance was expecting a child. She did not put off her journey to Sicily on that account; but she travelled more slowly and in her own time, starting out a month or two after her husband and moving by easy stages down the peninsula. Even so, for a woman of her age and in her condition, it was a dangerous undertaking. The days and weeks of being shaken and jolted over the rough tracks of Lombardy and the Marches took their toll; and when she reached the little town of Jesi, not far from Ancona, she felt the pains of childbirth upon her.

Ever since the beginning of her pregnancy, Constance had had one fixed idea. She knew that both her enemies and Henry's, on both sides of the Alps, would do everything they could to discredit the birth, citing her age and the long years of barrenness to claim that the child she was to bear could not really be hers; and she was determined that on this question there should be no possible room for doubt. She therefore had a large tent erected in the market square of Jesi, to which free entrance was allowed to any matron of the town who wished to witness the birth; and on the feast of St Stephen, 26 December, she brought forth her only son. A day or two later she showed herself in public in the same square, proudly suckling the child at her breast. The Hauteville spirit was not quite dead after all.

In the following century it was to appear again, more refulgently than ever, when that son, Frederick, grew to manhood. Though history may remember him as Emperor of the West, he himself never forgot that he was also King of Sicily, the grandson not only of Barbarossa but of Roger II as well. He showed it in the splendour of his court, in his lions and his leopards and his peacocks, in the Italian and Arabic poets he loved, in his classicizing architecture and his Apulian hunting lodges, and above all in that insatiable artistic and intellectual curiosity that was to earn him the appellation of *Stupor Mundi*, the Wonder of the World.

6

Stupor Mundi

━━━

KING HENRY OF Sicily did not last long, and it was just as well. He saw his new acquisition as an appendage, nothing more; and he treated it accordingly, looting and plundering it without mercy; a hundred and fifty mules were apparently needed to carry the accumulated treasure across the Alps.* It was not long before the people rose up against him, but his army was more than a match for them and the rebels were punished with sickening brutality. There were stories of Tancred's supporters being roasted alive or castrated; one member of the Hauteville family was said to have been crowned with a red-hot crown, which was then nailed into place. The reign of terror was still in progress when Henry died in 1197, aged thirty-two, probably of malaria caught on a hunting expedition – though, inevitably, there were dark suggestions of poison. His body was taken to Palermo Cathedral, where his tomb may still be seen.

His son, Frederick, was three years old. Following what was by now the established tradition, it was accepted that his mother would act as Regent; but Constance died only a year after her husband, having appointed Pope Innocent III as Frederick's guardian. It was not a happy choice – though it is difficult to see who else she might have picked – since Innocent, though he proved to be one of the greatest of all the Popes, was both too busy and too remote to be of much effect. For the next few years Sicily was governed by a succession of Henry's German barons. Their task was not easy – German was one of the few western European languages not

---

* How else could the glorious vestments of Roger II have ended up in the Kunsthistorisches Museum in Vienna?

spoken in Sicily, and they made no effort to learn anything else – but they soon proved as incompetent as they were ignorant. Before long there was a state of anarchy across the island. By this time the racial equality that had been such a feature of King Roger's reign was long since gone; it was now the Muslims who rebelled against their Christian brethren. In Agrigento, to take but one example, they converted the cathedral into a barracks and held the bishop prisoner for over a year.

None of this, however, appeared to affect the atmosphere of the court in Palermo at which Frederick spent his childhood and where he received an education as far removed from that normally given to German princes as could possibly be imagined. His personal tutor was probably Michael Scot, translator of Aristotle and Averroes, who is known to have spent several years in Palermo and was to become his close friend. As he grew older, it became impossible to find a subject which did not interest him. He would spend hours, not only in study but in long disputations on law or religion, philosophy or mathematics. Often, too, he would withdraw to one of his parks or country palaces, there to study the birds and animals that were to be a lifelong passion. Many years later he was to write a book on falconry, *De Arte Venandi cum Avibus*, which became a classic, displaying a knowledge and understanding of wildlife rare indeed in the thirteenth century. In appearance he was undistinguished – short and stocky, with a face almost as red as his hair and weak, short-sighted eyes – but his wit and charm were irresistible.

The physical energy fully matched the intellectual. In 1208, when Frederick was thirteen, a contemporary wrote:

> He is never idle, but passes the whole day in some occupation or other, and so that his vigour may increase with practice he strengthens his agile body with every kind of exercise and practice of arms. He either employs his weapons or carries them; drawing his shortsword, in whose use he is expert, he makes play of defending himself from attack. He is a good shot with the bow and often practises archery. He loves fast thoroughbred horses, and no one knows better than he how to curb them with the bridle and then set them at full gallop . . .
>
> To this is added a regal majesty and majestic features and mien,

to which are united a kindly and gracious air, a serene brow, brilliant eyes and expressive face, a burning spirit and a ready wit. Nevertheless his actions are sometimes odd and vulgar, though this is not due to nature but to contact with rough company . . . However he has virtue in advance of his age, and though not adult he is well versed in knowledge and has the gift of wisdom, which usually comes only with the passage of years. In him, then, the number of years does not count; nor is there need to await maturity, because as a man he is full of knowledge, and as a ruler of majesty.

Why, with all these qualities, was Frederick never loved by his subjects? Largely because they could never really understand him. Their ideal Emperor was more in the mould of Charlemagne: stately, paternalistic, his morals beyond reproach. Frederick loved to shock or to startle; a strong streak of self-indulgent exhibitionism was never far below the surface, and he was curiously insensitive to the feelings and susceptibilities of others. He could be cruel too; his treatment of his two wives was disgraceful, and his shamelessly dissolute life repelled many whose support and friendship would have been valuable to him.

Frederick came of age on his fourteenth birthday, 26 December 1208, and nine months later was married to Constance, daughter of Alfonso II of Aragon, ten years older than he and already a widow. She was the choice of Pope Innocent, and at least in the early days of their marriage Frederick does not seem to have shared the papal enthusiasm; but she brought five hundred armed knights in her train, and in view of the continuing unrest throughout the Kingdom he needed all the help he could get. She also introduced, with her ladies and troubadours, an element of worldly sophistication which had hitherto been lacking in Palermo. To Frederick, always alive to every fresh stimulus, there now opened up a whole new world, the world of courtly love. The marriage itself remained one of political convenience – Constance was largely ignored, although she duly presented her husband with a son, Henry, a year or two later – but it removed the rough edges; long before he was twenty, Frederick had acquired the social graces and the polished charm for which he would be famous for the rest of his life.

*

Early in June 1212 an embassy arrived in Palermo with a message from beyond the Alps. Once again, western Europe had been shown the perils of elective monarchy; since the death of Henry VI, Germany had been torn apart by a civil war among the various claimants to the imperial title. One of these, Otto the Welf, Duke of Brunswick, had actually been crowned Emperor by Pope Innocent in 1209, and two years later had taken possession of what was known as the Regno, the entire mainland part of Frederick's kingdom. Alas, he had gone too far: his invasion of the papal province of Tuscany had led to his instant excommunication, and in September 1211 a council of the leading German princes had met at Nuremberg and declared him deposed. It was they who had despatched the embassy with an invitation to Frederick to assume the vacant throne.

The invitation, as might be expected, created a considerable stir at the Sicilian court. Frederick's principal counsellors strongly advised against acceptance; so too did his wife. Except for his late father he had no ties with Germany; indeed, he had never yet set foot on German soil. His hold on his own kingdom was still far from secure; it was scarcely a year since Duke Otto had been threatening him from across the Strait of Messina. Was this really the moment to absent himself from Sicily for several months at the very least, for the sake of an honour which, however great, might yet prove illusory? On the other hand, a refusal would, he knew, be seen by the German princes as a deliberate snub, and could not fail to strengthen the position of his chief rival. Both in Italy and Germany, Otto still had plenty of support; having renounced none of his long-term ambitions, he was fully capable of launching a new campaign – and he would not make the same mistake twice. Here, surely, was an opportunity to deal him a knockout blow. It was not to be missed.

Pope Innocent, after some hesitation, gave his approval. Frederick's election would admittedly tighten the imperial grip to the north and south of the Papal States, and it was in order to emphasize the independence – at least in theory – of the Kingdom of Sicily from the Empire that the Pope insisted on Frederick's renunciation of the Sicilian throne in favour of his newborn son, with Queen Constance acting as Regent. Once these formalities had been settled,

Frederick's way was clear. At the end of February he sailed with a few trusted companions from Messina. His immediate destination, however, was not Germany but Rome; and there, on Easter Sunday 1212, he knelt before the Pope and performed the act of feudal homage to him – technically on behalf of his son – for the Sicilian Kingdom.

From Rome he sailed on in a Genoese galley, somehow eluding the fleet which the Pisans – staunch supporters of Duke Otto – had sent to intercept him. The Genoese, unlike their Pisan rivals, were enthusiastic imperialists, none more so than their leading family, the House of Doria, who put their principal palace at the disposal of the Emperor-elect until such time as the Alpine passes were once again open to enable him to complete his journey. Even then, however, his way was not clear. The Lombard plain was constantly patrolled by hostile Milanese, and it was one of these bands that surprised the imperial party as they were leaving Pavia. Frederick was lucky indeed to be able to leap on to one of the horses and, fording the river Lambro bareback, to make his way to friendly Cremona. By which route he finally crossed the Alps is not known, but with the beginning of autumn he was safely in Germany, and on 9 December 1212 one of the German archbishops crowned him King of Germany in Mainz. Two and a half years later, on 25 July 1215, upon the throne of Charlemagne in the cathedral of Aachen, he was crowned King of the Romans, the traditional title of the Emperor-elect. All that he now needed was a further imperial coronation by the Pope in Rome. Almost exactly a year before, on 27 July 1214, the army of King Philip Augustus of France had defeated that of Otto of Brunswick and King John of England at Bouvines, near Lille, effectively destroying all Otto's hope of opposing him. From that day his supremacy was unquestioned, and it was now that he announced his intention of taking the Cross.

Few acts in Frederick's life are to us today more incomprehensible. He had never been particularly pious; moreover, he had been brought up among Muslim scientists and scholars whose religion he respected and in whose language he was fluent. Indeed, there is plenty of reason to believe that he soon regretted his promise; he certainly showed no eagerness to fulfil it. He was to remain in Germany for another four years, spent largely in ensuring the succession to the Empire of his son, Henry, who in 1217 arrived with his mother from Sicily. It was not until the late summer of 1220 that his parents made their way back across the Alps, leaving the disconsolate little eight-year-old behind them. There followed a solemn progress through Italy, during which Frederick dispensed royal grants and diplomas with his usual largesse. In mid-November he and Constance arrived in Rome, and on the 22nd Pope Honorius laid the imperial crown on his head.

Immediately after this third coronation he returned to Sicily. His years in Germany had brought him the greatest secular title the world could bestow, but they had also showed him that he was at heart a man of the south, a Sicilian. Germany had been good to him, but he had never really liked the country or felt at home there. Of his thirty-eight years as Emperor, only nine were spent north of the Alps; throughout his reign he was to do all he could – though without conspicuous success – to shift the focus of the Empire to Italy, and it was in Italy that the main body of his life's work was to be done. He began it late in 1220, even before he had crossed the Strait of Messina, in the first important city within his northern frontier, Capua.

About the state of his kingdom he was under no illusions: ever since the death of William II in 1189 it had been in chaos. His father's reign of terror had only increased the unruliness and dissatisfaction; then there had been his own minority – his mother as Regent had barely succeeded in holding things together – followed by his long absence in Germany, during which the state had survived more in name than anything else. As the most urgent priority, order had to be restored; and it was with what are known as the Assizes of Capua that he took the first steps in doing so, promulgating a series of laws which laid the foundations for the national regeneration of the Kingdom of Sicily. Essentially, they involved a recentralization of power, with a return to the status quo existing at the time of King William's death. Frederick was particularly tough on the nobility: in future no holder of a fief could marry, nor could his children inherit, without the consent of the sovereign. And all castles built anywhere in the Kingdom since William's time were automatically forfeit to the crown.

The proceedings at Capua were repeated in the following months at Messina, Catania and Palermo. More laws were announced, regulating even private behaviour. Games of chance were forbidden; citizens were obliged to return home before the third evening bell; a special dress was prescribed for Jews, who were however under royal protection; they, and only they, were allowed to make loans, charging up to ten percent. Prostitutes were obliged to live outside the city walls. The Emperor then moved on to Syracuse, where he had serious business with the Genoese. Genoa had always been his friend, but as long ago as 1204 Genoese merchants had virtually taken possession of the city, from which they had spread their influence all over the island. One of the chief causes of the decline in Sicilian trade over the previous thirty years was the fact that most of it had fallen into the hands of foreigners; there was no chance of a return to prosperity while they remained in control. And so, despite the help he had received from the Genoese on his journey to Germany, Frederick acted with characteristic firmness. He threw them out. All the trading concessions that had been granted to Genoa, not only in Syracuse but in Palermo, Messina, Trapani and other trading centres across the island, were summarily withdrawn, while all Genoese depots and warehouses, with their contents, were confiscated.

But alas, there was another, far greater enemy than Genoa to be faced: the Muslims of western Sicily. Three-quarters of a century before, in the days of King Roger, the Arab community had been an integral part of the Kingdom. It had staffed the entire treasury and had provided most of the physicians and other men of science who had earned Norman Sicily its outstanding reputation in the field of scholarship. But those days were long gone. Already during the reign of William the Good much of the semi-autonomous Arab region had been granted to his Abbey of Monreale; now, with the final collapse of Norman power, the Arabs had found that they were no longer appreciated or respected. They had consequently been forced back, entrenching themselves in the wild and mountainous west, where Arab brigands and freebooters now terrorized the local Christian communities. Frederick's first campaign against them proved inconclusive; not until 1222 did his troops capture the

Saracen fortress of Iato, and with it the Muslim leader Ibn Abbad, who soon afterwards ended his days on the scaffold.

Not even Ibn Abbad's execution, however, marked the final solution to the problem. This came about only between 1222 and 1226, when Frederick adopted a still more drastic measure. He had already had practice in shifting populations: he had repeopled Malta, and settled considerable numbers of Lombards and Greeks in under-populated areas of Sicily. Now he removed the entire Muslim population of the rebellious western region – perhaps 15–20,000 people – altogether from the island, and resettled them at the other end of the Kingdom: at Lucera in northern Apulia, which became effectively a Muslim community, virtually every one of its Christian churches being replaced by a mosque. The town was not, it should be emphasized, in any sense a penal colony. Its citizens enjoyed complete liberty and the free exercise of their religion; and Frederick, who had been brought up with Muslims from his cradle, ultimately built a palace of his own there – a building in a distinctly oriental style which was to become one of his favourite residences.

The Saracens of Lucera, for their part, showed their new loyalty by providing him with his personal bodyguard. They also manned his principal weapons factory, producing blades of damascened steel that only Toledo could equal. Meanwhile, their women provided the Emperor with his harem: the Saracen dancing-girls who lived in considerable luxury in a wing of the palace, with their own staff of female servants and a body of eunuchs to see that they came to no harm. A number of these girls would accompany the Emperor on his constant travels, and although it was always maintained that they existed only to provide innocent entertainment for the imperial court there can be little doubt – as Gibbon remarks on the similar establishment kept by the Emperor Gordian – that they were in fact intended for use rather than ostentation.

The so-called Fifth Crusade, first launched in 1213, had been a flop. It had had as its object the capture of Damietta in Egypt, which it was hoped to exchange later for the Holy City itself. Damietta duly fell in November 1219, but the war dragged on for nearly two more years, and would have continued even longer had not the Crusading army been trapped by the Nile floods – from which it extricated itself only by surrender. With its failure, Frederick came under increasing pressure to honour his promise and initiate another Crusade – and also to take another wife. Constance had died in June 1221, and Pope Honorius suggested Yolande de Brienne, the hereditary Queen of Jerusalem, now twelve years old. Her title came from her mother, Maria – granddaughter of the Crusader King Amalric I – who at the age of seventeen had married the sexagenarian John of Brienne. John had promptly assumed the royal title. After his wife's early death a year or two later his claim to it was at least questionable, but he had continued to govern what was left of the kingdom as Regent for his little daughter Yolande.

Frederick was not at first enthusiastic. His proposed bride was penniless, and little more than a child; he was more than twice her age. As for her title, few were emptier: Jerusalem had been in Saracen hands for half a century. On the other hand, the kingship, purely titular as it was, would greatly strengthen his claim to the city when he eventually left on his long-postponed Crusade, originally sworn to seven years before. And so, after some deliberation, he agreed to the match. He agreed too, in the course of further discussions with the Pope, that the Crusade – to which the marriage was indissolubly linked – would set out on Ascension Day, 15 August 1227. Any further delay, Honorius made clear, would result in Frederick's excommunication.

It was in August 1225 that fourteen galleys of the imperial fleet arrived at Acre – the last surviving outpost of Crusader Outremer – to bring Yolande to Sicily. And so she embarked on the journey that was to take her to her new life, accompanied by a suite which included a female cousin several years her senior. Frederick, together with her father, was waiting for her at Brindisi, where their marriage took place in the cathedral on 9 November. It was, alas, ill-fated. On the following day the Emperor left the city with his bride, without previously warning his new father-in-law; by the time John caught up with them he was informed by his tearful daughter that her husband had already seduced her cousin. When they reached Palermo the poor girl was immediately packed off to the palace harem. Her father, meanwhile, had been coldly informed that he was no longer Regent. Still less did he have any further right to the title of king.

Pope Honorius died in 1227. His successor, Gregory IX, already an old man, started as he meant to go on. 'Take heed,' he wrote to Frederick soon after his accession, 'that you do not place your intellect, which you have in common with the angels, below your senses, which you have in common with brutes and plants.' To the Emperor, whose debauches were rapidly becoming legendary, it was an effective shot across the bows. By this time, the Crusade was at last gathering its forces. A constant stream of young German knights was crossing the Alps and pouring down the pilgrim roads of Italy to join the Emperor in Apulia, whence the army was to take ship for the Holy Land. But then, in the savage heat of an Apulian August, an epidemic broke out. It may have been typhoid, it may have been cholera; but it swept relentlessly through the Crusader camp. And now Frederick himself succumbed to the dread virus. He sailed from Brindisi regardless; but a day or two later he realized that he was too ill to continue. He sent the surviving Crusaders ahead, to make what preparations they could. He himself returned to Italy, promising to follow when he was sufficiently recovered – at the latest by May 1228. Ambassadors were simultaneously despatched to Rome, to explain the situation to the Pope.

Gregory, however, refused to receive them. Instead, in a blistering encyclical, he accused the Emperor of having blatantly disregarded his crusading vows. Had he not, after repeated postponements, himself set a new date for his departure? Had he not foreseen that, with thousands of soldiers and pilgrims crowded together in the summer heat, an epidemic was inevitable? And who was to say that he had really contracted the disease? Was this not a further attempt to wriggle out of his obligations? On 29 September he declared Frederick excommunicate.

In doing so, however, he created for himself a new problem. It was self-evident that excommunicates could not lead Crusades, which was precisely what Frederick intended to do. The Pope had badly overplayed his hand. Frederick had addressed an open letter to all who had taken the Cross, explaining his position quietly and reasonably – setting, in short, an example to the Holy Father of the tone which he would have been well advised to adopt himself. The letter had its effect. When, on Easter Sunday 1228, Gregory launched into a furious sermon against the Emperor, his Roman congregation rioted; hounded from the city, he was obliged to seek refuge in Viterbo. From there he continued his campaign, but whereas only a few months before he had been urgently calling on Frederick to leave on the Crusade, he was now in the ludicrous position of preaching equally urgently against it – knowing as he did that, if the Emperor were to return victorious, papal prestige would sustain a blow from which it would take a long time to recover.

The story of Frederick's Crusade can be quickly told. Saladin's old empire was now in the hands of three brothers of his own tribe, the House of Ayyub; one of them, al-Kamil, Sultan of Egypt, hearing of Frederick's imminent departure, had sent him an appeal: if his brother, al-Mu'azzam, could only be driven from his seat in Damascus, he himself would be in a position to restore to the Emperor the lost territory of the Kingdom of Jerusalem. Word had since come of Mu'azzam's death, so it might be that al-Kamil's enthusiasm for an alliance had somewhat faded; still, Frederick had been dealt something of a trump card, and he was determined to play it. On his arrival in Tyre at the end of 1228, he sent an embassy to al-Kamil, who was gradually gaining possession of his dead brother's lands and deeply regretting his former offer. The envoys pointed out that the Emperor had come only on the Sultan's invitation; now that the whole world knew he was here, how could he be seen to leave empty-handed? The resulting loss of prestige might prove fatal, and al-Kamil would never be able to find himself another Christian ally. As for Jerusalem, it was nowadays a relatively insignificant city, defenceless and largely depopulated; even from the religious point of view it was far less important to Islam than it was to Christendom. Would its surrender not be a small price to pay for peaceful relations between Muslim and Christian – and, incidentally, for Frederick's own immediate departure?

There were no threats – none, at least, outwardly expressed. But the imperial army was on the spot, and its strength was considerable. The Sultan was in an impossible position. There was the

Emperor on his very doorstep, waiting to collect what had been promised and unlikely to leave until he had got it. Finally al-Kamil capitulated, agreeing to a ten-year treaty on certain conditions. First, Jerusalem must remain undefended. The Temple Mount, with the Dome of the Rock and the al-Aqsa Mosque opposite it, might be visited by Christians but must remain in Muslim hands, together with Hebron. The Christians could have their other principal shrines of Bethlehem and Nazareth, on the understanding that they would be linked to the Christian cities of the coast only by a narrow corridor running through what would continue to be Muslim territory. On Saturday, 17 March 1229, Frederick – still under sentence of excommunication – entered Jerusalem and formally took possession of the city. On the following day, in open defiance of the papal ban, he attended Mass in the Church of the Holy Sepulchre, deliberately wearing his imperial crown. He had effectively achieved everything he had set out to achieve, and had done so without the shedding of a drop of Christian or Muslim blood.

Among the Christian community, a degree of rejoicing might have been expected; instead, the reaction was one of fury. Frederick, while still under the ban of the Church, had dared to set foot in the most sacred shrine of Christendom, which he had won in collusion with the Sultan of Egypt. The Patriarch of Jerusalem, who had studiously ignored the Emperor ever since his arrival, now showed his displeasure by putting the entire city under an interdict. Church services were forbidden; pilgrims visiting the Holy Places could no longer count on the remission of their sins. The local barons were outraged that they had not been consulted. How, they asked themselves, were they expected to retain the territories that Frederick had so dubiously acquired once the imperial army had returned to the west?

The last straw, to priests and laymen alike, was the Emperor's obvious interest in – and admiration for – both the Muslim faith and Islamic civilization as a whole. He insisted, for example, on visiting the Dome of the Rock – of whose architecture he made a detailed study – and the al-Aqsa Mosque, where he is said to have expressed bitter disappointment at not having heard the call to prayer. (The Sultan had ordered the muezzins to be silent as a sign of respect.) As always, he questioned every educated Muslim he met – about his faith, his calling, his way of life or anything else that occurred to him. To the Christians of Outremer, such an attitude was profoundly shocking; even the Emperor's superb Arabic was held against him. With every day that he remained in Jerusalem his unpopularity grew, and when he moved on to Acre – narrowly escaping an ambush by the Templars on the way – the city was on the verge of rebellion. He ordered his fleet to be ready to sail on 1 May, and reached Brindisi on 10 June 1229.

He found his kingdom in a state of helpless confusion. His old enemy Gregory IX had taken advantage of his absence to launch what almost amounted to another Crusade against him, writing to the princes and churches of western Europe demanding men and money for an all-out attack, both in Germany and in Italy. In Germany the Pope's attempts to establish a rival Emperor in the person of Otto of Brunswick had had little effect. In Italy, on the other hand, he had organized an armed invasion with the object of driving Frederick out of the south once and for all, so that the whole territory could be ruled directly from Rome. Furious fighting was at that moment in progress in the Abruzzi and around Capua, while several cities in Apulia, believing the rumours – deliberately circulated by papal agents – of Frederick's death, were in open revolt. To encourage others to follow their example, Gregory had recently published an edict releasing all the Emperor's subjects from their oaths of allegiance.

The situation could hardly have been more desperate, yet from the moment of Frederick's arrival the tide began to turn. Here was the Emperor once again among his people, not dead but triumphant, having recovered without bloodshed the Holy Places for Christendom. Frederick's achievement may not have impressed the Christian communities of Outremer, but to the people of south Italy and Sicily it appeared in a very different light. Meanwhile, many people were profoundly shocked that the Pope himself should have attacked the lands of an absent Crusader. Louis IX, King of France, was frankly appalled. Moreover, with his return to his kingdom, Frederick himself instantly became a changed man. Gone were the anger, the bluster, the insecurity that he had showed time and time again in the East. He was back now in the land he knew and loved; once again, he was in control. All that summer he spent tirelessly on campaign, and by the end of October the papal army was broken.

Gregory IX, however, was not, and the reconciliation between the two was a long, difficult and painful process. In the months that followed Frederick made concession after concession, knowing as he did that the obstinate old Pope still retained his most damaging weapon. The Emperor was still excommunicate: a serious embarrassment, a permanent reproach and a potentially dangerous diplomatic liability. As a Christian too – insofar as he was one – Frederick would have had no wish to die under the ban of the Church. But still Gregory prevaricated; it was not until July 1230 that, very reluctantly, he agreed to a peace treaty – it was signed at Ceprano at the end of August – and lifted his sentence. Two months later still, the two men dined together in the papal palace at Anagni. The dinner, one feels, must have been far from convivial, at least at first; but Frederick was capable of enormous charm when he wanted to use it, and the Pope seems to have been genuinely gratified that the Holy Roman Emperor should have taken the trouble to visit him, informally and without pomp. So ended yet another of those Herculean struggles between Emperor and Pope, on which the history of medieval Europe so frequently seems to turn.

Of course, it was not really over. Six years later a new Lombard revolt – inspired as ever by Gregory – called the Emperor north. At Cortenuova in 1237 he smashed the revived League and avenged his grandfather Frederick Barbarossa's historic defeat at Legnano, thus earning for himself yet another excommunication. Pope Gregory died at last, in 1241. If his successor, the hopeless old Celestine IV, had lived, Frederick's worries might have been almost at an end, but after just seventeen days Celestine followed Gregory to the grave. Frederick did everything he could to influence the next election, but in vain: the Genoese cardinal Sinibaldo dei Fieschi, who in June 1243 became Pope Innocent IV, proved if anything an even more determined adversary than Gregory had been. Only two years after his accession, at a General Council in Lyons, he declared the already excommunicated Frederick deposed, stripping him of all his dignities and titles.

But Emperors could not be thrown out so easily. This final ban, which Louis IX of France and Henry III of England – now the Emperor's brother-in-law* – both refused to recognize, made little immediate difference to Frederick's position. The Hohenstaufen name retained immense prestige in Germany, while in Sicily and the Regno his endless peregrinations, accompanied by his harem and, quite often, his remarkable menagerie, had ensured him a consistently high profile to the point where he seemed omnipresent, part of life itself. Loftily ignoring the papal pronouncement, he continued the struggle; and it was still in progress when in December 1250 at Castel Fiorentino in Apulia he was seized by a violent attack of dysentery. He died, dressed in the habit of a Cistercian monk, on Tuesday, 13 December, just thirteen days short of his fifty-sixth birthday. His body was taken to Palermo where, at his request, it was buried in the cathedral, in the magnificent porphyry sarcophagus that had been prepared for his grandfather Roger II but had till then remained unoccupied.

'The Papacy,' wrote Sir Steven Runciman, 'in all its long history had never met an adversary so formidable as Frederick II of Hohenstaufen.' Perhaps it was no wonder that Dante relegated him to the sixth circle of hell. Politically, too, he had been a failure. His dream had been to make Italy and Sicily a united kingdom within the Empire, with its capital in Rome. The overriding purpose of the Papacy, aided by the cities and towns of Lombardy, had been to ensure that that dream should never be realized. And the Papacy had won. But it was not for his political achievements that Frederick is remembered as the most remarkable European ruler between Charlemagne and Napoleon, still less for his work in Germany, which he never visited when he could avoid it. What earned him the title of *Stupor Mundi* was the sheer force of his intellectual and physical personality. Not for nothing were Frederick Barbarossa and Roger II his grandfathers. Both were themselves great men; but

---

* In 1235 Frederick had married as his third wife Isabella of England, daughter of King John.

both, in their own fields, he surpassed. From Barbarossa he derived the tireless energy, the military skill, the courage and the Augustan concept of empire to which he devoted his life; to Roger and his Sicilian upbringing he owed the limitless breadth of his mind and interests, his extraordinary gift for languages and his passionate love of art and science. In 1224 he founded the University of Naples, one of the oldest in the world and still known as the Università Federico II. A poet among poets, his was the circle in which the sonnet was invented and Italian vernacular literature was born; his burning curiosity over the nature of the physical and metaphysical worlds kept him in contact or correspondence with thinkers of every creed; while the surviving sculptures from the triumphal gate at Capua, which he designed himself, testify alike to his skill as an architect and his munificence as a patron. He has a good claim to the title of the first of the Renaissance princes, two centuries before his time.

7

The Vespers

~~~~~~

DEPRIVED OF FREDERICK'S firm hand at the helm, Sicily quickly sank back into chaos and confusion. Something – it may perhaps have been a legacy from their Arab past – always prevented the Sicilians from achieving any semblance of unity; almost all their major cities were riven by internal strife, and the result was something like a multilateral civil war. The barons took over, each one fighting for himself; thus, while feudalism on the mainland was slowly fading away, in Sicily it tightened its hold. Agriculture suffered badly in consequence, and the population dramatically decreased; it has been calculated that over the next two centuries it may have fallen by as much as a half.

No fewer than ten of Frederick's children and grandchildren perished in prison or met with violent deaths. His eldest son, Henry, who became King Henry VII of Germany – he was never crowned Emperor – rebelled against his father and died in prison in 1242. Conrad, the son by Yolande of Jerusalem whom he had therefore named as his heir, did his best to re-establish order; but he was obliged to spend most of his time in Germany, and the Regno was entrusted to Frederick's bastard son Manfred, the favourite of his eleven illegitimate children, whom his father had made Prince of Taranto. When Conrad died of malaria at the age of twenty-six only four years after his father, Manfred, after refusing to surrender Sicily to Innocent IV, took over the Regency on the part of his half-brother's two-year-old son, Conradin. The Pope, predictably furious, excommunicated him forthwith, and searched frantically for other suitable candidates for the throne. Richard of Cornwall, brother of the English King Henry III, was at one time the favourite, but although he was the richest man in England he found the price too high and refused to take up the challenge; it was, he said, like being offered the moon on condition that it was unhooked from the sky. Another offer had been made in 1253 to King Henry's eight-year-old son, Edmund of Lancaster, who had rather surprisingly accepted and had been formally invested by a Papal Legate with the Kingdom. For ten years Edmund called himself 'By the Grace of God King of Sicily' and even sent the Bishop of Hereford to collect taxes from his new subjects; but the idea was soon seen by everybody to be a non-starter and no more was heard of it.

Manfred, meanwhile, had extended his power over the greater part of south Italy. Pope Alexander IV, who in 1254 had succeeded the odious Innocent and to whom Manfred appeared every bit as dangerous as his father had been, had sent an army against him, which Manfred had almost effortlessly defeated. He was a worthy scion of his father. Unlike Frederick, he was astonishingly good-looking; moreover, he had inherited all his father's love of learning and of literature, as well as his devastating personal charm. He recreated Frederick's brilliant court, founded the Apulian port of Manfredonia and married Helena, the daughter of Michael II, Despot of Epirus, an alliance which gained him the island of Corfu and a considerable stretch of the Albanian coast. Another daughter, Constance, became the wife of Peter, heir to the throne of Aragon – a marriage that was to prove a good deal more significant than at first appeared. Finally, in August 1258, Manfred prevailed upon the Sicilian baronage to proclaim him King.

But Pope Alexander had not given up. Gentle and easy-going as he was, he would not – could not – ever recognize a Hohenstaufen, and he devoted most of the seven years of his pontificate to seeking an 'athlete of Christ' who would rid southern Italy once and for all of that hated dynasty. As far as he was concerned, the throne of Sicily was vacant, and he was still trying to find a suitable candidate when he died in 1261 at Viterbo – where, to avoid the factional strife in Rome, he had spent much of his pontificate. And it was in Viterbo that, after three months of inconclusive deliberations, the cardinals elected a rank outsider to the papal throne – the Patriarch of Jerusalem, who happened to be visiting the Curia in his official capacity. Jacques Pantaléon was a Frenchman, the son of a poor cobbler in Troyes. He took the name of Urban IV, and his eye soon fell on one of his own: a compatriot and, in addition, a man of quite outstanding ability, Charles of Anjou.

The brother of King Louis IX – St Louis – Charles was now thirty-five. In 1246 he had acquired through his wife the county of Provence, which had brought him untold wealth; he was also lord of the thriving port of Marseille. To this cold, cruel, immensely able and vastly ambitious opportunist the Pope was now offering a chance not to be missed. The army which Charles was to lead against Manfred was to be officially designated a Crusade – which meant that it would be as always something of a ragbag, with the usual mixture of adventurers hoping to secure fiefdoms in the Regno, pilgrims seeking the remission of their sins and ruffians out quite simply for plunder. With them, however, was an impressive number of knights from all over western Europe – French, German, Spanish, Italian and Provençal, with even a few Englishmen thrown in for good measure – who, Charles firmly believed, would be more than a match for anything that Manfred could fling against them.

On 6 January 1266 Charles of Anjou was crowned in Rome – not by Urban's successor, Clement IV,★ but by five of his cardinals – as King of Sicily; less than a month later, on 3 February, his army crossed the frontier of the Regno. This time there was to be no long campaign. The two armies met on the 26th outside Benevento, and it was all over quite quickly. Manfred, courageous as always, stood his ground and went down fighting; but his troops, hopelessly outnumbered, soon fled the field. Few of them survived. The bridge over the Calore was soon blocked; a man in armour had no chance against the swollen river waters. Queen Helena and Manfred's three sons tried to escape across the Adriatic to Epirus, but they were arrested while waiting for a boat and imprisoned in Nocera. Helena died there five years later, not yet thirty. The boys, too, remained in prison till their deaths. One was still there in 1307.

★ Neither Urban nor Clement ever went near Rome, preferring the greater comfort of Anagni or Viterbo.

The Crusade was over, or very nearly. Two years later young Conradin, 'beautiful as Absalom', made a last desperate attempt to save the situation, leading an army of Germans, Italians and Spaniards across the Alps. He marched by way of Verona, Pisa, Siena and Viterbo to Rome, where he was given a tumultuous reception; then he led his army on in search of Charles. They met at the border village of Tagliacozzo. This time the battle, fought on 23 August 1268, resulted in hideous slaughter on both sides. At one moment, indeed, it seemed that the vast majority of the Angevins had been killed and the remainder had taken flight, and Conradin was congratulating himself on his victory. But Charles had prepared an elaborate ambush. Suddenly, from behind a fold in the hills, he led nearly a thousand of his finest cavalry at full gallop against Conradin and those of his knights who were gathered around the Hohenstaufen banners. They were unprepared, outnumbered and taken completely by surprise. Conradin escaped from the field and actually reached Rome, but was captured soon afterwards. There followed a show trial in Naples, after which, on 29 October, the young prince was taken down to the marketplace and publicly beheaded. He was just sixteen years old.

The Hohenstaufen line in Italy was at an end; and so was something else that in the long term was far more to be regretted: Sicily's golden age. Its decline could be traced back for several decades – to that Christmas Day in 1194 when Henry VI was crowned King. His son Frederick always maintained that he loved the island above all his other dominions, but as he grew older he spent less and less time there and more and more in Apulia, where his great hunting lodge of Castel del Monte still stands today. This was not only a matter of personal preference; there were also practical political considerations. In Norman days, when the Kingdom consisted chiefly of Sicily and south Italy, it made sense to govern it from Palermo; but once the King-Emperor ruled also over north Italy and, in theory at least, over much of northern Europe, the old capital was simply too remote. The Strait of Messina, though only a couple of miles across and of considerable importance to Palermitan trade, now became more of an obstacle than an advantage, while Frederick's chief preoccupations – his problems in Germany and his constant struggle with the Papacy – were, to the average Sicilian, of little concern.

Manfred too had preferred the mainland. He had established his principal residences in Naples and Lucera, and had seldom visited Sicily after his coronation. This was a serious mistake: had he been content to settle in Palermo, while always keeping a stern eye on the Regno in the manner of his Norman forebears, he might have saved the island from its sad decline and founded there a lasting dynasty of his own. But Manfred never quite emerged from the gigantic shadow of his father; somehow he always felt that he was worthy of greater things. He too had ambitions in north Italy, and perhaps beyond. Sicily was not big enough for him, and they both suffered in consequence.

With the coming of the Angevins, it seemed as though the island would sink back still further into obscurity. Charles of Anjou at first showed minimal interest in Sicily, concentrating his attention instead on Tuscany – of which Pope Clement IV had nominated him Imperial Vicar – where there was almost constant fighting between the two great factions of medieval Italy, the Guelfs and the Ghibellines. But the Sicilians were not so easily ignored. In the late summer of 1267 they rose in revolt. It was a good two years before order was restored, and the severity of the punishments inflicted on innocent and guilty alike left a legacy of resentment and hostility that were all too soon to be made manifest. So too did Charles's subsequent reorganization of the Kingdom, very much on the French model. French, henceforth, was the language of government. The King refused to accept that either Manfred or Conradin – or even Frederick after his formal deposition by Pope Innocent in 1245 – had been lawful Kings of Sicily. All their legislation, together with all their grants of land, were therefore null and void. If a landowner could not satisfactorily prove that he had owned his property before 1245, that property was forfeit. All this confiscated land, together with further confiscations from the convicted rebels, were either kept by Charles for himself or distributed among his friends, nearly all of them Frenchmen or Provençaux. Once again – one is tempted to write 'as always' – the Sicilians lost out.

By about 1270 Charles of Anjou had brought much of the Italian peninsula under his control – a task which was made a good deal easier for him after Clement's death in 1268 by the inability of the cardinals to elect a successor. Thanks to his considerable influence in the Curia, he was able to keep the papal throne unoccupied for the next three years, thus gaining for himself a totally free hand in Italy.* On the whole he governed well. He was a first-class administrator and he worked hard, moving perpetually around his kingdom while his scribes and secretaries followed as best they could, taking a personal interest in every detail that was brought to his notice; only towards the end of his life did he begin to concentrate the government in Naples and make it a capital in something more than name.

Sicily, however, remained in a state of neglect. The recent revolt still rankled. The ports were left empty; the industries received little encouragement. The royal estates were well looked after, as might have been expected; but for the average Sicilian there was only one conclusion to be drawn – that he now belonged to an obscure and unimportant province, for which its ruler had long since ceased to care. In the last fifteen years of Charles's reign, despite all his interminable peregrinations around the Regno, he set foot in Sicily precisely once. As he was then on his way to join his brother Louis in Tunis he could hardly have avoided it; even so, the visit was limited to a few days. All this was uncharacteristically shortsighted of him; he did not lack intelligence, and he should have seen that by his neglect he was laying up trouble for the future. The Sicilians had their pride, and their memories were long.

For those who detested the House of Anjou and all it stood for, there was after the death of Conradin one rallying point: the court of King Peter III of Aragon. In 1262 Peter had married Manfred's daughter Constance, who was now the sole representative in the south of the Hohenstaufen cause; and increasing numbers of refugees from Sicily and the Regno were finding their way to his court at Barcelona. Among them was one of the great conspirators of his

* The interregnum ended only when the authorities at Viterbo (where the conclave was being held) actually removed the roof of the palace in which the cardinals were deliberating.

age. His name was John of Procida. He had studied medicine in his native city of Salerno and, as the Emperor's personal physician, had attended Frederick on his deathbed. Later he had entered the service of Manfred. He had fought with Conradin at Tagliacozzo, after which he had travelled to Germany with the intention of persuading another of Frederick II's grandsons to invade Italy and restore the Hohenstaufen line. Only when this plan failed did he move with his two sons to Barcelona. Constance, he believed, was the one last hope. King Peter gave him a warm welcome and made him Chancellor of the Kingdom, in which capacity he could concentrate on a great conspiracy to secure the Angevin downfall.

There is a remarkable legend, which appears in the works of both Petrarch and Boccaccio, to the effect that John then travelled in disguise around the courts of Europe to gain support for his cause, visiting the Emperor Michael VIII Palaeologus in Constantinople and returning with vast quantities of Byzantine gold. It is almost certainly untrue: by this time he was nearly seventy, and in both the years in question, 1279 and 1280, his signature regularly appears on documents issuing from the Aragonese chancery. It may well be, however, that someone else – perhaps one of his sons – made the journeys in his name. There was certainly some contact between Barcelona and Constantinople, where Michael was aware that Charles of Anjou was at that very moment preparing a major expedition against his Empire. He was consequently eager to take the immediate offensive, before that expedition could be launched. Peter, on the other hand, naturally advocated waiting until it was well on its way.

In fact the timing was in the hands of neither King nor Emperor, but of the Sicilians themselves. By 1282 the Angevins had made themselves cordially detested throughout the Regno, both for the severity of their taxation and for the arrogance of their conduct; and when on the evening of Easter Monday, 30 March 1282, a drunken French sergeant began importuning a Sicilian woman outside the church of Santo Spirito just as the bells were ringing for vespers, her countrymen's anger boiled over. The sergeant was set upon by her husband and killed; the murder led to a riot, the riot to a massacre; 2,000 Frenchmen were dead by morning.

The rising spread like wildfire. On 30 August King Peter and his army landed at Trapani, arriving in Palermo three days later. The formal coronation for which he had hoped proved impossible: the Archbishop of Palermo was dead, the pro-Angevin Archbishop of Monreale had most sensibly disappeared; Peter had to be content with a simple proclamation of his kingship. This he acknowledged with a public promise to observe the rights and liberties of his new subjects, calling upon all the able-bodied men of Palermo and its surroundings to march with him to Messina, where the French were still holding out. The response, we are told, was immediate and enthusiastic. For all good Palermitans – who detested the Messinans and the French in equal measure – the opportunity was too good to resist.

In Messina Charles had personally assumed command; and it was there, on 17 September, that he received ambassadors from King Peter. By now he realized that the Spanish conquest was a virtual fait accompli. He had no wish to risk a pitched battle with what he suspected was a vastly superior force; still less did he wish to be trapped on the island himself. He therefore told the ambassadors that while he naturally rejected their master's claims he was prepared, at least temporarily, to evacuate his forces to the mainland. For Peter, who had deliberately delayed his advance, this was exactly what he wanted to hear. He too was anxious to avoid bloodshed. All that was necessary now was to allow the Angevins a week or two to get their entire army across the Strait; he would then have won the island without striking a blow.

He was of course fully aware that he could not count on the continued loyalty of the Sicilian barons; and he had been warned in particular about one of them, a certain Alaimo of Lentini, Captain of Messina, who had already betrayed both King Manfred and King Charles. Alaimo's wife, Machalda, was, it appeared, even worse than her husband. When Peter arrived, dog-tired, at the little village of Santa Lucia near Milazzo where he had arranged to spend the night, he was horrified to find her waiting for him. As an excuse for her presence she had brought him the keys of Catania; but it was soon all too clear that her real purpose was to audition for the part of royal mistress. Poor Peter had an acutely embarrassing evening. He escaped only with a long disquisition on his love for and loyalty to

Queen Constance – which was not, we are told, an argument that Machalda found attractive. Henceforth she made no secret of her jealousy of the Queen, and did all she could to influence her husband against the royal couple.

Whether or not Alaimo knew of his wife's actions, he was for the moment cooperative enough, welcoming Peter to Messina and encouraging him to do the Angevins as much harm as he could. This proved to be considerable. Peter's fleet had now reached Messina; the Angevins were only just across the Strait in Reggio and, thanks to the precipitation with which they had been obliged to sail, still sadly disorganized. Mid-October saw two naval battles; the second, fought off Nicotera on the 14th, resulted in the capture of twenty-one French galleys on their way from Naples, loaded to the gunwales with armaments. There were several other engagements to follow in the next few years; one of them, fought on 5 June 1284 off Castellammare, resulted in the capture of Charles's son and heir, the Prince of Salerno.

Charles naturally refused to recognize his defeat, even going so far as to propose deciding the fate of Sicily by single combat with Peter, the confrontation to take place under English protection at Bordeaux, several weeks' journey away. Peter rather surprisingly accepted, though in subsequent negotiations it was decided that since Charles was already fifty-five – an old man by the standards of the time – and Peter only forty, it would be fairer if each monarch were accompanied by a hundred carefully chosen knights to fight beside him. The date for the great contest was fixed for Tuesday, 1 June 1283; unfortunately – or perhaps fortunately – the precise hour was not specified. The Aragonese arrived early in the morning, to find no sign of Charles. Peter accordingly announced that his was the victory, his cowardly opponent having failed to put in an appearance. Charles rode up a few hours later and claimed that, as there was now no sign of Peter, the victory was his. The two never met. The cost to both, in time as well as money, was considerable; but honour was saved on both sides.

Meanwhile, the Regno was split down the middle, and – since Charles steadfastly refused to renounce his title of King of Sicily – the legend of the Two Sicilies was born, Charles reigning in

Naples and Peter in Palermo, each determined to expel the other
and to reunify the country. But Charles's reputation was gone. His
empire had been built on sand. He had ceased to be a world power.
There could no longer be any question of an expedition against
Constantinople. On 7 January 1285 he died at Foggia. For twenty
years he had dominated the Mediterranean, possessed by both an
insatiable ambition and a driving energy that allowed him no rest.
He was genuinely pious, but his piety brought him no humility,
since he always saw himself as God's chosen instrument. Nor did
it bring him humanity, for he believed implicitly that the French
were a master race and made no attempt to understand the thoughts
and feelings of his non-French subjects; he thus consistently underestimated his enemies, and particularly the House of Aragon. Nor,
finally, did it bring him compassion: his execution of the sixteen-
year-old Conradin had shocked all Europe, and was held against
him all his life. He might on occasion have been admired; he could
never have been loved.

Perhaps his greatest mistake was to have neglected Sicily and the
Sicilians. They had annoyed him with a long and stubborn rebellion early in his reign; once that had been put down they simply
bored him. Poor, and therefore basically unprofitable, they were
moreover a mongrel people, an unhealthy mixture of Latin, Greek
and Arab – not, he somehow felt, to be taken very seriously. That
was why he never once paid a significant visit to the island. It
would have been a surprise indeed had he been told that it would
be the Sicilians – with only a very little help from their friends –
who would ultimately bring him down.

It is never a good beginning to a reign if the successor to the throne
chances to be in prison. Charles's heir was his son the Prince of
Salerno, who now became Charles II and was nicknamed 'the Lame'
(*le Boiteux*). He had been captured by the Aragonese admiral Roger
of Lauria in 1284, and was still being held prisoner when his father
died. The war, meanwhile, was by no means over; indeed, it was
to continue well into the next century. The Kings of France –
Charles of Anjou's nephew Philip III the Bold, and Philip's son
and successor, Philip IV the Fair – although they were respectively

the husband and son of Peter's sister Isabella, were to continue for reasons of family honour in their attempts to recover Sicily for themselves.

The Papacy too had to look to its prestige, since Sicily and the Regno had been granted to Charles of Anjou by Pope Urban. That was why, immediately after the Vespers, Pope Martin IV – another Frenchman – had excommunicated Peter and laid the island under an interdict. Shortly afterwards he went even further, declaring Peter deposed and deprived of his dominions, which he theoretically bestowed on King Philip's younger son, the Count of Valois. The Sicilians, on the other hand, seemed perfectly happy to accept Spanish rule. Their rebellion had been directed not against foreign occupation as such, merely against that of Charles, who had usurped the Kingdom, taxed them without mercy and treated them as second-class citizens in their own island. Peter's wife, Constance of Hohenstaufen, on the other hand, was their legitimate Queen. Besides, a distant ruler half-way across the Mediterranean was surely preferable to one on their very doorstep.

Their loss, however, was greater than they knew. The Pope's interdict was to last for a century – although, being largely ignored, it probably did more harm to the reputation of the Papacy than it did to the Sicilians – and for the next four hundred years their island was to be politically attached not to the Italian peninsula but to the Iberian. Their cultural and intellectual life suffered additionally because they were henceforth cut off from the University of Naples, which was all the more important to them in that they possessed no similar institution of their own. Economically, too, they were impoverished. Messina, and to a lesser extent Palermo, both lost their commercial contacts with Italian ports.

But there was a far, far greater deprivation to come. Italy was now on the threshold of her Renaissance. Dante had been born in 1265, Giotto two years later. The next three centuries were to see an explosion of national genius unlike anything the world had ever witnessed. Had Sicily remained Italian she could have shared in it all; she might even have made an important contribution of her own. Instead, she became Spanish. In all but architecture, the Italian Renaissance was largely to pass her by.

With one huge, dazzling exception: Antonello da Messina. Born in 1430, Antonello studied in Naples, where in the middle of the fifteenth century Flemish painting was all the rage. Giorgio Vasari – who mistakenly credits him with the introduction of oil painting into Italy – tells us that he was originally inspired by a magnificent triptych by Jan van Eyck, painted for the Genoese Battista Lomellini but now, alas, vanished without trace; and indeed his style is often more reminiscent of Flanders than of the warm south. He certainly exercised an enormous influence on Italian painting; the critic John Pope-Hennessy described him as 'the first Italian painter for whom the individual portrait was an art form in its own right'. As well as Naples, he is known to have worked in Milan and Venice; but Messina remained his home, and it was there, sometime in February 1479, that he died.

There must have been many occasions when King Peter of Aragon devoutly wished that he had stayed at home. Since the death of Frederick II Sicily had shown itself to be virtually ungovernable; Peter, who could not even claim papal authority for his conquest as Charles of Anjou had done, found himself dependent on the local baronage and was consequently obliged to tread with extreme care. He returned the seat of government from the Angevin stronghold of Messina to Palermo; he publicly undertook that Sicily should continue as a separate kingdom rather than being merged with Aragon, as most Sicilians had feared it would; he even went so far as to promise that after his death the two crowns should be allotted to two different members of his family. These moves were popular enough; on the other hand, in furtherance of Peter's long-term intention of conquering the whole of the Regno, the Aragonese and Sicilian fleets were amalgamated. Thus it was that many who had taken part in the rebellion of 1282 felt that their efforts had been largely in vain: they were no more independent now than they had been under the Angevins, while their government was as arbitrary as ever. They watched powerless while large estates were granted to a new Spanish feudal aristocracy, just as they had been formerly granted to the French.

Peter died on 2 November 1285, just ten months after his arch-enemy Charles of Anjou. (Dante, for some reason, has them singing harmoniously together outside the gates of Purgatory.) As promised, he divided his kingdom, leaving Aragon to his eldest son, the twenty-one-year-old Alfonso III – who was betrothed to Eleanor, daughter of King Edward I of England – while Sicily went to his second son, James. And there were two more deaths in that fateful year. The first, on 28 March, was that of Pope Martin. His pontificate had been a disaster. Of course the Papacy was committed to the Angevin cause; to have broken that commitment would have been tantamount to an admission that it had been wrong. But a wiser man with a modicum of diplomatic understanding might have been able to steer a less blinkered path and save it – and the French themselves – from humiliation. Martin was succeeded by the seventy-five-year-old Honorius IV,* a noble Roman so paralysed by gout that he was obliged to say Mass seated on a stool and needed a mechanical device to raise his hands from the altar. He too saw no alternative to the Angevins; but he was determined to restore peace to Italy, even if it took a war to do so.

Then, on 5 October, it was the turn of Philip the Bold of France, who died at Perpignan of a fever that had already carried off several thousand from an army that he had led against Aragon that summer. This had been yet another humiliating fiasco, from which both France and the Papacy were to take a long time to recover. Philip was succeeded by his son, Philip IV the Fair. Although still only seventeen, the young prince already possessed an acute political brain. Until now his sympathies had been frankly with the Aragonese, and he had vehemently opposed his father's support of Charles of Anjou; after his accession, however, he began to change his mind and to look on the claims of his brother Charles of Valois with a more favourable eye. After all, he was now King of France; how could he not support the French cause?

King James I of Sicily† was crowned at Palermo in 1286. Immediately after the ceremony he sent an embassy to Pope Honorius, offering him homage and requesting confirmation of his kingship. The Pope's reply was to excommunicate him together

---

* He was, incidentally, the last Pope to have been married before his ordination.
† In Spain he was James II.

with his mother, Constance of Hohenstaufen, and to put all Sicily under an interdict; the Bishops of Nicastro and Cefalù, who had officiated at his coronation, were summoned to Rome to explain themselves. The papal attitude to the island could hardly have been made much clearer. Honorius was on the warpath. He now ordered an invasion of Sicily, which duly took place in the spring of 1287. It proved a disaster. A substantial French and papal fleet left Brindisi and landed between Catania and Syracuse. By the end of June it was still besieging the same insignificant little town when it was attacked by Roger of Lauria, who captured forty-eight galleys bearing a large number of important French and Provençal nobles. They were eventually released, but only after payment of a swingeing ransom.

It is perhaps worth saying a little more about Roger of Lauria, who was probably the most successful and talented admiral of the Middle Ages. He had been born in 1245, into a south Italian family unshakably loyal to the Hohenstaufen; after the execution of young Conradin in 1268 they fled to Barcelona. There King Peter knighted him, and in 1282 appointed him commander of the Aragonese fleet. Over the next twenty years he fought at least six major naval battles, winning every one of them. After the accession of Peter's third son, Frederick III, in 1296, however, Roger transferred his loyalty to the Angevins, and in his last engagement – the Battle of Ponza in June 1300 – he defeated and captured King Frederick himself.

The attempted papal invasion had been a fiasco, but Honorius was spared the shame: he died in April 1287. There followed a ten-month interregnum, during which those members of the College of Cardinals – and there were many – hostile to the French struggled to block the election of another pro-Angevin Pope. Meanwhile, thanks to the mediation of King Edward I of England, poor Charles II of Anjou made a bid for liberty. It cost him 50,000 silver marks, in addition to which he was obliged to leave three of his sons – luckily he had fourteen children – and sixty Provençal nobles as hostages. In return he promised to work for a peace which would satisfy King Alfonso and King James on the one hand and Philip of France, Charles of Valois and the Pope on the other. It was something of a tall order, but it was a great improvement on prison. The bad news was that, if within three years he had not succeeded, he had had to promise to forfeit the County of Provence or to return to captivity.

Alas, he was due for another disappointment. This time it was the King of France who made difficulties. He much disliked the bit about Provence. By this time, too, a new Pope had at last been elected: the Franciscan Nicholas IV. He too objected to the proposed arrangement. There was only one thing for it: King Edward of England must return to the negotiating table, and the two sides must think again. They did, and by the Treaty of Canfranc, signed in October 1288, Charles obtained his liberty at last, on much the same terms as before. This involved his going directly to France, there to discuss peace – and the future of Sicily – with King Philip.

On his arrival at the French court, Charles's reception was decidedly chilly. Philip had no wish to make peace with Aragon; indeed, the Aragonese ambassadors who had accompanied Charles were placed under immediate arrest. Charles left as soon as he could and returned to Italy, where he found Pope Nicholas at Rieti and was much embarrassed when Nicholas insisted on crowning him King of Sicily on the spot. King Alfonso was predictably furious, but grudgingly accepted a two-year truce. Charles then hurried back to France to see how King Philip and Charles of Valois could best be satisfied.

This time he triumphed. A few months later, on 18 May 1290, his daughter Margaret married Valois, bringing as her dowry the counties of Anjou and Maine. In return her bridegroom agreed to renounce his claims and make peace with Aragon. All this was confirmed in a treaty signed at Brignoles in February 1291, Alfonso agreeing to go as soon as possible to Rome to confirm his reconciliation with the Pope. The date was set for June; but just before his departure he was stricken by a sudden fever and died, aged only twenty-six. Owing to his excommunication he had been unable to marry his English princess, and so died childless. His heir was consequently his brother James, King of Sicily. By the terms of his father's will, however, James was now obliged to pass Sicily on to his younger brother, Frederick.

But James refused. He agreed to accept Frederick as his Viceroy; he himself, however, was determined to remain King. Pope Nicholas's reaction was to excommunicate him, but in April 1292 the Pope died in his turn, having been no more successful in restoring the Angevins than his predecessor. This time the interregnum lasted for twenty-seven months, during which James – as Alfonso had before him – grew increasingly disillusioned with Sicily. The Kingdom of Aragon presented problems enough; was this endlessly troublesome island – divided, rebellious and chaotic – really worth hanging on to? The Angevins, unaccountably enough, seemed to want it, and Europe was unlikely to be truly at peace until they got it. Given adequate compensation, might it not be wiser simply to hand it over?

The question was still troubling him when the twelve living cardinals decided to bestow the Triple Crown on one of the most unsuitable men ever to occupy, however briefly, the papal throne. We may suspect the intervention of Charles II, who had ambitious plans for Europe and needed a Pope who would give him no trouble; but even he would surely have drawn the line at Celestine V, a terrified old peasant of eighty-five, who had lived for more than six decades as a hermit in the Abruzzi. Celestine barely knew what had hit him. The duties of the Papacy – political, diplomatic and administrative – he never began to understand, so simply ignored. He seldom agreed to receive any of his cardinals, whose worldliness and sophistication were well above his head; when he did so, they were obliged to abandon their elegant Latin and adopt the crude vernacular that was the only language that he understood. No wonder he lasted for just five months, then wisely announced his abdication – until 2013, the only one in papal history. Poor Celestine: he is usually identified with the unnamed figure whom Dante meets in the third canto of the *Inferno* and accuses of having made through cowardice *il gran rifiuto* – the great refusal. In fact he was no coward; he simply wanted to return to the hermitage that he should never have left.

Given a free hand by Pope Celestine, Charles had been busy. He now believed that he could recover Sicily if he played his cards right, and the immensely able new Pope, Boniface VIII, helped him to do so. On 12 June 1295 a peace was signed with King James at Anagni. James would free Charles's hostage sons and marry Charles's daughter Blanche; meanwhile, one of Charles's sons would marry James's sister Violante. James's brother Frederick would be given the hand of Catherine of Courtenay, daughter of Philip I, titular Emperor of Constantinople,★ with a considerable sum of money with which to finance the reconquest of the Byzantine Empire. King Philip of France and Charles of Valois would renounce their claims on Aragon. King James, together with his mother, his brothers and all his subjects, would be received back into the bosom of the Church and would hand over Sicily, together with his mainland conquests, to the Holy See, on whose behalf it would be held by the House of Anjou. The way seemed clear at last for Charles to return to the island as its ruler.

All this was fine as far as it went; but nobody had consulted the Sicilians. They had expelled the Angevins little more than ten years before, and were certainly not going to have them back. At the end of 1295 they sent a mission to James at Barcelona to make their position clear. First, they would have Frederick as their King rather than as James's Viceroy; this effectively dethroned James and emphasized Sicily's separate identity. Second, if anyone made any attempt to bring back the French, they would fight to the death. Frederick was in a quandary. He was under enormous pressure. Even John of Procida, now nearly eighty, and Roger of Lauria advised him to accept the treaty, wash his hands of Sicily altogether and allow the Angevins to return. At the same time, how could he possibly let his subjects down – and what would happen if he did? He was saved by Catherine of Courtenay. She wisely refused to involve herself in what was clearly an unspeakable can of worms, and turned him down flat. Without her participation the whole treaty collapsed. Charles of Anjou was no nearer

★ When the Greek Emperors of Constantinople were expelled by the Fourth Crusade in 1204, they were followed by a succession of seven 'Latin' (Frankish) Emperors. The last of these, Baldwin II, was of the Courtenay family, which continued to claim the imperial title long after Michael Palaeologus had recovered the Empire for the Greeks in 1261.

the throne after all, and Frederick was crowned as King Frederick III.*

His coronation did not prevent the reconciliation of the Kingdom of Aragon with that of Naples and with the Pope. King James duly married Charles II's daughter, Blanche of Anjou, and in 1297 he and his family – apart of course from Frederick, who remained in Sicily – travelled to meet Pope Boniface in Rome, where the Infanta Violante was married to Charles's heir, Robert, and King James was additionally invested with the islands of Corsica and Sardinia. Sicily now stood alone; with France, Aragon and the Papacy ranged against it, its future outlook was grim indeed. And yet, oddly enough, this alarming opposition did it relatively little harm. The next two years saw a few desultory raids on the island, during which Catania fell into the hands of Robert, and King James, after a long and unsuccessful siege of Syracuse, was soundly defeated by his brother Frederick. In October 1299 Charles's fourth son, Philip of Taranto, landed in the west of the island, hoping to oblige Frederick to fight on two fronts, but Sicilian intelligence was better than he thought; Frederick was ready for him, routed his invasion force and took him prisoner.

The stalemate, however, continued. James returned home, the Angevins failed to advance much beyond Catania; but Frederick was incapable, try as he might, of expelling the invaders from Sicily once and for all. At last, in July 1301, Violante managed to persuade her husband, Robert, to agree to a year's truce. When this expired Charles of Valois made one more attempt on the island, capturing Termini in the north and unsuccessfully besieging Sciacca in the south; but he was soon called back to France. By this time the Sicilian summer was at its height, everyone was bored with so much inconsequential fighting, and on 31 August Charles, Robert and Frederick signed a treaty of peace at Caltabellotta, a small town up in the hills behind Sciacca.

The Treaty of Caltabellotta was something of a milestone in Sicilian history, though in fact it was little more than a recognition

---

* He was actually only the second Frederick to reign in Sicily, but being a successor to Frederick II – his great-grandfather – he had little choice.

of the uneasy status quo. The Angevins agreed to withdraw all their troops from Sicily, the Sicilians to remove all theirs from the mainland. Frederick was to bear the title of King of Trinacria (which in fact he hardly ever used) so that the Angevins could still call themselves Kings of Sicily. To seal the agreement, Frederick released Charles's son Philip of Taranto, whom he had been holding prisoner at Cefalù, and agreed to marry Eleanora, Charles's youngest daughter. From his point of view, the treaty included one unwelcome clause: that he was to be King for his lifetime only, and that after his death his crown would revert to the Angevins. But he was not unduly worried; he was still only thirty, and that was a problem that could be dealt with later on. The important thing was that he was now reconciled with his brother James and the rest of his family, and that he could at last settle down to rule his country in comparative peace.

The Sicilians too rejoiced. In the twenty years since the Vespers they had suffered much, but on one point they had remained immovable: they would in no circumstances accept French or Angevin rule. The House of Aragon, on the other hand, they were happy to welcome: what disaffection there had been in the early days after King Peter's arrival was almost gone, and Frederick was becoming ever more popular. They were further reassured by the additional promises that he made at the time of his coronation. He would summon a parliament every year on All Saints' Day. He undertook never to leave the island or to make war or peace 'without the full knowledge and consent of the Sicilians'. All taxes would have to be prescribed by law or agreed by parliament. The fact that Frederick no longer had any interest in the Italian mainland was seen only as an advantage; it meant that no longer would his subjects feel like second-class citizens. Henceforth he would be able to concentrate exclusively on *them*.

But the War of the Sicilian Vespers had repercussions far beyond Sicily. Its effects were felt by the whole of Europe. From the death of Frederick II in 1250 to the coronation of Prince Henry of Luxembourg in 1312 there was no crowned Holy Roman Emperor, so the Papacy had at first looked to the most powerful prince in Europe, Charles of Anjou, to provide it with material strength.

Charles, however, had done nothing of the kind; indeed, he had soon proved as dangerous to the Church as ever the Hohenstaufen had been, effortlessly dominating his compatriots Urban IV and Clement IV and making full use of the three-year interregnum, which he had in some degree engineered. Thus, in the absence of both a Pope and an Emperor, he could pursue his career unchecked. There were admittedly two subsequent popes – Gregory X and Nicholas III – who had, as Italians, refused to allow the Papacy to be a mere puppet of the French; but despite their opposition Charles was still able to see himself as a future Emperor – and an Emperor of the East as well as the West, since Byzantium had scarcely begun to recover after the Fourth Crusade and could not possibly have withstood the great army which he intended to lead against it.

Thanks to the people of Sicily, that great army was never sent; the Byzantine Empire was to survive for the best part of another two centuries and Charles himself was to end in failure, taking the medieval Papacy with him in his fall. Europe – indeed Christendom – was never the same again. And Europe remembered. More than three hundred years later King Henry IV of France tried to alarm the Spanish ambassador by boasting of how much damage he could do to Spain's Italian dominions. 'I shall breakfast at Milan,' he said, 'and I shall dine at Rome.' 'Then,' replied the ambassador with a smile, 'Your Majesty will doubtless be in Sicily in time for Vespers.'

8

The Domination of Spain

— ◆ —

PEACE, IN FOURTEENTH-CENTURY Sicily, could never be anything more than comparative. The terms of the Caltabellotta treaty made it clear enough that the Angevins had not renounced their claim to the island, which they proposed to take over after Frederick III's death; and indeed war broke out again in 1312 and continued on and off for the next sixty years. Those years saw repeated raids, some of which assumed the scale of invasions, with quite substantial areas of coast and hinterland temporarily in enemy hands then lost again. The fighting went up and down – there were even occasions when Frederick's troops were engaged on the mainland. And yet, all the time, there was something half-hearted about it. Its sheer inconclusiveness sapped enthusiasm. At Messina in particular, where there had always been a degree of sympathy for the French cause, trade with Calabria and Naples was a tempting prospect, and had the additional advantage of doing down Palermo; and many a peace-loving Sicilian must have asked himself if an Angevin return might not be a small price to pay for peace.

The Sicilian barons, too, remained a perennial problem. They thrived on war, cared little if at all for Sicilian independence and often sided openly with the Angevins if they thought it was in their interest to do so. This was to some extent the fault of Frederick and his predecessors, all of whom had granted lands to their Aragonese or Catalan friends or servants. They had also made grants of lucrative privileges like forests and fisheries, tithes and tax collections. In theory, these were all held in trust, and were repayable by service to the King; but as time went by the barons, both Spanish and Sicilian, showed increasing reluctance to fulfil their feudal obligations, on occasion going so far as to claim outright possession. Some of them even became powerful enough to present a threat to the throne: the Ventimiglia, for example, not only controlled the cities of Trapani and Geraci but also possessed nineteen extensive fiefs all over the island; the Chiaramonte had only eight, but they included much of Palermo; the Moncada, as well as extensive estates in Sicily, also owned all Malta; and the Peralta held as a hereditary right the office of Grand Admiral. Frederick had promised an annual parliament of a kind that had been often held by his predecessors, but nobody could be bothered to hold one – they were all doing far too well without. Soon, too, they took over the administration of justice, despite the fact that hardly any were educated and the majority completely illiterate. In several parts of the island the royal writ no longer ran; the barons' word was law.

On 25 June 1337 Frederick died at Paternò, some dozen miles northwest of Catania. Though in war he frequently showed considerable physical courage – he had proved his moral worth when he stood out alone against the Angevins, the Pope and his own family in 1295–96 – he was at heart a gentle, cultivated man who wrote poetry in Catalan, but who ultimately lacked the force of character necessary to impose his will over his ungovernable subjects and thus to rescue his country from its steady decline. He was succeeded by Peter – the eldest son of his nine legitimate children* – whom he had had crowned as his co-ruler as early as 1321. We know little of the reign of Peter II – the records are maddeningly few and uninformative – except that the war continued in its desultory way and the barons were more rebellious than ever; indeed, they probably gave him a good deal more trouble than the House of Anjou.

Peter died in his turn – suddenly, at Calascibetta in the very heart of Sicily – on 15 August 1342, leaving the throne to his five-year-old son, Louis. Just five years later, disaster struck: the Black Death, which was brought to the island on a Genoese galley from the Levant. The famous fresco known as *The Triumph of Death* – perhaps one of the greatest late Gothic paintings in all Italy – from

---

* He had at least five illegitimate ones as well.

the Palazzo Sclafani in Palermo* in fact dates from the 1440s, but the century following the first appearance of the epidemic saw several further outbreaks, and this fearsome work must unquestionably have been inspired by one or more of them. The picture is dominated by the tremendous figure of Death, riding a semi-skeletal horse through the night, his right arm raised as if wielding a whip; beneath him is a cluster of the dead: bishops, popes, lords and ladies, even a minstrel with his lute. Above and a little behind is one of the most sinister greyhounds ever painted.

Of the Sicilian casualties even approximate figures are lacking; but in Europe as a whole the plague is believed to have carried off roughly one person in three, and there is no reason to think that Sicily was more fortunate. One of the certain victims was John, Duke of Randazzo, who shared the Regency with Louis's mother, Elizabeth of Carinthia, and was one of the few really effective governors of the century; another was Elizabeth's daughter Constance, who took over the Regency on her mother's death in 1352; yet another, later victim was Louis himself, who was stricken in 1355 and died on 16 October, aged seventeen. He was buried, with his father and grandfather, in Palermo Cathedral.

King Louis was, as might have been expected, childless. He was succeeded by his fourteen-year-old brother, Frederick IV.† Frederick was known, rather unkindly, as 'the Simple', a title he in no way deserved. But he was certainly unfortunate. Few kings in all history have inherited a realm more hopelessly chaotic. When he achieved his majority in 1357 Sicily was still on its knees after the Black Death; the surviving barons, however, and the Kingdom of Naples were as troublesome as ever they had been. By this time the former had split into two main factions, known as the Latins, led by the Chiaramonte, and the Catalans, represented by the Ventimiglia. Once the two families had actually intermarried, but the marriage had been childless and had

---

* It can now be seen in the Regional Gallery of Palermo in Palazzo Abatellis. To facilitate its transfer it was cut into four pieces, a procedure that proved disastrous when the paint fell away along the division lines; but it remains unforgettable.

† See p. 145n. In this book they will be Frederick III and IV respectively.

led to nullity proceedings. These in turn had involved accusations of sterility and counteraccusations of impotence. Honour was consequently at stake, and civil war had been the result. Thenceforth the two kept well apart. The Chiaramonte joined the Angevins in Naples and returned with an army which devastated much of the southern coast of the island. Meanwhile, the Ventimiglia attacked their enemy's strongholds in the north, starving the populations into submission. In the years that followed, the luckless King was briefly captured by both the Catalans and the Latins, and was even obliged to pawn the crown jewels.

But civil war – particularly when it is accompanied by intermittent foreign wars as well – cannot go on for ever, and in 1371 Frederick sent envoys to Naples to discuss terms for a lasting peace. These proved more favourable than he might have expected, boiling down as they did to the fact that he could continue as King of an independent Sicily on condition that he called himself King of Trinacria and paid an annual tribute to Naples. Pope Gregory XI, at that moment preparing to transfer the Papacy back to Rome after its seventy years at Avignon, also gave the agreement his blessing, provided only that Frederick acknowledged the feudal suzerainty of the Holy See, a legal technicality to which the King had no objection.

Frederick died in 1377. Though twice married he had only one child, a daughter named Maria who was fourteen years old at the time of his death. He entrusted her to his Grand Justiciar, Count Artale di Alagona, who had by this time become leader of the Catalan baronage. In the absence of a ruler it was agreed to divide the island into four major 'vicariates', to be administered by the four principal baronial families. Alagona would govern the east from Catania; Guglielmo Peralta the south from Sciacca; Francesco Ventimiglia, Count of Geraci, would be responsible for most of the north – but not, however, for Palermo, where Manfredi Chiaramonte held sway in a vast mansion that made the now empty royal palace look humble indeed. Needless to say, none of the four 'vicars' trusted the others for a moment, and the arrangement did not last very long.

Why at this point anyone wished to take on the thankless task of reigning in Sicily was not immediately clear; nevertheless, Maria now suddenly became a major diplomatic pawn among the princely houses of Europe. The Kingdom of Naples had never given up its claim to the island, but now, for reasons of his own, Alagona decided to bestow the hand of the young princess upon Giangaleazzo Visconti of Milan – making the additional mistake of announcing his intention in advance. On hearing the news another of the leading barons, Raimondo Moncada, already furious that he had not been numbered among the vicars and horrified by the idea of introducing the Milanese into the *mêlée*, kidnapped the girl from her guardian's castle at Catania and shipped her off to Barcelona, where she was married – probably in 1390 – to Martin, the son of the future King of Aragon Martin I★ by his wife, Maria López de Luna.

The ink was scarcely dry on the wedding contract when Martin, determined that Sicily should once again be lawfully subjected to the throne of Aragon, began – with the enthusiastic support of his father – to raise an army. Just as his predecessors had done, he promised Sicilian fiefs, pensions and high offices of state to those who were prepared to join him, even going so far as to offer pardons for past crimes (excepting, as always, heresy) – a practice previously reserved for popes proclaiming Crusades. The expedition set sail early in 1392, under the command of Martin I's right-hand man, Bernardo Cabrera, who had sold several of his estates in Catalonia in order to equip soldiers at his own expense. Despite the obvious fact that if his campaign succeeded it would categorically put an end to Sicilian independence, two of the four vicars, Ventimiglia and Peralta, offered no resistance; Chiaramonte, on the other hand, made it clear that he was ready to fight. For a full month Palermo lay under siege; but on 5 April Chiaramonte met Martin and

---

★ Great-grandson of Alfonso III, from whom the throne of Aragon had passed in 1291 to his brother James II, in 1327 to James's son Alfonso IV, in 1336 to Alfonso's son Peter IV and in 1387 to Peter's son John I. John's brother Martin was to reign until 1410. He died – of uncontrollable laughter at a joke by his jester, having just eaten a whole goose – with no surviving legitimate heirs, and the line which had begun with Wilfred the Hairy, Count of Barcelona in the ninth century, finally died out.

Cabrera at Monreale. He and his followers doubtless expected to make some sort of agreement; they were astonished to find themselves under arrest and imprisoned. The followers were later released, but Chiaramonte was condemned as a rebel and on 1 June was beheaded outside his own palace, his vast estates being bestowed on Cabrera.

Sicilian resistance continued for another three or four years, but by 1396 it was all over. Artale di Alagona had fled the island and Martin reigned supreme. To restore law and order, however, seemed an impossible task: a century of near-anarchy had taken a heavy toll. Martin did all he could to re-establish the King's authority. He regained from the barons Agrigento, Lentini, Licata and Corleone, as well as the island of Malta. He also tried to draw up a new feudal register – itself a major challenge, since most of the records had been lost or destroyed – recovering strategic castles and re-asserting crown rights wherever possible. Finally he abrogated the provisions of the 1372 treaty, firmly adopting the title *Rex Siciliae*. But whole regions of the island remained outside his control – and the barons knew it.

Fortunately for him, the Papacy too was in turmoil – suffering the worst crisis in its history. The Neapolitan Pope Urban VI, formerly a quiet, competent civil servant, had suddenly lost his wits and turned into a raging tyrant, having six of his cardinals brutally tortured and five of them subsequently executed. At this point a group of French cardinals, declaring that his election was invalid – it had in fact been perfectly canonical – declared him deposed and elected a successor, a Swiss who took the name of Clement VII. Each Pope then excommunicated the other, and Clement retired to Avignon, which the Papacy had left only a quarter of a century before.

The Church had been able to tolerate a papacy in exile, but the existence of two rival popes, one in Avignon and one in Rome, created a major problem indeed. Pope Urban died in 1389, Pope Clement – technically he is now seen by the Church as an antipope, though he himself would have been horrified by the description – outliving him by five years. Never for a second did he doubt the validity of his own election, and it was a bitter disappointment to him when on Urban's death the ensuing conclave did not recognize him as the legitimate Pope. Instead, they insanely elected another Neapolitan as Boniface IX. In his last years, while still at Avignon, Clement was put under considerable pressure to agree to a solution whereby both popes should resign and open the way to a new conclave, but was still stubbornly resisting when he died, of a sudden apoplexy, in 1394. It would have been so easy to end the schism; all that was required was that when one of the popes died, his conclave should refuse to elect a successor, so leaving the survivor in undisputed authority. But Rome had passed up the chance in 1387, and Avignon in 1394 did no better. They now proceeded unanimously to elect the Aragonese cardinal Pedro de Luna, who took the name of Benedict XIII.

Benedict was almost certainly in some way related to King Martin through his wife, Maria López de Luna; but amid all this confusion – it was to continue until 1417 – Martin seems to have had no difficulty in repudiating the papal suzerainty which had been a condition of the treaty of 1372. Indeed he went further, reclaiming the post of Apostolic Legate, which empowered him to appoint bishops and generally to administer the affairs of the Sicilian Church. But he had still not broken the power of the barons. Those who had actively opposed him had been firmly dealt with – Chiaramonte executed, the body of Francesco Ventimiglia tied to a horse's tail and dragged, the heart still beating, along the street before being hacked to pieces. But the Moncada, who had given the King their support from the start, had been richly rewarded by the grant of the Alagona estates, and several other baronial families continued to flourish.

Martin also revived the old institution of regular parliaments, which Frederick III had promised but which had quickly died out through lack of interest. They were never particularly democratic: their principal function was to listen to the King while he presented his views on the internal situation or made his wishes known. The parliamentarians could make suggestions or present petitions: that fewer Catalans and more native Sicilians should be appointed to government posts, for example, or that Sicilian laws should be observed when they conflicted with Catalan ones. But there was no question of legislation; the laws came down from above, proclaimed by royal decree.

It is rare indeed for a father to succeed a son on a throne; but when Martin I died – in 1409, while campaigning in Sardinia – leaving no legitimate heir,★ his father assumed the crown, so that Martin I of Aragon became Martin II of Sicily. Neither the Pope nor the barons – let alone the ordinary Sicilians – were consulted, and nobody objected that now, for the first time since Peter III well over a century before and in defiance of his promise, the crowns of Aragon and Sicily were united in a single ruler. But the situation did not last long. Martin the father lived only one year longer than Martin the son, whose death had left him childless. Suddenly both thrones were vacant. In Sicily the Regency was taken over by Martin I's second wife, Blanche of Navarre; but Cabrera refused categorically to accept her, and the island rapidly subsided into its habitual chaos. An attempt was made to hold a parliament at Taormina, which decided to appoint a committee with the purpose of choosing a king. It also proposed that Sicily should once again put herself under the protection of the Church; but when the antipope John XXIII,† hearing of this suggestion, declared that the rightful King of Sicily was the perfectly appalling King Ladislas of Naples, the entire island was horrified and the idea was not mentioned again.

While the Sicilians were bickering, a new King was elected in Spain. In 1412 nine delegates representing the three kingdoms of Aragon, Catalonia and Valencia met at Caspe near Zaragoza and voted for Ferdinand of Trastámara, the younger son of King John I of Castile and Eleanor of Aragon, and thus a nephew of Martin I on his mother's side. Naturally he claimed the title of King of

---

★ Of his two legitimate sons, Peter died before his second birthday, Martin before his first.

† In 1416 that same John XXIII was arrested, put on trial for his countless crimes and duly condemned. As Edward Gibbon gleefully noted, 'the most scandalous charges were suppressed: the Vicar of Christ was only accused of piracy, murder, rape, sodomy and incest.' In the circumstances it seems somewhat surprising that Cardinal Angelo Roncalli, when elected to the Papacy in October 1958, should have chosen the same name.

Sicily, and this time there was no objection from his island subjects; they were too tired to care. They accepted the fact that their new ruler would in all probability never set foot on their shores, and that they would in future be ruled by Viceroys. This was in itself something of a recognition that they were a separate kingdom; but it meant also that for as long as the situation lasted they could no longer hope to function as an independent country or as an effective presence in the Mediterranean.

They were not to know that the situation was to last for some four hundred years.

King Ferdinand did not have long to make his mark on his new realm. In 1416, only four years after his election at Caspe, he died aged thirty-six. His son Alfonso V, by contrast, was to reign for the next forty-two years, the concluding fifteen of them from Naples. The full story of his conquest of that city is far too long and complicated to go into here; the salient fact is that in 1421 the childless Queen Joanna of Naples had adopted him and named him as her heir. Joanna had succeeded her fiendishly cruel brother Ladislas in 1414. In the following year she had married James of Bourbon, who kept her in a state of semi-confinement, murdered her lover and imprisoned her chief captain, Muzio Attendolo Sforza; but his arrogance drove the local barons to rebellion and they expelled him. There followed a still worse tangle of intrigue between Joanna and her menfolk – Sforza, Joanna's new lover Giovanni Caracciolo, Alfonso of Aragon and Louis III of Anjou, whom Joanna had now nominated as her heir in place of Alfonso – ruffians all, whom we now find pitted against one another in every possible combination. Though Joanna died, lamented by no one, in 1435, it was another eight years before Alfonso finally proved victorious and achieved papal recognition as King of Naples.

Nor did he stop there. Most of his remaining years were devoted to one war after another – against Florence and Venice, Milan and Genoa – in which he demanded and received considerable help from Sicily, not always to the island's advantage. In 1446 a Venetian fleet actually entered Syracuse harbour and set fire to every ship in it. But in other respects Alfonso was very unlike his predecessors.

He may not have been quite a Renaissance man, but at least he had been touched by Renaissance fire. He founded a university in Catania – the first that Sicily had ever known – and established a school of Greek at Messina. And all his life he was a generous patron of the arts – even though he could not always afford to be.

For money remained a perennial problem. Too much of Sicily was enfeoffed to the barons, although many of them commuted their feudal service into monetary payments. Such crown estates as had survived also brought in a useful income, as did the tuna fisheries (which paid a substantial royalty) and various profitable exports, particularly wheat and other cereals. But all this was still nowhere near enough, and Alfonso stopped at nothing to bring in more. High-sounding titles and offices of state were invented simply so that they could be sold to the highest bidder; tax farming was practised on a vast scale; pardons could be bought for the most heinous crimes, as could licences to mint money. Foreign merchants flocked to the island, especially Catalans and Genoese; the Venetians kept a consul in Palermo and even had their own church. The English too were represented; in the following century they would have consuls at both Messina and Trapani – which, as the nearest port to Spain, had increased dramatically in size until it rivalled Catania and those two bitter rivals, Messina and Palermo.

When Alfonso died in 1458, he once again split his kingdom into two. Naples he hived off to his bastard son Ferdinand; the rest of his realm went to his brother John II, who instantly decreed that Aragon and Sicily should be eternally and indissolubly wedded. Shortly after John's accession a parliament was held at Caltagirone, where various petitions from the barons were addressed to the new King. He accepted one requesting the reduction of their military service, and another which sought to limit the acquisition of territories and castles in the island to Sicilians alone. He refused, on the other hand, a request that the viceroyalty should always be awarded to the King's eldest son. Nor would he agree to make peace with the Turks – who had captured Constantinople only five years before – nor to allow Sicilian merchants to trade with them; henceforth Muslim shipping was to be forbidden within sixty miles of the Sicilian coast.

On the whole Sicily seems to have been content with her new master. Her people did not demur when John sought financial contributions to help him to subdue the Moors of Granada; indeed, in his twenty-one-year reign they stood up to him only once – in 1478, when he urgently needed money for his continuing war against the Turks. The King and his Viceroy were fully aware that their hostility towards the Ottoman Empire was not shared by the Sicilians, who were only too happy to trade with Turkish merchants when permitted; and despite every effort made at persuasion – and, one suspects, not a little intimidation – the parliament stubbornly refused. The Viceroy had worked so hard and had identified himself so completely with the whole affair that he had to be replaced. This little story is worth repeating for one reason only; it shows that the Sicilian parliament was – to the King's surprise and very probably to its own – capable, if need be, of asserting itself. Had it continued occasionally to do so it might well have developed into a responsible and effective body; alas, it never did.

The accession of John's son Ferdinand in 1479 was of immense historic importance, since Ferdinand was already married to Queen Isabella of Castile. This marriage united the two kingdoms and created a third – that of Spain itself. Sicily thus suffered a further loss of importance. But a worse misfortune lay ahead. In 1487 there arrived the first members of the dreaded Spanish Inquisition. This had been established by Ferdinand and Isabella as early as 1481 – with the blessing of Pope Sixtus IV – and remained under their direct control. It was intended principally to ensure the orthodoxy of those who had recently been persuaded to convert to Christianity from Judaism or Islam; and after the royal decrees of 1492 and 1501 – which ordered Jews and Muslims to convert or leave the country – it substantially tightened its grip. Few converts slept soundly in their beds for fear of accusations that they were secretly observing the old customs, the punishment for which was burning at the stake.

Both the Inquisition and the expulsion decrees struck Sicily hard. The Muslim population, which had once been a majority in the island, was now relatively small, but the Jews were many; in the cities and towns they may well have constituted more than a tenth of the population. And Sicily needed them: they were active as merchants, as metalworkers and weavers, and especially as doctors and of course moneylenders. Doctors tend to be popular among the people; but moneylenders are less so and there were, after the middle of the century when interest rates climbed above ten percent, occasional outbreaks of anti-Semitism. None the less, the citizens of Palermo appealed to Spain on behalf of their native Jews, protesting that they were doing no harm and begging that they might be allowed to remain. Their request went unheeded.

History shows us all too many cases of Jewish persecution, and in every case the persecuting country ends up impoverished. Spain and Sicily were no exception. We do not know the numbers involved – how many Jews decided to emigrate rather than deny their faith and how many 'converted' – although the converts too lost much of their property, and even then were never safe from the Inquisition. But whatever the proportions, there can be no doubt that Sicily – like Nazi Germany in more recent years – lost a vast number of her most skilled, talented and intelligent citizens. And her economy suffered accordingly.

Another somewhat unsettling trend made itself evident during the sixteenth century's opening decade: a steady increase in royal authority. For well over two centuries the barons had had things very much their own way. Thanks to corruption, carelessness on the part of the authorities or quite often simply the passage of time, many of them held estates that were technically crown property, or had long since been allowed to forget their feudal obligations. But those days were over. With every passing year it became more evident that King Ferdinand was gradually tightening his grip. This was confirmed in 1509, with the appointment as Viceroy of a general named Ugo Moncada, who was bent on the conquest of North Africa and saw Sicily as the obvious springboard. From the beginning the barons hated him. Not only did he show them no respect; on his arrival he instituted searching enquiries as to their legal positions – in many cases with extremely embarrassing results. Arrests were made, frequently leading to imprisonment; fiefs were confiscated, including several that had been formally claimed by the Church. Meanwhile, the Inquisition was making its presence increasingly felt, particularly after it began burning its victims alive in the public squares.

Ferdinand's death in January 1516 brought matters to a head. Did this automatically deprive the detested Moncada of his authority? No one was quite sure, but when soon afterwards he dissolved the parliament he had recently called, some of its members reassembled at Termini on their own initiative. Here once again was a tentative show of independence; but before any conclusions could be drawn there occurred a far greater one – a full-scale popular revolution in Palermo. When the mob reached the point of removing the cannons from the city's bastions and training them on the Viceroy's palace, Moncada fled to Messina. The building was sacked and looted, the surviving archives burnt.

The people of Messina, who could always be trusted to oppose those of Palermo, gave the terrified Viceroy a warm welcome, assuring him of their full support. He knew, however, that he could never return to the capital, and sent a message to the new King Charles,* recommending him to appoint an Italian as his successor. Charles duly selected a Neapolitan nobleman, the Count of Monteleone; but if he thought that the Count would bring peace to the island he was to be disappointed. After only the briefest lull, the revolution broke out anew, under an impoverished minor nobleman named Squarcialupo; and the second outbreak was worse than the first. Soon Monteleone in his turn was obliged to seek refuge in Messina, but some of his entourage were not so lucky: they were first castrated, then flung out of the palace windows. Squarcialupo managed to control the rabble for a week or two, but was then assassinated while praying at Mass and the revolt caved in. Monteleone returned to Palermo and punished the ringleaders just as cruelly as Moncada would have done. A third, French-inspired uprising in 1523 was no more successful; the bodies of its ringleaders were quartered and then suspended in iron cages from the palace windows. All that this seven-year unrest had proved was that the Sicilians would never be able to put up any serious resistance to

---

* Despite two wives, Ferdinand left no legitimate male heirs. The throne therefore went to his grandson Charles, the future Emperor Charles V.

the power of Spain. They lacked the cohesion and the discipline, as well as any positive or constructive ideas for what they wanted to put in its place. By now, too, the power of Spain was very much more than that; it was the power of the Holy Roman Empire.

Charles of Habsburg, born in 1500 to the Emperor Maximilian's son Philip the Handsome and to Ferdinand and Isabella's daughter Joanna the Mad, had inherited neither of his parents' primary attributes. His appearance was ungainly, with the characteristically outsize Habsburg chin and protruding lower lip; he suffered too from an appalling stammer, regularly showering his interlocutors with spittle. He had no imagination, no ideas of his own; few rulers have ever been so utterly devoid of charm. What saved him was his innate goodness of heart and, as he grew older, a tough sagacity and shrewdness. He was also, in his quiet way, quite remarkably tenacious, wearing away those who opposed him by sheer determination and endurance. Though by far the most powerful prince in the civilized world, he never enjoyed his empire in the way that his contemporaries Henry VIII of England and Francis I of France enjoyed their kingdoms – or, indeed, Pope Leo X his papacy;* and when he finally abandoned his throne for a monastery, few of his subjects can have been greatly surprised.

His inheritance was vast, but he did not inherit it all simultaneously. First came the Low Countries, formerly Burgundian, which his grandfather Maximilian had acquired through his marriage to Mary of Burgundy. After the death of his father in 1506 he had been brought up by his aunt Margaret of Savoy, Regent of the Netherlands; from the age of fifteen he had ruled them himself. Already by that time his mother, Joanna, now hopelessly insane, was being held under the restraint that she was to endure for more than half a century; technically, however, she remained Queen of Castile, while Ferdinand ruled as Regent in her name. On Ferdinand's death, despite her condition, he left her his own crowns of Aragon and the Two Sicilies, awarding the Regency to Charles.

* 'God has given us the Papacy,' Leo wrote to his brother Giuliano dei Medici soon after his accession, 'let us now enjoy it.'

The government of Castile, on the other hand, he entrusted to the octogenarian Cardinal Archbishop of Toledo, Francisco Ximenes – though one of the Archbishop's first acts was to proclaim Charles King, conjointly with his mother.

The young king who, at the age of seventeen, landed on the coast of Asturias and saw his Spanish kingdom for the first time was still a Netherlander through and through, utterly ignorant of the habits, the customs, even the language of his new subjects. He did not make a good start. The Spaniards saw him as the foreigner he was, and deeply resented the hordes of Flemish officials who now flooded the country. Rebellion was never far below the surface. Ximenes, who had done everything possible to smooth his master's path, was elbowed aside by the Flemings and not even allowed a meeting with the King; he was simply ordered back to his diocese. Two months later he was dead, and Charles was in full authority throughout the country. He did his best, as always; but he was quite unable to control his ambitious and endlessly grasping countrymen, while the Spanish Cortes (parliament) left him in no doubt that he was there on sufferance, and would be tolerated only for so long as he did its bidding.

The Spain that Charles inherited was very different from that of his grandparents; the events of the last decade of the fifteenth century had changed the civilized world. On 17 April 1492 Ferdinand and Isabella had given their formal approval to Christopher Columbus for his voyage, putting at his disposal three tiny caravels – the largest of them little more than 100 feet long. Moreover, just four years before the *Niña*, the *Pinta* and the *Santa Maria* set sail, the Portuguese Bartholomew Diaz had rounded the Cape of Storms (renamed by John II of Portugal the Cape of Good Hope); just six years afterwards, on 20 May 1498, his compatriot Vasco da Gama had dropped anchor at Calicut on the Malabar coast. Not only had he found a continuous sea route to India; he had proved that Portuguese ships were capable – just – of getting there and back.

The stories of these three great adventurers are not ours; what is important to us is the effect they had on the fortunes of the Mediterranean. Henceforth the writing was on the wall. Until now, even if the Turks did not make trouble – as they usually did – all cargoes bound for the further east had to be unloaded in Alexandria or some Levantine port. Thence they would be either transported overland to the pirate-infested Red Sea or consigned to some shambling camel caravan across Central Asia which might take three or four years to reach its destination. Now, merchants could look forward to a time when they could sail from Lisbon – or London – and arrive in India or Cathay in the same vessel. Meanwhile, thanks to Columbus and those who followed him, the New World was proving infinitely more profitable than the Old, possessed as it was of fabulous wealth, the lion's share of which went to Spain – and legally too. Within only seven months of Columbus's first landfall, the Borgia Pope Alexander VI – himself a Spaniard – had issued the first of his five bulls settling the competing claims of Spain and Portugal over the newly discovered territories; within twenty-five years the galleons were regularly returning to their homeland loaded to the gunwales with loot. No wonder the successors of Ferdinand and Isabella had their eyes fixed so firmly on the west.

It was not immediately apparent that this sudden opening up of the oceans on both sides had dealt trade in the Mediterranean what would prove to be a paralysing blow. Gradually, however, men realized that, at least from the commercial point of view, the Middle Sea had become a backwater. East of the Adriatic the Turks now allowed passage to western ships reluctantly or not at all. To the west, it was still indispensable to Italy; but France was nowadays finding her northern ports on the English Channel a good deal more useful than Marseille or Toulon, while Spain, now entering her years of greatness, had other, tastier fish to fry. Not for another three centuries, until the building of the Suez Canal, would the Mediterranean regain its old importance as a world thoroughfare.

And Sicily, as always, was the loser.

9

Piracy and Revolution

~~~

FOR ALL THE excitement of her newfound wealth, Spain could not completely ignore her European responsibilities. Her chief enemies were the French and, of course, the Turks – though she also had to fight occasional wars with just about everyone else, including the English and the Portuguese, the Germans and the Dutch, and on occasion even the Papacy. None of these wars except those against the Turks had anything to do with Sicily, though the island was always obliged to make its contribution, whether in money, manpower or agricultural produce.

The second half of the fifteenth century, as we have seen, witnessed two cataclysmic events, one at each end of the Middle Sea: in the east, the fall of Constantinople to the Turks in 1453 – with the consequent closure of the Black Sea and, ultimately, much of the eastern Mediterranean – and in the west the gradual expulsion of the Moors from Spain in the years following 1492. Both led to a proliferation of rootless vagabonds – in the east Christians, in the west Muslims – all of them ruined, disaffected and longing for revenge; and many of them adopted the buccaneering life. The Christians would normally establish their bases in the central Mediterranean – in Sicily, or Malta, or among the countless islands off the Dalmatian coast. The Muslims, on the other hand, could only join their coreligionists in North Africa. Between Tangier and Tunis there were some 1,200 miles and, in what was still for the most part a moderately fertile and well-watered coastal strip, several almost tideless natural harbours ideal for their purposes. And so the legend of the Barbary Coast was born.

Until the middle of the century, the Sicilians had maintained friendly relations with North Africa, and there was profitable commerce in both directions. After the fall of Constantinople, however, conflict between the Spaniards and the Turks became inevitable and Sicily, instead of occupying the centre of the main trade route between Europe and Africa, found herself in what almost amounted to a no-man's-land. Her parliaments consistently petitioned Spain to be allowed to preserve the old commercial links with the cities of the coast, but the ultra-Catholic Ferdinand refused to allow his subjects any dealings with the infidel, and such trade as continued to exist was carried on largely by smugglers or pirates.

Of these pirates by far the most powerful were Kheir-ed-Din Barbarossa and his brother Aruj. Born on the island of Mytilene (the modern Lesbos) to a retired Greek janissary – like all janissaries, he had at first been a Christian before his forcible conversion to Islam – they possessed not a drop of Turkish, Arab or Berber blood, a fact to which their famous red beards offered still more cogent testimony. Acting on behalf of the Ottoman Sultan Selim I, they effortlessly conquered Algiers as early as 1516. Aruj died two years later; Kheir-ed-Din, however, went from strength to strength, ruling Algiers and its province technically in the Sultan's name but in fact wielding absolute power in the region. In 1534 he had the temerity to attack Tunisia, toppling the local sultan Moulay Hassan and annexing his kingdom; but here he overreached himself. He might have seen that the Emperor Charles V could not conceivably accept the annexation of a country less than a hundred miles away from the two most prosperous ports of western Sicily – Trapani and Marsala – and only a very little more from Palermo itself. The idle and pleasure-loving Moulay Hassan had constituted no danger, but now that Barbarossa was in Tunis the Emperor's own hold on Sicily was seriously threatened.

As soon as he heard the news, Charles began to plan a huge expedition to recover the city. His invasion fleet would number ships from Spain, Naples, Sicily, Sardinia, Genoa and Malta, which – with Tripoli – he had given in 1530 to the Knights of St John following their eviction from Rhodes. The Spanish contingent – estimated at some four hundred ships – sailed from Barcelona for Tunis at the end of May 1535. Against such an armada Barbarossa knew that he had no hope of retaining his hold on the city. On

14 July the fortress of La Goletta that defended the inner harbour was stormed by the Knights, and a week later a considerable number of Christian prisoners – there are said to have been 12,000, but this sounds unlikely – managed to smash their way to freedom and flung themselves on their erstwhile captors. Tunis was effectively won – and now it was Barbarossa's turn to flee. Moulay Hassan was formally reinstated in the empty shell of his city and the Spaniards, having repaired and refortified La Goletta, declared it Spanish territory and equipped it with a permanent garrison. The expedition, the victorious Christians all agreed, had been a huge success. Tunis was once again in friendly hands, Sicily was again secure, thousands of their coreligionists had been freed from captivity and – best of all, perhaps – the formerly invincible Barbarossa had been conclusively defeated.

Or so they thought. In fact, the great corsair was in mid-career. He was to score several more major victories, including, in 1541, one that resulted in the almost total destruction of another Spanish invasion fleet, directed this time against Algiers. He also annexed in the name of the Turkish Sultan – now Süleyman the Magnificent – many formerly Venetian islands. Soon Süleyman gave him the command of the entire Ottoman navy; the erstwhile pirate was now Supreme Admiral. He died in 1546 – peacefully in Istanbul, where his tomb may still be seen.

After Barbarossa's death the fighting went on, with the Turks launching a series of devastating raids along the Sicilian and North African coasts. In 1551 – only five years after the old corsair's death – they took Tripoli, and in 1560 destroyed twenty-four out of forty-eight Spanish and Sicilian galleys off Djerba. The pendulum swung back briefly in 1565, when the Knights of Malta heroically defended their island for four months against everything that Sultan Süleyman could throw against it; once again, however, theirs was an isolated triumph. Ten years later, Venetian Cyprus was to fall to Süleyman's son Selim; its commander, Marcantonio Bragadin, was subjected to appalling tortures, culminating in his being flayed alive. Of the old Venetian trading colonies of the Mediterranean, only Crete remained.

In 1571 Christian Europe took its revenge, when Spain, Venice and the Papacy smashed the Turkish navy at Lepanto, Sicilian ships as usual playing their part. But – the question is still being debated today – was Lepanto indeed, as many have claimed, the greatest naval engagement between Actium – fought only some sixty miles away – and Trafalgar? In England and America, admittedly, its continued fame rests largely on G. K. Chesterton's thunderous – if gloriously inaccurate – poem; but in the Catholic countries of the Mediterranean it has broken the barriers of history and passed into legend. Does it, one wonders, altogether deserve its reputation?

Technically and tactically, yes. It was the last major battle ever fought exclusively with oared galleys; after 1571, naval warfare was never the same again. Politically, on the other hand, it was a flash in the pan. The battle did not, as its victors hoped, mark the end of the pendulum's swing, the point where Christian fortunes suddenly turned, gathering force until the Turks could be swept back into the Asian heartland whence they had come. Instead, those Turks were to capture Tunis in the following year, leaving Oran as the only port along the entire coast remaining in Spanish hands. Venice did not regain Cyprus; only two years later she was to conclude a separate peace, relinquishing all her claims to the island. Nor did Lepanto mean the end of her losses; in the following century Crete, after a twenty-two-year siege, was to go the same way. As for Spain, she did not even appreciably increase her control of the central Mediterranean; only seventeen years afterwards, the historic defeat of her Great Armada by the English was to deal her sea power a blow from which it would not quickly recover. And, try as she might, she was never able to break the links between Constantinople and the Moorish princes of North Africa; within a few years the Turks were to drive every Spaniard from Tunis, make vassals of the local rulers and reduce the area – as they had already reduced most of Algeria to the west and Tripolitania to the east – to the status of an Ottoman province.

But the real importance of Lepanto, for all those Christians who rejoiced in those exultant October days, was moral. The heavy black cloud which had overshadowed them for two centuries and which since 1453 had grown steadily more threatening, to the point where they felt that their days were numbered – that cloud had suddenly lifted. From one moment to the next, hope had been reborn. The Venetians were eager to follow up their victory at once; the Turk must be given no rest, no time to catch his breath or to repair his shattered forces. This was the message that they propounded to their Spanish and papal allies, but their arguments fell on deaf ears. Don John of Austria, King Philip's bastard half-brother and the Captain-General of the combined fleet, would probably have been only too happy to press on through the winter, but his orders from Philip were clear. The allied forces would meet again in the spring; till then, he must bid them farewell. He had no choice but to return with his fleet to Messina.

In the years after Lepanto, piracy along the Barbary Coast continued unabated. Sicily suffered; in her dangerously exposed position she could hardly have done otherwise. At this time she was enduring two or three major attacks each year; no farmhouse within ten miles of the sea was safe, and in 1559 and 1574 there were raids on the outskirts of Palermo itself. On the other hand, she probably gave as good as she got: of the worst offenders among the corsairs, rather more than half seem to have been Christians, including a good many Sicilian privateers. The Knights of St John too, despite the huge Maltese crosses that they wore with such pride, were by no means averse to piracy and smuggling on a formidable scale. Spain did everything possible to dress up the whole thing as a Crusade, but of course it was nothing of the kind: the Turks had many a Christian working or fighting on their side. In 1535 Francis I of France had actually allied himself with Barbarossa, and in 1543 had allowed the Turkish fleet to winter in the harbour of Toulon; and – though few were aware of the fact – there was even a brief moment when Charles V himself considered abandoning Algiers and the greater part of Tunis and Tripoli to the old pirate. Fortunately, he thought better of it.

The fact of the matter is that Charles was becoming bored with the Barbary Coast. Obviously, it could never be reconquered; and the constant need to protect Spanish interests was proving ruinously expensive in ships and manpower while achieving only very moderate success. In any case, by the time of his abdication in 1556 and the

succession of his son Philip II, the political situation was beginning
to change; and by the end of the 1570s Philip saw that he must
cut his losses in the Mediterranean and concentrate his strength in
northern Europe for deployment against his new enemies, England
and the Netherlands. Now Sicily was left practically undefended,
and the raids from the Barbary pirates became worse than ever –
worse still after the defeat of the Armada in 1588, when Philip's
entire navy was lost and for many years Spain effectively ceased to
be a maritime power.

Why, it might be asked, did the Sicilians not make a greater
effort to defend themselves, or indeed to take the offensive against
their enemies? Largely, because they no longer possessed a proper
navy. Their last, of which they could be genuinely proud, had been
the creation of King Roger, some three hundred years before. But
after the end of Sicilian independence there was little incentive to
build ships – an industry that Roger had largely confined to his
mainland territories, where there were plenty of good navigable
rivers for transporting timber from the inland forests down to the
shore. In Sicily such rivers did not exist. This is not to say that
there was no shipbuilding at all on the island: the industry continued
after a fashion, principally in Palermo and Messina, and oared galleys
were still the rule. But galleys needed crews, and these were increasingly hard to find. They called for six men to each oar, some two
hundred in all for a large vessel. Some were slaves or convicts, some
were press-ganged, some were so-called volunteers. If food ran
short, one or two of them might be thrown overboard. All were
chained night and day.

Meanwhile, piracy no longer stopped at the Strait of Gibraltar:
the corsairs, both Christian and Muslim, had found a new and
highly lucrative occupation – that of slave-running along the West
African coast, subsequently exporting the captured slaves to Europe.
Once again, the Sicilians were deeply involved – and, as far as we
can judge, with a clear conscience. Had not the Emperor himself
decreed that all infidels taken at sea could be considered slaves?
Surely, then, the same must apply to those rounded up on land.
So profitable was the trade that the slavers saw no reason to confine
their activities to infidels; by the 1580s, several captains – including

at least two Englishmen – were doing excellent business buying and selling Christian prisoners along the coast.

As the above pages must have made more than clear, life for those living anywhere around the Sicilian littoral must have been unsettling indeed; but for those living anywhere else on the island it can have been very little safer. Sicily under Spanish domination remained as lawless as it had always been. Brigandage was rife; in many areas it was considered inadvisable to travel in groups of less than twenty. The brigands were for the most part peasants from the interior, who saw little of Spanish officialdom and cared less. They lived as they had always lived. The existing system of justice, as they well knew, invariably favoured the rich and privileged; they preferred to follow a counter-system of their own. If it was corrupt, it was no more corrupt than the colonial government under the Viceroy. If it was violent, it was no more violent than the baronage. The story is told of two rival baronial families, the di Luna and the Perollo, who were constantly at each other's throats over the control of Sciacca. Each had its own private army of brigands. When in the 1520s the Viceroy appointed a special officer to control them the luckless man was almost immediately assassinated; his naked body lay for days in the street before anybody dared touch it. The di Lunas then took over the town, massacring many of the Perollos and their followers. It is interesting to note that the head of the di Luna clan, who was primarily responsible for these outrages, was the nephew of the Medici Pope Leo X. He and his family remained unpunished.

The barons, clearly, had no respect for the Viceroy; but neither – more often than not – did anyone else. Whether Spanish or Sicilian, the Viceroys were almost invariably open to bribes. They also tended to set atrocious examples to those they attempted to govern: many made no secret of the fact that they were there for what they could get. Several, indeed, became extremely successful privateers and amassed considerable fortunes. The Church was richer still; in the late sixteenth century the Archbishop of Monreale – always, incidentally, a Spaniard, as were most of the senior prelates – received at least four times the salary of the Viceroy, and possessed no fewer than seventy-two fiefs. His colleagues the Archbishop of Palermo and the Bishop of Catania did very nearly as well. In other fields, too, the activities of the priesthood and religious houses left much to be desired. There were parts of Sicily in which married clergy were the rule rather than the exception; and, on more than one occasion, regulations had to be promulgated forbidding the serenading of convents by monks from neighbouring monasteries.

Separate from the Church but working closely with it was the Inquisition. The Inquisitors were appointed directly by the King of Spain; they maintained their own police force and their own special prisons. Often they would send the King secret reports on the Viceroy, and occasionally would be used by him to countermand the Viceroy's orders; not surprisingly, there was considerable friction between the two authorities. The Inquisition brooked no interference. Torture was allowed, and indeed encouraged. If the victims died during the process there was nothing to be done about it: it was the judgement of God. Even survival might well be only temporary; one might emerge from the torture chamber only to be publicly burnt at the stake. The Inquisitors attacked heresy wherever they thought they found it, frequently persecuting former Jews and Muslims whose families had long since converted to Christianity. Jewish merchants residing temporarily in the larger towns were obliged to wear a badge, their Muslim colleagues a turban. A measure of tolerance was shown to the countless thousands of Greeks who professed the Orthodox religion; there were too many of them, and they had lived in Sicily too long. Protestants, on the other hand – especially Lutherans – found life not only hard but dangerous.

For many Sicilians – and in particular good law-abiding Catholics, living in the interior and following a respectable and moderately profitable trade – life under Spanish domination was probably agreeable enough; but this cannot alter the fact that, particularly during the sixteenth and seventeenth centuries, Sicily was a desperately unhappy island. Only once in all her long history had she been united and at the same time independent, and that was under the twelfth-century Norman Kings, whose successive reigns had lasted less than seventy years. Since then, thanks to her Angevin and

Spanish masters, she had become hopelessly demoralized and deeply corrupt. She had no national pride, no loyalties, no solidarity, no discipline. In consequence she vegetated, suffering much and achieving nothing apart from the occasional unsuccessful revolution, until, at the beginning of the eighteenth century in Utrecht, she finally escaped from the Spanish frying pan – only to fall ultimately into the Bourbon fire.

Sicily's hero in the first quarter of the seventeenth century was Pedro Téllez-Girón, 3rd Duke of Osuna. After an early career as a soldier and diplomat – he is said to have been a member of the embassy sent by King Philip III to the English King James I in 1604 to sign the recently concluded peace treaty – he arrived in Palermo in 1611 as Viceroy, and was appalled by what he saw. Within a fortnight, the streets were cleared of beggars and scores of suspicious characters had been imprisoned or expelled. The carrying of stilettos was forbidden, even to the aristocracy. The right of asylum in any of the city's three hundred churches was withdrawn, criminals could no longer buy their freedom, and a special confraternity was established to reconcile the family feuds that cast such a blight over Sicilian life. Next, Osuna turned his attention to defence. Finding that there was barely a single seaworthy vessel in the fleet, he ordered the construction of twelve new galleys on the English model, and when they were ready he used them for an extremely profitable war against the Barbary states.

The economy proved a more intractable problem. Osuna's examination of the treasury ledgers disclosed that about a third of the annual revenue was completely unaccounted for. He immediately instituted a new system of tight restrictions and controls, simultaneously negotiating a substantial loan from the Genoese. Within a couple of years he had restored government credit. In Palermo and Messina the banks – some of which had long since been closed – were reopened for business. The people of Messina lodged a furious protest at his actions, claiming that they were not bound to pay any taxes levied without their consent, and offering 20,000 scudi to Osuna to say no more about it. Osuna rejected the offer, telling King Philip IV that this was the sixth time in fifty years that they had refused to pay perfectly legitimate taxes, and that if they were allowed to continue they would soon be an independent state.★ He then went himself to Messina, arrested the city fathers and brought them back in chains to Palermo, where he imprisoned them in solitary confinement at their own expense.

Osuna was not only a brilliant administrator; he was also an enthusiastic patron of the arts, and particularly of architecture. To the horror of the Inquisition, he welcomed the new Italian theatre to Palermo, willingly consenting that it should perform on Sundays and raising no objection to the presentation of women on the stage. He was particularly keen on the carnival, even attempting to make the wearing of masks compulsory. Unlike the vast majority of Viceroys he was genuinely popular, and when he left in 1616 the Palermitans – if not the Messinesi – were sorry indeed to see him go.

Fortunately he was not in Sicily for either of the two worst outbreaks of bubonic plague. In 1575 it was said that Messina lost half its population; in 1624 it was the turn of Palermo, when the plague arrived on ships bringing Christian slaves back from Tunis. Thousands died, including the Viceroy, Emanuel Filibert of Savoy; Anthony van Dyck, who was painting his portrait at the time, escaped to the mainland with not a moment to spare. The relics of S. Cristina and S. Ninfa were carried daily through the streets, probably serving only to spread the infection; but at the critical moment S. Rosalia – believed by many to be a niece of King William the Good – appeared to a hunter on Monte Pellegrino and, pointing out that she had never received a proper Christian burial, showed him the cave in which her remains lay. They were retrieved at once, and proved considerably more efficacious than those of her sister saints, whom she forthwith replaced as patron of the city.

Almost as disastrous as the plague itself was the Thirty Years' War, one of the longest and most destructive conflicts in European

---

★ In fact the Messinesi, increasingly concerned at the rise of Palermo, would have welcomed a separation. In 1629 they offered a million *scudi* to Spain if she would divide the island into two at the Salso River, with twin Viceroys in Palermo and Messina. The King, Philip IV, was tempted, but declined.

history. Beginning in 1618 as a religious war fought between Catholics and Protestants in the Holy Roman Empire, it gradually spread across most of the continent, becoming all the time less confessional and more a continuation of the age-old feuding between the houses of Bourbon and Habsburg. For most Sicilians, however, the only important thing about the war was its expense. Parliament was by now meeting at least once – often twice – a year, and was invariably confronted with huge tax demands from Spain. Sicily tried hard to meet them; virtually no scheme or proposal was turned down if it promised to make money. Important posts in government were sold for huge sums, as were places in the aristocracy: the right to add the word 'Don' before a name could be bought for a hundred *scudi*; for more distinguished titles the prices rose astronomically. Pardon for all crimes – always excepting treason – was put up for sale. The Agadian (Egadi) Islands off Trapani* were bought by the Pallavicini–Rusconi family of Genoa for 160,000 *scudi*. Nor was it only money that was needed; there was manpower as well. Off sailed Osuna's new galleys, crewed largely by Sicilians. Finally the pips squeaked: the Viceroy was obliged to report to his master that that was it – not another *maravedi* was to be found.

The Thirty Years' War was not to end until 1648; but meanwhile the economic situation in Sicily continued to worsen, and dissatisfaction grew. The root of the trouble was social and agricultural rather than political. Sicily was essentially a producer of wheat; and wheat was notoriously vulnerable to the whims of nature. An unexpectedly dry spring; two or three bad harvests in a row; a plague of locusts; a consignment accidentally exposed to dampness; all these misfortunes – and many others – could bring about catastrophe. Thanks to recent increases in population, there was now insufficient storage capacity; and the farmers, once they had enough for themselves, tended to export their surpluses to Spain, Venice, Crete or anywhere else from which they could expect considerably higher prices than their countrymen could afford. Already in 1644 the quality of the bread had had to be reduced; two years later

* Principally Favignana and Levanzo.

Messina was forced to cut the subsidized bread ration. Then in February 1647 the heavy rains destroyed the newly sown seed and the whole process of sowing had to be repeated – by those fortunate enough to have any seed left. This disaster was followed in March and April by a savage drought. The towns were thronged with beggars; in the countryside men, women and children were dying of starvation.

The revolt broke out in May, after days of penitential processions during which the participants would flog themselves with chains until their backs streamed with blood. We are told that there was even a special procession of the city's prostitutes, who were politely received and offered refreshment by the Princess of Trabia in her palace. But in the middle of the month the atmosphere changed. The church bells summoned the people to the public squares, the Archbishop armed his clergy, the city hall was set on fire. In the ensuing riots, many other buildings were also put to the torch and the streets, we are told, ran red with blood. Interestingly enough, there seems to have been little or no resentment against Spain itself; the indignation was directed principally against the Viceroy and the administration. By the following day, order was in part restored. Subsequent investigations suggested that the whole thing had been started by an escaped cutthroat named Nino La Pilosa. He was captured with the help of the artisan guilds, the so-called *maestranze*, and under torture made a somewhat astonishing confession: that his intention had been to make himself king, after which he proposed to distribute all the money belonging to the city bank and the Jesuits to the poor. We can only hope that this knowledge did not affect the sincerity of his Jesuit confessors, whose task was to give him comfort before he was publicly dismembered with red-hot pincers.

Perhaps it is worth saying a little more about these *maestranze* which, growing up in the sixteenth century, had in the past hundred years gained considerable power. Their original purposes were the same as those of all the other European guilds: to protect the interests of their particular trades, to train apprentices and to look after those members who were too old or too sick to look after themselves. In Sicily, however, where the degree of general lawlessness was appreciably greater than anywhere else, they had developed into societies which administered their own rough justice – much as the Mafia was to do in more recent times.

The nobles of Palermo, meanwhile, had taken refuge in their various estates, the further away the better; and though the city was now quiet they showed no inclination to return. The Viceroy, the 5th Marquis of los Vélez, finding himself abandoned by all his principal supporters, now departed on what was described as a pilgrimage. Typically enough the city of Messina, which had put money and armed troops at his disposal to help him against its detested rival, now offered to accommodate him permanently, together with his court; but their offer was seen for what it was and rejected.

The Viceroy had not been much use, but he had been better than nothing; Palermo was now left without any semblance of government, and with food and money shorter than ever. It was saved by the *maestranze*. On 12 August 1647 they – and particularly the guilds of fishermen and leatherworkers – took over the effective administration of the city, imposing emergency levies on windows and balconies, wine and tobacco, beef and – perhaps surprisingly – snuff. They also produced a new leader, a certain Giuseppe d'Alesi. D'Alesi – by profession a goldsmith – had been associated with La Pilosa, and had narrowly escaped capture. He had fled to Naples, arriving there just in time to take part in a remarkably similar uprising led by a charismatic rabble-rouser known as Masaniello; but he was soon back in Palermo, and it was not long before he had taken control. The Viceroy was dragged back from his pilgrimage, but not for long. A week or two later d'Alesi and his men took over the royal palace. Los Vélez panicked and fled.

Giuseppe d'Alesi was a very different character from La Pilosa. He hated violence and was genuinely loyal to Spain. He forbade any more destruction, made looting a capital offence and ordered the immediate reopening of the city bank. He tracked down the Viceroy, offered him safe conduct and begged him to return – which, rather reluctantly, he did. Now at least a legitimate government was possible, and d'Alesi was in a strong enough position to compel los Vélez to enact a number of vitally necessary reforms.

He had deserved well of his country; it is sad to have to report that at this point he somehow forfeited his popularity, and that during a renewed outbreak of fighting at the end of August he was pursued and eventually run to earth in a sewer. He was killed on the spot, his house was demolished and his head impaled on railings in the central piazza. For all he had done, it was a sad and shameful reward.

A week later the uprising was over. The Archbishop of Monreale absolved the people from the sin of revolution and publicly exorcized the central piazza, lest there should be any malevolent spirits still lurking. The food shortage was still acute; all the unemployed and all those who had lived for less than ten years in Palermo were ordered to leave the city at once, on pain of death. All stocks of wheat, wherever they might be, were to be declared to the authorities. Gambling was prohibited, as was the wearing of masks – though it is not immediately easy to see how these last two measures could have affected food supplies – and agricultural labourers were given a special dispensation to work on Sundays and feast days until the crisis was past.

Los Vélez, meanwhile, fell into a state of nervous prostration from which he never recovered; he died in November. His successor, Cardinal Giangiacomo Trivulzio, was a man of very different stamp. A firm authoritarian, he instituted a curfew throughout the city, demanded the surrender of all hand arms, and cleared a space around the royal palace so that the artillery would have an uninterrupted line of fire in any future emergency. Next, in order to make more business for the local tradesmen and to create new jobs, he ordered all the nobles to return from their places of refuge. Moreover, he allowed them to bring their hired retinues back with them. This last decision caused a degree of anxiety: these retinues tended to be made up of rough peasants, all more or less disreputable. But Trivulzio had established permanent bastions around the city, all of which had to be manned. How else was he to find sufficient men to do so?

If the history of the first half of the seventeenth century in Sicily is scarcely edifying, that of the second half is far, far worse. The basic situation remained unchanged – chronic food shortages, constant tax demands from Spain, the continued refusal of the nobility to pay its share. This last, of course, lay at the heart of Sicily's sufferings, but the Viceroys dared not insist; it was safer to raise money by the sale of titles and privileges, for which there was always an enthusiastic demand. Sixteen new princes were created in the 1670s, in the 1680s fourteen new dukes. Countless fiefs, and indeed several towns, were put up for auction.

The situation was still further aggravated by the traditional hostility that existed between Palermo and Messina. The two, it must be said, had little enough in common. The Messinesi, first of all, displayed a thundering superiority complex, claiming to have been recognized as the Sicilian capital in 270 BC. Secondly, they tended to consider themselves almost a part of Calabria; many of them owned property there, and they could be across the Strait in an hour or two; the journey to Palermo – on which they embarked as rarely as possible – might take them, by land or sea, up to three days. Even their dialect was more readily comprehensible on the mainland than it was in the capital. Besides, they had a different outlook on life. Palermo maintained a genuine aristocracy of the old school; the nobles of Messina were more like those of Venice, men of business and proud of it. For that reason most foreign trading houses preferred to keep their representatives there; the city boasted an English consul, even an English church.

One perennial bone of contention was whether the Viceroy should not spend half his time living in Messina rather than Palermo. The Messinesi felt extremely strongly about this, and had spent a good deal of money to bring it about; they had actually bought the privilege on more than one occasion from the King of Spain, and had built a special viceregal palace, together with a whole group of offices for the government and administration. The reason that these remained unoccupied was a remarkably simple one: Palermo was grander and more elegant. Socially speaking, it was also a good deal smarter; no wonder the Viceroys preferred it.

Messina was also generally unpopular, largely because it claimed the monopoly on silk, both raw and manufactured: a claim that was bitterly resented – and constantly challenged – not only in

Palermo but throughout Sicily. The claim was also impossible to enforce, and involved the sending of regular embassies to Spain, which the city could ill afford, requesting its confirmation. These problems were made still more acute when France also began to develop an ambitious silk trade, heavily sponsored by its government. For these and many other reasons, Messina's economy began to decline and her population to fall, and by 1670 the situation was causing serious concern. On 11 March 1669 there had already been one of the most violent eruptions of Mount Etna in all its history, a river of lava more than a mile across which five weeks later reached the walls of Catania, fifteen miles away. Then, in the opening year of the new decade, came the first of a long succession of disastrous harvests. Strict food rationing was imposed, but it was not long before the Viceroy, the Prince de Ligne, was receiving the first reports of deaths from starvation.

All this was certainly a contributory cause of the revolution which began at Messina in 1674, but it was not the only one. For obviously very different reasons, the well-to-do citizens were every bit as worried as were the poor. Not only was their money fast draining away; they watched with alarm while, at their expense, de Ligne constructed huge fortifications against the Turks, who in 1669 had captured Crete from the Venetians after a siege of twenty-two years, the longest in history. And then, as always, there was the spectre of Palermo, which had flourished as Messina declined and which was now demanding that its rival should be deprived of its immunities with regard to taxation and the silk industry. Spain, too, was causing anxiety: what had once been the most reactionary government in Europe was now introducing democratic reforms which, it was feared, could only breed unrest among the populace.

The incipient revolution, therefore, took a surprising form. Its leaders appealed to France, which was at that time at war with Spain. For Louis XIV, it need hardly be said, here was an opportunity not to be missed. He immediately sent out a contingent of French troops, led by the Duke of Vivonne – the brother of his current mistress – with the arguably optimistic title of Governor of Sicily. The duke arrived at Messina early in 1675. For the Viceroy de Ligne, there was one major consolation: the revolution remained concentrated at Messina, and showed no signs of spreading across the island. On the other hand, his attempts to raise a militia were almost laughably unsuccessful. Relatively few Sicilians bothered to answer his summons; of those who did, many of them proved worse than useless and many others deserted almost at once. The nobility proved very little better; after a year of attempted mobilization, there was still not one single regiment of Sicilian soldiery in existence. Such troops as de Ligne did manage to collect were nearly all Spanish or German. Most useful of all to him was the fleet provided by Spain's somewhat surprising ally, the Dutch, under their seventy-year-old admiral Michiel de Ruyter; the Sicilians were however shocked by the drunkenness and debauchery of the Dutch sailors ashore, while the Dutch were contemptuous of the apparent fecklessness of their hosts. It was largely due to the general Sicilian inefficiency that de Ruyter met his death in a minor engagement off Augusta.

Four hundred years before, the presence of unwanted French troops had sparked off the War of the Sicilian Vespers. It says much for the state into which the population had fallen that it now seemed to show no resistance to anything. Even in 1676, when the French navy destroyed the main Spanish and Sicilian fleet just off Palermo in the full sight of its citizens and the Archbishop was scared enough to train the castle cannon on to the main square rather than the ships at sea, a general apathy continued to reign. This apathy in the capital was the more surprising in that the French represented the interests exclusively of Messina, which had summoned them in the first place. Try as they might, they never succeeded in extending their power much beyond the city. King Louis, to whom the expedition proved a sad disappointment, actually went so far as to propose to give Sicily her complete political independence under a king of her own.

He had failed, however, to understand the people of Messina. To them independence was all very well, but they were much more interested in winning a lasting supremacy over Palermo. They accordingly sent ambassadors to Paris with their demands, which included the granting to their city all the rights of a free port, exempt from customs duties; the confirmation of her monopoly on silk exports; and above all the recognition of Messina as the capital city, the permanent residence of the Governor, his court and his administration. These demands came to Louis as something of a shock; he was not used to such table-thumping on the part of a subject city. The ambassadors were received coldly, provided with only two horses rather than the usual six for the carriage that brought them to Versailles, given precedence immediately behind the representatives of Malta and ultimately sent home empty-handed. The fact was that King Louis too was bored with Sicily. Messina, he now saw, had appealed to him under false pretences. Sicily had no intention of returning to French rule. His expeditionary force had achieved precisely nothing.

By 1677, the feeling was mutual. A number of villages had been destroyed in the fighting, a number of farms, olive and mulberry trees burnt to the ground. Prices had rocketed. The citizens had deeply resented – and frequently resisted – the billeting of French soldiers in their houses and the consequent threat to the honour of their wives and daughters. Venereal disease rocketed, the Messinesi being most unfairly blamed. They of course did not speak French, the French did not deign to learn Italian or Spanish; instead, they simply bossed the people around. Vivonne himself made no secret of his contempt for the local aristocracy, who were forever making demands and never lifting a finger for themselves.

It was not long before Louis decided on withdrawal. In the circumstances he might have considered a departure agreement that would, in some degree at least, have protected Messina against Spain and Palermo, both of which would obviously be eager for revenge. But he did nothing of the kind – and many of the senatorial families of Messina fled for their lives. France refused to receive them; they found shelter where they might, and never returned to their native city. Their houses were duly looted by the mob, but with disappointing results: they had taken all their money and most of their possessions – including as many bales of silk as they could carry – with them.

It is in its way appropriate that Messina should be the setting for Shakespeare's *Much Ado About Nothing*; for centuries the city had made trouble for the rest of Sicily, with absolutely no profit to itself; its last, idiotic, adventure had proved calamitous. Quite apart from the effect on the city and its people, it had cost Spain a mint of money and hundreds of men their lives. It deserved to be punished, and so it was. In 1679 the new Viceroy, the Count of Santisteban, demolished the city hall, symbolically ploughing up the entire site and sowing it with salt. The cathedral bell that had summoned the citizens to rebellion was melted down,* many of the cathedral's treasures were seized and destroyed. The local senate was abolished; so too was the university, which was replaced by a vast fortress commanding the entire city. Those rebel families who had elected to remain saw their houses and possessions sold off at public auction.

Messina undoubtedly deserved all it got; but Sicily also suffered. Effectively to destroy its second city – its first from the commercial point of view – was obvious folly. By the beginning of the 1690s – by which time Messina's population had dropped by more than half – attempts were made to repair some of the damage; but they had little real success. One of the most sensible proposals advanced to restore prosperity was to settle communities of foreign merchants in the city – Jews, Greeks, perhaps even Muslims; but the Inquisition soon scotched that, and Messina's slow *dégringolade* continued.

Meanwhile, at nine o'clock in the evening of 11 January 1693, there came one of Sicily's most dreadful earthquakes, the most powerful in Italian history. Its epicentre was in the southeast of the island, where at least seventy towns and cities were destroyed, Noto and Modica among them; Syracuse and Ragusa were badly damaged. Eyewitnesses report how the earth seemed to open up and swallow crowds of people whole; how rivers would suddenly vanish and new ones appear as if by magic; how giant tidal waves and tsunamis devastated the coastal villages. The darkness of the winter night increased the general terror: tens of thousands leaped from their beds and fled to the countryside. The total casualties were estimated at about 60,000, including almost two-thirds of the population of Catania, where Sicily's only remaining university was completely

---

* Giacomo Serpotta (see below) used the metal for a statue of the Spanish King trampling the hydra of rebellion.

wiped out. Altogether some five percent of the island's inhabitants are believed to have perished, either that night or in the weeks afterwards, when they would die of their wounds or – worse still – of later infection.

But even earthquakes can occasionally have their uses; and without the catastrophe of 1693 we should not have had three of the love-liest baroque towns in Sicily, towns almost entirely rebuilt after the devastation. They are Noto, Ragusa and Modica, all three in the far southeast of the island.* Old Noto was effectively destroyed and was rebuilt on a new site some five miles to the south, nearer the sea. The town plan was an interesting one, with three parallel streets traversing the slope of a gentle hillside, while a number of narrower streets ran up and down the hill, intersecting them at right angles. Three piazzas were built along the main street, each with a church on the higher side. The result is the most beautiful city in Sicily, made lovelier still by its glorious honey-coloured stone, which seems to absorb and then radiate the almost constant sunshine. The cath-edral is probably the most spectacular of the ecclesiastical buildings, thanks largely to the tremendous flight of steps which leads up to it; it is one of the latest of the great buildings of the city, having been completed only in 1770. But the cathedral is only the begin-ning. There is the now deconsecrated Montevergine, which looms dramatically over one of the narrow cross-streets as if it is going to swallow it up; there is the wonderful convex curve of S. Domenico; and for amateurs of the baroque there are S. Salvatore and the Jesuit church of the Collegio (though I have to say that when I last saw them some years ago they were not looking their best). But in Noto, as in Venice, the ultimate miracle is the city itself.

Ragusa is divided into two. After the earthquake some of the survivors planned a new city due west of the old one, but others preferred to stay where they were and rebuild on the spot. The new city need not detain us long. Its cathedral, built immediately after the earthquake, forms the centre; it is a fine enough building, but not a patch on that of Ragusa Ibla, as the city on the old site

---

* The whole area has been designated by the United Nations as a World Heritage Site, and quite right too.

is now called. Those who are interested in early antiquity may like to visit the archaeological museum to see a curious stone sculpture dating from the late seventh century BC known as the Warrior of Castiglione; it was discovered by a local farmer in 1999.

Ragusa Ibla is a delightful old town of a lovely mellow stone, similar – though not identical – to that of Noto and in a remarkable state of preservation. It is built on a long, narrow ridge that runs from west to east between two deep gorges. Its supreme masterpiece is the Duomo of S. Giorgio, the work of the brilliant Rosario Gagliardi, who described himself as *ingegniere della città di Noto e sua Valle* – the Val di Noto comprising the entire southeastern third of the island. The Duomo stands at the top of a vast flight of steps, rising up three storeys to the belfry, the freestanding columns that are such a feature of the design providing wonderful chiaroscuro effects as the sun moves around it. (The rather unfortunate dome, set on tall columns, which covers the crossing is fortunately invisible from the front.) A little further to the east, S. Giuseppe looks like a slightly more modest version of its neighbour – so much so that there is good reason for thinking that this is also the work of Gagliardi. Before leaving Ragusa Ibla it is worth taking a short stroll and looking at the several lovely old palaces – and in particular their balconies, often carried by those grotesque monsters which were so favoured all over the island.

Should you drive from Ragusa to Modica, you will cross the Guerrieri bridge and will be rewarded by a spectacular first glimpse of your destination, seen from a height of almost 1,000 feet. The city, like its neighbour, is split into two, upper and lower; half-way up the hill stands the magnificent church of S. Giorgio. Ragusa's S. Giorgio was impressive enough; Modica's – also almost certainly by the great Gagliardi – beats it at its own game. Both stand at the head of a magnificent flight of steps; but whereas those in Ragusa number perhaps fifty at the most, Modica boasts five times as many, descending right down the hill to the road below. And here the church extends to five bays across, as opposed to the three at Ragusa.

The Modica S. Giorgio has always had a bitter rival, the church of S. Pietro. After the earthquake Charles II of Spain had given orders that only one of the two churches should be rebuilt; this could then be dedicated to both saints and the ill feeling would be forgotten. Unfortunately the royal command was ignored – that was the sort of thing that happened to Charles II – and it was not long before the new S. Giorgio and the new S. Pietro were once again at each other's throats. S. Pietro is undeniably magnificent; but, despite the splendid statues of the Apostles that line the steps, its façade strikes one as disappointingly flat. It is Gagliardi's S. Giorgio that is the ultimate showstopper – for many of us the most beautiful baroque church in Sicily, in one of the loveliest and most remote corners of the island.

This is perhaps the moment – while we are on the subject – to mention one more artist, a contemporary of Gagliardi but one who seems to have confined his activities largely to Palermo and its neighbourhood. He was not an architect but a worker in stucco, and his name was Giacomo Serpotta. The great Professor Rudolph Wittkower described him as 'a meteor in the Sicilian sky'. The three small oratories in Palermo which he decorated prove him to be the greatest stuccoist that ever lived; but he was also entirely his own man. Although he was naturally influenced by Italian models, not once in his seventy-six years (1656–1732), so far as is known, did he ever leave Sicily.* None of his three oratories – the other two are those of S. Lorenzo and S. Domenico – should on any account be missed; but the first and most important is that attached to the Dominican church of S. Cita. Along the side wall, the windows are framed with a riot of putti and allegorical figures, and under each, also in plaster, is what appears to be a tiny stage set depicting a biblical scene.

All this would be more than enough to justify the journey, but it is the end wall that constitutes the ultimate tour de force. It is virtually covered by a billowing stucco curtain, supported by a whole regiment of putti, into which are set more miniature biblical scenes; these, however, surround a larger and more ornate frame which depicts no less an event than the Battle of Lepanto. This historic naval engagement owes its presence here to the fact that

---

* Anthony Blunt suggests that he may have travelled to Rome when about twenty, but there is no written evidence.

the defeat of the Turks was, as everybody knows, due to the miraculous intercession of the Virgin, whom we see enthroned above the Christian navies.

On Friday, 1 November 1700, King Charles II of Spain died at the age of thirty-nine in his palace in Madrid. He had lived far too long. Weak in body and mind, he had come to the throne at the age of four on the death of his father, Philip IV, and one glance at the luckless child had been enough to convince the court of his total inadequacy for the tasks that lay ahead of him. Charles looked like the caricature of a Habsburg, his chin and lower jaw projecting so far that his lower teeth could make no contact with the upper ones. He was always ill, to the point where many suspected witchcraft. Few of his subjects believed for an instant that he would grow up to assume power over his immense dominions. But grow up he did; the consequence was that from the day of his accession in 1665 and for the next thirty-five years Spain was effectively a great monarchy without a monarch. Government of the country was left to a succession of prime ministers of varying ability, to the Church and to the Church's principal instrument, the Inquisition.

It came as no surprise that Charles, despite two so-called marriages, had failed to produce any offspring, and as the century drew to a close the question of the succession grew steadily in importance. His siblings were all dead. Of his aunts – the two daughters of his grandfather Philip III – the elder, Anne, had been married to Louis XIII of France; the younger, Maria, to the Emperor Ferdinand III of Austria. Anne had in due course given birth to the future Louis XIV, Maria to the Emperor Leopold I. Throughout the first nine months of 1700 the chanceries of Europe were busy indeed; then, on 3 October, the dying King put his tremulous signature to a new will, by the terms of which he left all his dominions without exception to Louis XIV's seventeen-year-old grandson, Philip Duke of Anjou. A month later he was dead.

Louis lost no time. In February 1701 the Duke of Anjou entered Madrid as King Philip V of Spain, and French troops occupied the Spanish Netherlands. To England, Holland and the Holy Roman Empire such a situation could not be accepted: it meant the union of the two mightiest nations in Europe, dangerously upsetting the balance of power. If Spain were to pass from the hands of the weakest monarch in Europe into those of the strongest, who could tell what the result might be? They knew exactly whom they wanted as King of Spain: the Archduke Charles, brother of the Austrian Emperor Joseph I. And so there began what was known as the War of the Spanish Succession, which was to last for the next fourteen years.

From the people of Palermo – if not perhaps those of Messina – one might have expected demonstrations, or active protests; after all, their island was to be transferred from one great nation to another, without any pretence of consultation. And they had no cause to love the French, whom they had already once forcibly expelled. It was true that over four centuries had passed since the Vespers, but these had now become a part of Sicilian folklore; they were certainly not forgotten. And yet there was scarcely a murmur. Sicily, it seemed, had grown accustomed to its colonial status; all it wanted was to be left alone. The Viceroy – currently the Portuguese Duke of Veraguas – proclaimed three days' festivities, in which nobles and people alike dutifully participated before going obediently home.

While the war continued, the long-term fate of Sicily hung in the balance. There was a moment in 1707, when Austrian troops arrived in Calabria and prepared to invade the island. Now at last the prospect of a whole new lot of invaders, of whom the Sicilians knew nothing, sparked off riots in Palermo – especially when it was proposed to use an Irish regiment, under the command of a soldier of fortune named Colonel Mahony, to garrison the city. There were a few unpleasant scenes, and at one moment the *maestranze* – those same guilds who had distinguished themselves sixty years before – took over the government, not unsuccessfully. But, apart from a few isolated raids, the threatened invasion never occurred. Just in time, the warring powers called a halt, laid down their arms and assembled in the Dutch city of Utrecht – where, quite simply, they redrew the map of Europe.

10

The Coming of the Bourbons

W HAT IS GENERALLY known as the Treaty of Utrecht, negotiations for which began in 1712, was in fact a whole series
of treaties through which the European powers attempted once
again to regulate their mutual relations. Only one of the many
agreements concerns us here: the decision to transfer Sicily to the
Spanish King Philip V's father-in-law, Duke Victor Amadeus of
Savoy. The idea had been accepted largely on the insistence of the
British, who were uneasy at the thought of Sicily joining Naples
in Austrian hands and who argued that the Duke had deserved a
reward by changing sides during the war.* The only objection was
raised, somewhat unexpectedly, by Queen Anne, who disliked seeing
countries being shuffled around without their consultation or
consent; but her ministers quickly overruled her.

Victor Amadeus was of course delighted. He arrived in Palermo
on a British ship in October 1713, and was shortly afterwards crowned
King of Sicily – and, somewhat improbably, of Jerusalem† – in the
cathedral. Over Jerusalem he had of course no power at all; even
in Sicily he controlled only nine-tenths of the island, the powers
at Utrecht having deliberately left King Philip all his personal estates,
which were administered by Spanish officials and exempt from both
taxation and Sicilian law. None the less, Victor Amadeus was the
first royal presence on the island since 1535. The Sicilian nobility

* This habit was to become something of a *spécialité de la maison*. I well remember
my father rocking with laughter when Italy joined the Allies in 1943 and quoting
– I think – Palmerston, who said, 'there has never yet been a war in which the
House of Savoy ended on the same side as that on which it began – except on
those occasions when it changed twice in between.'
† An old legacy from the Emperor Frederick II's day.

welcomed their new monarch, expecting as they did so that he would settle in the city and set up a proper court there. The people in general received him with their usual apathy. They had had so many rulers over the centuries; this one would probably be no better and no worse than the rest.

He actually made a serious effort to be better. He stayed on the island for a year, travelled fairly widely – though not into the impenetrably deep interior – and tried hard to understand the character and customs of his subjects. He reopened the University of Catania and introduced new industries wherever he could, establishing factories for paper and glass, doing his best to revive agriculture and shipbuilding. But it was no use: he had to contend not only with the rich, who continued to set their faces against any innovations that might adversely affect their privileges, but also – and far worse – with the universal corruption, idleness and lack of initiative that were the result of four centuries of foreign domination. There was also the perennial grievance: just as in former centuries the Sicilians had grumbled about the sudden influxes of Spaniards or Frenchmen who would take over the senior offices of government, so now they protested at the flood of Piedmontese civil servants and accountants whom the King had introduced in an attempt to restore order to the chaotic national finances.

Such protests, Victor Amadeus knew, were inevitable; he could take them in his stride. But he knew too that the Sicilians had rebelled twice in the previous century, and were perfectly capable, if pressed too far, of doing so again. Wisely, he treated the barons in particular with extreme caution. So long as they continued to enjoy their traditional immunities and privileges, they would give no trouble; if, on the other hand, these were in any way threatened, the consequences could be serious indeed. When the time came for him to return to Piedmont, he must have felt that the Sicilian cause was hopeless. Family vendettas were as many and frequent as ever; banditry was everywhere. The people were essentially ungovernable.

Moreover, he had failed utterly to gain their affection. The Sicilians loved colour and display; they had long been accustomed to the pomp and splendour surrounding the Spanish Viceroys, representing – as only Viceroys could – one of the richest and most powerful nations in the world. Victor Amadeus was not a man for finery. A natural puritan, he hated ceremonial and dressed more like a man of the people than a monarch, preferring a walking stick to a sword. He was also distressingly parsimonious; gone were the ostentatious parades and the lavish receptions which had been such a feature of life for the aristocracy of Palermo. No wonder that children a hundred years later were still throwing stones at dummies bearing his name.

Soon after his return to Turin, he received another humiliation, this time from the Pope. The origins of the quarrel with Clement XI go back to the old Spanish times and need not concern us here; but the consequence was that in 1715 a papal bull entitled *Romanus Pontifex* put an end to the six-hundred-year tradition whereby the Kings of Sicily were also automatically the Papal Legates. The Pope also instructed all Sicilian clergy to refuse taxation. Many obeyed, only to be punished by exile or imprisonment and confiscation of their property. Churches were closed, bishoprics left vacant, and all good Christians adjured to defy royal authority. The more sensible naturally ignored the ban; the monks of a monastery near Agrigento, on the other hand, prepared to defend themselves against the King's representatives with the well-tried weapon of boiling oil, employed for the first time since the Middle Ages. The Sicilians, who had always been proud of their status as Papal Legates, tended to blame the trouble on the House of Savoy rather than the Papacy. To them, it was just another nail in the Piedmontese coffin. To Victor Amadeus, it was just another nail in theirs.★

By this time, he was bitterly regretting that he had ever accepted the Sicilian crown; fortunately it soon proved remarkably easy to surrender. In 1715 the recently widowed King Philip of Spain took as his second wife Elisabeth Farnese, the twenty-two-year-old niece and stepdaughter of the Duke of Parma. The new queen was

---

★ Gradually, of course, the situation returned to near-normal; but all was not entirely well until 1728, when Pope Benedict XIII restored a modified version of the legateship 'in perpetuity'.

undistinguished by beauty, education or experience, but she had a will of iron and she knew what she wanted. Instantly, all French influence vanished from the Spanish court; it became Italian through and through. Determined to recover all Italian-speaking territories for Spain, Elisabeth moved first against Sardinia, part of the Empire. In August 1717 she sent her fleet out from Barcelona and by the end of November the island was hers. Then, emboldened by this easy success, she directed the ships straight on to Sicily. On 1 July 1718 Spanish troops were landed near Palermo, where – simply because they were not Piedmontese – they received a warm welcome.

Back in Turin, Victor Amadeus was of course loud in his protests; but we may imagine that they had a slightly hollow ring. Far more sincere in his objections was the Emperor Charles VI, who had strongly opposed the grant of Sicily to Piedmont in the first place; Naples was by now part of his empire, and he was anxious to unite the island with the city as in the past. Charles had recently concluded an agreement between Britain and France. He himself had no navy, but Britain did; and so it was that a British fleet under Admiral Sir George Byng hastened to Sicily, where it annihilated the Spanish fleet off Cape Passero, at the island's southeast corner. Unfortunately Britain was not at that time technically at war with Spain; Byng's action thus created a tidal wave of indignation, the effects of which were to be felt throughout Europe. Its results, however, were clear: that the British would intercept any reinforcements sent from Spain, while Austrian troops would be permitted to cross the Strait without opposition.

Once again Sicily became a battlefield. Austrians and Spaniards pursued each other backwards and forwards across the island, ravaging the villages and fields as they went. The battle they fought at Francavilla – a few miles inland from Taormina – on 20 June 1719 was probably the most important engagement on the island since Roman times. The fighting continued throughout the day, the Austrians making three separate attacks on the fortified Spanish positions but being driven back each time; their commander, the Count de Mercy, was gravely wounded (though he survived to fight again). The Spanish artillery played a crucial role in the battle – as did the cavalry, whose counterattack when evening fell removed all hopes of an Austrian victory. The Austrians fell back, leaving over 3,000 dead and wounded on the field. Spanish losses were about 2,000. The imperial forces, however, had one decisive advantage: the British navy, which could keep them fully supplied with all they needed. Gradually they gained the upper hand. The Spaniards as they retreated pursued a scorched earth policy, destroying everything behind them; but in 1720 they at last surrendered, and the subsequent Treaty of London confirmed Sicily as an integral part of the Holy Roman Empire.

As for Victor Amadeus, he submitted with relief to the inevitable, gave up his kingdom with good grace and willingly accepted that of Sardinia in its stead. Compared with Sicily, his new acquisition was of little importance indeed, but it was a lot less trouble. It also enabled him to continue to call himself King. That is why from 1720, when he formally took possession of the island, until 1861, when his distant cousin Victor Emmanuel II became first king of a united Italy, he and his successors were always known as Kings of Sardinia, while continuing to reign from their ancestral capital at Turin.

Austria's rule in Sicily lasted just twice as long as that of Piedmont, but the story was much the same. The Sicilians as usual offered no resistance to their new masters, but they disliked them from the start. The first barrier was linguistic – Piedmontese had been bad enough, but German was far, far worse. The underlying trouble was, however, that Sicily, after four centuries of Spanish occupation, was itself Spanish at heart; it had got used to the easygoing ways of Spain, a considerable proportion of its population was of Spanish origin, and the Spanish language was almost everywhere understood. Any other occupying power was bound to be resented, its attempts at reform frustrated at every turn. The Austrians did their best. They drew up plans for the reform of the tax system, but these proved impossible to apply. They tried to restore the standing and reputation of Messina, making it once again a free port; but the foreign merchants, encouraged by those of Palermo, still stayed away – they could do better elsewhere. The Emperor made an effort to revive the silver and alum mines, but the Sicilians refused or were unable to work them; when skilled labour was imported from Saxony and Hungary the local peasantry made life for the foreign miners so difficult that they soon returned home. Attempts were made to begin or to revive several other industries; they all failed. Year by year, the mutual disenchantment grew; and when after fourteen years Sicily returned to Spanish hands, it is to be suspected that the Emperor, like Victor Amadeus before him, felt nothing but relief.

Queen Elisabeth cared not a jot for the Treaty of London. In her eyes Sicily was rightfully the property of Spain, and she was determined to recover it as soon as possible. The task proved easier than expected. In 1731 her uncle Antonio Farnese died suddenly, and one of her greatest ambitions was realized the following year when her sixteen-year-old son Don Carlos – with a mother like his, he was despite his name far more of an Italian than a Spaniard – left his native land, which he was not to see again for nearly thirty years, and sailed with a retinue two hundred and fifty strong for Italy, where he was formally installed as Duke of Parma and Piacenza★ and Grand Prince of Tuscany. He was not, it must be admitted, a particularly impressive youth. A strict Jesuit education had given him four languages besides his own and an adequate knowledge of history, but he was in no sense an intellectual, far preferring hunting and shooting to any other pursuits. Short and round-shouldered, he had a huge nose and reminded one acute observer of a very distinguished ram. But he was bright and good-natured, and possessed of a certain charm which was to stand him in good stead in the years to come.

Now Parma, Piacenza and Tuscany were all very well; but, for Elisabeth Farnese, they were nowhere near enough. In November 1733 she signed a treaty with Louis XV; the following month a French army of 40,000 crossed the Alps and occupied Lombardy, while a Spanish force of 30,000 landed at Livorno. Against such strength the imperial Viceroy, with some 7,000 men under arms,

★ Parma and Piacenza had been papal fiefs since 1545, when Pope Paul III had bestowed them on Pierluigi Farnese, the eldest and most dissolute of the four sons he had fathered since becoming a cardinal at twenty-five.

was powerless; he garrisoned the three Neapolitan castles – Ovo, Nuovo and S. Elmo – and then fled to Apulia with his leading generals. The castles were duly besieged, but with extreme gentility. 'The besieged,' an eyewitness reported, 'no less considerate of the city than the besiegers, make signs with a handkerchief when they decide to fire, and give warning with a loud voice so that the populace can withdraw, and when these are out of danger they proceed. Before destroying a small house, they allowed time for the furniture to be removed.' It was in fact a token resistance; Don Carlos was welcomed every inch of the way and made his triumphal entry into Naples on 10 May 1734, to the sound of trumpets and a crowd cheering him to the echo.

Now it was the turn of Sicily. Here the imperial garrisons of Messina, Syracuse and Trapani showed rather more determination than their mainland colleagues, holding out for some six months before the food and water ran out; but Sicilians everywhere welcomed their most recent invaders just as warmly as the people of Naples had done. On 3 July 1735, with Trapani not yet surrendered, Charles – as we must now call him – was crowned (after furious protests from Messina) in Palermo Cathedral, the nineteenth king to receive his coronation there since the founding of the monarchy by King Roger the Norman. The celebrations continued for four full days, after which he sailed back to Naples.

Once more, Naples and Sicily were a single kingdom. Two years later, in 1737, further diplomatic negotiations resulted in both good and bad news for Spain. The good news was that the Emperor formally renounced all his claims to the Kingdom of Naples, provided only that it was never to be united with the Spanish crown. In other words, should Charles ever succeed to the throne of Spain, he would have to pass on Naples to his next of kin, whoever that might be. The bad news was that Spain was obliged to surrender Parma and Piacenza to the Emperor and Tuscany to Duke Francis of Lorraine, husband of the future Empress Maria Theresa. But even this pill was delicately sugared, for Charles received permission to remove all the personal property of the Farnese family from the two duchies before he left. Everything was brought to Naples – superb pictures and furniture, whole libraries of books and archives, even a marble staircase. Now more than ever it had been, Naples was a great European capital; the long succession of Viceroys had at last given place to a King.

That King, however, needed a Queen. On the question of who she should be he expressed no opinion. As the ever-dutiful son of his parents – and particularly of his mother – he was perfectly ready to leave the selection to them; he asked only that they should decide as quickly as possible. Elisabeth Farnese's ultimate choice was, perhaps, a curious one. The Princess Maria Amalia was the daughter of Augustus III, the Saxon King of Poland – a crown he had won only after having forcibly dethroned Louis XV's father-in-law, Stanislaus Leszczynski. The marriage would not be popular with the French, for a start.

There were other disadvantages too. First, the bride was still under thirteen (though unusually well developed for her age) and could not consequently be married without a papal dispensation; second, she was quite shatteringly plain, even before the smallpox that was soon to disfigure her yet further. The poet Thomas Gray, who was doing the Grand Tour in 1738 with his friend Horace Walpole, considered the young King and Queen 'as ugly a little pair as one can see'. The Président Charles de Brosses* thought she had 'a malicious air, with her bullet nose, her crayfish features and magpie voice'. But it hardly mattered. Maria Amalia spoke excellent French and Italian besides her native German, and shared to the full her husband's passion for hunting. Before long the two of them had fallen deeply in love. When, soon after Maria Amalia's arrival he was taken on a tour of the royal palace, de Brosses noted 'that there was no bed in the King's apartment, so punctual is he in sleeping in the Queen's'. When in 1760 she was to die aged only thirty-six, Charles was heartbroken. His mother and several friends urged him to marry one of the daughters of Louis XV, but he refused to listen. Despite her appallingly bad temper – which

---

* The presidency of Charles de Brosses (1709–77) was only that of the Parlement of Dijon; but he has somehow always managed to keep his title. President or not, he is a consistently interesting and amusing writer, whose views are always worthy of respect.

he never seemed to mind, although it had grown worse with her almost continual pregnancies – Maria Amalia had been the love of his life. Before and during his marriage he had never looked at another woman; he would not do so now.

One thing only had clouded their conjugal happiness: their eldest son. The Queen had already given birth to five girls, four of whom had died in infancy, before she produced Philip, Duke of Calabria, in June 1747. At first he seemed healthy enough; but he was soon giving cause for alarm. 'There is something in his eyes,' reported the Sardinian ambassador, 'that does not harmonize with the rest of his features. I have been assured that although he is seven years old he does not speak, and that he can scarcely utter a word . . . [he] has been violently attacked by his usual convulsions and does not look as if he will reach maturity.' Fortunately the Queen was to bear four more sons (and two more daughters), so the succession was assured.

Once King Charles had returned to Naples after his coronation in 1735, Sicily returned to its old ways. The Sicilians had never allowed themselves to become Austrianized, resisting all Austrian attempts to subvert them just as they had resisted those of Piedmont. After four centuries of Spanish occupation they remained essentially Spanish, and the fact that they were now ruled from Naples rather than from Madrid at first made remarkably little difference. The King, for all his Italianate ways, was by birth a Spaniard; large areas of Sicily remained in Spanish hands; the upper classes and those with any pretensions to gentility continued to speak Spanish as they had for generations; carnivals and religious processions continued in the Spanish manner; and although Italian was somewhat reluctantly adopted for official documents in the 1760s, bullfighting continued until well into the nineteenth century.

But times were changing. In August 1759 the Spanish King Ferdinand VI died aged forty-six. His mental powers had never been strong, and the death in the previous year of his beloved wife, the perfectly hideous Maria Barbara of Braganza, had plunged him into desperate melancholy. He refused to be shaved or to change his clothes, and would sit motionless for eighteen hours at a stretch.

Strangely enough, he had been a surprisingly good king – though much of the credit for this should properly go to his wife. Together, he and Maria Barbara had restored the national finances – which his predecessor Philip V and Elisabeth Farnese had left in hopeless confusion – had built up a formidable fleet, had enthusiastically encouraged the arts and sciences and had clamped down on the Inquisition, putting an end to the public autos-da-fé that so shocked eighteenth-century Europe. Many a monarch has done worse.

His kingdom now passed to his half-brother Charles, who was consequently obliged to transfer that of Naples to another member of his family. His eldest son, Philip, was, alas, all too obviously out of the running; his second son – also called Charles – was made Prince of Asturias and formally designated heir to the Spanish throne; Naples he therefore gave to his third son, Ferdinand, then a child of eight. These dispensations completed, he and Maria Amalia, together with their four eldest children – there was no room for the two youngest, who travelled on a separate ship – set sail for Barcelona. On 9 December they reached Madrid, where the King was reunited with his formidable mother – who had been acting as Regent – for the first time since his departure twenty-eight years before. The two embraced affectionately, but Charles soon made it clear that he was now his own man and that he had no intention of allowing Elisabeth any influence over state affairs. She made no objection; she was by now grossly fat and almost blind. She soon returned to her palace at San Ildefonso, and never – even after the death of Maria Amalia only three months later – returned to Madrid.

Although Charles may not have been exceptionally intelligent, he was industrious, conscientious, deeply pious and utterly honest; and he left his kingdom considerably more prosperous than he had found it. As he himself wrote in 1750:

> This year I have finished paying all the debts contracted during the last war* and still have 300,000 ducats in savings to put in my treasury. To prove this I have refused the usual *donativo* [voted tax] from the Sicilian Parliament, a larger sum than any voted previously,

* The War of the Austrian Succession (1740–48).

telling them that I had no present need of it, and that they were to save it until it was required. Apart from which I have revoked a tax and devote all my attention to improving the welfare of my subjects, since I wish to save my soul and go to Heaven.

Naples he transformed. It was now one of the most magnificent capitals in Europe. He had a mania for building. At the very beginning of his reign he had established the San Carlo Opera House, although opera bored him stiff. This he had followed with the immense hunting lodges of Portici, Capodimonte, Torre del Greco and – later – the vast palace of Caserta, comparable to Schönbrunn or even Versailles. Towards the end of his reign he also started work on what was known as the Reale Albergo dei Poveri, of which the front is 354 metres long and which was intended to house, feed and educate the poor of the city. Inevitably, however, he found himself thwarted again and again by the unyielding conservatism of his subjects, and especially that of the Church. In 1740, for example, he had encouraged Jews to settle in the capital; but the priests and friars stirred up the people against them, and when the influential Jesuit Father Pepe assured him that he would never have a son so long as he allowed a single Jew to remain, he reluctantly gave in. For just seven years the Jews had been welcome in the Kingdom; after 1747 they were banned once again.

Unfortunately, apart from his generosity with regard to the *donativo* and two useful trade agreements with Tunisia and the Ottoman Empire, Charles did very little for Sicily. After his coronation visit he never returned to the island; Maria Amalia never saw it at all. The only trace left of King Charles III was his statue, and even that was made of bronze which had been previously used for a similar one of the Austrian Emperor, melted down after it was no longer needed.

But can we really blame him for his neglect? Would the Sicilians have received more attention from their sovereign if they had shown the slightest inclination to help themselves? Very likely; they never did. Every effort at reform was instantly blocked by the parliament. There was a moment when King Charles established what was called the Supreme Magistracy of Trade, which was to control inter alia customs duties, mines, fisheries, food supplies and the salt industry. Unfortunately it was so constituted that the barons could be outvoted by the civil servants and the merchants together – which was more than enough to condemn it. Its activities were blocked at every turn and after a few years Charles accepted defeat.

The failure of this magistracy was especially unfortunate, since it would almost certainly have improved the state of the island's roads, which were a good deal worse than they had been in Roman times. Just outside Palermo were a few miles of paved thoroughfare; but for much of the eighteenth century the only means of travel elsewhere was by the occasional mule track or drovers' path, which involved fording rivers impassable in the rainy season. Wheeled traffic was out of the question; the 225-mile journey on land from Trapani to Messina would normally take a good three weeks. No wonder that most people preferred to travel by sea. The effect on agriculture and industry can easily be imagined: how was an inland farmer or manufacturer to get his produce to the nearest market, let alone to the coast? On administration too: how could a Viceroy properly govern an island of which well over half was utterly inaccessible?

And these were only a few of the problems that Sicily presented to those who tried to assist it. Sooner or later they all came to the same conclusion: the place was impossible; the best thing to do was to leave it alone.

If we are to follow the fortunes of Sicily, we must, clearly, follow those of its King; and since the King of Sicily elected to live in Naples, it is on Naples that the spotlight must now be turned. The first problem with that King was his title. He was Ferdinand III of Sicily, Ferdinand IV of Naples. Later he was also to be Ferdinand I of the Two Sicilies. The second problem was his character. Although he lived to be seventy-four he remained throughout his life an overgrown schoolboy, and an unusually stupid one at that. In his youth a Bohemian Jesuit appeared every morning at eight to teach him Latin, French and German, but as the Sardinian Minister pointed out, 'His Majesty profits little by it, for he speaks only Neapolitan.'

Like his father he had but a single real interest, hunting; unlike his father he had no feelings of responsibility, and very little conscience. He boasted that he had never read a book. When not in the saddle he spent his time in rough and boisterous horseplay that the average boy grows out of at the age of nine or ten; Ferdinand never grew out of it at all. Fortunately for him, he had the common touch – less fortunately, it was the only touch that he did have – and was greatly loved by the populace, among whom he spent as much time as he could. The state continued to be governed by its Chief Minister, the lugubrious Marchese Bernardo Tanucci, who dictated his every move and actually kept the Royal Seal to ensure that His Majesty did nothing without his approval.

In 1764, when Ferdinand was thirteen, there had arrived a new Envoy Extraordinary to the Kingdom of the Two Sicilies, Sir William Hamilton. He was the fourth son of Lord Archibald Hamilton, sometime Governor of Jamaica. It was said that his mother had been the mistress of the son of George II, Frederick Prince of Wales, who was to die before his father; the rumour may well have been true, since young William grew up with Frederick's son, the future King George III, who would always refer to him as 'my foster brother'. Born in January 1731, he had spent a short time in the army and then in 1761 had become a Member of Parliament; but in early 1764, hearing that the current Envoy in Naples was to be promoted to Madrid, he applied for the post. It was to be his for the next thirty-six years. In the superb Neapolitan climate his always frail wife, Catherine – with whom he shared a passion for music – soon recovered much of her health, while his own duties left him plenty of time to pursue his interest in art and to build up what was to become his astonishing collection of antiquities. He also made a close study of Vesuvius, and enjoyed nothing more than taking interested visitors on expeditions to the summit.

King Ferdinand, meanwhile, had married. It had long been decided that his bride should be one of the eleven daughters of the Empress Maria Theresa of Austria.* The first selected, the eleven-year-old Archduchess Joanna, died of smallpox; the choice then fell on

---

* She and her husband, the Emperor Francis I, also had five sons.

Archduchess Maria Josepha, who was vivacious, healthy and, we are told, of unusual intelligence. This last quality was perhaps unfortunate in the circumstances, as her mother was all too well aware; 'I look on poor Josepha as a sacrifice to politics,' she wrote. But the sacrifice was to be a magnificent one. The princess, now aged sixteen, was equipped with a hundred dresses from Paris; and by October 1767 thirty-four royal coaches, nine one-horse carriages, four luggage wagons and fourteen litters were ready for departure. A few days before, Maria Theresa had insisted that her daughter should descend into the family vault to pay her last respects to her father, the Emperor Francis I, who had died in 1765. The poor girl hated these visits, but reluctantly complied. It was rumoured that she was there infected by the body of her sister-in-law – the wife of her eldest brother, the future Emperor Joseph II – who had succumbed to smallpox a few weeks before; however that may be, she was soon showing symptoms of the disease. She died on 15 October, the day before her intended departure.

When the news reached Naples, the King was informed that it would be unseemly if he were to go hunting; he must spend the day in the palace at Portici. It seems almost unbelievable that, to while away the time, he decided to celebrate a mock funeral of his dead fiancée; but so he did. One of the courtiers was dressed as the princess and laid out on a bier, with chocolate drops on his face and hands to represent smallpox pustules. The cortège then proceeded through the palace, with Ferdinand as chief mourner.*

The King's letter of condolence to Maria Theresa – doubtless drafted by Tanucci – begged her to make available another of her daughters. There remained two alternatives: the Archduchesses Maria Amalia and Maria Carolina. Portraits of both were sent – not to Naples but to Madrid – and Maria Carolina was chosen. Nineteen months younger than her bridegroom, she was the Empress's tenth daughter and had been brought up with the eleventh and last, the future Marie Antoinette of France. She could hardly have been

---

* Reported in the *Historical Memoirs* of Sir Nathaniel Wraxall, who claims to have heard it from Sir William Hamilton.

more unlike the quiet and docile Josepha; indeed, Maria Theresa used to say that of all her daughters Maria Carolina was the most like herself. Imperious and often arrogant, she was every inch a queen; and she too was formidably intelligent. When on her way to Naples she passed through Bologna, the British minister Sir Horace Mann wrote to his friend Horace Walpole:

> It is feared that her extreme delicacy and good sense will only make her feel the more the want of both in her Royal Consort, whose deficiency in both has made many people interpret it as an organical defect approaching madness on some occasions. But Lord Stormont assures me it proceeds totally from the want of education; and that he is now what many school-boys are in England at ten years old. If so, the scandalous neglect may be repaired by his most excellently well-bred queen.

Ferdinand was there to receive his bride at the Neapolitan border, whence he escorted her to the palace at Caserta. The wedding night seems to have left him unmoved. He got up early as usual to go hunting; typically, in that particular milieu, his entourage asked him how things had gone. Equally typically, His Majesty replied, '*Dorme come una' ammazzata, et suda come un porco*' – 'she sleeps as if she had been murdered and sweats like a pig.' Before long, however, he had radically changed his tune. He admired – indeed, he was astonished by – his young wife's energy, her enterprise and, not least, her gentleness and thoughtfulness towards himself. His only criticism of her was that she read too many books – a practice of which he violently disapproved.

It was fortunate for Maria Carolina – we have to remember that she was still barely seventeen – that she had an excellent sense of humour; without it she would have gone under. As she confessed to her old governess in Vienna, she knew that she could never love her husband or look up to him as a dutiful wife should. On the other hand, she had become quite fond of him; his character, though often ridiculously childish, was not as bad as she had expected; he was, as she later described him to her brother, *ein recht guter Narr* – 'a right good fool'. She did not mind his ugliness – or if she did, she would soon get used to it; what irritated her was that he seemed to think he was good-looking. He often bored her to distraction; secretly she longed for Vienna and home. Still, she was a queen, and if she played her cards properly she could make herself a fairly powerful one. At the time of her marriage her mother had been careful to stipulate that as soon as she gave birth to a son she must be a member of the Privy Council; it was to take her seven years, but she would dominate that Council for the next forty.

In 1769 the Emperor Joseph came to Naples to visit his sister; his are the best descriptions we have of Neapolitan court life, and indeed of the King himself:

> He has muscular arms and wrists, and his coarse brown hands are very dirty since he never wears gloves when he rides or hunts. His head is relatively small, surmounted by a forest of coffee-coloured hair, which he never powders, a nose which begins in his forehead and gradually swells in a straight line as far as his mouth, which is very large with a jutting lower lip, filled with fairly good but irregular teeth . . .
>
> Although an ugly prince, he is not absolutely repulsive. His skin is fairly smooth and firm, of a yellowish pallor. He is clean apart from his hands; and at least he does not stink . . .
>
> I wanted to attempt a general conversation, but the King proposed some parlour games . . . The five or six court ladies, my sister, the King and I began to play blind man's buff and other games . . . Throughout, the King distributes blows and smacks the ladies' behinds without distinction . . . There is a continuous tussle with the ladies, who are inured to it and throw themselves sprawling on the floor. This never fails to amuse the King, who bursts into uproarious laughter. As he seldom speaks without shouting and has a piercing voice like a shrill falsetto, one can distinguish it among a thousand . . .

Then there was a court ball, at which

> the King gave me a great salute with all his might on my behind at the moment I least expected it, in the presence of more than four people. For an age I had the honour of carrying him on my back, and more than twenty times he came and put his arms over my shoulders, slackening his whole body so that it dragged after

me . . . Our departure for this ball was truly singular . . . The march began with solemnity and good order . . . But apparently the King was bored with this procession, for he began to shout like the postillions and kick bottoms lustily right and left, which seemed the signal to start galloping. The whole court, big and small, ministers, old men, galloped away while the King chased them in front of him, always shouting at the top of his voice. The French ambassador Choiseul unhappily found himself in the King's path and received a punch in passing. Weak as he is, his nose collided with the wall.

During an official visit to the Certosa of San Martino, the King

scoured the innermost recesses of the monastery, committing a thousand childish follies which ended in the kitchen, where he started to cook an omelette . . . All the gentlemen of the party had the honour of being treated, either to water which he flung in their faces, or to ices which he spilled in their pockets, or to marmalade which he put in their hats. Even the ambassador Kaunitz was not exempted. He has the misfortune to be ticklish, which amuses the King, who makes him yell.

It is interesting to speculate on how this sort of behaviour could be endured by the super-sophisticated Sir William Hamilton. He seems at any rate gradually to have got used to it, and it was after all a small price to pay for the delightful life he led in Naples. But much unhappiness was in store for him. August 1782 saw the death of his beloved Catherine. 'I must ever feel the loss,' he wrote to his niece Mary, 'of the most amiable, the most gentle and the most virtuous companion that ever man was blest with.' In the following year he returned to England on leave, and made a brief trip to Scotland with his nephew Charles Greville, Member of Parliament for Warwick and the younger son of his sister Elizabeth. It was now that he made his first acquaintance with Greville's mistress, Emma Hart.

Emma's origins were humble, to say the least. The daughter of a blacksmith who died when she was two months old, she was at first brought up by her mother and by the age of twelve was already working as a housemaid. Domestic service, however, did not last long. A year or two later she had found employment as a dancer in the 'Temple of Health', an establishment run by a Scottish quack doctor named James Graham. Among its other attractions was an electric bed which gave its occupants mild shocks, thus – according to Dr Graham, who made a fortune out of it – ensuring early conception. Then, at the age of fifteen, she was taken up by Sir Harry Featherstonehaugh, who hired her as a 'hostess' for his friends at Uppark in Sussex, where she earned her keep, we are told, by dancing naked on the dining table. She never cared much for Sir Harry, though she did conceive a daughter* by him; more to her taste was his friend Greville, with whom she lived until she was eighteen.

It was then, in 1783, that the relationship came to an end. Greville had by this time exhausted his considerable fortune and needed a rich wife – an ambition to which Emma constituted a serious stumbling block. What was he to do with her? Then came a brainwave: why not unload her on to his sad and lonely uncle? Sir William welcomed the idea. He needed a wife, not only for his bed but as a hostess for his salon, and Emma – who was famous for her beauty, having already been painted half a dozen times by George Romney – would, he had no doubt, be an immense success in Neapolitan society. He accepted his nephew's suggestion with enthusiasm, happily agreeing to pay the expenses of her journey to Italy.

Emma, on the other hand, was less pleased. Greville had not dared to tell her the truth. He had suggested only that she should go to Naples on an extended holiday while he was away in Scotland on business, and she was furious when Sir William – who was now in his early fifties and more than twice her age – gently informed her that the new arrangement was to be permanent and that she was to be his resident mistress. But there – he was a man of considerable wealth and charm, he lived in a beautiful house in a beautiful

---

* This girl, known as Emma Carew, was taken away soon after her birth and was raised independently by a Mr and Mrs Blackburn. For a few years she paid occasional visits to her mother; later she became a governess, and spent much of her life abroad.

city, and he promised to keep her in a style even grander than that to which she was accustomed. She soon realized that this was the greatest stroke of good luck that had ever befallen her.

Since Emma's mother had accompanied her – for the sake of appearances – as a chaperone, there was no reason to hurry over the marriage, which took place only in 1791. Sir William was sixty, she was twenty-six. No matter – now at last she was Lady Hamilton, the name by which she is best remembered and which she was to carry for the rest of her life. By this time Sir William had schooled her in French and Italian, in singing and in dancing; her beauty, her irresistible charm and an extraordinary theatrical talent did the rest.

And she was indeed a success. No less a personage than Johann Wolfgang von Goethe, who spent two years in Italy between 1786 and 1788, was enraptured by her performance of what she called her 'attitudes':

Hamilton is a person of universal taste, and after having wandered through the whole realm of creation has found rest at last in a most beautiful companion, a masterpiece of the great artist Nature . . . She is an Englishwoman about twenty years old . . . The old knight has had a Greek costume made for her, which becomes her extremely. Dressed in this and letting her hair loose and taking a couple of shawls, she exhibits every possible variety of posture, expression and look, so that at last the spectator almost fancies it a dream. One beholds there in perfection, in movement, in ravishing variety, all that the greatest artists have rejoiced in being able to produce. Standing, kneeling, sitting, lying down, grave or sad, playful, exulting, repentant, wanton, menacing, anxious – all mental states follow rapidly one after the other. With wonderful taste she suits the folding of her veil to each expression, and with the same handkerchief makes every kind of head-dress. The old knight holds the light for her, and enters into the exhibition with his whole soul. He thinks he can discern in her a resemblance to all the most famous antiques, all the beautiful profiles on the Sicilian coins – indeed, of the Apollo Belvedere itself. This much at any rate is certain – the entertainment is unique. We spent two evenings at it with thorough enjoyment.

As for her singing, it was good enough some years later for her to take on one of the solo parts in Haydn's *Nelson Mass*. She even at one point received an offer – which she decided not to accept – to sing leading roles at the Madrid Opera. She was, in short, a phenomenon, and it is no exaggeration to say that she took the staid, unimaginative society of Naples by storm.

Among her conquests were the King and Queen. She and her husband would often dine with them *en famille*, after which she and Ferdinand would sing duets. Louise Vigée Le Brun, who painted her portrait – having fled to Italy with her daughter to escape the French Revolution – maintained that she used to feed the Queen with little titbits of political gossip; she certainly wrote to her former lover Greville:

> Send me some news, political and private; for, against my will, owing to my situation here I am got into politics, and I wish to have news for our dear much-loved Queen, whom I adore. Nor can I live without her, for she is to me another friend and everything . . . Her heart is most excellent and strictly good and upright . . .

Poor Maria Carolina needed all the comfort she could get. With the French Revolution now in full spate, she was sick with anxiety over her sister Marie Antoinette; and in March 1792 came the news of the sudden death of her brother, the Emperor Leopold.★ Had he lived, he might just possibly have been able to save the French monarchy; the only other ruler eager to do so was King Gustavus III of Sweden, but he was assassinated before the month was over. True, her eldest daughter was now Empress – she had married Leopold's son Francis in 1790 – but there was little that either of them could do to help the sad, imprisoned queen.

The situation deteriorated steadily throughout the summer, and on 20 November the Sardinian ambassador reported to his government:

> It has been decided that a French squadron should sail to Naples and Civitavecchia to attack and pillage these places . . . This squadron, which is now supposed to be in Leghorn, may reach Naples within two days . . . This has sufficed to create indescribable alarm. The

★ Formerly Grand Duke of Tuscany, Leopold had succeeded his parents Francis I and Maria Theresa in 1790.

Chevalier Acton* certainly has great qualities . . . but he is very poorly supported . . . His Majesty repairs daily to the hunt as if nothing was happening; most of the minister's subordinates are of a revolting mediocrity. He has to arrange everything and struggle incessantly against intrigue, ignorance and ill-will. In the meantime everybody is so terrified that each thinks of saving his property and running away.

The squadron duly arrived on 12 December, thirteen strong. The admiral commanding wanted to hand the King an ultimatum that Acton be sent to France as a hostage – 'within an hour General Acton must be in my power or Naples will be destroyed' – but he was eventually calmed down, ultimately agreeing to settle for the King's recognition of the French Republic and the sending of an ambassador to Paris. After only twenty-eight hours the ships sailed for Sardinia; it was unfortunate indeed for them that on the following day they ran into a tempest off Civitavecchia – breaking the flagship's mainmast – and were obliged to limp back to Naples for repairs.

Little more than two months later came the news that on 21 January 1793 King Louis XVI had been executed by the guillotine. All Naples was in mourning, and the requiem Mass held in the cathedral was attended by the King and Queen and the entire court. Maria Carolina, in spite of being already a grandmother, was now pregnant for the eighteenth time. Her anguish was greater than ever. 'I hear horrible details,' she wrote on 5 March, 'from that infernal Paris';

At every moment, every noise and cry, every time they enter her room, my unfortunate sister kneels, prays and prepares for death. The inhuman brutes that surround her amuse themselves in this manner: day and night they bellow on purpose to terrorize her and make her fear death a thousand times. Death is what one may wish for the poor soul, and it is what I pray God to send her that she may cease to suffer . . .

* Commodore John Acton – later Sir John Acton, baronet – had arrived in Naples in 1778 to reorganize the Sicilian navy. Such was his ability that he had quickly risen to be Chief Minister.

Marie Antoinette's sufferings continued until 16 October, when they were brought to an end by the guillotine in the Place de la Concorde. Exactly five weeks before, on 11 September, the British warship HMS *Agamemnon* had cast anchor in Naples with despatches for Sir William Hamilton, which her commanding officer delivered in person. The two had a short conversation, after which Sir William summoned his wife. He was, he said, about to introduce to her a small man who might not be very handsome but who, he believed, 'would one day astonish the world'.

It is now that Captain Horatio Nelson, RN, enters our story.

II

Napoleon, Nelson and the Hamiltons

— —

CAPTAIN NELSON WAS now thirty-five. His effect on Sir William was the more remarkable in that he was at that moment in the last stages of exhaustion. He had set foot on shore only twice in the past four months, during which he and his crew had been without fresh meat, fruit or vegetables. He was however greatly cheered by his reception in Naples, where he was invited to dinner at the palace and was placed on the King's right. Since he spoke not a word of any foreign language, Emma interpreted for him. One cannot help wondering whether he did not fall in love with her there and then; she was radiantly beautiful, bursting with charm – and after all it was a long time since he had seen a woman.

The despatches that he had brought for Sir William were concerned with the port of Toulon, which had been occupied a week or two before by French royalist, British and Spanish forces. It was now under heavy siege by the army of the Republic and in desperate need of reinforcements, which it was hoped that Naples could provide. Acton immediately promised to send 6,000 men, who headed off with all speed. But it was too late: Toulon was doomed, and on 18 December the British ships weighed anchor and headed for the open sea. There was no doubt to whom credit for the French victory belonged. It had been won through the genius of another young captain – he was actually only twenty-four – Napoleon Bonaparte, who had virtually taken charge of the whole operation. His (theoretically) commanding officer, Jacques-François Dugommier, had already sent urgent advice to the War Minister in Paris: '*Récompensez, avancez ce jeune homme; car, si l'on était ingrat vers lui, il s'avancerait de lui-même.'**

Little did Dugommier know how prophetic his words were. In March 1795 Napoleon launched his first prolonged campaign, which was also to prove one of his greatest. It did not immediately threaten Naples; its purpose was first to mop up northern Italy, then to advance through the Tyrol into Austria and finally to join the army of the Rhine, carrying the war into Bavaria. It started with an advance into Piedmont. Nobody – except possibly Bonaparte himself – could have foreseen the measure and speed of his success; almost every day brought news of another victory. Towards the end of April Piedmont was annexed to France, King Charles Emmanuel IV abdicating and retiring to Sardinia, which remained under his authority. On 8 May the French crossed the Po; on the 15th Bonaparte made his formal entry into Milan.

His army was of course living off the conquered land, requisitioning food and accommodation as necessary, but for the members of the Directory in Paris this was not enough. Their instructions were to levy huge contributions both from the Italian states and from the Church, not just money to support the troops but works of art to send back to Paris; and Napoleon obeyed them to the letter. The neutral Duke of Parma, to take but one example, was obliged to hand over two million French *livres* and twenty of his best pictures, to be chosen personally by the Commander-in-Chief; few of the major towns escaped having to surrender their Raphaels, their Titians and their Leonardos. Many of these found their way to the Louvre or to other French museums; some of them still hang there today.

With the occupation of Milan all Lombardy was now in French hands, save only Mantua – which, thanks to determined Austrian resistance, held out till February 1797. Now at last the way was clear for the invasion of Austria. True, it lay across the neutral territory of Venice, but that could not be helped. The Republic

---

* 'Reward this young man, and promote him; for if his services are not recognized, he will promote himself.'

sent two envoys to plead with Napoleon, but he answered with a furious diatribe, leaving them persuaded that no accommodation was possible and ending with those terrible words which were soon to echo in the heart of every Venetian: '*Io sarò un Attila per lo stato veneto*' – 'I shall be an Attila to the Venetian state.' On Friday, 12 May 1797, the Great Council of the Republic met for the last time. The Doge was just completing his opening speech when the sound of firing was heard outside the palace. At once, all was in confusion. To those present, those sounds could mean one thing only: the popular rising that they had so long dreaded had begun. Within minutes, the true source of the firing had been established: some of the Dalmatian troops, who were being removed from the city on Bonaparte's orders, had symbolically discharged their muskets into the air as a parting salute. But reassurances were useless; the panic had begun. Leaving their all too distinctive robes of office behind them, the remaining legislators of the Venetian Republic slipped discreetly out of the palace by the side doors. The *Serenissima* had lasted well over a thousand years; for much of that time she had been the acknowledged mistress of the Mediterranean. Her end could hardly have been more ignominious. The last tragedy of Venice was not her death; it was the manner in which she died.

When Napoleon Bonaparte signed the Treaty of Campo Formio on 17 October, he passed Venice and the Veneto over to Austria; he himself, however, had no regrets. Though he had never set foot in the city, he had always hated Venice and all it stood for; and he believed – probably rightly – that he could master Italy for so long as the peninsula remained divided. Meanwhile, there was peace throughout continental Europe. Only England remained an enemy. Should it now be invaded and destroyed? The Directory was in favour of the plan; it was Bonaparte himself who, after the best part of a year's consideration, decided against it, on strategic grounds. The French navy was, he knew, in a deplorable state, with no commander who could hold a candle to Hood, Rodney or St Vincent – still less to Nelson.

The alternative was Egypt. He would land at Alexandria with an army of 20–25,000 and occupy Cairo. From there a further expedition could be launched against British India – possibly even through a hastily dug canal at Suez. Once again the Directory gave its willing approval. Not only would the proposal keep the army employed and their terrifying young general at a safe distance from Paris; it also offered an opportunity to take over the British role in India, while providing France with an important new colony in the eastern Mediterranean. Finally, it would achieve a major diversion of English sea power to the east, which might make the delayed invasion possible after all.

Napoleon, it need hardly be said, accepted the command with enthusiasm. Determined that his expedition should have objectives other than the purely political and military, he recruited no fewer than 167 *savants* to accompany it, including scientists, mathematicians, astronomers, engineers, architects, painters and draughtsmen. Egypt had preserved her ancient mysteries for too long; she was a fruit more than ready for the plucking. The country had been effectively under the Mamelukes* since 1250. In 1517 it had been conquered by the Turks and absorbed into the Ottoman Empire, of which it still technically remained a part; a century later, however, the Mamelukes were back in control. A French invasion would doubtless evoke an indignant protest from the Sultan in Constantinople; but his empire, though not yet known as 'the sick man of Europe', was a decadent and demoralized shadow of its former self and unlikely to represent much of a threat. Unfortunately there were other risks a good deal more serious. The three hundred French transport ships were poorly armed, their crews practically untrained. True, they had an escort of twenty-seven ships of the line† and frigates, but Nelson was already known to be cruising in the Mediterranean. Were he to intercept them, their chances of escape – and those of the 31,000 men aboard them – would be negligible.

Napoleon left Toulon in his flagship *L'Orient* on 19 May 1798. His first objective was Malta. Since 1530 the island had been in the possession of the Knights of St John. They had conscientiously

---

* The Mamelukes had begun as a huge corps of soldiers, mostly Georgian or Circassian, bought as boy slaves and trained as crack cavalrymen. They had destroyed the Ayyubid dynasty in 1250 and established a new one of their own.
† Ships of the line were the largest category of naval vessels, being those fit to stand in the line of battle.

maintained their hospital and had heroically withstood the dreadful Turkish siege of 1565, but since then they had grown soft. They were 550 strong, but more than half of them were French and many more were too old to fight; and after a two-day token resistance they surrendered. Napoleon continued his journey, on the night of 1 July arriving at Alexandria, where the crumbling walls and tiny garrison could do little to delay the inevitable. It was the same when they reached Cairo. Mameluke swords, however valiantly wielded, were no match for French musketry; the so-called Battle of the Pyramids was a walkover.

Nelson, meanwhile, had been pursuing the French ships across the Mediterranean. Napoleon had in fact left Malta on 19 June; misled by information from a Genoese vessel that he had departed three days earlier, Nelson had hastened to Alexandria; then, finding no trace of the French fleet, he had sailed again on the 29th to search for it along the coast of Syria. As a result of this confusion it was only on 1 August that he returned to Egypt, to find thirteen French men-of-war – he himself had fourteen – and four frigates anchored in a two-mile line in Aboukir Bay, one of the mouths of the Nile. But they were still nine miles distant and it was already mid-afternoon: it would take another two hours to reach them, and a lot longer still to draw up his own ships in a regular line of battle. Night encounters in those days were hazardous things; there was a danger of running aground in unknown waters, and a worse one of firing into one's fellows by mistake. Most admirals, in such circumstances, would have waited till morning; Nelson, however, seeing that the French were unprepared and that there was a favourable northwest wind running, decided on an immediate attack. He began by sending four ships inshore along one side of the French line, while he himself in his flagship, HMS *Vanguard*, led a parallel attack down the offshore side. Each enemy vessel was thus subjected to a simultaneous cannonade from both sides. That was at about six o'clock; the ensuing battle lasted through the night. By dawn all the French ships but four had been destroyed or captured, including their flagship, *L'Orient*. That vessel still lies beneath the waters of the bay, together with all the treasure looted from the palaces and churches of Malta.

The Battle of Aboukir Bay – or, as it is sometimes called, the Battle of the Nile – fought on 1–2 August 1798, was one of the most brilliant victories of Nelson's career. At a stroke he had not only destroyed the French fleet; he had severed Napoleon's line of communication with France, leaving him marooned and frustrating all the French plans of conquest in the Middle East. Thanks to him, the great Egyptian expedition – which had included a brief and equally unsuccessful foray into Palestine – was a flop. As always, Napoleon did his best to dress up defeat as victory. Turkish prisoners were paraded, captured Turkish flags proudly displayed. But no one, least of all the Egyptians, was fooled. For the first time in his career – but not the last – Napoleon deserted his army, leaving it to get home as best it could, and at five o'clock in the morning of 22 August 1799, slipped stealthily from his camp and sailed for France. Not even his successor in command, General Jean-Baptiste Kléber, knew of his departure until he was safely away.

The news of Nelson's victory on the Nile was received with jubilation at the court of Naples. The situation there was still rapidly deteriorating. The French were now in Rome, where Napoleon's brother Joseph Bonaparte was ambassador. General Louis Berthier had marched in with an army in February 1798 and, meeting no opposition, had occupied the city. Churches, palaces and villas had been plundered. A new republic had been proclaimed in the Forum. Pope Pius VI, aged eighty, had been abominably treated – his rings torn forcibly from his fingers – and had been carried off to France, where he died soon afterwards.

What was Naples to do? Here were the French on her very doorstep; what was to prevent them from crossing the frontier, and who could stop them if they did? With Napoleon's seizure of Malta the threat loomed larger still; as Nelson himself was to remark, 'Malta is the direct road to Sicily.' No wonder that the Neapolitans rejoiced when they heard of his victory on the Nile, or that Hamilton should have written to him:

Come here for God's sake my dear friend, as soon as the service will permit you. A pleasant apartment is ready for you in my house,

and Emma is looking out for the softest pillows to repose the few
wearied limbs you have left . . .

Nelson arrived in Naples towards the end of September, to a
hero's welcome. He was seen not only as one who had gained a
magnificent victory over the French navy, but as the deliverer of
the city from imminent invasion. More than five hundred boats
and barges surrounded the *Vanguard* as she entered the bay. The
Hamiltons came on board, and Emma performed the affecting scene
she had been rehearsing for the past three weeks. As Nelson reported
to his wife,

> Up flew her ladyship, and exclaiming, 'Oh God, is it possible?' she
> fell into my arm [*sic*] more dead than alive. Tears, however, soon
> set matters to rights.

The King followed, but not Maria Carolina, who was mourning the
death of her youngest daughter. She did, however, together with all
her court ladies, wear special sashes bearing the words 'Viva Nelson'.
A few days later, on the 29th, the Hamiltons were hosts at a magnificent banquet for 1,800 guests to celebrate the hero's fortieth birthday;
but the party, so far as Nelson was concerned, was not a success. On
the following morning he wrote to Lord St Vincent:

> I trust, my Lord, in a week we shall all be at sea . . . I am very
> unwell, and the miserable conduct of this Court is not likely to
> cool my irritable temper. It is a country of fiddlers and poets, whores
> and scoundrels.

And indeed, the next three months were a nightmare. It was
decided, however, to take the offensive. The Austrian field marshal
Baron Karl Mack von Leiberich★ arrived in early October 1798 to
assume command of the Neapolitan forces, which duly marched
north, a quivering King among them. (The fact that he had omitted
to declare war on France does not seem to have occurred to him.)
Their avowed purpose was to restore the Papacy and to liberate
Rome from the French. Needless to say they proved quite incapable

---

★ 'Whose reputation as a fine strategist will ever remain a mystery' – Acton, *The
Bourbons of Naples.*

of doing either, and by early December more and more of them, officers and men alike, had shed their uniforms and returned to their homes. The Queen – her sister's dreadful fate always in her mind – wrote several times to Emma Hamilton deploring their cowardice, but after her husband deserted in his turn there were no more letters on the subject. On 18 December there arrived a despatch from an utterly demoralized Mack, confessing that his army – which had not yet fought a single battle – was now in full retreat and imploring Their Majesties to leave for Sicily while there was still time. 'I do not know,' wrote Nelson to the Minister at Constantinople, 'that the whole Royal Family, with 3,000 Neapolitan émigrés, will not be under the protection of the King's flag this night.'

And indeed it was. Maria Carolina had been packing for the last three days, sending all her clothes, jewels and other valuables by night to the British Embassy, where Emma passed them on to the *Vanguard*'s crew. The royal party, with Acton and a number of others, eventually slipped out of the palace at nine o'clock in the evening of Friday, 21 December 1798. They were not alone; most of the English and French families then in Naples were eager to join them. The total number of refugees was probably nearer two thousand than Nelson's estimate of three, but still enough to consti-tute a serious evacuation problem. Fortunately a number of other ships were also waiting in the roads, including one Portuguese and two Neapolitan men-of-war, some twenty locally recruited merchantmen and two smaller Greek vessels thoughtfully chartered by Sir William.

The weather, meanwhile, could hardly have been worse. The wind had increased to gale strength, the journey in rowboats out to the ships seemed interminable, and many of their frozen, rain-soaked passengers were in a state of collapse long before they dragged themselves on board in the early hours of the following morning. Nelson accommodated the royal family as best he could. His own cabin he put at the disposal of the ladies and children; the gentlemen were packed into the wardroom, while the ship, though still at anchor, pitched and rolled as if it were on the high seas. This torment continued for the next forty-eight hours: owing to the continuing tempest and the usual Neapolitan confusion, the convoy remained penned up in the bay.

Meanwhile, the people of Naples had learnt with horror of their King's imminent departure. It had been announced that he was travelling to Sicily only to collect reinforcements – but what reinforcements could Sicily possibly provide? Endless deputations and delegations were rowed out to the *Vanguard*, imploring His Majesty to stay, but Ferdinand was firm. His subjects, he said, had betrayed him; he would return only after they had made proof of their loyalty. Meanwhile, to remain in his capital would be to endanger his life.

Only on Sunday evening, 23 December, did the convoy finally weigh anchor. The weather was no better; indeed on the following day – Christmas Eve – Nelson recorded that 'it blew harder than I have ever experienced since I have been at sea'. The sails were torn to shreds; preparations were even made to cut away the main-mast. Among the distinguished passengers in the *Vanguard* there was something close to panic; only Emma Hamilton and one of the King's stewards kept their heads. Emma in particular was superb: tending the groaning Queen, comforting the royal children as if they were her own, giving them her own bed linen when neces-sary. Nelson could not conceal his admiration, emphasizing in a letter that she never once went to bed during her whole time on board. As for Sir William, he was found in his cabin with a loaded pistol in each hand – since, he explained to his wife, he was deter-mined not to perish 'with the guggle-guggle-guggle of salt water in his throat'. The Austrian ambassador, Count Esterhazy, threw his jewelled snuffbox over the side since it bore a miniature of his mistress in the nude, considering it 'highly impious to keep about his person so profane an article, when (as he thought) on the verge of eternity'.

Quite apart from the weather, Christmas Day 1798 was marked by tragedy. That evening little Prince Carlo Alberto, aged six, died of exhaustion in Emma's arms. It was not till two o'clock in the morning of the 26th that the *Vanguard* and its companions finally dropped anchor in the harbour of Palermo. Maria Carolina, unable to remain another minute on board, disembarked at once and was driven to Palazzo Colli, the royal residence. The King, on the other hand, slept soundly and ate a hearty breakfast before making, for the first time, his formal entry into his kingdom's second capital. The warmth of his reception there delighted him – though his wife described it as 'without frantic enthusiasm'. He seemed utterly unconcerned, either by the loss of Naples or by the death of his son. The situation, he maintained, would right itself soon enough; meanwhile Sicily promised to be excellent hunting country and he proposed to enjoy it.

Considering that the people of Palermo had until now never once clapped eyes on their King or Queen, their enthusiasm – if such it was – for their two sovereigns was remarkable. Hope of material profit doubtless played its part, yet much of it was probably due to the fact that at last they no longer felt provincial; at least for as long as the royal family remained in Sicily, Palermo – not Naples – was the true capital of the Kingdom. To the family itself, on the other hand, Palazzo Colli – their official residence – came as a nasty shock. Dark and dripping with damp, it had not been lived in for years – and whose fault, the King and Queen might have asked themselves, was that? Moreover, it had no resident domestic staff. Neither did it even possess fireplaces; during the mild Palermo winters, these were not normally necessary, but the winter of 1798–99 was perishingly cold – the coldest indeed on record. There were not even any carpets. The Palermitan authorities had been given little or no advance warning of their sovereigns' arrival and the first few days must have been hellish, particularly after that nightmare voyage. Maria Carolina made no secret of her feelings. She wrote to the Duca di Gallo, Neapolitan ambassador in Vienna:

> I have lived too long, and grief is killing me . . . I am sure I cannot continue to live in this way and doubt if I shall survive . . . My daughter-in-law has consumption and cannot live. Concerning their father I should be silent. He feels nothing but self-love and hardly feels that. He should realize that he has lost the best part of his Crown, of his revenue; but he is aware only of the novelties which amuse him, without thinking that we are reduced to a quarter of our income, dishonoured, unhappy and dragging others into the

same misfortune . . . Everything here repels me. Our provinces, Sorrento – I would prefer any other place.

Were Ferdinand and Maria Carolina justified in leaving Naples as and when they did? The answer is probably yes; they were certainly not guilty of the charges of cowardice that have so frequently been laid against them. Had they remained to face expulsion or even violent death, that would have been the end of their dynasty. By their withdrawal to Palermo, where they were still sovereign, they kept their royal status intact and – if and when the situation on the mainland improved – were well placed for any possible reinstatement. It should be remembered too that in leaving they were following the advice of Nelson himself. He, meanwhile, had moved in with the Hamiltons. He was utterly exhausted, and not yet completely recovered from a head wound sustained at Aboukir Bay. He was quarrelling with the Admiralty, and his relationship with his wife was also causing him serious concern. He desperately needed emotional support – and Emma Hamilton gave it him. Her long experience as a courtesan did the rest. It was almost certainly now, in Sicily, that their celebrated affair began.

When the French troops under General Jean-Etienne Championnet arrived in Naples in mid-January 1799, they found the populace a good deal more spirited than the army. The mob – the *lazzaroni* – was prepared to attack the invaders tooth and nail, and for three days there was bitter house-to-house fighting. In the end the *lazzaroni* had of course to give in, but not before they had stormed and gutted the royal palace. They had done so with a clear – or almost clear – conscience. Was their King not known as *il re lazzarone*, in other words one of themselves? And even if he had abandoned them, would he not have preferred his treasures to go to his own subjects rather than to his French enemies? When at last peace was restored, a French officer remarked that if Bonaparte had been there in person he would probably have left not one stone of the city standing on another; it was fortunate indeed that Championnet was a moderate and humane man. Quietly and diplomatically he established what was known as the Parthenopean Republic, on the French revolutionary model. It was officially proclaimed on 23

January, and acquired a number of loyal Italian adherents – though it was perfectly obvious to all that it had been the result of conquest, and that the French army of occupation was its only support.

The news of the sack of the royal palace caused poor Maria Carolina still greater distress. Worst of all, perhaps, her husband had turned against her, blaming her for forcing him into that shameful campaign and for saddling him with the hopeless General Mack. Early in February there were riots in Palermo in protest against the spiralling costs of food. She wrote again to Gallo:

> Palermo is in full ferment and I expect grave events. Having neither troops nor arms, lacking everything, I am ready for anything and quite desperate. Here the priests are completely corrupted, the people savage, the nobility more than uncertain and of questionable loyalty. The people and clergy might let us leave if we promised to agree to the establishment of a republic. But the nobility would oppose our departure because they would be ruined, and they dread the democratization of the country. They would prefer to rise and put themselves at the head of the movement and have us massacred, ourselves and all Neapolitans . . .

But hope was at hand, nearer than she knew. Cardinal Fabrizio Ruffo was already over sixty. He had been papal treasurer to Pope Pius VI, but when all his suggested reforms had been rejected as too radical he had retired to Naples, whence he had duly followed the court to Palermo. He now proposed a landing in his native Calabria, first to defend it from any further French advance – as well as from Italian republicanism – and ultimately to recover Naples for its King. This would, he emphasized, be nothing less than a Crusade, and he had no doubt whatever that all his fellow Calabrians would rally to the Cross.

With the wholehearted support of the King, the Queen and Acton, Ruffo landed as planned on 7 February, with just eight companions. He had no arms or ammunition; his only equipment was a banner, bearing the royal arms on one side and a cross on the other, inscribed with the words '*In hoc signo vinces*.'* This he

---

* 'Under this sign will you conquer', the words that Constantine the Great claimed to have seen in the sky before the Battle of the Milvian Bridge in 312.

hoisted from the balcony of his brother's nearby villa while he issued an encyclical letter to all the neighbouring bishops, clergy, magistrates and persons of note, calling upon each one of them to defend his religion, his King, his fatherland and the honour of his family. How the various addressees reacted to this summons is unfortunately not recorded; but eighty armed *lazzaroni* joined him almost at once, and by the end of the month the strength of the 'Christian Army of the Holy Faith' had risen to 17,000. Ruffo was a born leader, and quickly won their love and trust; in 1799, wrote his secretary-biographer Sacchinelli, 'there was not a miserable peasant in all Calabria but had a crucifix on one side of his bed, a gun on the other.' On 1 March the Cardinal was able to establish his headquarters in the important city of Monteleone, the seat of the provincial treasury; it provided him with 10,000 ducats and eleven magnificent horses. Catanzaro followed, and then Cotrone. Admittedly, he had his problems. His ramshackle army was totally without discipline, his 'Crusaders' comporting themselves no better than their medieval predecessors; Cotrone, for example, was delivered over to a sack from which it never recovered. Such atrocities could not but damage his reputation, though he personally was mild and merciful, always preferring peaceful conversion to violence. But his momentum was unstoppable, and his successes encouraged other, similar movements throughout south Italy. He himself, having recovered the whole of Calabria, marched eastwards into Apulia, where he had similar success. By the beginning of June he was at the gates of Naples – which, owing to a blockade of the bay by a British fleet, was now on the brink of starvation.

On 11 June, hearing of the Cardinal's approach, the people of Naples broke out in open rebellion. There was fighting throughout the city. Desperate for food, mercilessly bombarded by the French from the S. Elmo, Nuovo and Ovo castles, the *lazzaroni* fell on every Jacobin, French or Italian, that they could lay their hands on, with unbridled barbarity. There are accounts of unspeakable atrocities: of dismemberment and cannibalism, of severed heads paraded on pikes or kicked around like footballs, of women suspected of Jacobinism being subjected to ghastly humiliations. The horrified Cardinal did what he could, but many of his own men had plunged joyfully into the bloodbath; in any case, against mob hysteria he was powerless. The orgy of destruction continued for a week. Negotiations were seriously impeded by the inability of the commanders of the three castles to communicate with one another, and it was only on the 19th that the French formally capitulated. The terms, thanks to Ruffo, were remarkably generous. The garrisons could, if they wished, return to Toulon. They could remain in the three castles while the necessary ships were prepared, after which they could march out with all the honours of war.

The wisdom of such a policy was obvious; Charles Lock, the British consul in Palermo, wrote that he considered that 'it effectually swept the Kingdom of the disaffected.' But it was against the stated policy of the King and Queen, who insisted – with the enthusiastic support of the Hamiltons – that no mercy be shown to any of the Jacobin survivors. Ruffo and his friends saw all too clearly the danger of bringing home a royal couple who thought only of revenge, but there was little they could do; and the arrival of Nelson, with eighteen ships of the line, on the 24th hardly improved the situation. He had been on a fruitless search for the Franco-Spanish fleet which was said to be bound for Naples with vital reinforcements; returning, he had called in at Palermo to confer with Ferdinand and Maria Carolina and had quietly embarked the Hamiltons. His task was now to enforce the King's wishes in Naples. As the *Foudroyant* sailed into the bay and she saw the flags of surrender on the castles, Emma is said to have cried, 'Haul down those flags of truce! No truce with the rebels!'

Her husband was still more unhappy, but for a different reason. He had never objected to Emma's relationship with Nelson – he seems if anything to have been rather proud of it; far more distressing was the news now brought to him of the ship *Colossus*, which had been wrecked on its way to England, carrying with it his entire collection of Greek and Roman antiquities, to which he had devoted his life. Rightly or wrongly, he held the French responsible – making him more vindictive than ever.

As for Nelson, it need hardly be said that he was firmly on the monarchist side. Politically he was extraordinarily naïve, his knowledge of the situation in Naples being limited to the highly tendentious opinions he had picked up from the King and Queen and the Hamiltons. As a down-to-earth, right-wing English Protestant he deeply mistrusted Cardinal Ruffo, and on his arrival in Naples had no hesitation in overruling him, insisting – as his friends also insisted – on the unconditional surrender of all the rebels. Some 1,500, whom Ruffo had saved from the mob and to whom he had given refuge in the municipal granaries, marched out according to the terms of the capitulation, expecting safe conduct to their homes. To their astonishment they were put under immediate arrest, and many were executed. Not surprisingly, Ruffo resigned, but the question persists: was it Nelson who gave the order? Probably not personally. All that we know of his character suggests that he would never knowingly have done such a thing; but the Hamiltons' influence was paramount, and he always accepted their point of view.

He has also been condemned, with a good deal more justification, for his treatment of Commodore Francesco Caracciolo, the former senior officer of the Neapolitan navy who had transferred his allegiance to the republicans. After ten days on the run in disguise, Caracciolo had been found hiding in a well and was brought before Nelson on the *Foudroyant*. At ten in the morning of 30 June he was court-martialled, at noon he was found guilty and condemned to death, and at five in the afternoon he was hanged from the yardarm. There his body remained until sunset, when the rope was cut and it fell into the sea. He had been allowed no witnesses for his defence, no priest to hear his last confession. His request to be shot rather than hanged was refused outright. Traitor he may have been, but he had deserved better than that. Why had Nelson allowed it? Simply because of his infatuation with Emma. With a ship and the ocean beneath him he was invincible, infallible; on land he was literally out of his element, and when in the arms of his mistress little better than a child.

Leaving Maria Carolina – to her considerable frustration – in Palermo, the King returned to Naples on a Neapolitan frigate in the first week of July. His subjects gave him a warm welcome – whatever happened, he never lost his personal popularity – but thanks to his intransigence hostilities had been resumed and the French were still firing from St Elmo. On the afternoon of his arrival he boarded the *Foudroyant*, and for the next four weeks never once set foot on shore. It was during this time that an extraordinary incident occurred; a local fisherman reported that he had seen the body of Caracciolo swimming towards Naples. At first nobody believed him, but soon the body was spotted from the *Foudroyant*, rapidly approaching in the strong current. It proved indeed to be that of Caracciolo; owing to the weights which had been attached to his feet it was floating upright in the water. The King, intensely superstitious, was horrified; he partly recovered only when the chaplain assured him that Caracciolo had returned to implore his pardon and to be given a Christian burial. He at once gave orders that the body was to be towed ashore, where it was buried in the church of S. Maria la Catena.

By the end of the month the last of the rebels had surrendered. The French were returned to Toulon; the Neapolitans were put in irons to await their trial. Cardinal Ruffo had received little gratitude for having saved the monarchy – all the credit had somehow been given to Nelson – but in recognition of his past services he was now appointed Lieutenant and Captain-General of the Realm. There were those who believed that after the repudiation of his solemn treaty he should not have accepted the post; but he remained as loyal as ever to his monarch, and had no desire to stand on his honour if he could still prove useful. His appointment meant in practice that he was president of what was known as the *Suprema Giunta*, the Supreme Committee. Under this were two other committees of judges, one to try the military, the other the civilians. Much has been written about the deliberations of these committees, to demonstrate the cruelty and inhumanity of the Bourbons. In the event, their deliberations seem to have been remarkably merciful. Out of some 8,000 political prisoners, 105 were condemned to death (six were later reprieved), 222 were condemned to life imprisonment, 322 to shorter terms, 288 to deportation and 67 to exile, from which many were to return. The rest were set free.

And that was the end of the flatulently named Parthenopean Republic. It had sought to inflict, by means of conquest, a form of government that the country and people did not want and which was already largely discredited even in France. Had it survived, it could have retained power only through violence or the threat of violence. The resulting police state would have been far worse than anything created by the Bourbons.

In the first week of August 1799 King Ferdinand, with the Hamiltons as always in tow, set sail on the *Foudroyant* for Sicily. Never, during his forty years on the throne of Naples, had he believed that he had enemies in the city; now he knew that he did, and the knowledge had shaken him to the core. Henceforth he preferred the safety of Palermo. On the 8th he sailed into its harbour with Nelson at his side. The Queen came on board with their children, and that afternoon the whole party disembarked to a salute of twenty-one guns before driving in state amid cheering crowds to a solemn Te Deum in the cathedral. For the next three days the city was *en fête*, the feast day of its patron saint, S. Rosalia, having been postponed for a month pending His Majesty's arrival.

Now it was time for rewards. For Emma, the Queen had a diamond necklace with her portrait in miniature and the inscription '*Eterna Gratitudine*', plus two coaches filled with fine dresses to replace those she had lost in her flight from Naples; for Sir William, a portrait of the King set in jewels. Nelson received the Sicilian dukedom of Bronte, which brought in an annual revenue of some 3,000 pounds, together with the diamond-hilted sword which Louis XIV had given Ferdinand's grandfather Philip V. Golden snuffboxes, watches and rings were freely distributed among his officers.

For Ferdinand and Maria Carolina, for the Hamiltons and for Nelson, life now continued much as it had before – except that there was no longer any cogent reason to stay in Palermo. The Queen yearned for Naples; the King, on the other hand, had worked himself up about it until dislike had turned to detestation. Never, he said, would he willingly go back. It was perhaps this more than anything else which led to a marked deterioration in the previously cordial relations between Ferdinand and Maria Carolina. The King also became almost pathologically mean, allowing his family barely enough money to live on and paying his staff only with the greatest reluctance. His wife, however, possessed one small secret weapon. She knew that her husband was notoriously susceptible to a woman's arms, especially if they were covered in white shoulder-length gloves. According to Count Roger de Damas, a French émigré now a member of the Neapolitan court:

> His brain becomes exalted when he sees a glove well stretched over a beautifully shaped arm. It is a mania he has always had and which has never varied. How many affairs of the greatest importance have I seen settled by the Queen's care to pull her gloves over her pretty arms while discussing the question which engrossed her! I have seen the King take notice of this, smile, and grant her wish.

She was, for all that, desperately unhappy, and spent her days writing interminable, self-pitying letters to everyone she could think of.

It was at this time that Ferdinand conferred what was to become his greatest gift to Sicily. In 1802, only some four years after Edward Jenner had published his first observations on vaccination, he had invited an English doctor to the island to demonstrate the new technique. So successful was it that he gave orders for medical centres to be opened in every town, and for vaccination to be made compulsory. He was indeed vaccinated himself – and a Te Deum was sung in Palermo Cathedral when he survived.

Superficially, life at court was as brilliant as ever, with balls, concerts and supper parties which were nearly always followed by cards. Stakes were high, with Emma Hamilton among the most reckless of the players, Nelson always beside her though often more than half asleep. Visitors were often shocked by his public display of devotion; one of them, Lady Elgin, gave it as her opinion that it was high time for the entire *ménage à trois* to go home. 'It is really humiliating,' she wrote, 'to see Lord Nelson, he seems quite dying and yet as if he had no other thought than her.' To her husband Nelson looked 'very old, has lost his upper teeth, sees ill of one eye,★ and has a film coming over both of them'.

The Hamiltons, while from the political point of view advocating the King's return to Naples, were in fact perfectly content where

★ His right eye had been badly damaged during fighting off Corsica in 1794. He eventually lost the sight in it altogether.

they were. Sir William, being accredited personally to Ferdinand, was required to remain with him, and Naples may well have held poignant memories after the loss of his beloved antiquities. A far sadder fate was Nelson's. He was to remain ashore in Palermo until June 1800, ten months in which his infatuation with Emma Hamilton not only sapped his morale but even seems to have adversely affected both his conscience and his sense of duty. For the first half of that period he was acting Commander-in-Chief, Mediterranean, but he left virtually all the work to his subordinates. He was not there to intercept Napoleon Bonaparte when he slipped out of Egypt; had he made the effort and succeeded, history might have taken a very different turn. His colleagues grew increasingly concerned for him and disturbing reports reached London, where the Admiralty began to lose patience and the First Lord, Lord Spencer, very nearly relieved him of his command. In January 1800 his superior, Lord Keith, returned to duty and ordered Nelson to join him in an inspection of the blockade of Malta, but the admiral returned almost at once to Palermo, where Emma – now shamelessly pregnant – received him publicly with open arms.

For Maria Carolina, the 1800s had a disastrous beginning. After thirty-six years in Naples and Palermo Sir William Hamilton was recalled to London, while Nelson's Mediterranean command also came to an end. There was little that the poor Queen could do about Nelson, but she refused to contemplate the prospect of Palermo without the Hamiltons and was determined not to let them go without a fight. In this she was enthusiastically supported by Emma, who had no wish to leave the glamour of the court and the almost perpetual sunshine for the comparative gloom of England, living alone with a man thirty-four years her senior; but the task was by no means easy. First, there was the attitude of the King. Though fond of Hamilton he had taken a deep dislike to Emma and he refused absolutely to intervene. Second, Sir William's successor was already on his way.

The Hon. Sir Arthur Paget, the third son of Lord Uxbridge,*

---

* His elder brother Henry, 1st Marquess of Anglesey, was the famous 'Old One-Leg' who lost his leg at Waterloo while serving as second-in-command to the Duke of Wellington.

arrived in Palermo in March to a distinctly cool reception. From the start, the Hamiltons were determined to get rid of him, making his life – even the presentation of his credentials – as difficult as possible. He wrote to the Foreign Secretary, Lord Grenville:

> After waiting near 3 quarters of an hour H.S.M.* came into the room where I was, attended by Sir William and Lady Hamilton, Lord Nelson, etc., and where the whole court were, and spoke one or two sentences to me. I really, my Lord, should not mention this had it not happened that the Russian Minister who had taken the same step as myself was invited to a private Audience which lasted over an hour. This circumstance, coupled with the very disadvantageous manner in which Her Sicilian Majesty has on every occasion expressed herself of me made me imagine that she would do everything in her power to have me removed.

He had only one friend at court who seemed to be prepared to treat him with reasonable civility: Sir John Acton, who had done more than anyone else to keep the Sicilian Kingdom on a relatively even keel. But in 1799 Acton, now sixty-four, had married – by special papal dispensation – his thirteen-year-old niece, and his dedication to his work was beginning to suffer. Everywhere, discontent was smouldering. The Neapolitans were calling for the return of their King; Ferdinand was refusing point-blank to go. Maria Carolina had set her heart on a journey to Vienna; Ferdinand was longing to see the last of her, but Acton opposed the idea, both on grounds of expense and also because he was worried about the political damage she could do; he did not trust her an inch. Ultimately, however, the King and Queen got their way. Paget reported:

> The Queen of Naples is certainly going to Vienna. These two Courts are always kicking and splashing at one another and she is going to endeavour to reconcile matters, but I have some idea that she might as well save herself the trouble, as I apprehend that M. de Thugut† cannot bear her . . . She takes two or three daughters with her who will be sold to the best bidder.

---

* His Sicilian Majesty.
† The Austrian Foreign Secretary.

At last all was ready. Nelson and the Hamiltons had just returned from a short trip to Malta, the recent blockade of which had been successful; the island was now, at its own request, a British dominion. All the Queen's efforts to delay their departure had failed, so on 10 June they all sailed in the *Foudroyant*, including the ten-year-old Prince Leopold and the Princesses Christine and Amélie, aged twenty-one and eighteen respectively. There could obviously be no question of the family travelling to Vienna unescorted; it was understood that Nelson and the Hamiltons should travel with them, all the way. They reached Livorno on the 14th; but a serious problem had arisen. Bonaparte – by now First Consul – had once again invaded Italy, and on the day before the *Foudroyant*'s arrival had encountered the Austrian army at Marengo. First reports, reaching Leghorn the following day, suggested that the Austrians had won a decisive victory. Had they done so, it would probably have spelled the end of Napoleon's career; but that evening the appearance of French reinforcements totalling 6,000 men, all fresh and rested, turned the scale. By nightfall the Austrians were in full retreat.★

Now, for the Queen and her children, the onward journey to Vienna was to say the least uncertain. They waited in Livorno for nearly a month, Maria Carolina always fearing that she would have to return to Palermo. Nelson, meanwhile, was showing serious insubordination, refusing his orders to join the main fleet. Under Emma's influence, he seemed to be rapidly going to pieces. 'It is really melancholy,' noted Sir John Moore, who happened to be passing through the city at that time, 'to see a brave and good man, who has deserved well of his country, cutting so pitiful a figure.' At last Lord Keith, his commander-in-chief, went to Leghorn himself 'to be bored by Lord Nelson for permission to take the Queen to Palermo, and Princes and Princesses to all parts of the Globe'. Lady Hamilton, he added, had had command of the fleet long enough.

It was finally decided that the party should travel first to Florence

---

★ When the news reached Rome, there was a sudden change from celebration to lamentation – which, incidentally, lends additional poignancy to Act II of Puccini's *Tosca*.

and thence to Ancona, where they would pick up a ship to take them to Trieste. They left Leghorn on 13 July. It was a dangerous journey: many of the roads were largely destroyed and on several occasions they had to pass within a very few miles of the French forces. At Ancona they found transport with a small Russian squadron, for which Nelson could not hide his contempt; a strong gust, he said, would have capsized the lot of them. But they reached Vienna at last, and after three weeks Nelson and the Hamiltons finally bade the Queen farewell and left for Prague, Dresden, Dessau and Hamburg. From there they caught a packet ship to Great Yarmouth, where they arrived on 6 November. Another hero's welcome awaited Nelson, but he now had the problem of his wife, Fanny. Around Christmas she issued an ultimatum: her husband must now make the final choice between her and Emma. Inevitably, he chose Emma.

The year 1801 began well, with the birth in January of their daughter Horatia. All too soon afterwards, however, Nelson was summoned back to sea – first to the Channel Fleet and then to the Baltic and the Battle of Copenhagen. On his return to London he was made a viscount and bought a somewhat ramshackle house at Merton – then a separate parish, now a part of suburban Wimbledon – where the *ménage à trois* continued until the death of Sir William in 1803. Shortly after that, the war with France was resumed and Nelson was summoned back to the Mediterranean. It was another two years before Trafalgar, but he never saw Emma again.

Poor Emma: in her widowhood she was desperately lonely. Despite her late husband's distinction, his careful instructions to provide for her and Horatia were ignored, and the small pension that he had been able to leave her was soon exhausted. After his death, their few friends fell away; in the eyes of society she was a fallen woman. She took to drink, and in 1813 served a year with Horatia in the debtors' prison in Southwark before moving to France to escape her creditors. There she spent her last years in penury, finally dying at Calais in 1815. She was forty-nine.

12

Joseph and Joachim

$\sim\!\!\sim$

IT WAS A joy and an immense relief for Maria Carolina to be back in her beloved Vienna. Ten years had passed since she had seen her eldest daughter, Maria Teresa – who had married the future Emperor Francis II in 1790 – and she was now able to meet the first five of her grandchildren. If, however, she had expected to influence Francis in his struggle with Napoleon Bonaparte, she was to be disappointed. The Emperor kept his distance; the situation was quite bad enough without an interfering mother-in-law. Napoleon had expected him to sue for peace after the disaster of Marengo, but he had recently signed a treaty with Britain whereby, in return for a subsidy of two and a half million pounds, he had undertaken not to do so before February 1801. The result was another, even more decisive victory for the French at Hohenlinden, twenty miles east of Munich, in December 1800, when the Austrians were thrown back with almost 20,000 casualties. In a fortnight their retreating army was driven two hundred miles towards Vienna. On Christmas Day the desperate Francis signed a new armistice, and when in January 1801 another French army began pushing the Austrians out of northern Italy, he was ready for peace. He delayed for another week or two in deference to the British, then on 9 February signed the Treaty of Lunéville, which effectively took Austria out of the war. The French acquired Belgium, Luxembourg and the left bank of the Rhine. Britain and Naples – whose interests the Austrians had entirely ignored at Lunéville – were now the only two nations still at war with Napoleon.

Meanwhile, in Palermo King Ferdinand was under increasing pressure, both from Sir Arthur Paget and from his Neapolitan subjects, to return to Naples. He fought it hard; the very idea was hateful to him. He believed, or pretended to believe, that his life would be in serious danger; the fact was that he infinitely preferred his quiet life in Sicily, where – particularly now that the Queen was gone – he could leave all the unpleasant business to Acton and hunt to his heart's content. At last he decided to send over to the mainland his son and heir, the Hereditary Prince Francis, with his wife, Maria Clementina of Austria, the Emperor's sister. They were both twenty-three years old, and passionately in love. 'Her husband is her husband two or three times in twenty-four hours,' wrote the Queen, 'he adores her in every sense of the word. He says she loves him, and assuredly she shows and demands many proofs of love.' For the Neapolitans – who had hoped for his father – it was very much a second best, but when the royal couple arrived on 31 January 1801 they received a magnificent welcome, and when the smiling Princess appeared on the palace balcony and held up each of her two children in turn she, and they, were cheered to the echo.

But no amount of celebration could conceal the fact that Napoleon was still at war with Naples, and that Naples was at his mercy. At last a peace treaty was agreed, and was signed in Florence on 28 March. Naples was forced to surrender the island of Elba and part of the adjacent mainland, to withdraw her troops from the Papal States, to close all her ports to British shipping, to free all French and republican prisoners and to allow the stationing of French troops, at her own expense, on her territory for a year. This last provision resulted in the arrival of 10,000 men under General Jean-de-Dieu Soult, who occupied the ports of Otranto, Taranto and Brindisi to improve his communications with the army that Napoleon had abandoned in Egypt in 1799 and that was still waiting to return home. Finally, in May, a French ambassador, Baron Charles-Jean-Marie Alquier – who had actually been a member of the Convention which voted for the execution of Louis XVI – presented his credentials to the Hereditary Prince. The rest of the diplomatic corps – apart from the Russian minister – remained with the King in Palermo. Britain was now Napoleon's only declared enemy.

November of that same disastrous year of 1801 saw the death of Maria Clementina at the age of only twenty-four, probably of tuberculosis. Just four months before, her baby son had died shortly before his first birthday. Her husband was broken-hearted, but a new wife was quickly found for him. She was his cousin Maria Isabel, daughter of Charles IV of Spain;* it was further agreed that, in a double ceremony, the bride's brother, the Prince of the Asturias – the future Ferdinand VII – would marry the groom's sister, Princess Maria Antonietta. Maria Carolina was furious at her son's choice of bride; she had always detested the Spanish Bourbons, and had hoped that all her children would marry safe, respectable Austrians. She was also shocked. 'I have seen it in his own handwriting to the General [Acton],' she wrote, 'only ten days after the death of his virtuous wife, saying that this long celibacy oppressed him. I blush that this is my son.' She may well have blushed still more deeply at the realization that his intended wife was just thirteen.

While Naples mourned the death of the young princess, Napoleon was hard at work. Not only was he reorganizing the new French Republic; he also had to establish effective governments in Italy, Holland, Germany and Switzerland. In such circumstances he could not for the moment continue active hostilities with Britain. Negotiations were long and hard, but a peace treaty was finally signed at Amiens in March 1802. It was the only one ever concluded between Britain and Bonaparte, and it lasted only a year; its principal provision was that France should withdraw her forces from the Kingdom of Naples while Britain should withdraw hers from Egypt. The island of Minorca, which had for the past century been batted about like a shuttlecock between Britain and Spain, became Spanish for good. Another provision, that Britain should leave Malta within three months and return it to the Knights, was – for reasons that are shortly to become clear – never implemented.

Napoleon was naturally anxious, as he had been in Egypt, to dress up his withdrawal from Naples, making it look as far as possible like a victory. He wisely sent his brother-in-law Joachim Murat,

---

* At least in theory. It was generally believed in Spain that her father was Manuel de Godoy, Prime Minister 1792–7 and 1801–08 and long-term lover of Queen Maria Luisa.

with the rank of ambassador extraordinary, to supervise the operation; no one was better suited to the job. The Neapolitans had expected some drab and colourless republican; Murat – charismatic, dashing, always resplendent in his superbly cut uniforms – could not fail to impress. He was given a magnificent reception at the royal palace at Caserta, where, with elaborate ceremony, he presented the Hereditary Prince with a brace of pistols made at Versailles. Such was the splendour of the spectacle that many of those present concluded that republican days might be nearly over and that France might soon be a monarchy again. Little did they know how soon they would be proved right.

With the French gone, there was no conceivable reason for King Ferdinand to stay in Sicily. He continued to procrastinate as long as he could, but finally gave in. After an absence of more than two and a half years, on 27 June 1802 he entered Naples from Portici on horseback. It was said that the population of the city was almost doubled by the crowds who flocked from all over his kingdom to welcome him. What he had done to deserve his astonishing popularity is not altogether clear; it was something to do with the way the *re lazzarone* identified with the humblest of his subjects. The *lazzaroni* surrounded him, gave him a four-hour ovation and nearly pulled him from his horse in their excitement. For him at least, his renewed life in Naples promised to be a good deal more agreeable than he had feared.

The Queen, however, continued to dread it, and characteristically made no secret of the fact. She was detained in Vienna by an agonizing operation for piles, and eventually arrived in Naples on 17 August, almost in secret. She shared none of her husband's popularity, and made no effort to endear herself to a public she despised. The forthcoming double marriage offered her little consolation or comfort. She loved her daughter Antonietta, now departing for Spain, whom she was afraid she would never see again; for her son Francis, awaiting his new wife in Naples, she felt only repugnance. He seemed to have no interest in anything but sex, and no one at court showed the slightest interest in him.

In fact, both marriages turned out worse than even Maria Carolina had feared. 'Antonietta,' she wrote, 'is in despair. She left with the most sanguine expectations, but that is all over. Her husband has a hideous face, a terrifying voice, and is an utter simpleton. The life there is abominable, like that of five centuries ago.' The Princess, despite strict instructions from the Neapolitan ambassador to write only the happiest letters home, confessed to her mother that she would have preferred a convent. All this was bad enough; but when the court in Naples first set eyes on the child bride of the Hereditary Prince it was collectively horrified. The King described her as 'little, and round as a ball'; the Queen, as usual, did not mince her words:

> Not Bourbon in the least, but white and red, with black eyes. She is very stout and sturdy, yet her legs are very short. So much for her exterior. The rest cannot be described because I myself cannot understand it. She is null in every respect – knowledge, ideas, curiosity. Nothing, absolutely nothing. She speaks a little Spanish but neither Italian nor French, and only monosyllables, yes or no, indiscriminately. She smiles all the time, whether she is pleased or not . . . Francis's child aged four has far more intelligence. It is incredible. Francis has engaged masters to teach her Italian and the rudiments of geography and arithmetic. She knows nothing except a little piano. I have tried to praise and enliven her. She feels nothing; she merely laughs.

Two, however, could play at that game. To Queen Maria Luisa of Spain, her new daughter-in-law was 'that offscouring of her mother, that poisonous viper, that animal bursting with spleen and venom instead of blood, that diabolical serpent'. She firmly believed that Maria Carolina intended her daughter to poison her, and when the poor girl died aged twenty-one – after two miscarriages – there were dark rumours that she herself had been poisoned by her mother-in-law. Maria Carolina, of course, had no doubt in her mind at all.

By the late spring of 1803, the Treaty of Amiens was obviously on its last legs. Bonaparte had annexed Piedmont and Elba and had occupied Switzerland; where would he turn next? A recent report in the French *Moniteur* by a certain Colonel Sebastiani maintained that 6,000 French soldiers would easily suffice to conquer Egypt. Napoleon's first attempt to do so had been a moderately humiliating failure; could he really be contemplating a second? The very possibility was enough to persuade the British government not to abandon Malta after all. News of this change of heart threw Napoleon into a fury. He himself broke agreements and treaties when it suited him; he did not permit it in others. On 18 May he declared war on England; on the 31st he notified the government of Naples that he would be sending an army of 13,000 to garrison Apulia – naturally, at Neapolitan expense – under General Laurent de Gouvion-Saint-Cyr. By this time, owing largely to the efforts of his ambassador, Charles-Jean-Marie Alquier, he had a new reason for treating the Kingdom the way he did: Sir John Acton. He wrote to the Queen:

> What must I think of the Kingdom of Naples . . . when I see at the head of its entire administration a man who is alien to the country, and who has concentrated in England his wealth and all his affections? In the meantime the kingdom is governed less by the will and principles of its Sovereign than by those of this minister. I have therefore decided as a wise precaution to consider Naples as a country ruled by an English minister.

Ironically enough, the Queen agreed – though she was naturally careful not to say so. She hated Acton, and had long been intriguing against him. Without him, she believed, she would have her husband's ear; once again she would enjoy the influence she craved. But Ferdinand was adamant. If his chief minister were to resign, he said, he himself would abdicate. He trusted Acton more than any man alive – far more, certainly, than his wife – and would listen to no criticisms, least of all from her.

Just at this time there arrived in Naples a new British ambassador, Hugh Elliot.* He had sailed as far as Gibraltar with Nelson, who had recently been appointed to the Mediterranean command, and

---

* Sir Arthur Paget had been transferred to Vienna. Elliot never received the customary knighthood, having blotted his copybook by fighting a duel with his wife's lover early in his career.

who had doubtless given him the fullest possible briefing on what he could expect – including dire warnings about Sicily. Nelson had already written to Acton about the island, which he saw as central to the monarchy – more central, even, than Naples itself. If the city were conquered, he maintained, Sicily might still be saved; if Sicily were lost, it would mean the end of the Kingdom. Thus, from the beginning, Elliot had no delusions. A strong man himself, he considerably strengthened Acton's resolve. If Napoleon insisted on his demands that Neapolitan ports should be closed to British shipping, he must be quietly informed – and we can sense Nelson's influence here – that the British would occupy Messina. It was essential, on the other hand, to do nothing precipitate: Britain would be powerless if Saint-Cyr took it upon himself to march on the capital. Meanwhile, the shore defences of both Sicily and Calabria would be redoubled, and gunboats would be assembled at Messina to prevent any attempt at invasion. Finally, HMS *Gibraltar* would remain in Neapolitan waters, to protect – and if necessary once again to remove – the royal family in the event of an emergency.

As 1803 turned to 1804, Alquier and Saint-Cyr stepped up their pressure on the Queen. Not a day passed without protests or complaints from the ambassador or new outrages on the part of the general – who was acting like a dictator in Apulia, riding roughshod over government regulations, billeting troops wherever he liked, emptying the granaries and even ordering the execution of Neapolitan citizens. Both continued to demand the removal of Acton, who – goaded beyond endurance – finally submitted his resignation. The King as usual flew into a rage and threatened to leave at once for Sicily; but when he learned that Napoleon had decided to declare war unless the Chief Minister left the capital within a matter of days he reluctantly agreed to accept what was presented as a compromise: Acton would retire to Palermo with a generous pension and an extensive estate at Modica, but would effectively retain his position, with all important reports and despatches being forwarded to him. His so-called successors would thus be little more than under-secretaries.

Such an arrangement might have saved Acton's face, and indeed that of the court; but it could not possibly have worked. The

minister had never been popular and had made no effort to mix
with the local aristocracy; the fact remained, however, that he had
been virtually omnipotent in the country for a quarter of a century
and had made himself irreplaceable. Henceforth there was no guiding
hand at the helm; worse still, there was no one to control the
Queen. 'The King,' she wrote,

> is always at Belvedere. He comes here occasionally for a few minutes.
> At other times I go there, which is very trying in the awful heat
> and dust. We are entirely separated and have to write each other
> everything . . . The Prince attends the councils in his father's absence,
> and I attend them only on the King's account . . . The King dislikes
> the city and longs for solitude, as he cannot adapt or subject himself
> to the supremacy of the French and be ordered about by them or
> Bonaparte. He only sighs for Sicily, which he prefers as he has never
> been offended and insulted there. In fact he is in a state of fury
> which depresses me. He is very determined not to receive Alquier's
> credentials but to let his son represent him . . . because he declares
> he would have convulsions or a stroke, which would kill him . . .
>
> We have heard that General Acton arrived in Palermo on the
> 31st [May 1804]. He received an ovation, and the Sicilians say: 'A
> man persecuted by France must be incorruptible.'

Only after Napoleon had crowned himself Emperor on 2
December 1804 did Maria Carolina enjoy one small compensation.
Thenceforth, whenever Alquier – that ardent republican who had
voted for Louis XVI's execution – called on her, she took delight
in emphasizing his altered status, smiling sweetly as the words 'The
Emperor, *your master*' rolled trippingly off her tongue.

On 26 May 1805, in Milan Cathedral, Napoleon Bonaparte
crowned himself for the second time – on this occasion with the
Iron Crown of Lombardy, proclaiming himself King of Italy. To
Ferdinand and Maria Carolina, such an act seemed a direct threat
to their own title; weak as they were, they demanded an explan-
ation. Napoleon was predictably furious, the more so when he heard
of the recent landing of a considerable Russian force at Corfu, and
of the arrival of British reinforcements at Malta. Subsequently, when
he received the Neapolitan ambassador, the mild-mannered Prince
of Cardito, he subjected him to the sort of harangue for which he

was rapidly becoming famous, calling Maria Carolina a lesbian and condemning her as 'the worst Messalina of the age'. That British ship still riding in the bay, he declared, would not prevent her from being dethroned. When these words were reported back to her, she concluded that a French attack was imminent. She had two allies, the British and the Russians, who had promised to defend the Kingdom – the Russians going so far as to send two generals, rather surprisingly named Lacy and Oppermann, to investigate the military situation for themselves. Neither commanded much respect; the King thought them laughable, and made no attempt to conceal the fact. Lacy was Irish by birth, though he was far happier in Russian than in English, which he spoke with a heavy Irish brogue. Immensely old, he used to pull a nightcap from his pocket and go sound asleep at meetings. Oppermann was an Alsatian who never stopped complaining. It was he who took all the decisions.

With the somewhat grudging assistance of these two, the Queen – though she knew that there was little hope of repelling a full-scale invasion – was able to conclude a second agreement in September, whereby the Tsar would send a further considerable force, to be supplemented by 6,000 British troops from Malta. This agreement was perhaps not as favourable as it appeared; with St Petersburg so far distant, Naples would be at the absolute mercy of the Russians on the spot. A week or two later, however, there came encouraging news from Paris: the French troops would leave the Kingdom within a month. In return Ferdinand was strictly to maintain his neutral status, forbidding all ships of belligerent nations to enter his ports. Nor was he to appoint any French émigré, or a subject of any power hostile to France, to any military command. All that this really meant was that Napoleon believed Saint-Cyr and his men to be more useful in Lombardy than in Apulia; but at least it gained a little time.

And time was short. On 19 November the first Russian convoy sailed into the bay. Shortly afterwards, 7,000 British troops landed at Castellammare – some twenty miles to the southeast of Naples – and some 13,000 Russians and Albanians at the city itself. The Neapolitan army – such as it was – amounted to just under 10,000; but its morale was low, and its discipline poor. A last-minute recruiting campaign proved little short of disastrous, with men deliberately mutilating themselves to avoid the call-up. Maria Carolina welcomed the new arrivals, delighted that the situation was at last coming to a head; Ferdinand, for once wiser than his Queen, knew that his country was doomed. He now thought only of getting back to Sicily, consoling himself with the reflection that he had left not a single wild boar for the French. There is a story of an Albanian colonel whom he chanced to meet on his return from hunting.

'Where are you going?' asked the King.
'To Abruzzo,' the colonel replied.
'What for?'
'To enter the campaign.'
'Against whom?'
'The French, Your Majesty.'
'God help you,' muttered the King as he rode off.

On 2 December 1805, in one of the most fateful victories of his career, Napoleon's army of 68,000 triumphed over a combined force of 90,000 Austrians and Russians at Austerlitz in Moravia. On the day after Christmas, by the terms of a treaty signed at Pressburg (now Bratislava), Austria was obliged to return to France, inter alia, all the Venetian territories she had acquired in 1797 at Campo Formio – to constitute, with the coasts of Istria and Dalmatia, part of the new Napoleonic Kingdom of Italy. The Emperor had refused to admit into the treaty any stipulations on behalf of Naples; indeed, on the day it was signed he had declared his intention 'to hurl from the throne that criminal woman who has so shamelessly violated everything that is sacred among men'. In a subsequent proclamation to his army he continued: 'Shall we trust again a court without loyalty, without honour, without sense? No, no! The dynasty of Naples has ceased to reign: its existence is incompatible with the peace of Europe and the honour of my crown.'

The news of Austerlitz seems to have caused near panic in the hearts and minds of the Russians, who decided on an immediate withdrawal to Calabria. The British general, Sir James Craig, disagreed but followed their lead anyway. Maria Carolina was as furious as only she could be. She had half-expected as much from the Russians, but in the British such conduct was unforgivable:

> The smell of gunpowder sickens the feeble organs of General Craig, who therefore wishes to avoid the chance of getting even a whiff. I hope he will go and become a monk, after having dishonoured his country and made it lose all influence in the commerce of the Mediterranean, the Levant and Egypt; they will feel the effect of this step for a long time to come. I am entirely *disanglomanized*.

Then, on 10 January 1806, the allied generals changed their minds. They would not after all defend even Calabria; they would go home instead. For King Ferdinand, that was enough: how could Naples possibly stand up to an army that had defeated the Austrian Empire? On 23 January he sailed for Sicily, leaving the Queen and the Hereditary Prince to do the best they could. Little more than a fortnight later the Prince announced his own departure for Calabria, 'to co-ordinate all possible measures', and now at last Maria Carolina realized that the situation was hopeless and that she could do no more in Naples. Together with her two unmarried daughters, her daughter-in-law the Hereditary Princess, her two granddaughters and eleven members of the court, on the afternoon of 11 February she embarked on the Neapolitan frigate *Archimede* to face the winter miseries of Palermo. Even then her troubles were not over. The weather was little better than it had been on her previous journey, with Nelson and the Hamiltons. A violent storm dispersed the convoy, and twenty-six of the transport ships were driven on to the coast, where they were either captured by the French or surrendered to them. Several lost everything they possessed; all the government records fell into enemy hands. It was five dreadful days before the *Archimede*, now almost alone, dropped anchor in Palermo harbour.

The royal party had left only just in time; it was, somewhat inappropriately, St Valentine's Day when, under drenching rain, a French division under General Louis Partouneaux entered Naples. This proved to be the vanguard of an army of 40,000 under Marshal André Masséna, with the Emperor's elder brother Joseph Bonaparte as his personal representative. There was no resistance. Whereas, seven years previously, the *lazzaroni* had fought like tigers and caused appalling carnage, this time they were listless and apathetic, making no protest when Joseph staged his own procession on the following day and took up his residence in the royal palace. Six weeks later, on 30 March, Joseph was proclaimed King. What Sir Harold Acton describes as 'the dazed and doddering regency' was concerned only with preserving the peace. Having received strict instructions not to surrender its three principal castles it instantly handed over all three, together with the islands of Ischia and Procida, to ensure that the French should receive a friendly reception.

'Naples captured, everything will fall,' Napoleon wrote to Joseph. Not for the first time, however, he had underestimated his enemy. Calabria proved a very much harder nut to crack. On 1 July 1806 a British force from Palermo under General Sir John Stuart, consisting of 4,800 infantry and sixteen guns, disembarked on the west coast; three days later it attacked a French force near the village of Maida, and after a savage assault with bayonets put it to flight. The victory was welcomed with enthusiasm, not only locally but also in England, where the battlefield is still remembered in the name of Maida Vale.* There were those who complained that if Stuart had continued his march to the north 'nothing could have stopped him short of Naples', but they tended to forget that his tiny army was exhausted by heat and malaria. As it was he succeeded in indefinitely post-poning the intended French invasion of Sicily – surely achievement enough. But the achievement had to be consolidated. Sicily was now – apart from Sardinia – the only part of Italy not under French occupation, and it was obviously in the British interest to keep it that way. It was consequently put under British military protection, with some 10,000 troops distributed across the island.

Unfortunately the fall – after a heroic resistance lasting six months – of the city of Gaeta, together with Masséna's decision to concen-trate far greater forces against him, obliged Stuart to re-embark his troops in September. This meant that guerrilla warfare now took over, with the usual atrocities perpetrated on both sides. The Calabrians cherished no deep love for the Bourbons, but they vastly

---

* Until a few years ago there stood at the southern end of Maida Vale a pub named the *Hero of Maida*, with a portrait of General Stuart on its sign.

preferred them to the French invaders; besides, had not the Pope refused to recognize Joseph Bonaparte as their king? They were of peasant stock, and when the fighting began they pulled no punches.

As for Sicily, an island ruled solely by King Ferdinand and Queen Maria Carolina would probably have presented Masséna with few problems. Nelson was dead, and on their arrival in Palermo the royal family had had a far cooler reception than on their previous visit. The Sicilians by now knew their sovereign all too well, and were fully conscious of the fact that Ferdinand saw their island as nothing more than a hunting reserve and an occasional funkhole. In the Palatine Chapel he had even destroyed a number of superb twelfth-century mosaics simply to give himself more convenient access to the building. Moreover, all the principal administrative posts had been taken over by Neapolitans, and many Sicilians – including in particular the younger sons of the nobility – found themselves unemployed. In such circumstances, a French invasion might have met with little enough resistance.

But the true situation was very different. First of all, Ferdinand had invited the British to take over the defence of the island – which was just as well, as they would have done so anyway – and the Strait of Messina was now constantly patrolled by British gunboats. Secondly, the British had taken over a good deal more than Sicily's defence; in all but name they were now masters of the island itself, with more than 17,000 soldiers and some thirty civilian consuls or vice-consuls stationed across it. Sicily also enjoyed a direct subsidy from Britain, to say nothing of a number of sizable loans and a good deal of private investment; the impact on the formerly sluggish Sicilian economy can well be imagined. It brought with it a wave of extreme Anglophilia: the swells of Palermo now affected to speak the Sicilian dialect with a strong English accent.

The return of the royal family to Palermo was welcomed by one man above all: Sir John Acton. It was now well over a year since his exile to Sicily, and by the time of the Queen's arrival he had regained all his previous authority. Maria Carolina had always loathed him, and their meeting, she wrote, was 'a scene of violent recrimination and tears'. Acton, she noted, considered the Calabrian campaign a waste of time and money (although, thanks to the determination of the Queen, it was to continue indecisively for another four years); he was far more interested in saving Sicily than he was in recovering Naples. Thanks to him, the British troops had already occupied a number of forts around Messina and the northeast; he had also written to Admiral Lord Collingwood – who had succeeded Nelson as Commander-in-Chief, Mediterranean – asking him for a fleet to defend the island.

Collingwood had another, still greater, objective: to prevent the French Atlantic fleet from entering the Mediterranean at all. But he sent a remarkable substitute. Rear-Admiral Sir Sidney Smith put new life into the Sicilian court. He already boasted a splendid war record, having given Napoleon a hard time during the siege of Acre in 1799, when he had anchored his ships in shallow water alongside the coast and used them to fire broadsides into the French camp. Energetic, exuberant and extremely noisy, he found instant favour with the Queen, who thought she had found another Nelson. 'Schmidt', as she invariably called him, was determined not to disappoint her. On 11 May he sailed into the Bay of Naples. Obviously he had no wish to bombard the city; but he captured Capri and, a short while afterwards, the island of Ponza – which was soon to become a hotbed of royalist conspiracy and intrigue. He also delighted the Queen by dropping guerrilla leaders secretly along the Calabrian coast with proc- lamations inciting revolt against the French, and by sending arms and provisions to Gaeta, which was still heroically holding out. On 28 June she invested him with supreme authority over all Neapolitan–Sicilian forces on land and sea; accepting the commis- sion, Smith promised her that he would now 'dare to do more than Bonaparte would venture to imagine'.

It was perhaps inevitable that Sir Sidney would prove somewhat less popular among his English colleagues. The June investiture, which was performed without any consultation with Sir John Stuart, not surprisingly threw Stuart into a fury. Fortunately for all concerned he was almost immediately transferred, to be succeeded by General Henry Fox who – already a sick man – left most of the decisions to be taken by his second-in-command and eventual successor, Sir

John Moore. But Moore found Smith every bit as irritating as had Stuart; worse, he believed him to be doing irreparable harm by

> his interference in Calabria, where in his imagination he is directing the operations of armies, but where in reality he is only encouraging murder and rapine, and keeping up amongst that unhappy people, whom we have no intention to support, a spirit of revolt which will bring upon them the more severe vengeance of the French government. As long as Sir Sidney had money, he distributed it profusely; and now, with as little judgement, he is distributing arms, ammunition and provisions . . .

All the chroniclers agree that the Calabrians needed no encouragement from Sir Sidney. Even without his interference the campaign was still more nightmarish than such campaigns normally are, with unspeakable atrocities on both sides followed by hideous reprisals; in the piazza of the little town of Cassano, to take but a single example, fifty-two Italians were shot by their own compatriots. Most, however, were firmly against the French. They were primitive, passionate and God-fearing; and the Pope's refusal to recognize Joseph Bonaparte as King was enough to make up their minds. Joseph's subsequent suppression of all the monasteries and convents in the region confirmed them still further.

Sir Sidney's recall in January 1807 came as an immense relief to virtually all his compatriots in Sicily. Now it was only the Queen who longed for action. This was the moment, she believed, for a full-scale attack on Naples. All her advisers, British and Sicilian, tried to persuade her – in the politest possible terms – that she was wrong, but she refused to listen. As Hugh Elliot had pointed out, 'Her Sicilian Majesty . . . with great susceptibility of temper, of a lively, imaginative and active enterprising spirit, does not, or perhaps does not choose to, see the difficulties which oppose the attainment of any favourite object.' Eventually, owing entirely to her determination, a force of some 4,000 men under General Prince Louis of Hesse-Philippsthal – hero of the recent siege of Gaeta – crossed the Strait of Messina and began their advance through Calabria; almost at once, however, the expedition ended in disaster. In the course of a single brief engagement near Mileto the Prince lost

1,633 men and six pieces of artillery. Maria Carolina took the news tragically – as she always did – but refused to see that the fiasco was in any way her fault. Her ardour remained undimmed.

In July 1807 Sir Arthur Paget called briefly at Palermo on his way to his new posting at Constantinople. He had hoped to avoid the Queen, but she had had prior word of his arrival and summoned him at once to the palace. She harangued him for two hours, complaining about the English in general and Sir John Moore in particular. 'Upon the whole,' he wrote afterwards,

> next to possessing the island, Bonaparte himself could hardly wish the situation of affairs in it to be different . . . it appeared to be the decided opinion of both Generals Fox and Moore that no faith whatever is to be placed in the Sicilian government, administered as it now is, and so long as the Queen directs its Councils, and that the Sicilian army, if it is so to be called, is in so wretched a state, that no useful co-operation is under the present circumstances reasonably to be expected from it.

Maria Carolina had also been profoundly shaken by the Treaty of Tilsit, which Napoleon and Tsar Alexander I had signed in July 1807 on a raft in the middle of the Neman River. The Tsar, her former ally, had agreed to recognize Joseph Bonaparte as King of Naples; 'I await my death warrant,' she wrote. She was, however, still recovering from a far greater blow: the death two months before of her eldest daughter, Maria Teresa, wife of the Austrian Emperor.* When the Emperor married again only eight months later – having compounded his sin by his own recognition of Joseph Bonaparte – the last emotional ties with his former mother-in-law were broken; henceforth the two corresponded as little as possible, and then in the most formal terms.

The Treaty of Tilsit had, at least for the moment, settled the future of eastern Europe. Napoleon was now able to look west, to the Iberian peninsula. Portugal had been quickly dealt with; in the autumn of 1807, when the Portuguese had refused to close their ports to British shipping, he had sent in an army of 30,000. The Portuguese royal family had instantly fled to Brazil, leaving the French in possession of the country. Much of the invading army

---

* She had been named after her maternal grandmother, the Empress Maria Theresa.

had then moved into northern Spain, while the Emperor despatched his brother-in-law Joachim Murat to occupy Madrid and to bring the Spanish King Charles IV and his son Fernando* to meet him at Bayonne. There, on 5 May 1808, Charles and Fernando simultaneously abdicated their rights to the throne, Napoleon promising in exchange that Spain should remain Roman Catholic and independent, under a ruler whom he would shortly name. Soon afterwards, he did so; and the name was that of his brother Joseph.

Joseph had started well enough in Naples; on his brother's orders he had initiated a programme of dismantling the vast feudal estates and had done his best to regularize the financial, educational and judicial systems. But he had never been happy there, and when Napoleon offered him the crown of Spain he was only too glad to accept. Alas, his new reign was doomed before it had even begun. On 2 May, even before the joint abdication of their monarchs, the people of Madrid had risen against the invaders.† The rising was quickly and brutally suppressed, but other provincial insurrections sprang up all over Spain, whose people as always demonstrated their superb capacity for guerrilla warfare. On 23 July the French general Pierre Dupont was obliged to surrender with his entire army. The rebels now advanced on Madrid and expelled Joseph a few weeks later.

On the Emperor's orders Joachim Murat was to replace Joseph on the throne of Naples. Murat had hoped to be given Spain for himself; failing that he would have been quite happy with Poland or Westphalia. Naples, he felt, was hardly worthy of him, and his wife, Caroline – Napoleon's sister – felt much the same; the Neapolitan crown, she claimed, was too small for her head. As a result they decided to spend the heat of summer in the Pyrenees; only in September did they formally take over their new kingdom. Meanwhile in June there had landed at Messina the future 'King of the French', Louis-Philippe, Duke of Orléans, as suitor for the

---

* There are too many Ferdinands. To avoid confusion, let us stick to the Spanish version of his name.

† Goya's great painting *The Third of May* and his subsequent series of prints known as *The Disasters of War* illustrate this rebellion.

hand of Princess Maria Amalia, now twenty-eight and the last of the Queen's daughters to remain unmarried.* As the son of 'Philippe-Egalité' – who had wholeheartedly espoused the revolution before he too ended up on the guillotine – he was desperately trying to redeem himself; marriage with a Bourbon was just what he wanted. Many years later he remembered:

> Admiral Collingwood . . . was careful to warn me: 'If you go to Palermo, God preserve you from Queen Caroline! She is certainly the wickedest woman He has ever created.' It is true that she was no angel, but personally I was well pleased with her . . . As soon as my arrival was announced, she waited for me on the palace steps, and when I introduced myself to her she took my hand and, without a word, led me to her apartment. There, in a window embrasure, she held my head between her hands and gazed at me awhile without speaking. 'I ought to hate you,' she said at last, 'as you have fought against us: in spite of that I have a liking for you. You came here to marry my daughter; well, I shall not hinder you, but tell me frankly what part you took in the French Revolution. I forgive you everything in advance, on condition I know everything.'

The Prince apparently did exactly what he was told. In 1791, at the age of eighteen, he had in fact fought with extreme bravery against the Austrians and Prussians; but with the coming of the Reign of Terror he had wisely decided to leave. He had spent the next fifteen years in exile. True to her word, Maria Carolina gave her blessing to the marriage, which took place in the unlikely setting of the King's bedroom, to which Ferdinand had been confined since falling downstairs some weeks before; the ceremony was repeated, however, a day or two later in all the splendour of the Palatine Chapel. 'Naughty Amalia has married the Duke of Orleans,' wrote Maria Carolina. 'They have nothing to live on, are poor but happy and love each other infinitely.' They did indeed; the marriage was to prove an enduringly happy one, producing ten children, and

---

* The last but one, Princess Maria Cristina, had married Duke Charles Felix, brother and heir of the King of Sardinia, the previous year. Harold Acton claims that they 'spent more time on their knees in chapels and churches than in the bridal chamber'. Certainly they produced no issue after forty-two years of marriage.

in 1830 Maria Amalia, as her husband's consort, was to become Queen of the French. By that time her mother was long dead – but how happy she would have been.

After the arrival on 6 September 1808 of 'Joachim Napoleon, by the grace of God and by the Constitution of the State, King of the Two Sicilies, Grand Admiral of the Empire' Naples became uncomfortably like Ruritania. With the superb uniforms that he designed himself, his flamboyance, his swagger and his sheer panache, Murat's new subjects found him hard indeed to resist. His initial reluctance was quickly overcome, and he flung himself heart and soul into the task of dragging Naples into the nineteenth century, replacing its old, somewhat slap-happy laws with the rigours of the *Code Napoléon*. His wife, Napoleon's youngest sister Caroline, was perhaps in the circumstances a little unfortunately named; but, like her namesake in Palermo, she was immensely energetic, highly ambitious and determined to rule.

The island of Capri is not normally seen as a blot on the landscape. To Joachim and Caroline, however, that is exactly what it was. Still held by the Bourbons, it seemed confident of remaining so; such at least was the apparent conviction of the commander of its garrison, Hudson Lowe – later to be Napoleon's gaoler on St Helena – who on arrival had ordered 'four dozen champagne, three dozen burgundy of three years old, three dozen burgundy of four years old, six dozen of the best wines such as Frontignan, and any others which may be held in good estimation'. Alas, he was never to enjoy them. Early in October 1808 the French attacked at Anacapri. Lowe, whose garrison consisted exclusively of Corsicans and Maltese, managed to hold out for two long weeks, daily expecting the appearance of HMS *Ambuscade* or some other naval vessel; but none came, and on the 16th, his provisions – if not his cellar – exhausted, he was obliged to surrender.

The capture of Capri made no real difference to the political situation, except to enable Murat to celebrate it as only he could,*

---

* Much to Napoleon's irritation, he actually rode in state to the cathedral to pay homage to the patron saint, S. Gennaro.

and still further to increase Maria Carolina's mounting fury with the British. Nothing would shake her firm conviction that Naples was a powder keg about to explode. 'I do not think,' she wrote in April 1809, 'that the recovery of Naples will be difficult . . . The whole of Italy is ready to unite, to expel the oppressors.' Just how wrong she was became clear two months later, when a small British fleet led by an extremely reluctant Sir John Stuart sailed into the bay and the Neapolitans showed not the faintest sign of insurrection. In one of the smallest naval battles in history – it featured one British frigate and one French – the British vessel came off worse; and the two islands of Ischia and Procida, which had been briefly captured, were now hastily evacuated. The sad little expedition then returned to Sicily.

13

The End of the Murats

$\sim$

MARIA CAROLINA BECAME extremely fond of her new son-in-law. He was intelligent and energetic, in marked contrast to the curiously colourless Hereditary Prince – among whose chief interests sex had by now given place to dairy farming – and he proved invaluable in smoothing relations between her and the Sicilian barons, whom she instinctively mistrusted. He even managed to persuade her to bring a few of the local nobility into the government. But with increasing age – in 1810 she was fifty-eight – she was becoming ever more autocratic and suspicious of those around her. She herself made no attempt to conceal the fact that she considered Sicily a mere staging post, to be endured only while Naples remained in enemy hands; on the other hand, she knew perfectly well that her old allies the British had now lost interest in recovering her lost capital; all they wanted was to preserve Sicilian independence – which meant effectively running the island themselves. She could not accept the fact that they were her only ally, with whom good relations were of paramount importance.

As for her original countrymen the Austrians, she despaired of them. By the Peace of Schönbrunn which they had signed in October 1809, they had recognized all Napoleon's conquests, an action which in her view 'had destroyed the House of Austria'. But worse was to come. Only five months later, Napoleon married her eldest granddaughter, the Archduchess Marie Louise. 'I have said goodbye for ever,' she wrote, 'to my native land, which I have loved so deeply. If the tyrant and his concubine (for she is only that) meet with the fate of tyrants, what will be left for the Emperor's other children but the infamy of this alliance?' Her horror was incontestably genuine; but it would have been characteristic of her, after the initial shock was over, to try and use the marriage for her own ends, and – not for the first time – to attempt, through her granddaughter, secret communications with Napoleon. Such overtures were indeed widely suspected, and not only by the British; they were fully shared by Joachim Murat in Naples, who had consistently opposed the marriage since he believed that it might prevent his invasion of Sicily, preparations for which were already well under way. He reported the 'rumours' to his master, who – to his intense irritation – refused either to confirm or deny them.

In fact, as things turned out, the projected invasion proved a fiasco. This was in no way due to the machinations of Maria Carolina; the real reason was that Napoleon himself was only luke-warm, fearing that a French army in Sicily might find itself held there by the British fleet – which was, since Trafalgar, many times stronger than the French. It was even rumoured that General Paul Grenier, Murat's chief of staff who commanded two divisions in Calabria, had received strict orders – from Paris rather than Naples – on no account to cross the Strait. For this reason, when a single division of 3,000 Neapolitans and Corsicans landed just south of Messina on 18 September 1810 it received no help from the main-land and hastily re-embarked, leaving 800 Corsicans behind. Napoleon – whose fault this largely seems to have been – was furious, and blamed his brother-in-law; Murat tried, unsuccessfully, to defend himself; and by the end of the year relations between the two were not far off breaking point.

Much the same was true of those between the Queen and the Sicilian barons. They were all too well aware of the contempt in which she held their island. Already on 28 July they had approached the British ambassador in Palermo, Lord Amherst, seeking his help in obtaining for Sicily a constitution 'as nearly similar as possible to that of Great Britain'. Their own constitution would have sufficed, they pointed out, if it had been properly adhered to; but – as Amherst wrote to the Foreign Secretary, Lord Wellesley –

> they complain that the King has already been guilty of gross viola-
> tions of the institutions under which he holds his crown, and that
> they have no security against a tyranny wholly repugnant to the

original freedom enjoyed by the inhabitants of Sicily. They announce their intention of urging their demands on the King by the legal organ of his Parliament; but they foresee an opposition on the part of their sovereign which nothing will overcome but the interposition of England; and which, if England refuses to interfere, will drive them into rebellion, and perhaps ultimately into the arms of France.

Since he himself had determined to resign, he ended by recommending to Wellesley that his successor should be empowered to control the influence of the Queen, to demand that the Neapolitan army should be put under the command of a British general and to insist that the Sicilian government should be administered by Sicilians.

At this point it becomes hard to believe that Maria Carolina was still completely sane. Both the Duke of Orleans and Maria Amalia pleaded with her to be more moderate and not to condemn as Jacobins all those who dared disagree with her, but as always she refused to listen. In July 1811 five of the leading barons, including their principal spokesman the Prince of Belmonte, were arrested and deported to various small islands 'for preparing to disturb the public peace'. Louis-Philippe was summoned to the palace but, fearing to suffer a similar fate, refused to go. His horse stood ready saddled in case he had to take refuge in the country, though this fortunately proved unnecessary.

But now at last the Queen met her match. Lord William Bentinck had arrived in Palermo four days after the arrest of the barons, as both ambassador to the Sicilian court and commander-in-chief of the British forces on the island. The son of that third Duke of Portland who was twice Prime Minister, he had been Governor of Madras at twenty-nine and had then returned to Europe to fight in the Peninsular War, having been promoted to the rank of Lieutenant-General at thirty-four after the Battle of Corunna. He was now thirty-six. He had been thoroughly briefed by Amherst and others, and – determined not to take any nonsense from Maria Carolina – he began as he meant to continue. But even he seems to have been surprised by the strength of her opposition to everything he proposed. Within a month of his arrival he had returned to London to obtain yet wider powers.

On 16 September, while he was still away, the Queen suffered an apoplectic stroke.* Any other woman of her age would have sought peace and quiet for a gentle convalescence; she, as soon as she was able, was back at her desk, plunged once more into the fray. She was desperately weak, befuddled by opium and no longer able to face Bentinck – who returned on 7 December – with quite the energy that she had formerly shown; but her determination was undiminished, and he decided to waste no more time. He now spelt out his demands, making it clear that the annual subsidy being paid by the British would be suspended until all of them were satisfied. First and most important was the supreme command of Neapolitan–Sicilian forces, which he himself proposed to assume; among the rest were the return of Belmonte and his colleagues from exile and the formation of a new ministry under the Prince of Cassaro. Neither the King nor the Queen were to be involved in the administration. Should there be any objections, Bentinck declared that he would not hesitate to ship off both of them – and if necessary the Hereditary Prince as well – to Malta, putting the Prince's two-year-old son on the throne under the Regency of the Duke of Orleans. Fortunately, this last threat had its effect; but Bentinck had already sent orders to the British detachments in Messina, Milazzo and Trapani to march on Palermo when, on 16 January 1812, the King formally transferred his authority to his son.

The new ruler was far from ideal. He was neat, methodical and bureaucratic, a conscientious husband and father, and would doubtless have made a moderately competent manager of a local bank; but of political understanding, let alone of courage or charisma, he possessed not a shred. His instinctive caution, timidity and 'littleness of mind' frequently drove Bentinck to distraction; but – at least for the moment – he served his purpose.

One of the first actions of the Prince Vicar – as the Hereditary Prince was now called, since he was standing in for his father – was to recall the exiled barons, three of whom were immediately

---

* The story was that, when an emetic failed to work, she had drunk twenty-four glasses of water.

appointed to serve in the new government, the Prince of Belmonte as Minister of Foreign Affairs. The most important task before them, as Bentinck emphasized, was to draft the new constitution, based on the British model and abolishing the feudalism that had for so long been the bane of Sicilian life. The next was to get rid of the Queen. Her health was now rapidly deteriorating, but she was intriguing with all her old determination against the new ministry. She was also developing persecution mania. 'The French government murdered my sister,' she said to the British consul, Robert Fagan, 'and I am convinced that your government intends to do the same to me – probably in England.' Perhaps for this reason, she was fighting like a tiger to remain in Palermo, and her husband and son took her side – not because they did not deplore her behaviour as much as anyone but simply because they had always deferred to her and found the habit difficult, if not impossible, to break.

At one moment Bentinck decided to request an audience with Ferdinand, in the hope of persuading him to reason with his wife and to explain to her the harm she was doing; he was simply refused an audience. The only channel of communication open to him was through the royal confessor, Father Caccamo, who was happy to reveal Ferdinand's true feelings about his wife. His Majesty was, he said, forever writing to her '*andate via, andate via!*'* and had described his marriage of forty-four years as a 'martyrdom'. But, as he put it, 'he had not the heart or the courage to force his wife out of the island.' His son the Prince Vicar felt much the same way.

Not that the Prince's relations with his mother were in any way friendly; rather the reverse. She had never forgiven him for accepting the Regency; she had called him a revolutionary and a traitor; and when on the evening of 26 September 1812 he fell suddenly and seriously ill, her first reaction – before worrying about his health – was that he must immediately resign. The symptoms, as Bentinck reported to the British Foreign Minister Lord Castlereagh, were suggestive of poison, and 'general suspicion was fixed on the Queen' – a suspicion fully shared by the Prince himself. When Bentinck

* 'Go away, go away!'

suggested to his doctor that the illness might be due to the unwonted heat, the patient, trembling with fever, cried out, '*Ce n'est pas la chaleur, c'est ma mère, ma mère!*'* It turned out not to have been deliberate poisoning after all, but the Prince never altogether recovered; his illness left him prematurely aged – bent, grey-faced and shuffling.

Meanwhile, in July 1812, the new constitution had been drafted and duly promulgated. Its fifteen articles granted the people of Sicily an autonomy that they had never before enjoyed. Executive and legislative powers were rigidly separated, and the feudal practices that had been observed for some seven hundred years were finally abolished. All this proved, however, surprisingly good news for the Bourbons, at least in Naples. There was increasing anti-French feeling in the city, where Murat was effectively a dictator, while Ferdinand – hard as it may be to believe – was seen as an enlightened constitutional monarch. In the country, by contrast, the constitution was a good deal less popular; the people seemed simply unable to take it in. Many of the barons, too, who had actually voted for it were horrified to find their former powers and privileges gone for ever.

On 5 January 1813 Maria Carolina made one last desperate attempt to save the monarchy as she saw it. Secretly joining her husband at his hunting lodge near Ficuzza, she urged him to annul the new constitution, 'an unwieldy machine which deprived him of his authority', and to take up once again the reins of government. He was, as always, putty in her hands, and when he returned to Palermo on 6 February he had made up his mind to do so. His subjects were delighted. We read that despite heavy rain more than a hundred carriages went to meet him three miles outside the city, and that a vast crowd was waiting to acclaim him in the palace square. On 9 March he announced his intention of resuming the government of Sicily, and after the next morning's thanksgiving service the crowd tried to unharness the horses and pull his carriage themselves. His idleness and interminable absences had clearly done nothing to diminish his people's love for him.

But such love was no longer enough. In Bentinck's eyes, Sicily

---

* 'It's not the heat, it's my mother, my mother!'

was now rapidly declining into chaos. When he called on the King two days later, diplomatic etiquette and even common politeness were forgotten. Angrily, he informed Ferdinand that he now considered him just as much an enemy of England as was the Queen. 'Your Majesty,' he thundered, 'will repent of his conduct.' The King, who hated rows and was always deeply upset by them, developed a violent headache and went to his room to lie down; at this point, however, the Governor of Palermo burst in on him with alarming news: 8,000 British troops had entered the city and now controlled all the main strategic points. Meanwhile the barons, understandably furious at Ferdinand's volte-face, were also threatening to rise in rebellion unless the Queen left Sicily and the King swore to uphold the constitution in every detail.

By now Ferdinand was at the end of his tether. On 16 March he had a long conversation with the Duke of Orleans. Louis-Philippe too refused to pull his punches. He reminded his father-in-law that with Bentinck in his present mood he was in imminent personal danger. If he allowed the present situation to lapse into war, all his treaties with England would be rendered null and void; the only laws observed would be the laws of war, and Sicily would be treated like any other conquered territory. The King protested that he had no illusions. The crisis had had a disastrous effect on his health; he could neither eat nor sleep. 'Perhaps Lord William is about to arrive with his troops, to plant guns in the square and fire grapeshot at my windows. Oh Jesus, Mary! I want none of his cannonades, you know – I want none of them at all.'

The following day he surrendered. In a letter to his son he restored the Vicariate and promised to take no more independent action without British consent. There remained the Queen. She had retired to Castelvetrano in the far west of the island where, it need hardly be said, she was plotting an insurrection. But Bentinck had had enough. He sent his second-in-command, General Robert Macfarlane, to Castelvetrano with 5,000 men. Maria Carolina received the general with her usual tirade, referring to Bentinck as *'quella bestia feroce'*.* Macfarlane was not unimpressed, and later

---

* 'That furious beast'.

remarked that she was terrible in her rage; but she was beaten and she knew it. She wrote Bentinck a proud and passionate letter, telling him that she had decided to yield only for the sake of her husband and family and demanding generous financial concessions amounting to one million pounds sterling. Then, at long last, she started making preparations for her departure.

She had already written some months before to her son-in-law the Austrian Emperor, seeking his permission to return to Vienna. The request had been unwelcome – Prince Metternich, the Foreign Minister, had violently opposed it, on the undeniable grounds that she was a compulsive intriguer who would only cause mischief – but the Emperor, while agreeing with him, simply did not feel that he could refuse. The Queen accordingly planned to travel, with her son Prince Leopold, first to Constantinople on board HMS *Unity*, which Bentinck had arranged to be put at her disposal, together with two ships of the line as protection against the Algerian pirates who infested the central Mediterranean. The squadron set sail from Mazara on 14 June. It put in for two weeks at the Ionian island of Zante (Zakynthos) and eventually reached Constantinople on 13 September. There the Queen chartered a merchant ship for Odessa, where she was held up by quarantine for two more months.

Her journey had already been long and frustrating enough; but the worst was still to come. In the early nineteenth century eastern Europe boasted few inns, and certainly none suitable for a queen and her retinue. Fortunately the Polish aristocracy was available to make good the deficit for much of the way; later, however, the royal coach broke an axle and overturned, and repairs were still in progress when the weather suddenly deteriorated. An hour or two later the land was in the grip of a blizzard. Shelter was eventually found in a peasant hovel. 'Only the Queen,' wrote an eyewitness, 'displayed serenity and good humour; she joked about the accident and . . . caressed the children of the household, asking their parents through an interpreter a few benevolent questions.'

She reached Vienna on 2 February 1814. Metternich had ordered her to remain at least six miles away from the court, but she ignored him. 'Let us see,' she said, 'if they will drive the last daughter of Maria Theresa from Schönbrunn.' They did not, and she and Leopold settled at Hetzendorf, only two and a half miles from the palace. This did not however imply any improved relations with her son-in-law the Emperor. Bored to tears by her constant complaining and her bottomless self-pity, he avoided her as much as humanly possible – not that she herself had any desire to see the man who had recognized Murat on the throne of Naples and given his pledge to keep him there. When her granddaughter Marie Louise returned to Vienna in May – having refused to accompany her husband to Elba – she at first gave her a chilly reception, not because she had married Napoleon but because she had deserted him. She was well aware of the lengths to which the girl's father had gone in order to persuade her to do so; she nevertheless gave it as her opinion that Marie Louise should have returned to her husband, if necessary by tying her sheets together and escaping in disguise. 'That,' she said, 'is what I would have done in her place. When one is married it is for life.'

Having effectively dealt with both the King and the Queen and given Sicily its admirable new constitution, Bentinck – who never forgot that he was also a soldier – decided to obey a recent summons to go and join Wellington's army in Catalonia. His brief campaign there was not a success; it certainly did nothing to enhance his military reputation. On 12 September 1813 he was soundly defeated by an army under Napoleon's Marshal Suchet, and was soon afterwards obliged to resign his command and return to Sicily, where he arrived on 3 October. He soon realized that he should never have left. As he wrote to Castlereagh,

> I am convinced that such is the weakness of the Hereditary Prince, and such will be the incapacity of any set of men who may be placed at the head of the government; such also the silly and depraved character of the people, that it will be impossible for the British political authority ever to absent himself.

He found the island once again in chaos. There were, for a start, violent arguments about the constitution, the full text of which had not yet been published. Belmonte, whom he had once described as 'the main hope of his country', had broken with his uncle and erstwhile colleague the Prince of Castelnuovo and caused a great rift which had split their party in two. In parliament, meanwhile, hamfisted attempts to control prices were arousing such storms of protest as to lead to riots in Palermo and elsewhere. Fortunately the resident British troops were able to restore order; two of the ringleaders were hanged. To make matters worse, the plague had broken out in Malta and dark rumours were being spread that the British intended deliberately to introduce it into Sicily.

Bentinck saw that he had no choice but to resume dictatorial powers. He held no brief for despotism, he announced, but it was preferable to anarchy. He prorogued parliament, which the Prince Vicar obediently dissolved, formed a new ministry and issued a proclamation that all 'disturbers of the public peace, assassins and other foes of the Constitution' would be summarily punished by martial law. He then set out on an extended tour of the island – his first – visiting all the larger cities and towns and explaining the immense benefits that the constitution would bring in its train. Finally he crossed to the mainland, the better to consider the problem of Joachim Murat.

Murat had had some difficult decisions to make. After his defeat at Leipzig on 16 October 1813 Napoleon was clearly a spent force; if Murat wished to cling on to his kingdom – which he did, very much – he would need a new ally; and he was in little doubt as to who this ally would be. He was delighted when, towards the end of the year, Prince Metternich sent an ambassador, General Count Neipperg, to discuss the future with him and, if possible, to negotiate a treaty. The incentive he offered was tempting indeed: if Murat were now to join the allies, Austria would not only guarantee his throne; it would support his claim to extend his Italian kingdom. The only person who might have been expected to oppose this plan was his wife, Queen Caroline; she was after all Napoleon's sister. On the other hand, she had also been Metternich's mistress and was well aware on which side her bread was buttered. She gave her enthusiastic support, and on 11 January 1814 a treaty was duly signed. In a secret clause Murat renounced all claim to Sicily, while Austria promised to do her best to persuade King Ferdinand similarly to renounce his claim to Naples.

Whether it was because he loathed the idea of an Austrian presence in Italy or whether he simply despised Murat for his disloyalty, Bentinck made no secret of his contempt for the agreement. It was lamentable, he wrote, 'to see such advantages given to a man whose whole life had been a crime, who had been the active accomplice of Bonaparte for years, and who now deserted his benefactor through his own ambition and under the pressure of necessity'. But Castlereagh ordered him to negotiate an armistice between Sicily and Naples, and he had no course but to comply – though he was careful to avoid any formula which might be taken as recognition of Joachim Murat as King. In fact Murat probably cared little whether he did so or not; his sights were by now set a good deal higher – to make himself ruler of the entire Italian peninsula. As he marched north with his army to join the other allies, he and his soldiers scattered leaflets in all the villages through which they passed, calling on the Italian people to rally to his flag. Meanwhile Queen Caroline, who had remained behind as Regent, showed herself considerably more anti-French than her husband. He was already carefully avoiding any active engagements with the French army; she, on the other hand, expelled all French officials from the Kingdom and closed Neapolitan ports to all French shipping.

At this point Bentinck seriously forgot himself. Abandoning every pretence of diplomacy, he decided to support the cause of Italian independence, landed with a considerable Anglo-Sicilian force at Livorno and there delivered a proclamation urging all Italians to vindicate their rights to be free. On 15 March he actually confronted Murat at Reggio Emilia. If, he threatened, Murat did not instantly withdraw his troops from Tuscany, he – Bentinck – would drive them out himself, restore the legitimate Grand Duke Ferdinand III and invade Naples under the Bourbon flag. Leaving Murat no time to answer, he marched his army up the coast to Genoa, where the French garrison immediately surrendered. According to his own account, he restored the old republic; according to the Genoese, they did so themselves; in any event, another corner of the Napoleonic empire crumbled away.

By now things were moving quickly. On 31 March the Allies entered Paris; 2 April saw the *Acte de déchéance de l'Empereur*, which declared Napoleon deposed. On that same day he abdicated in favour of his infant son, with Marie Louise as Regent; this, however, the Allies refused to accept; an unconditional abdication followed two days later. On 23 April Maria Amalia wrote in her diary:

> My husband suddenly came into my room shouting 'Bonaparte is finished. Louis XVIII has been restored, and I am leaving on this ship which has come to fetch me.' I fell senseless in his arms.

Louis-Philippe then hurried on to tell his father-in-law. Ferdinand burst into tears of joy and gratitude. Already he began to feel that he was back in Naples. It was Belmonte who had suggested that with the fall of Napoleon there was no longer any reason why the King should not return to the throne. Aware that only the year before he had promised not to do so without British consent, Ferdinand made great play of asking Bentinck's permission. Bentinck personally absolved him from his promise and on 4 July he returned to his capital, as always amid cheering crowds. Lord William Bentinck was not among them. His conduct in recent months had not gone unnoticed by the British government. Just twelve days later he left Sicily for ever.

Maria Carolina was naturally overjoyed when she heard of her husband's triumph. Despite the horrors of her journey to Vienna, she now determined to hurry back to Sicily to share it; it was arranged that a ship should sail at once for Trieste to fetch her. It sailed, however, in vain. Just before midnight on 7 September 1814, her maid thought she heard a summons and went to her room. She found her mistress unconscious, her hand reaching out for the bell-cord. It was another stroke, and this time it was fatal. She was sixty-two.

The reactions to the Queen's death in Vienna and in Palermo make an interesting contrast. In Vienna, the great Congress was already in progress; there were balls almost every night. The court mourned, but no one else did. The French Foreign Minister Talleyrand* wrote to Louis XVIII: 'The Queen of Naples is scarcely

---

* Charles-Maurice de Talleyrand-Périgord, by now sixty, had had an astonishing

regretted. Her death seems to have put M. de Metternich more at ease.' In Palermo, on the other hand, all the theatres were closed for a month and official mourning continued for six. Requiem Masses were held in every church in the city. In Naples the Murats actually suspended an official reception when the news arrived. King Ferdinand himself set a less edifying example. On 27 November, at the age of sixty-three – less than three months after his wife's death – he married his longtime mistress, the forty-four-year-old Princess of Partanna, who now became, in the incomprehensible Sicilian fashion, Duchess of Floridia. Despite the seven children she had borne to her late husband, she was rumoured in Palermo to have distributed her favours unusually widely; the Hereditary Prince in particular had made no secret of his disapproval, earning his father's famous rejoinder, '*Penza a Mammeta, figlio mio, penza a Mammeta!*'* But she was a welcome change after Maria Carolina, always smiling and cheerful, taking absolutely no interest in politics and keeping Ferdinand – as everyone could see – blissfully happy.

There was a bad moment for almost everyone – including those attending the Congress of Vienna – at the end of February 1815, when Napoleon escaped from Elba, gathered an army largely composed of Louis XVIII's forces that had been sent to stop him, and marched triumphantly on Paris. A principal exception was Joachim Murat, who rallied at once to his old chief and saw (or thought he saw) his opportunity of creating a united Italy – with himself, it need hardly be said, at its head. With an army of some 40,000 he advanced on Milan, once again calling on all patriotic Italians to rally to his flag. Alas for him, there was no response. The people had had enough of fighting. One or two of them

career. Having first entered the Church, he had risen to the rank of bishop. Later he had represented his government in London, working hard in the cause of Anglo-French relations; but after the execution of Louis XVI and Marie Antoinette he had sought refuge in America, where he had remained for two years. Returning to Paris, he was appointed Foreign Minister under the Directory, and soon became Napoleon's principal adviser on foreign policy; eventually, however, disgusted by the Emperor's insatiable ambition, he began secretly to plan for a Bourbon restoration. With the accession of Louis XVIII in 1814, he found himself once again Foreign Minister.

* 'Think of your Mama, my boy, think of your Mama!'

gave him a friendly wave, but that was all. The Austrians at first retired before him, having too few troops in the area; but by April they were once again on the offensive and on 3 May, at Tolentino in the Marches, they met Murat in pitched battle. He fought – as he always did – with exemplary courage; but he was hopelessly outnumbered, and having lost 4,000 men and all his artillery had no option but to withdraw. A fortnight later he returned, exhausted, to Naples.

His wife, Caroline, had held the city together as best she could. Like him, she had never lacked courage. An Anglo-Sicilian fleet under Commodore Sir George Campbell was anchored in the bay, continually threatening bombardment, while the *lazzaroni* of the city were becoming increasingly restive, longing as they were for the return of a king who spoke their language and was, in their eyes, one of them. Caroline, however, had refused to leave, driving daily through the streets to show that she was still in confident control. In fact, she knew as well as her husband that their great adventure was over. All that they could hope for now was a settle-ment with the Allies that would allow them to keep what was left of their dignity. This was signed at Casalanza, near Capua, on 20 May. It provided for the return to the throne of Naples of King Ferdinand, who pardoned his former enemies, military and political, resuming his reign with a completely clean sheet.

Murat was not one of the signatories. He had removed his splendid uniform and, in modest civilian clothes and accompanied only by a few officers and his valet, had ridden out of the city on the previous day. By then his wife, with her four children and two English governesses, had embarked with Commodore Campbell in HMS *Tremendous*, en route to Trieste. According to one of the governesses, Miss Catherine Davies, she had been 'allowed to take whatever she thought proper from the palace with her'. This included 'a favourite cow with one horn, named Caroline after herself, that she might have milk for the children during the voyage'. The former Queen had one further humiliation to suffer before she was free of Neapolitan waters: she passed King Ferdinand's ship as it was about to enter the bay. Campbell made no attempt to conceal it from her, and explained that he must fire a twenty-one-gun salute as His Majesty went by – 'a piece of ceremony,' she later commented, 'that we could very well have dispensed with'.

Meanwhile, all Naples was *en fête*. Prince Leopold arrived on the 22nd from Vienna; when he went to give thanks to the city's patron saint, S. Gennaro – whose blood predictably liquefied, dead on time – the assembled crowds were astonished at the simplicity of his dress, accustomed as they were to the comic-opera splendour of Murat's uniforms. Their astonishment was fully shared by the court when they saw the utter transformation that the royal palace had undergone at the hands of Queen Caroline, filled as it now was with furniture and pictures which she had brought from the Elysée Palace in Paris and which she had nonchalantly left behind.*

On 7 June Ferdinand landed at Portici, having weathered a severe storm which he jokingly attributed to Caroline. He was as over-excited as a child, laughing and crying by turns and vowing to build a great new church to be dedicated to St Francis of Paola, who had spread his cloak over the sea and, using it as a sail, had miraculously crossed the Strait from Calabria to Sicily.† His formal entry into Naples was equally emotional, as the huge crowds waved and cheered and the tears poured down his cheeks. His simplicity and his obvious happiness impressed them far more than all Joachim Murat's finery; here again, at long last, was their rightful king whom they had known and loved for well over half a century. Less than a fortnight later, on the 19th, his appearance in the royal box at the specially decorated and illuminated San Carlo Opera was the scene of a still more magnificent ovation.

The rejoicing would have been more enthusiastic still had anyone yet been aware of what had happened on the previous day. Napoleon Bonaparte had been defeated at Waterloo. Only one unpleasant Napoleonic shadow still remained: Murat, who had fled to Corsica. Early in October he landed in Calabria, at the little seaport of

* Prince Leopold is said to have exclaimed to the King, 'Oh my dear father, if only you had stayed away another ten years!'
† The church still stands, on the west side of the Piazza del Plebiscito. It was originally planned by Murat as a tribute to Napoleon, but was continued by Ferdinand as a church.

Pizzo. Why he continued to believe that he had only to show himself to gain the immediate support of all around him we shall never understand; but there in Pizzo, at eleven o'clock on a Sunday morning, he disembarked in his most magnificent uniform and called upon the people to follow him. The attempt was, as might have been expected, a disaster. He was arrested, held for some days in the Aragonese castle which dominates the town, court-martialled on charges of inciting to civil war and bearing arms against the legitimate king and, on 13 October, executed by firing squad in the main hall of the castle. He met his end, we are told, with exemplary courage, refusing a chair or a blindfold and giving the command himself.

14

The *Carbonari* and the *Quarantotto*

‸

THE FINAL RETURN of the King to Naples allowed him to turn his attention to his own title. He had been Ferdinand III of Sicily but Ferdinand IV of Naples, which people found complicated and confusing. On 8 December 1816 he formally assumed the title of Ferdinand I of the Two Sicilies. There was, as we have seen, nothing new in this concept, which originally came about owing to Charles of Anjou's insistence on continuing to claim the title of King of Sicily, even after the island had been lost to the Kingdom of Aragon after the War of the Sicilian Vespers. It had, moreover, been decided by the Congress of Vienna that the Two Sicilies should continue as a single kingdom. In Sicily itself, however, the decree could not fail to be unpopular. It meant the end, after only four years, of both its constitution and its theoretical independence; and it condemned it in future to be – not for the first time – little more than a province of Naples. Financially, too, the departure of the court from Palermo dealt the island a heavy blow. Trade had been expanding in both directions, while foreign businesses – the vast majority of them British – had been steadily increasing in numbers; many of these now relocated to the mainland. British commercial influence henceforth survived principally in only two key industries: the wine trade in western Sicily, based on the town of Marsala, and the mining of sulphur, which was becoming ever more important as the Industrial Revolution took its course.

At the end of April 1819 the Emperor and Empress of Austria arrived in Naples on an official visit. Francis I* was now fifty-one.

---

* He had been Francis II of the Holy Roman Empire, but this had been dissolved in 1805 after Napoleon's victory at Austerlitz. He had now become the Emperor Francis I of Austria.

His second wife, Maria Teresa – the eldest daughter of Ferdinand and Maria Carolina – had died in 1807, having borne her husband twelve children;* the current Empress was his fourth, the daughter of the King of Bavaria; they had been married only two and a half years. With them, as always, was their Foreign Minister, Prince Metternich. Ferdinand – with his son Leopold, now Prince of Salerno, who was somewhat ill-advisedly married to his own niece, the Emperor's granddaughter Maria Clementina† – met their guests at the port of Gaeta; the former Hereditary Prince and his wife, now Duke and Duchess of Calabria, awaited them at the palace. There were extravagant celebrations in their honour – the huge dinner for more than a thousand at Capodimonte outshone, it was said, even the lavishness of the Murats. Other attractions included the ascent in a balloon of a fourteen-year-old girl, Mademoiselle Cecilia, which was not a total success; she was eventually retrieved from a distance of several miles, half-suffocated by smoke. (The outcome of a parachute drop by what Sir Harold Acton describes as 'a small unidentified quadruped' is unfortunately not recorded.)

At this point there appears in the story the figure of an immense Calabrian general named Guglielmo Pepe. Born in 1783, Pepe had first fought against the *Sanfedisti* of Cardinal Ruffo in 1800. Captured and exiled to France, he had joined Napoleon's army and subsequently shown himself to be a Bonapartist through and through, fighting for both Joseph Bonaparte and Joachim Murat and commanding a Neapolitan brigade during the Peninsular War in Spain. He had fought bravely for Murat at Tolentino and had reluctantly accepted the Treaty of Casalanza, by the terms of which he had retained his army rank. But he had spent his entire life fighting the Bourbons, and it was too late to transfer his loyalty. He now devoted himself, while ostensibly campaigning against brigands in the Capitanata,‡ to rallying the somewhat inchoate mass

---

* There were also several bastards. His final total was not far short of twenty.
† A fact to which the poor girl never became reconciled.
‡ That area of southeastern Italy around Foggia, including the great promontory of Monte Gargano.

of dissatisfied Italians known as the *carbonari* – 'the charcoal-burners' – and welding them into a national militia.

The *carbonari* were organized – insofar as they were organized at all – on the lines of Freemasons, split up into small, covert cells scattered across the peninsula. Even their objectives were far from identical: some were out-and-out republicans, others preferred constitutional monarchy; what they all hated was absolutism, the Bourbons, the Austrians and the Papacy. And they dreamed, almost all of them, of an independent, liberal, united Italy. In 1814 they had fought for the Sicilian constitution and had been outlawed by the Pope for their pains; in 1817 they had inspired risings in the Papal States. According to Pepe's memoirs – which may not be totally reliable – he had planned to take advantage of a military review of 5,000 men, to be held in the Emperor's honour at Avellino, to seize the imperial and royal party and hold it to ransom. What would have been the result of such a coup, if it had successfully taken place, is hard to imagine; fortunately, the Emperor and the King were warned at the last moment – not of the conspiracy, but simply that the Avellino road was in execrable condition and might well prove impassable. They thereupon gave up all idea of attending the review and returned to Naples.

For some time the *carbonari* had been rapidly increasing in numbers; according to Pepe, there were now over a quarter of a million in Italy alone, and we can be pretty sure that Sicily – with its long history of subversion and brigandage – would have contributed its full share. There was a general feeling of anticlimax after the Napoleonic Wars. The armies in particular were bored; they had little to do and promotion was slow. No wonder that so many drifted towards *carbonari* lodges. Gradually, too, the movement became more focussed, its aims grew a little clearer; and the first of these aims was to force the King to grant a constitution. In existing circumstances this was not going to be easy; the British ambassador Sir William A'Court reported that 'Naples was advancing slowly and silently to a degree of strength and importance never before possessed'; one of Ferdinand's principal generals, Pietro Colletta, who had served under Murat but, like Pepe, had been allowed to keep his rank, went further still:

King Ferdinand I, King of the Two Sicilies (Ferdinand IV of Naples): stupid and often childish, but beloved of his subjects.

Ferdinand's wife, Queen Maria Carolina: wilful and self-deluding to the point of madness, she was to make government of Naples virtually impossible.

King Ferdinand's carriage at the Piedigrotta Festival in Naples; Mount Vesuvius in the background.

Sir William Hamilton, *c.*1802,
Envoy Extraordinary to the
Kingdom of the Two Sicilies.

Admiral Lord Nelson, 1801,
by Sir William Beechey.

Emma Hamilton performing
her 'attitudes'. Painting by
Louise Vigée Le Brun, *c.*1790.

Napoleon's brother-in-law, the charismatic
and dashing Joachim Murat.

Murat's bedroom at the royal palace of Caserta.

Joseph Bonaparte, Napoleon's elder brother.

King Victor Emmanuel II, King of Piedmont and first King of Sicily, *c.*1870.

THE MAN IN POSSESSION.

V—r E—m—l. "I WONDER WHEN HE WILL OPEN THE DOOR."

There was a dangerous point in the Risorgimento when Garibaldi utterly overshadowed King Victor Emmanuel (though this worried Cavour much more than it did the King). Cartoon from *Punch*, 6 October 1860.

Count Camillo Cavour and Giuseppe Garibaldi detested each other. Cavour saw Garibaldi as an unprincipled adventurer and didn't trust him an inch, while Garibaldi never forgave Cavour for surrendering his birthplace, Nice, to France.

Cesare Mori, summoned to
Palermo by Mussolini in 1925
to 'eradicate the Mafia'.

Giuseppe ('Joe') Petrosino of the
New York Police Department,
murdered in Palermo in 1909 while
investigating criminal activities
between America and Sicily.

King Victor Emmanuel III and Queen Elena visit Messina
after the earthquake, December 1908.

Generals Sir Bernard Montgomery and George S. Patton, Sicily, 1943.
Two allied generals divided by deep personal dislike.

Notorious bandit Salvatore Giuliano with Don Vito Genovese (in U.S. Army uniform) serving as interpreter. Genovese was wanted by the FBI on several charges including murder.

Traditional Sicilian painted cart. The pictured battles between Christian knights and Saracens recall the days of the Norman Conquest, though in the popular imagination Charlemagne and Roland are also involved.

The puppet shows give
life to the same tradition.
They should on no
account be missed.

The rulers were benign, finance prospered, works of charity and public utility were undertaken, and the state was flourishing; the present was happy, the future appeared to be most happy, Naples was among the best governed kingdoms of Europe, which preserved a larger portion of the patrimony of new ideas for which so much blood had been shed.

It might be said that both these men were prejudiced; but so too were most of the *carbonari*. Naples, we can be sure, was something considerably less than a terrestrial paradise; but it possessed one important advantage in an absolute monarchy – a King who was beloved of his people. As a subsequent chief of police readily pointed out, the conspirators would probably have limited their activities to a few speeches and inflammatory posters, had it not been for Spain; but Spain gave them new encouragement.

Whether or not he was the son of King Charles IV or his mother's lover Manuel de Godoy, King Fernando VII of Spain had been a disaster. Napoleon had forced his abdication, with that of his father, in May 1808,* but in December 1813 – when the Emperor was still reeling after his defeat at Leipzig two months before – Fernando signed the Treaty of Valençay, allowing him to return to Spain. He almost immediately abolished the constitution and ruled the country with a small *camarilla* of favourites, changing his ministers every few months. 'The King,' wrote the German statesman Friedrich von Gentz in 1814, 'himself enters the houses of his prime ministers, arrests them and hands them over to their enemies.' Six weeks later he continued: 'The King has so debased himself that he has become no more than the leading police agent and prison warden of his country.'

By 1820 his country had had enough. On 1 January the army mutinied under one of its commanders, Rafael del Riego. Beginning in Galicia, the revolt quickly spread across Spain. On 7 March troops surrounded the royal palace in Madrid, and on the 10th Fernando capitulated. The mutineers should have got rid of him there and then; insanely, they decided to give him another chance. He was to remain in power till 1833, by which time he had been

* See p. 248.

responsible for a three-year reign of terror that sickened and horrified his subjects. Among its victims was del Riego, who was hanged in the Plaza de la Cebada. The King's last ten years are still known as the 'Ominous Decade'; harsh censorship was introduced, the university was reorganized on almost medieval lines, all opposition was suppressed, and a reactionary absolutism prevailed.

The mutiny, in short, was not a success. But it inspired the *carbonari* of Italy. Even then, they took their time; it was 1 July before a very small revolt – not much more than a hundred men – broke out in Avellino. The news arrived in Naples just as the Duke of Calabria and his wife were returning from Palermo, where the Duke had been a conscientious and highly respected Viceroy since 1815. The King, always happy when he was surrounded by his children, did not seem unduly alarmed, though he did object – most fortunately, as it turned out – when his ministers suggested sending General Pepe to settle the trouble. Pepe in fact remained in Naples till the 5th, when he rode out of the city at the head of half a company of infantry and seventy dragoons and, on arrival at Avellino, instantly assumed command of the rebel army. He then issued a proclamation, declaring that he and his men would not lay down their arms until the constitution was signed by the King. As there was at this point no constitution to sign, the Spanish one was arbitrarily chosen as a model; the fact that nobody had actually read it seems to have been considered of little importance.

On the very night of Pepe's departure, a party of five *carbonari* arrived at midnight at the royal palace and demanded to see the King. They at last agreed to settle for his secretary, the Duke of Ascoli, who assured them that His Majesty had already decided to grant a constitution. They then insisted that he had just two hours to do so. As it was by now one o'clock in the morning this seemed a little unreasonable; but early the next morning the King issued his own proclamation, to the effect that he had agreed to a constitutional government and that its details would be published within a week. Alas, this was not soon enough. The rebels wanted the Spanish constitution, and they wanted it now. A further decree was issued; the King signed it; and a new government was formed. Several of its members had served under Murat.

According to the Austrian minister, Prince Jablonowski, a revolution might have been expected on the moon rather than in Naples; in the words of A'Court, 'a kingdom in the highest degree flourishing and happy under the mildest of governments, and by no means oppressed by the weight of taxation, crumbles before a handful of insurgents that half a battalion of good soldiers would have crushed in an instant.' 'It is scarcely a fortnight,' he added, 'since I was assured both by the King and General Nugent* that the army might be securely reckoned upon from the General down to the lowest of the soldiers.'

The next move came from Pepe, who announced that he would make his triumphal entry into Naples on 8 July. It was in fact the 9th when he led some 14,000 men through the city to the palace: first the regular troops, then the *carbonari*. An English eyewitness, Richard Keppel Craven, was in Naples at the time and has left us with a full description:

> The spectacle displayed by the bands of provincial militia was singular in the extreme; as, though they were all most formidably armed, their weapons varied as much as their accoutrements: a very small proportion of them were in military uniform, the majority being habited according to the different costumes of their respective districts, which at the same time bore a very warlike aspect. It must be acknowledged that the cartridge belt, the sandalled legs, the broad stiletto, short musket and grey peaked hats, so peculiarly adapted by painters to the representation of banditti, seemed here to realise all the ideas which the inhabitants of the north have formed of such beings; and the sun-burnt complexions, and dark bushy hair and whiskers of the wearer, greatly contributed to render this resemblance more striking . . .
>
> Nearly all these individuals had been absent from their homes nine days, during which they had never slept in a bed, or even under a roof, but they all seemed in perfect good humour and spirits and

---

* The unusually named Laval Graf Nugent von Westmeath was an Irishman born in Prague, where his father was Governor. After twenty years in the Austrian army, he had taken over that of Naples in 1817 – a further indication of Ferdinand's subservience to Austria at this time.

appeared amply repaid for all the hardships they might have endured, by the success which had followed them.

The King, meanwhile – as was his usual practice at moments of crisis – had retired to bed, though even this did not spare him a visit from General Pepe, marked, so far as we can tell, by a degree of frostiness on both sides. On 13 July, however, he dragged himself upright and, in the royal chapel, took the constitutional oath.

In Vienna, reports of these events were received with considerable alarm. Such revolts were known to be contagious; was that of Naples not itself a secondary infection, caught from Spain? Was there not a serious risk that it might spread yet further afield, if not firmly prevented? Prince Metternich certainly thought so, and on 25 July he announced his intention of suppressing it, if necessary by armed force. His opinion was shared by Tsar Alexander I of Russia; the result was a conference of Austria's allies – the others were Britain, France and Prussia – to meet the following October at Troppau in Silesia.* In Britain, Lord Castlereagh was against any principle which would make the Allies 'the armed guardians of all thrones'; France was undecided; and it was therefore only the three eastern, autocratic powers who put their names to the resulting protocol. Before leaving, however, they decided to meet again in January at Laibach, nowadays better known as Ljubljana in Slovenia; and this time they agreed to invite King Ferdinand himself. Such an invitation, they thought, might even give him a chance to escape.

For indeed King Ferdinand was at this moment far from happy. Naples was still in an uproar. General Pepe was, according to A'Court, parading through the city 'at the head of an immense mob of people armed with guns, knives, sticks, clubs, swords, etc., carrying a tricolour flag . . . filling the streets with tumult and changing the cry of "King and Constitution" to that of "Liberty or Death".' In August there were reports of a plot to assassinate the King; Ferdinand was terrified – physical courage had never been his forte – and the Duchess of Floridia had secretly asked A'Court to summon one or two British ships which would be ready to rescue her husband,

* Now Opava in the Czech Republic.

herself and his family if it became necessary to do so. When two frigates duly appeared in the bay in early October the *carbonari* were predictably furious, and the Foreign Minister, the Duke of Campochiaro, was ordered to demand their removal. He was obliged to obey the instructions he had been given; but as he did so he murmured to A'Court: 'For heaven's sake ignore the notes I have to write about your squadron. If it leaves the Bay we are all lost.'

How, it may be asked, was news of the adoption in Naples of the Spanish constitution received in Sicily? The Sicilians were outraged. First, they had not been consulted; second, they had a perfectly good constitution of their own. And what had they to do with Naples anyway? They demanded nothing less than full independence. Riots broke out, and riots led to something dangerously approaching civil war. In Naples, the government acted quickly, sending out all the men that could be spared under the command of General Florestano Pepe, Guglielmo's considerably more reliable brother. Palermo was besieged, its water supplies cut off, and its people nearly died of thirst until, on 5 October, a capitulation was arranged. By the terms of the agreement Naples would take over the forts and strongholds, and the Spanish constitution would be accepted, at least for the moment. The parliament would be summoned to decide the question of unity or independence. Not that anything could be hoped from the parliament, whose members, wrote A'Court, 'occupy themselves with anything except what really demands attention. They had a long debate last week, which was pushed to a division, whether God was or was not the Legislator of the Universe. The question was decided in favour of the Deity by a small majority.'

Ferdinand had a hard time getting permission to leave Naples; but he succeeded at last, and on 13 December embarked with relief on HMS *Le Vengeur*. The weather was filthy, but anything was better than the *carbonari*. He eventually landed at Livorno on 21 December and spent Christmas in Florence with his nephew, the Grand Duke of Tuscany. His wife the Duchess sailed separately, but arrived soon after; she would stay in Florence until his return. After a week or so he set off again, passing through Bologna, Modena and Vicenza before turning east. The cold was intense and his hands were covered with chilblains, but he seemed not to mind; indeed, he preferred it to the intense, suffocating heat of the Austrian stoves which awaited him in Laibach and stopped him from sleeping.

The Congress opened on 26 January 1821. The Emperor Francis and Tsar Alexander were both present in person; Prussia had sent a plenipotentiary. Once again Britain stood aside, being represented only by its ambassador in Vienna, Lord Stewart, who was there more as an observer than anything else. France too remained lukewarm. Ferdinand failed to distinguish himself. Twice he had sworn to uphold a constitution; now he maintained that he had done so only under threat of force and that his oaths were consequently null and void. He raised no objection when Metternich suggested sending an imperial army to Naples; nothing else would have given him the courage to return.

The conclusion was – as everyone knew it would be – much the same as that reached at Troppau: a message was sent to the Regent to the effect that the *carbonari* revolt had endangered the peace of Europe, and that in consequence an Austrian army, with full Russian support, was already on its way to the beleaguered kingdom: as friends if that kingdom were to return to its former regime, as foes if it insisted on continuing on its present disastrous path. The Regent replied that the choice between these two alternatives was one which must be decided by the parliament, which would consider it urgently.

And the parliament voted for war. Had it allowed itself to be guided by common sense rather than by 'a frolic wind of bellicose enthusiasm',* it must have seen the foolhardiness of such an action. It was only six years before, at Tolentino, that the Austrians had destroyed Murat's army, compared with which the present *carbonari* force was a hopelessly undisciplined rabble. Guglielmo Pepe, who had himself fought at Tolentino, must have known as he marched off to the Abruzzi that he had not the faintest chance of victory – a truth which was demonstrated when, on 7 March, he decided to engage with the Austrian advance guard at Rieti. Before a shot had been fired his troops simply melted away. After that it was all

* Acton.

over quite quickly. He returned to Naples on the 15th to find that the parliament had already changed its mind and decided to submit to the King. A week later the Austrians marched into Naples. Most of the *carbonari* leaders could not be seen for dust, and the Regent was only too pleased to help them on their way. Pepe went off to London – he was to be back in Naples for the events of 1848 – as did several of his erstwhile colleagues, for whom A'Court had willingly provided passports to get them out of the way.

King Ferdinand had much enjoyed his trip to Laibach, and had subsequently rejoined his wife the Duchess in Florence as planned. Meanwhile, from this safe distance, he appointed a provisional government. When the Duke of Calabria showed the list of its members to A'Court, the ambassador was appalled. 'Such a choice,' he scoffed, 'was never before heard of! Hardly one under seventy, or with talent or capacity enough to govern a village!' Under pressure from Metternich and others, a formidable chief of police was appointed, the Prince of Canosa, who freely meted out punishment – often in the form of public floggings – to all those still suspected of *carbonari* tendencies; and by the late spring the King thought it safe to return. He did so on 15 May 1822, and was received with all the old enthusiasm. Presented with a list of thirty republicans sentenced to death, he pardoned twenty-eight of them. He had always been loved by his people, but now there was something more: he was seventy-one – an old man by the standards of the time – and he had become an institution. After his sixty-two years on the throne, few of his subjects – though they looked back with some distaste to the interruptions of Joseph Bonaparte and Murat – could remember the days of his predecessor.

One more task was left to him: a visit to the Congress of Verona the following October. He did not attach a great deal of importance to it; indeed, he delayed his departure from Naples till 22 October, two days after it had begun. Its primary interest was in any case events in Spain. Where his own kingdom was concerned, it was agreed that the Austrian army of occupation should be reduced to 35,000 men – its original numbers are uncertain – 'who would remain until public tranquillity was fully restored and the Neapolitan army was reorganized'. From Verona he travelled on to Vienna where, despite the coldest weather for many years, he passed the winter. There his simple – sometimes almost peasant – ways won all hearts. 'He seemed to enjoy himself tremendously here,' wrote the Baroness du Montet:

> His figure is patriarchal and very dignified without being majestic; his high stature, his fine white hair, his pronounced and venerable features would make him respected in whatever class of society he had been born. In a peasant's cottage or in the garb of a simple fisherman, one could not help honouring him as a grand old man. He speaks very loud and laughs uproariously; at the theatre, and especially at the Italian opera, he applauds with a ringing voice and beats time vigorously on the ledge of his box; at a performance of *The Barber of Seville* he shouted, '*Bravo, lazzarone, bravo!*' in his enthusiasm for Lablache, who used to sing one of the airs in so astonishing a manner.
>
> . . . The King of Naples is very devout; he fasts with extreme austerity, tells his rosary every day, and often listens to sermons. He has brought his confessor with him. This is a venerable and even very handsome Capuchin who refused the lodging prepared for him at Court to stay in a cell of the Capuchin convent. The King went to the crypt of this church to visit the tomb of the Queen, his wife . . . He rises very early in the morning, hears Mass, says a great many prayers, dines at mid-day, takes a nap, then plays cards for fairly high stakes with his favourites, from whom he exacts punctual payment within twenty-four hours, without any remission.

He always sent his Duchess a proportion of his winnings.

Ferdinand returned to Naples on 6 August 1823, having been away for nearly nine months. He found his kingdom still under Austrian occupation, yet for the most part prosperous and contented. Lady Blessington, who arrived at almost exactly the same time, though she fully shared the Bonapartist views of her lover, Count d'Orsay, was forced to confess: 'We are told that the Italians writhe under the despotism of their rulers; but nowhere have I seen such happy faces. Men, women and children, all appear to feel the influence of the delicious atmosphere in which they live; an atmosphere that seems to exclude care and sorrow.'

On 2 January 1825 the King went shooting as usual. The next day he complained of a slight cold and remained indoors; at his evening game of piquet with the Duchess he could barely keep awake and his speech sounded a little blurred. He refused to be bled, however, and asked only that he should not be called at his normal waking time of six a.m. His valet accordingly waited till eight before entering the bedroom. He found Ferdinand dead in bed of an apoplectic stroke, just as his wife Maria Carolina had died a little more than eleven years before. He was a week short of his seventy-fifth birthday.

King Francis I of the Two Sicilies, former Duke of Calabria, had always been curiously colourless. It was frequently pointed out that nobody took any notice of him – except, presumably, his two wives and many mistresses. His first wife, Maria Clementina of Austria, he had genuinely loved, and his heart was broken when she died in 1801. His second, Maria Isabella of Spain, was – if we are to believe his mother, Maria Carolina – almost as boring as he was. His five-year reign was almost devoid of incident. In his youth, such few ideas as he possessed suggested that he would show himself, as a ruler, rather more liberal than his father had been; but his views became steadily more conservative as he grew older. He resembled his father, too, in his indolence and his incorrigible reluctance to take any active part in the government of his country. His ministers were hardly more efficient – though his valet and the Queen's personal chambermaid, both of whom made a small fortune out of bribes, gradually acquired considerable political influence. Essentially, the Kingdom was run by the police and the army, and woe betide those citizens who fell foul of either one or the other. The army in particular helped itself to most of the revenue: St Ignatius of Loyola, founder of the Jesuits, who had died in 1556, was gazetted a field marshal on full pay; just where his salary went remains uncertain. So it was that in his short and deeply undistinguished reign, Francis I could boast one achievement only that was of genuine benefit to Naples: the withdrawal in 1827 of the Austrian army of occupation, the maintenance of which had been a heavy drain on treasury funds. For the rest, he lived in strict seclusion

– such was his morbid fear of assassination – surrounded by soldiers, his favourites and his mistresses. He enjoyed none of his father's popularity and died in 1830, unlamented.

Francis's son and successor, Ferdinand II of the Two Sicilies, seemed at first to be more a chip off the old block. Like his grandfather he mixed with the *lazzaroni*, spoke their dialect and endeared himself to them with his free and easy ways. The Sicilians too were disposed to welcome him. He had been born in Palermo, in 1810, while his father was Governor, and he was to make no fewer than four visits to Sicily in the first ten years of his reign. In consequence, he grew to know the island a good deal better than most Sicilians. His appointment of his younger brother Leopold – also Sicilian-born – as Governor was also popular. Hopes were additionally raised by the edict which he published on his accession, promising a fair and impartial administration of justice and a reform of the state finances. He drew attention to the corruption and the many other abuses which had so long afflicted the Kingdom and undertook to spare no effort in putting an end to them once and for all. His long-term goal, he concluded, was to govern his kingdom in such a way as to bring the greatest happiness to the greatest number of his subjects, while naturally respecting the rights of his fellow monarchs and those of the Roman Catholic Church.

These were noble sentiments indeed – but Sicily and the Sicilians were too strong for him. The crime rate was steadily increasing; the presence first of British and then of Austrian troops had afforded endless opportunities of stealing arms and ammunition. Brigandage extended up to the very walls of Palermo, Messina, Catania and the other major cities. Another practice which was to become something of a Sicilian speciality was the protection racket: people would pay good money not to have their water supplies cut off, their cattle stolen or destroyed, their sulphur mines incinerated. Those whose houses were robbed were often quietly informed of how, on payment of a hefty fee, their possessions might be returned to them. There was a spate, too, of kidnapping – not only of children but of prominent citizens as well. Here, in short, were all the ingredients of the modern-day Mafia. Only the name was still lacking.

Against abuses on such a scale there was little the government could do. The twenty-five separate police forces existing on the island numbered in total only some 300–350 men. They would do what they could, even making the occasional arrest; but when the offender was brought to court a little discreet bribery could almost certainly ensure his acquittal. More often than not, a judge would buy his position; it would then seem to him only natural to recoup his outlay as best he could. In despair, King Ferdinand tried to introduce a body of honest judges from Naples, but the experiment was not a success. First, they found the local dialect incomprehensible; they could understand nobody and nobody could understand them. Second, they were disgusted; according to one Neapolitan judge posted to Trapani, 'there is scarcely a single official here who does not prostrate himself before the aristocracy and who does not intend to profit from his post.'

And indeed the aristocracy had no cause for complaint; but everybody else did. Sicily was as much of a backwater as ever it had been; for anyone with ambition it offered no future at all. To take but one example, the composer Vincenzo Bellini – just like Alessandro Scarlatti a hundred and fifty years before him – was obliged to make his name abroad; to have remained in his birthplace of Catania would have condemned him to a lifetime of obscurity. Meanwhile, for the humbler townsfolk and peasantry, the situation was becoming desperate; many of the latter were already struggling against starvation. Nor was there any noticeable prospect of improvement; things, it seemed, could only get worse. In circumstances such as these, could a major social upheaval be anything more than a matter of time?

No one knew better than King Ferdinand II that Sicily was an open sore; but he was powerless to do anything about it. As one foreign ambassador lamented, 'although the King and his ministers are fully sensible of the evils which exist in Sicily, they do not possess sufficient talent or energy to meet them, and will leave things to take their chance.' Ferdinand did not quite do this; but, after five years of total failure to improve things, in 1835 he gave up all attempts at remedial legislation and, obviously smelling revolution in the air, resorted to repression. Foreign books were banned, a strict censorship imposed. Desperate measures such as these tend, all too often, to be counterproductive; and it was only two years later that a brief but quite serious revolt gave warning of worse things to come.

It began in 1837 with a sudden outbreak of cholera, a disease previously unknown in western Europe; and somehow the rumour spread that the infection had been deliberately introduced by the government. To us the very idea seems ridiculous; and yet, we are told, it was shared by several professors at Palermo University and even by the Archbishop himself. As men, women and children died in their thousands, panic spread the length and breadth of the island. On this occasion Palermo itself remained relatively quiet; at Syracuse, however, there were furious riots, in the course of which what little law and order there was broke down completely and several hundred more lost their lives. The most remarkable reaction was at Catania, where the demonstrations suddenly turned into demands for Sicilian independence. As usual, however, lack of discipline, cohesion and proper planning did the rebels in. After a few arrests and a few executions, Sicily settled back to her old ways.

Ferdinand returned there in the following year. He did what he could, re-establishing the University of Messina in order to increase the number of those qualified to become administrators and senior civil servants; somewhat pointedly, the previous practice whereby such jobs had been reserved for Sicilians was abandoned. Ferdinand himself felt strongly that this represented the only chance of eliminating the corruption and nepotism that were the bane of Sicilian life. The measure was reluctantly accepted; the King's attempts at land reform, however, immediately ran into serious trouble. Obviously, they were bound to involve the reduction of the huge estates, and thus the influence of the feudal aristocracy – and the latter result was the more dangerous in that the Bourbons were becoming increasingly unpopular in aristocratic circles, who were beginning to regret the supremacy of Naples and to argue instead for independence. Meanwhile, another idea was slowly developing: had the time not come for a radical political realignment? The old Spanish influence was on the wane; France was by now every bit as important, England – thanks to her considerable financial interests – still more so. But what, on the other hand, about Italy? Up and down the peninsula, the call for a united Italy was growing stronger every day: if this union were to occur, should Sicily not be a part of it?

When, on Wednesday, 12 January 1848 – the thirty-eighth birthday of Ferdinand II – the people of Palermo rose up against their Bourbon masters, they could have had no idea of what they were starting. As we have seen, risings in the Kingdom were nothing new, but they had all been relatively easily dealt with. What happened in 1848 – the *quarantotto*, as Italy remembers it – was something else. It was a revolution, and by the end of the year it had been followed by many other revolutions. In Italy alone, they occurred in Naples, Rome, Venice, Florence, Lucca, Parma, Modena and Milan; in northern and central Europe there were also those in Paris, Vienna, Cracow, Warsaw and Budapest.

Already, as the year opened, student riots had prompted the authorities to close the University of Palermo; several eminent citizens known for their liberal views had been arrested, and an unsigned manifesto was circulated calling on everyone to rise up on the King's birthday. When that day dawned and the demonstrations began, the streets emptied, shops closed, houses were barricaded. A large number of the insurgents were mountain brigands or simple peasants, few of whom probably had much idea of what they were fighting for; but they were thrilled to be able to break down the customs barriers and give themselves over to looting to their hearts' content. Many of the smaller villages and towns were devastated, as was much of the countryside.

The Bourbons had some 7,000 troops in the Palermo garrison, but they proved almost useless. Communications were atrocious, the roads execrable, and they could not be everywhere at once. In despair they decided to bombard the city – a decision which they soon had cause to regret, especially when a shell destroyed the municipal pawnbrokers, on which many families depended, aristocratic and plebeian alike. The infuriated mob fell on the royal palace, sacked it – sparing, thank heaven, the Palatine Chapel – and set fire to the state records and archives. Meanwhile, hundreds of prisoners were released from gaol. The garrison retreated, and soon returned to Naples. In the following days a committee of government was formed under the presidency of the seventy-year-old Sicilian patriot (and former Neapolitan Minister of Marine) Ruggiero Settimo; meanwhile, the revolt spread to all the main cities – except Messina, which held back through jealousy of Palermo – and well over a hundred villages, where the support of the peasantry had by now been assured with lavish promises of land. It encountered no opposition worthy of the name.

By the end of the month the island was virtually free of royal troops, and on 5 February Settimo announced that 'the evils of war had ceased, and that thenceforth an era of happiness had begun for Sicily'. He failed to mention that the citadel of Messina was still in Bourbon hands; none the less, it was clear to King Ferdinand that he had his back to the wall. Owing to the almost continuous demonstrations in Naples on the Sicilian model, on 29 January he offered a liberal constitution to both parts of his kingdom, providing for a bicameral legislature and a modest degree of franchise. 'The game is up,' wrote the horrified Austrian ambassador, Prince Schwarzenberg, to Metternich; 'the King and his ministers have completely lost their heads.' Metternich simply scribbled in the margin, 'I defy the ministers to lose what they have never possessed.'

The news that reached the King towards the end of February must have distressed him still more. In Paris his uncle, the 'Citizen King' Louis-Philippe, had been toppled on the 24th and a republic proclaimed. Now the landslide began. Ferdinand, who had enjoyed a brief popularity after his grant of a constitution, was more than ever execrated; liberal constitutions, it seemed, were no longer enough. The Sicilians, meanwhile, had refused his offer. 'Sicily,' they coldly informed him, 'does not demand new institutions, but the restoration of rights which have been hers for centuries.' In Palermo on 13 April he was declared deposed, the Bourbon flag being replaced by the revolutionary tricolour and the three-legged *triskelion*.

Sicily was now truly independent. The difficulty was that it lacked any machinery for self-government. Without an experienced hand at the helm, the old chaos and confusion grew worse than ever. Trade plummeted, unemployment soared, the legal system virtually collapsed. Towards the end of August, Ferdinand sent a combined military and naval force of some 20,000 under Field Marshal Prince Carlo Filangieri to restore comparative order on the island; and September saw a concerted land and sea attack on Messina. It was then that the city suffered heavy bombardment for eight hours – after it had already surrendered. The rebels fought back, and the age-old hatred between Neapolitans and Sicilians give rise to atrocities on both sides – to the point where the British and French admirals in Sicilian waters, revolted by the bloodshed and brutality, persuaded Ferdinand to grant a six-month armistice. Here, one might have thought, was an opportunity to end the stalemate, but every offer of settlement was rejected by the rebels out of hand. Had they been prepared to negotiate, they might have saved something from the wreckage; since they refused, more and more of their erstwhile supporters – for reasons of sheer self-preservation – turned back to the Bourbons. As a result, Filangieri was able to capture Taormina on 2 April 1849 and Catania five days later. On 15 May, without any difficulty, he entered Palermo.

By their inefficiency, their lack of unity and their refusal to compromise, the Sicilians had perfectly demonstrated how a revolution should not be run.

When the smoke cleared, Filangieri was appointed Governor of Sicily. Few tasks could have been more thankless, but he acquitted himself as well as he could. Ferdinand – now, after the bombardments of both Palermo and Messina, known as 'King Bomba' – had meanwhile lost his nerve completely. He had been badly frightened by the revolution, and no longer wished to have anything to do with Sicily or the new liberal and national ideas which were evidently taking hold. Once again he clamped down, and the island became effectively a police state. Freedom of movement was severely restricted, a still harsher censorship imposed; men could be arrested on suspicion only, and sent after little more than a token trial to the penal settlements on Lampedusa and other islands.

When William Ewart Gladstone visited Naples in 1850–51 and

found that the dissidents imprisoned by the government even included the legal adviser to the British Embassy he became seriously concerned; and when in February 1851 he was allowed to visit the prisons he was scandalized – and consequently published a blistering attack on what he described as 'the negation of God erected into a system of government'. This did immense harm to the Kingdom's reputation; inevitably, it was compared to its northern counterpart, the Kingdom of Piedmont, which stood for liberalism and progress and Italian unification. It did not gain by the comparison.

In 1856 Ferdinand was the victim of an attempted assassination by one of his own soldiers. The attempt failed, but the relatively slight wound that he sustained from the man's bayonet became infected, and many believed that he never altogether recovered. He lived for another three years, but when he died in May 1859 he was still under fifty. In the first part of his reign he had not been unpopular. He had done his best for Sicily, and although that best had not been good enough it is doubtful whether any other ruler could have done much better. He had, on the other hand, established telegraphic communications between Naples and Palermo. His navy had the first steamship in Italy, and he had also built the first railway. True, it at first ran only the ten kilometres between central Naples and Portici, but it was soon extended down the peninsula and it showed Ferdinand to be a good deal more progressive than his contemporary Pope Gregory XVI, for whom railways were *chemins d'enfer*,* banned from all papal territories. After 1848, however, his reputation collapsed. To his subjects he was to remain 'King Bomba' for the remaining eleven years of his life.

His son, Francis II, succeeded him at the age of twenty-three. Francis's reign, as we shall see, was to be both dramatic and extremely short. It was bound to be; for the Risorgimento was at hand.

---

* The French for 'railway' is *chemin de fer* ('iron road'). *Chemins d'enfer* means 'roads of hell'.

15

Risorgimento

HAD THE *QUARANTOTTO* been in vain? By the autumn of 1849 it certainly seemed so. The Austrians were back in Venice and in Lombardy; Pius IX – who had fled to Gaeta the previous year – had returned to a French-occupied Rome; in Naples, the sadly unreconstructed King Bomba had torn up the constitution and once more wielded absolute power; Florence, Modena and Parma, all under Austrian protection, were in much the same state. In the whole peninsula, only Piedmont remained free. Its King, Victor Emmanuel II, was short, squat and unusually ugly, principally interested – or so it seemed – in hunting and women. But he was a good deal more intelligent than he looked; despite his genuine shyness and awkwardness in public, politically speaking he missed very few tricks. It is hard to imagine the Risorgimento without him.

Yet even Victor Emmanuel might have foundered had it not been for his chief minister, Camillo Cavour, who came to power in 1852 and remained in control, with very brief intermissions, for the next nine years – years which were crucial for Italy. Cavour's appearance, like that of his master, was deceptive. Short and pot-bellied, with thinning hair, a blotchy complexion and a beard that carefully avoided his upper lip, he was shabbily dressed and, at first acquaintance, distinctly unimpressive. His mind, on the other hand, was like a rapier, and once he began to talk few were impervious to his charm. His political aim was simple: a united Italy, with Piedmont at its head. For this the first requirement was to get rid of Austria; and he now began to entertain the hope that the most recent comet on the international scene, the Emperor Napoleon III, might help him to do so.

Louis-Napoléon, nephew of Napoleon I, had become heir to the Bonapartist dynasty on the death of his exiled cousin – the so-called Napoleon II, Duke of Reichstadt – in Vienna in 1831. After the revolution of 1848, he had been the first elected president of the French Republic, then on 2 December 1851 he had staged a *coup d'état*, precisely one year after which he had himself become Emperor. By 1858, however, he was aware that his prestige and popularity were declining. He desperately needed a war – and a victorious war at that – to regain them, and Austria was the only potential enemy available. In July he and Cavour had a secret meeting, by the terms of which he promised to send an army into Italy in return for the cession of the County of Savoy and the city of Nice. The following spring he marched some 120,000 troops into Italy, with himself in personal command. There followed two tremendous battles, both of which were victories. The first was in May at Magenta, a small village west of Milan. Casualties were high on both sides, and would have been higher had not the Piedmontese unfortunately arrived some time after the battle was over. The second was a month later at Solferino, just south of Lake Garda, where well over a quarter of a million men were engaged. Here was the greatest battle since Leipzig in 1813, and the last in history where all the armies were under the personal command of their monarchs: Napoleon III, Victor Emmanuel and the Emperor Franz Josef of Austria. It was however a Pyrrhic victory; the French and Piedmontese lost almost as many men as the Austrians, and the outbreak of fever – probably typhus – that followed the battle accounted for thousands more deaths on both sides.*

Two weeks later Napoleon concluded a separate peace with Austria; and on 11 July 1859 the two emperors met at Villafranca near Verona, where the future of north and central Italy was decided in under an hour. Austria would keep Mantua and the fortress town of Peschiera at the extreme southern end of Lake Garda; the rest of Lombardy she would cede to France, who would pass it on to Piedmont. An

---

* The scenes of carnage made a deep impression on a young Swiss named Henri Dunant, who organized emergency aid for the wounded. Five years later, as a direct result of this experience, he founded the Red Cross.

Italian confederacy would be established under the honorary presidency of the Pope. Venice and Venetia, though members of the confederacy, would remain under Austrian sovereignty. Early in 1860 Cavour reached his own agreement with Napoleon; Piedmont would annex Tuscany, while surrendering Savoy and Nice to France. Plebiscites held soon afterwards confirmed the wisdom of these arrangements: in Savoy, for example, the voting was 130,500 to 235. Still, not everyone was in favour; and perhaps the angriest opponent of all was the greatest of Italy's patriots, Giuseppe Garibaldi – who, having been born in Nice, suddenly found himself a Frenchman.

Garibaldi was now fifty-three. He had started his professional life as a merchant seaman; in 1834 he had been involved in a mutiny, and a warrant had been issued for his arrest. Just in time he had managed to escape to France; meanwhile, in Turin, he was sentenced *in absentia* to death for high treason. After a brief spell in the French merchant navy he joined that of the Bey of Tunis, who offered him the post of commander-in-chief. This he declined, and in December 1835 sailed as second mate in a French brig bound for South America. There he was to stay for the next twelve years, the first four of them fighting for a small state, now forgotten, which was trying – unsuccessfully – to break away from Brazilian domination. In 1841 he and his Brazilian mistress trekked to Montevideo, where he was soon put in charge of the Uruguayan navy, also taking command of a legion of Italian exiles – the first of the Redshirts, with whom his name was to be ever afterwards associated. After his victory in the minor but heroic battle of San Antonio in 1846 his fame quickly spread to Europe. By now he had become a professional rebel, whose experience of guerrilla warfare was to stand him in good stead in the years to come.

The moment Garibaldi heard of the revolutions of 1848, he gathered sixty of his Redshirts and took the next ship back to Italy, where he fought his own private war against Austria and then, on hearing of the Pope's flight from Rome,* was elected to the new Assembly there; it was he who formally proposed that the city

---

* Pope Pius IX had fled to Gaeta in November 1848, as a result of his ill-advised 'Allocution' violently opposing the idea of a united Italy.

should become an independent republic. In June 1849, however, the French invaded Rome, and after a heroic resistance that lasted for nearly a month the defenders were forced to give in. Around midday on the 30th, Garibaldi appeared at the Assembly, covered in dust, his red shirt soaked in blood and sweat. Surrender, he declared, was out of the question. They must take to the hills: '*Dovunque saremo,*' he declared, '*colà sarà Roma.*'* But it was not to be. With his wife, Anita, and a few followers he sailed for Venice, the only Italian state where a newly declared republic was still fighting for survival; but their ship was intercepted by an Austrian warship and they were forced to disembark on a remote stretch of the coast – where, soon afterwards, his beloved Anita died in his arms. Temporarily, the spirit went out of him. Once again he left Italy and took ship for New York, there to begin his second period of American exile.

One of Garibaldi's closest political colleagues was a fiercely republican Sicilian lawyer named Francesco Crispi. Sentenced to death for his part in the events of 1848, he had managed to escape and in 1859, after a long period of exile in London, he had visited his homeland in disguise and under an assumed name. This visit had convinced him that it was ripe for revolution. The Bourbons were everywhere detested, and so widespread was the poverty that the vast majority had little or nothing to lose. A small armed expedition was all that was required, and the whole island would be up in arms. The only question was, who was to lead it? The name of Garibaldi immediately sprang to mind; he had returned from America in 1854, full of his old ardour and enthusiasm, and had fought magnificently at Solferino. But Garibaldi was hesitant. He was still seething over Villafranca, and he himself had rather a different dream: the capture of Nice and its restoration to Piedmont.

Thoughts of Nice, however, were soon to be indefinitely postponed. The Sicilians had never accepted the loss of their own state; they had rebelled in 1820, in 1837 and in 1848; and on 4 April 1860 there was yet another popular insurrection in Palermo. If all

---

* 'Wherever we are, there shall be Rome.'

had proceeded according to plan it would have been accompanied by a simultaneous rising among the aristocracy; but, as always in Sicily, something went badly wrong. The Neapolitan authorities had been secretly informed, and the insurgents found themselves surrounded almost before they had left their homes. All who were not killed instantly were executed later. The operation had been a disastrous failure; but it provided a spark for many others throughout northern Sicily, and the authorities could not cope with them all. Nor could they suppress the rumour that ran like wildfire across the island – adding fuel to the revolutionary flames – that Garibaldi was on his way.

At the time it was wishful thinking; Garibaldi was in fact busy collecting funds to buy 'a million rifles' – Colonel Samuel Colt had already sent a hundred of his superb revolvers from New York as a gesture of support – but when he heard the news of the insurrection he acted at once. Victor Emmanuel refused his request for a brigade from the Piedmontese army on the grounds that he was not at war with Naples, but within less than a month Garibaldi – now in Genoa – had assembled a formidable band of volunteers. 'The Thousand', they came to be called, though in fact 1,162 of them finally embarked. They represented a broad cross-section of Italian society. About half of them were professional men – some 250 lawyers, 100 doctors, 50 engineers, a number of university lecturers and a few priests – while the other half was drawn from the working classes. They included one woman – Crispi's wife Rosalia, disguised as a man. Some were still theoretically republicans, but their leader made it clear to them that they were fighting not just for Italy but also for King Victor Emmanuel – and this was no time to argue.

For Victor Emmanuel the situation was delicate, to say the least. In his heart he wished Garibaldi every success; indeed, he was a good deal more sympathetic than Cavour, who never quite overcame his distrust of so swashbuckling an adventurer. But the King well knew that to reveal those sympathies would be dangerous indeed. He had, fortunately, an excellent reason for not categorically disowning Garibaldi: the man was already a hero, by far the most popular figure in Italy. Nevertheless, if he were seen to be openly supporting him, not only Naples but France and Austria too would be up in arms. In such circumstances, while Garibaldi was recruiting his men and preparing his expedition all the authorities could do was to beg him to maintain the lowest possible profile while they looked the other way.

Garibaldi had managed to charter two steamships, the *Piemonte* and the *Lombardo*. At half-past eight on the evening of Saturday, 5 May, dressed in his usual red shirt, South American poncho and coloured scarf and armed with a sabre, a dagger and one of Colonel Colt's revolvers, he boarded the *Piemonte* in Genoa and sailed round to the neighbouring harbour of Quarto, where his followers were waiting. Now and now only did he send a message to the King:

> Sicily's cries of pain have reached my ears and moved my heart and the hearts of a few hundred of my comrades in arms. I have not encouraged an insurrection by my brothers in Sicily, but since they have risen up in the name of Italian unity, of which Your Majesty is the personification, against the most infamous tyranny of our age, I did not hesitate to accept the leadership of the expedition.

The two ships sailed at dawn on the following day.

Anxious to escape the attentions of the Bourbon navy and at the same time to avoid giving offence to Victor Emmanuel by invading his territorial waters around the island of Sardinia, Garibaldi headed west for many miles, to the point where several of his followers thought he was heading for Tunisia or Malta rather than Sicily; but he turned south at last and – after a dangerous moment when his two ships almost rammed each other in the dark – reached Marsala on the morning of 11 May. He found it completely undefended, so that his followers were able to pass an undisturbed night in the town before moving on the next day. On the 14th, at Salemi, he addressed the populace and formally assumed the dictatorship of Sicily in the name of the King. His speech, we are told, drew thunderous applause. It was on the following day, on a hill known as Pianto Romano just outside Calatafimi and only a mile or two from the temple of Segesta, that he and his men found the Bourbon army awaiting them.

The battle was fought on 15 May and lasted several hours, most of the fighting being hand-to-hand, with bayonets rather than rifles. Garibaldi knew that he was massively outnumbered; on the other hand, he could count on a huge psychological advantage. To every Italian, his army of Redshirts – with its whole string of victories in South America as well as in Italy – was by now of almost legendary fame, its members often credited by the peasantry with a magic invulnerability to bullets. The Bourbon troops were frightened, and had little stomach for the fight: the Thousand were championing an ideal in which they all passionately believed, under a leader whose extraordinary charisma was a constant inspiration. If they could win this first battle, Garibaldi told them, there was a strong possibility that the opposition would melt away; then, in just a week or two, they would be masters of Sicily.

Militarily, it was a close thing: 32 insurgents killed, as against 36 of the Neapolitans, with perhaps 150 wounded on each side. Morally, however, there was no doubt of the victory. Garibaldi was to be proved right. There was no more obstruction before Palermo; on the contrary, thousands of Sicilians rallied to his colours, while the Bourbon army had to fight its way back to the capital through a countryside already in revolt. At Partinico it took four hours of fighting – with artillery – to clear its way through the town. Those soldiers who were killed were torn to pieces.

But Palermo was still garrisoned by 21,000 troops, including a considerable number of Austrian and Bavarian mercenaries. Even though Garibaldi was counting on the population to rise up against them, the odds against him were still overwhelming. The original Thousand had now been reduced to about 750, and the new, largely peasant, volunteers who were joining him every day were too untrained and undisciplined to be of much use. A frontal attack was clearly out of the question; approaching by a circuitous path through the surrounding mountains, at dawn on 26 May he entered the suburbs of Palermo. The Bourbon military command, expecting him to attack along the Monreale road, had stationed nearly all their troops to the north and west of the city; approaching as he did from the southeast, he encountered no opposition. Nor, however, had he expected to be greeted by three British and two American naval officers from the ships which happened to be in the harbour, still less by the Hungarian correspondent for the London *Times*, which had been devoting daily articles to his progress.

For by now Garibaldi's expedition had caught the imagination of the world. In England especially, the excitement mounted day by day. Appeals for funds were launched; Charles Dickens and Florence Nightingale were among the contributors. The Royal Small-Arms Factory in Enfield sent an artillery gun, duty free. In France, extracts from Garibaldi's memoirs were published in *Le Siècle* after careful editing by Alexandre Dumas himself.* In America, the *New York Times* compared Garibaldi to Washington, while the *New York Daily Tribune* published a blistering attack on the Bourbons by the paper's London correspondent, Karl Marx. In Russia, interest was not confined to the intelligentsia of Moscow and St Petersburg; Mikhail Bakunin, who was at that time in exile in Siberia, reported that the march of the Thousand was being followed with passionate interest in Irkutsk.

Palermo in 1860 had a population of some 160,000. In recent months Sicily had been effectively a police state; the Palermitans were at first frightened and unwilling to show themselves. Soon, however, as they heard the bells of celebration ringing, they emerged into the streets and began to erect barricades; here at last was an insurrection which promised to topple the Bourbons for ever. The fighting went on for three days, with the Neapolitan ships in the harbour subjecting the city to heavy bombardment. On 28 May 2,000 prisoners escaped from the Vicaria prison. Some, whose offences were political, headed straight for the barricades; but the overwhelming majority were dangerous criminals. Garibaldi, in his capacity as legitimate dictator, decreed that all theft or looting should be punishable by death.

On the morning of the 30th the seventy-three-year-old General Ferdinando Lanza, commanding the Neapolitan forces, invited Garibaldi to a meeting on a British warship, HMS *Hannibal*. The two agreed on an immediate ceasefire, which was prolonged for the next few days while the negotiations continued. During this

---

* When this task was completed Dumas hurried to Palermo on his yacht, arriving in early June.

time, we are told, the Bourbons were planning to assassinate Garibaldi, and a Calabrian brigand had actually been brought to Palermo for the purpose. But so impressed was General Lanza by the man's charisma, so captivated by his charm, that the operation was called off. When at last agreement was reached it was signed on behalf of the insurgents by Crispi as 'Secretary of State for the provisional government of Sicily' – an important recognition. No further instructions were received from Naples, and on 6 June Lanza capitulated. A fortnight later, not a single Neapolitan soldier was left in Palermo. In little over a month, a handful of poorly armed and largely untrained men had brought one of the greatest royal houses of Europe to its knees.

After the victory in Palermo, that handful amounted to a few hundred exhausted men, carrying sorely outdated rifles and running seriously short of ammunition. Fortunately, additional arms and equipment were on the way. On 7 June 1,500 new rifles and munitions arrived from Malta; ten days later, three American steamships docked at Castellammare carrying 3,500 new volunteers, with another 8,000 rifles and 400,000 cartridges. Another 2,000 men landed on 6 July. Garibaldi's only major disappointment was in the Sicilians themselves. On his arrival in Palermo he had immediately issued a proclamation, calling every young or middle-aged man to the colours; but the Bourbons had formally exempted the island from conscription, the harvest was approaching and there was little response.

On the other hand he was now – for the first time in his long career – in sole command of an army; and that army had work to do. The Bourbons had withdrawn from Palermo, but they had not surrendered; they still had 18,000 men in Messina, with smaller garrisons in Milazzo, Augusta and Syracuse. Leaving Palermo in mid-July, Garibaldi led his troops across the island to Milazzo – where, on Friday, 20 July, he attacked. His force numbered nearly 5,000; that of the Bourbons perhaps 4,700, together with a unit of cavalry and eight guns.

The battle that followed was long and hard, fought in crippling heat. Around noon, Garibaldi narrowly escaped death when a cavalry captain lunged at him with his sabre; fortunately the man's horse was shot in the nick of time; Garibaldi parried the blow and killed the rider. Both sides were now dropping from exhaustion, but the fighting remained indecisive. It was mid-afternoon when Garibaldi suddenly realized what he had to do. Lying out in the roadstead was his only warship – the ten-gun steam corvette *Veloce*, which had defected from the Bourbon fleet and had since been renamed the *Tüköry*, after a Hungarian hero who had been killed on the Palermo barricades. He ran down to the beach, jumped into a boat and rowed out to the vessel, which at his command bombarded the Neapolitan troops. Taken by surprise, they panicked and made a rush for the ancient castle. The town, left undefended, was overrun by the insurgents. Garibaldi rode in on his horse, Marsala, then dismounted in the garden of a church, where he laid his saddle on the ground for a pillow and immediately fell asleep.

The castle was not large – certainly not able to accommodate over 4,000 men, with little food or water, in the heat of a Sicilian midsummer. When on 23 July a Neapolitan naval squadron appeared off the coast, Garibaldi prepared to resist; but he soon learned that the commander had come to negotiate the surrender of the castle and to repatriate the troops within it. On the following day agreement was reached. The exhausted men, nearly dying of thirst, dragged themselves down to the ships and the squadron returned to Naples. Garibaldi kept the guns, munitions, horses – and half the mules.

In terms of manpower, the insurgents' losses far exceeded those of the Bourbon army – 800 to around 150 – but the Bourbons had lost Sicily as well. Now at last the island was free. None the less it had to be governed; and Garibaldi, with his temporary dictatorial powers, was careful always to emphasize that it was soon to take its place as part of a united Italy. He was, however, more a general than a statesman; and he was fortunate indeed in having Francesco Crispi at his side. Crispi was a Sicilian, a lawyer, and a highly intelligent man; no one understood the island better than he. Already after the Battle of Calatafimi he had appointed a governor to each of the twenty-four districts into which Sicily was divided, with powers to reorganize the local administrations in whatever ways they considered necessary. When on 2 June Garibaldi formed a regular government with six ministries, Crispi took over the two most important, that of the Interior and the Treasury. Sicily further confirmed its independence by appointing its own diplomatic missions in Turin, Paris and London.

Garibaldi himself concentrated on winning popular support. He arranged for the payment of compensation for bomb damage, for the adoption of war orphans and for regular financial assistance to the poorest families. He showed almost exaggerated respect for the Church, visiting monasteries and convents, kissing crucifixes and attending, on 15 July, the festival of Palermo's patron saint, Santa Rosalia, in the cathedral. Dressed in his red shirt, he seated himself on the royal throne, thus assuming the office of Apostolic Legate which was by tradition the prerogative of the Kings of Sicily. During the reading of the Gospel, he held his sword unsheathed as a symbol of his readiness to defend the Church.

What, now, was the next step? When was Sicily to be formally annexed to Victor Emmanuel's rapidly growing kingdom? For Cavour, the sooner the better; but this idea was hotly opposed by Garibaldi and Crispi. To all intents and purposes, they argued, Sicily was already part of the Kingdom. The Sicilians certainly assumed as much, and the long legal technicalities could surely wait until the rest of the fighting was over. They were worried, too – though they took care not to say so – that, if the island were legally absorbed into Italy, Cavour might use his new authority to forbid them to use it as a bridgehead from which to advance on Naples, Rome and Venice.

These fears were by no means groundless. On 1 August 1860 Cavour wrote in desperation to his *chef de cabinet* and close friend Costantino Nigra:

> If Garibaldi can pass to the mainland and take possession of Naples as he has of Sicily and Palermo, he becomes the absolute master of the situation . . . King Victor Emmanuel loses almost all his prestige; to most Italians he is simply the friend of Garibaldi. He will probably keep his crown, but that crown will shine only with the reflected light that a heroic adventurer chooses to throw on it . . . The King cannot take the crown of Italy from the hands of Garibaldi; it would lie too unsteadily on his head . . .
>
> We must ensure that the government of Naples falls before

Garibaldi sets foot on the mainland . . . The moment the King is gone, we must take the government into our own hands in the name of order and humanity, while snatching from Garibaldi's hands the supreme direction of the Italian movement.

This brave, you may say audacious, measure will provoke cries of horror from Europe, will cause serious diplomatic complications, may even involve us at a somewhat later stage in a war with Austria. But it saves our revolution, and it preserves for the Italian movement that quality which is at once its glory and its strength: the quality of nationhood, and of monarchy.

There were further complications too. The first was political: the Bourbons had withdrawn their troops from Sicily, but they still claimed the island as theirs. On 25 June King Francis restored the constitution granted by his father in 1848 and promised Sicily new political and economic advances. He even tried to open negotiations with the Kingdom of Sardinia, though Victor Emmanuel, not surprisingly, prevaricated. The second complication was domestic: a peasant revolt was looming. Garibaldi and his followers – excepting only Crispi – had assumed that the problems affecting Sicily and the *mezzogiorno** were much the same as those of the north; they did not begin to understand why what they saw as a campaign for unification should have become a class struggle. But so it had. In the words of a young friar, liberty was not enough for those who were without bread; this was a war of the oppressed against the oppressors, who were to be found not only at the court but in every city and town. What was needed was something more than just the fall of the Bourbons. Already some of the large estates were being forcibly occupied by the peasantry; that summer Garibaldi received an appeal from the British consul in Messina to send a military force to protect the extensive lands at Bronte that were still owned by the descendants of Lord Nelson. Unhesitatingly, he did so; mass arrests and executions followed.

Cavour had already persuaded Victor Emmanuel to write officially to Garibaldi asking him not to invade the mainland. The King had done so, but he was a good deal more optimistic over the probable

---

* Literally, the midday, but the normal Italian word for southern Italy.

outcome of such an invasion than was his chief minister, and seems also to have been less concerned with his own personal prestige. He had therefore followed up his letter with another, private note for Garibaldi to the effect that these official instructions might perhaps usefully be ignored. This note contained, at least in its draft form, the following passage:

> The General must reply that he is full of devotion and reverence for the King, and would like to be able to follow his advice; but his duties to Italy will not allow him to give undertakings not to assist the Neapolitans when they appeal to him to take action to free them from a government in which loyal men and good Italians can place no trust. Thus, regretfully, he must retain complete freedom of action.

Garibaldi did indeed reply in such terms. Making use of his secret direct line to the King, he then informed him at the end of July that he had decided to cross the Strait on 15 August or even before, and requested that he be sent 10,000 rifles, with bayonets, before his departure. The King – whose optimism was growing every day – ordered that everything possible should be done to satisfy the general's demands. He also advised Garibaldi to keep the Neapolitan army intact, so that it could be united with that of Piedmont in the event of an Austrian attempt to recover Lombardy. Francis II should be allowed to leave Naples unharmed.

The Strait of Messina is only three kilometres across, but it presented a formidable obstacle. The Bourbon army – still intact – numbered 80,000 men, some 16,000 of whom were strung out along the Calabrian coast; and the Bourbon navy had complete command of the sea. A trial attempt at a crossing on the night of 8 August was a hopeless failure, and even after the arrival a few days later of two more steamships and 2,000 additional volunteers from Genoa it seemed to many that the expedition had reached the end of the road. Garibaldi, however, evolved a plan: the Strait must be avoided altogether. The two vessels were consequently despatched to the bay of Giardini-Naxos*, some fifty kilometres to the south of Taormina,

---

* Founded in 734 BC, it was the oldest Greek colony in Sicily.

where they faced the open sea. When Garibaldi arrived on the afternoon of the 18th, he found 4,200 volunteers already on board. A small leak in one of the ships was hastily repaired by blocking it with cow dung, and the expedition sailed that evening. By dawn they were in Calabria.

It would have been better if they could have begun their long march at once, but the men desperately needed rest. Those who had come straight from Genoa had not slept for three days, and shortage of space on board had obliged them to stand throughout the night. Lying exhausted on the beach, they were thus easy prey to the two Bourbon warships which, alerted by telegraph, had appeared off the coast and immediately opened fire. Many were killed or wounded, and when on the evening of the 19th the party set off, its numbers were down to about 3,600. That, however, was the last of the disasters. They marched without incident the thirty kilometres to Reggio, which they took after a short but furious battle. As they continued through Calabria, the Bourbon opposition melted away. There is a delightful account of Garibaldi strolling among the humiliated Neapolitan soldiers, reminding them that they too were Italians and inviting them to join him. Meanwhile the Neapolitan fleet had left the Strait, enabling yet more volunteers to cross directly from Sicily. By now, too, rebellions were breaking out in Potenza, Foggia and Bari. Not that the advance was easy; it was some two hundred miles of rough track from Reggio to Naples; the men were exhausted; the heat was merciless; water was short.

But at least there was no more fighting. King Francis was panic-stricken. The British diplomat Odo Russell, at that time serving on a mission to Naples, had reported that when Garibaldi had entered Palermo the King 'telegraphed five times in twenty-four hours for the Pope's blessing'. Francis knew that his army was incapable of further resistance to the seemingly invincible Redshirts, and that he himself was equally incapable of breathing further life into it; the only alternative was flight. On 6 September he took ship for Gaeta.

On the same day Garibaldi reached Salerno, some fifty miles from Naples. There he received an invitation to enter the city, delivered personally by the mayor and the commander of the National Guard. He accepted at once. He was fully aware that he might well have to deal with the few thousand loyal Bourbon soldiers who remained in the fortresses and barracks, but that was a risk he was ready to face: he did not trust Cavour an inch, and feared a preemptive strike.

He arrived in Naples, surprisingly, on King Bomba's railway. Since its inauguration in 1839 it had been extended southwards and now reached as far as Vietri, on the coast near Amalfi. Garibaldi immediately requisitioned all the rolling stock he could find and filled it with his army. He himself, with six companions, climbed into an open carriage and advanced slowly among the dense crowds that lined the track. When the train reached Portici he was strongly advised to go no further; the guns in the forts, it was believed, were already aiming at the railway station. He refused, however, to listen; and at half past one on 7 September the train trundled into Naples. That evening he addressed a cheering populace from the balcony of the royal palace, thanking the Neapolitans 'in the name of all Italy which, owing to their cooperation, had at last become a nation'. It was a shameless lie – they had not lifted a finger – but he doubtless felt that a little flattery at this stage would do no harm. There followed a service of thanksgiving in the cathedral – at which the Cardinal, a keen supporter of the Bourbons, was conspicuous by his absence – after which Garibaldi was taken by carriage to the Palazzo d'Angri, which had been put at his disposal for as long as he wanted it. Still the cheering continued outside his windows, until one of his officers emerged on a balcony and signalled that the great man would appreciate a little sleep.

He made no attempt to move into the royal palace, remaining in the palazzo, where he occupied a small upper room with a simple iron bedstead, between ten and eleven every morning receiving calls there from anyone who wished to speak to him. Many of his visitors were foreign journalists, since he had now become the hero of Europe. In London alone, nearly half a million prints of his portrait were sold, and as early as 1861 Messrs Peek Frean of Bermondsey launched their new firm with the Garibaldi biscuit – better known as the 'squashed fly' – which has remained popular ever since.

★

For the next two months Garibaldi ruled Naples and Sicily as a dictator. Meanwhile, he was planning his next step, which was to be an immediate march on Rome and the Papal States. This step, however, was never taken. Cavour, having been unable to prevent his invasion of the mainland and knowing full well that – with a French army still occupying Rome – to allow him to continue might well mean war with France, was now determined to stop him in his tracks. It was for his own sake too: those Redshirts would have found the superbly trained French troops a very different prop-osition from anything that they had so far encountered, and Italy might well have lost everything she had gained in the past two years. Finally, there was his old nagging concern over personal prestige. Garibaldi was now far more popular than Victor Emmanuel himself, and there was always a lurking danger that he might be persuaded to desert the King of Sardinia and espouse the republican cause.

Garibaldi was of course well aware of Cavour's hostility, just as he believed in the King's tacit support; and soon after his arrival in Naples he had even gone so far as publicly to demand the Chief Minister's resignation; but in doing so he had badly overplayed his hand. Victor Emmanuel, realizing that he could no longer continue to play off the two men against each other, found it safer to accept the policy of his government. None of this, however, nor any number of letters – inspired by Cavour – from distinguished foreigners ranging from the Hungarian patriot Lajos Kossuth to the British social reformer Lord Shaftesbury, weakened Garibaldi's resolve to march on Rome. The only argument that could have had an effect was the one that eventually did so: *force majeure*.

So it was that, not long after Garibaldi left Naples on the first stage of his intended advance to Rome, he found two formidable armies ranged against him: the Piedmontese and, surprisingly, the Neapolitan. In spite of its recent reverses in Sicily and Calabria – which were due far more to the incompetence of the generals than to the shortcomings of the troops themselves, who had fought with great courage at Calatafimi and Milazzo – King Francis's army was still essentially intact. Remarkably few had defected to the insur-gents, and the King had been able to recruit more during his self-imposed exile in Gaeta. They were now occupying the fortified city of Capua, some fifteen miles to the north of Naples; Garibaldi accordingly made his headquarters at Caserta, just seven or eight miles away. He knew that he was in a weak position; he would have to move with caution.

At this particular moment a dispute broke out in Sicily on the subject of the island's annexation. On 19 September Garibaldi had to make a quick visit to Palermo – and one of his generals, a Hungarian named Stefano Türr, saw (or thought he saw) his chance. He marched on Capua, sending a separate force of 300 to occupy the little town of Caiazzo, on a hilltop just above the Volturno River. The Bourbon army easily drove them back and then, two days later with a force of 7,000, launched their own full-scale attack on the town, to which Garibaldi – now returned from Sicily – had sent a further 600 men. Caiazzo fell. Garibaldi, fighting himself always in the front line, lost 250 men he could ill afford – dead, wounded or taken prisoner. The Bourbons had won their first victory. Perhaps the pendulum, at long last, had begun to swing.

On the first day of October, however, he had his revenge. Known nowadays by the name of the river Volturno, the battle was fought just outside Capua, around the little village and abbey of S. Angelo in Formis on the slopes of Mount Tifata.★ It was an expensive victory – some 1,400 killed or wounded – but it saved Italy. Once again the defeat of the Bourbon army was due to the ineptitude of its generals. As Garibaldi explained in his subsequent analysis of the battle, had they adopted a different strategy they could have reached Naples with very few losses and much, if not all, of his own work would have been undone.

Meanwhile a second army was already on the march. Cavour, determined to recapture the initiative, had launched an invasion of his own into the papal territories of Umbria and the Marches. Leaving Rome untouched, he had neatly avoided antagonizing France and, quite possibly, Austria; he had also opened the way

---

★ It is something of a miracle that the church of S. Angelo was not destroyed. It is the grandest monument in all Campania, its interior walls covered in eleventh-century frescoes by Greek artists from Byzantium and their Italian pupils. All are in a quite astonishing state of preservation.

into the south, where he could claim that the Piedmontese were urgently needed to save Naples from the forces of revolution. Most important of all, he had at least partly removed the barrier of the Papal States which, so long as it lasted, split Italy into two parts and made unification impossible. The campaign itself was unspectacular but effective. The Piedmontese overcame a spirited resistance at Perugia, scored a small victory over a papal army near the village of Castelfidardo near Loreto and a rather larger one when, after five days' fighting, they captured Ancona, taking 7,000 prisoners – including the commander of the papal forces, the French General Christophe de Lamoricière. That was the end of the papal army; henceforth it gave no further trouble.

Victor Emmanuel himself, accompanied by his long-term mistress Rosina Vercellana – dressed, we are told, to kill – now came to take titular command of his army. From that moment Garibaldi's star began to set. The Battle of the Volturno had already persuaded him that a march on Rome was no longer a possibility; and now, with the King himself on the way, he saw that his rule in the south must come to an end. This was confirmed on 21 October 1860, when plebiscites were held in the Kingdom of Naples and in Sicily, in Umbria and in the Marches, on whether voters wished their land to form an integral part of Italy under Victor Emmanuel. The votes in favour were overwhelming: in Sicily 432,053 voted in favour, 667 against.

This all but unanimous vote obviously needs some explaining. Few of the voters had the faintest idea of what it was all about, nor was there time or the technology to educate them. Those who were against the motion were subjected to often intolerable pressure not to vote. Many peasants feared that they were being approached for military service and fled at once to the hills; others thought that they were just being asked to express their admiration of Garibaldi. But none of this mattered. The receiving officers perfectly understood what was required of them – and delivered it.

When it was realized that the effect of the referendum had been to end the dictatorship of Garibaldi and to transfer all his powers to the government in Turin many Sicilians, who had seen him as a hero and a liberator, made no secret of their disgust. Still greater offence was caused when, on the all-important subject of regional self-government, Cavour went back on his word. It appeared that there was to be no autonomy for Sicily after all. Alas, he was a northerner through and through, with no knowledge – let alone understanding – of the customs and institutions of the south. Looking at Sicily – where he had never been – from the safe distance of Turin, some six hundred miles away even as the crow flies, he concluded that what the island needed was a good dose of northern discipline. The following years would show just how wrong he was.

Garibaldi for his part gave in gracefully. On the 26th he met the King at Teano, and on 7 November the two of them entered Naples side by side in the royal carriage. He asked one favour only: to be allowed to govern Naples and Sicily for a year as the King's representative. But the request was refused. He was after all a dangerous radical and anticlerical, who still dreamed of capturing Rome from the Pope and making it the capital of Italy. In an attempt to sugar the pill, Victor Emmanuel offered him the rank of full general together with a splendid estate, a ship and several other privileges, but Garibaldi would have none of them. He remained a revolutionary, and for as long as Austria still occupied Venice and the Veneto – and the Pope continued as temporal ruler in Rome – he was determined to preserve his freedom of action. On 9 November he sailed for his farm on the tiny island of Caprera off the Sardinian coast. He took with him only a little money – borrowed, since he had made none during his months of power – a few packets of sugar and coffee, and a bag of seeds for his garden.

On Passion Sunday, 17 March 1861, Victor Emmanuel II was proclaimed King of Italy. Old Massimo d'Azeglio, Cavour's predecessor as Chief Minister, is reported to have said when he heard the news: '*L'Italia è fatta: restano a fare gli italiani*.'* But although the first half of the statement was true – an Italian nation had indeed come into existence, even if it was not yet quite complete – the second half was truer still. Francis II kept up his resistance; the country had been divided since the end of the Roman Empire,

---

* 'Italy is made; now we have to make the Italians.'

and few indeed of Italy's 22 million people thought of themselves as Italians. North and south had virtually nothing in common, with radically different standards of living – as indeed they still have today. New roads and railways had to be built as a matter of urgency. A national army and navy had somehow to be created, together with a single legal system, civil administration and common currency. In the meantime there was no alternative to the adoption of Piedmontese institutions; but this forcible 'Piedmontization' was widely resented and did little to help the cause of unity. Even the King's decision to continue to call himself 'the Second' caused offence. As the first King of a united Italy he was surely Victor Emmanuel I; was the Risorgimento really the rebirth of Italy, or was it simply the conquest of Italy by the House of Savoy?

Less than three months after the royal proclamation Cavour was dead. He had spent his last weeks in furious debate over the future of Rome – in which, it should be recorded, he had never once set foot. All the other major Italian cities, he argued, had been independent municipalities, each fighting its own corner; only Rome, as the seat of the Church, had remained above such rivalries. But though the Pope must be asked to surrender his temporal power, papal independence must at all costs be guaranteed – what was necessary was 'a free church in a free state'. He encountered a good deal of opposition – the most vitriolic from Garibaldi, who emerged from Caprera in April, strode into the Roman Assembly in his red shirt and grey poncho and let loose a stream of invective at the man who, he thundered, had sold off half his country to the French and done his best to prevent the invasion of the Two Sicilies. But alas – he succeeded only in confirming the general view that however brilliant a general he might be, he was certainly no statesman; Cavour easily won the vote of confidence that followed. It was his last political victory. He died suddenly on 6 June 1861, of a massive stroke. He was just fifty years old.

If Camillo Cavour had lived just one more decade he would have seen the last two pieces of the Italian jigsaw fitted into place. Where Rome was concerned, the situation was not helped by Garibaldi, who in 1862 made a faintly ridiculous attempt to repeat his triumph of two years before. Adopting the slogan 'Rome or death!', he raised 3,000 volunteers in Palermo, with whom he took possession of a complaisant Catania; then in August, having commandeered a couple of local steamers, he crossed with his men to Calabria and began another march on Rome. This time, however, government troops were ready for him. He had got no further than the Aspromonte massif in the extreme south of Calabria – the toe of Italy – when they attacked. Fearing a civil war, Garibaldi ordered his men not to return the fire; there were a few casualties none the less, he himself having his right ankle shattered. He was arrested and sent in a gunboat to Naples – where he was promptly set at liberty. After all, he was still a hero. The government did not dare take action against him.

The story can be very briefly completed. In 1866 the Prussian Chancellor Otto von Bismarck found Austria to be a serious obstacle to the realization of his dream of uniting all the German states into a single empire. He therefore forged an alliance with the new Kingdom of Italy: the two would attack Austria simultaneously on two fronts. In the event of victory, Italy's reward would be Venice and the Veneto. A single battle was enough. It was fought on 3 July at Sadowa – also known by its German name of Königgrätz – some sixty-five miles northeast of Prague, and it engaged the greatest number of troops – some 330,000 – ever assembled on a European battlefield. The Prussian victory was total. It bankrupted the military resources of the Emperor Franz Josef and opened the way to Vienna. The ensuing armistice duly resulted in the cession of the promised territory. Venice was no longer the independent republic that she had once been, but she was at least an Italian city rather than an Austrian one; and Italy could boast a new and economically invaluable port on the northern Adriatic.

The unity of Italy, however, could not be achieved without Rome; and Rome too was acquired by courtesy of Bismarck, who had cunningly drawn France into a war by his threat to place a prince of the ruling Prussian House of Hohenzollern on the throne of Spain – a proposal clearly unacceptable to the French, who would have then found themselves completely surrounded by Germany. War was therefore declared – by France, not Prussia – on

15 July 1870. It was to prove a bitter struggle; Napoleon III was going to need every soldier he had for the fighting that lay ahead. Thus, by the end of August, not one French soldier remained in Rome. Pope Pius IX was left defenceless. Napoleon's defeat at Sedan on 1 September spelled the end of the Second Empire; and on 20 September the Italian army entered the Holy City. The Pope withdrew inside the walls of the Vatican, where he remained for the last eight years of his life. The plebiscite that was held shortly afterwards registered 133,681 votes in favour of the incorporation of Rome into the new kingdom and 1,507 against. Rome was now part of Italy, not by right of conquest but by the will of its people;* and the Kingdom of Italy, under its sovereign King Victor Emmanuel II, finally took its place among the nations of Europe.

As the voting figures showed, the Sicilians were as happy as their new compatriots. They were, after all, a good deal more Italian than Spanish, and even though their King was a Piedmontese – a man of the mountains rather than of the sea, and hailing from as far from Sicily as it was possible to go while remaining an Italian – there seemed a fair chance that they would be allowed to play a larger part in their own affairs than they had in the past. They hoped so, anyway.

* The Vatican City has been an independent state only since 1929. We should also perhaps mention the still independent Most Serene Republic of San Marino, which covers only twenty-four square miles and numbers only some 30,000 nationals, but dates its beginning to the year 301 AD and is thus in theory the oldest surviving sovereign state in the world. During the Risorgimento it served as a refuge for many people persecuted because of their support for unification, as a result of which Garibaldi granted its wish not to be incorporated into the new Italian state.

16

The Mafia and Mussolini

IN SICILIAN EYES, the unification of Italy had – largely on account of the blunders made in Turin – got off to a deplorable start. The new Italian government was hated, perhaps, even more than that of the Bourbons before it. The people of Sicily deeply resented not only the refusal of their promised autonomy but the summary dismissal of Garibaldi, with barely a word of thanks or congratulation on his astonishing achievement. Cavour's distrust of the dauntless old hero had induced him to sabotage his reputation in every way he could. The government of the island had been put in the hands of men whom Garibaldi had despised; his many extremely sensible recommendations had been deliberately ignored.* What Cavour had forgotten was the man's enormous popularity: moreover, he had utterly failed to understand that belief, in the hearts of all Sicilians, that it was *they* who, on 4 April 1860, had taken the first step towards the liberation and unification of Italy. Was annexation – to Piedmont, of all places – now to be their reward?

The officials sent from Turin to set Sicily to rights were equally disillusioned by what they found. They had expected a sadder, poorer version of Piedmont; here instead was another world, speaking another language, operating on a completely different system. It did not even share the moral values of the north. Nepotism, for example, was not considered remotely wrong; on the contrary, it was the duty of any respectable man to do as much as he possibly could for his family and friends.† Patronage, too, was right and natural; it affected

---

* He had, for example, recommended a regional assembly for Sicily. Eighty-five years later, Sicily got one.

† At Monreale in 1875 almost all the municipal employees were relatives of the mayor.

all transactions, all agreements, and it extended in a vast network from one end of the island to the other. And there were other problems too: the powerful but deeply reactionary clergy, for example, many of whom longed for a Bourbon restoration; or those potentially dangerous groups of revolutionaries who dreamed of an independent Sicilian republic. In such circumstances a fair and efficient administration was clearly impossible; those luckless bureaucrats whose business it was to attempt it could only shrug their shoulders and, at the earliest possible moment, apply for a transfer.

After 1870, all the bitterness and resentment that continued to seethe in Sicily against Piedmont was redirected against the Kingdom of Italy itself and, in particular, against the two hated institutions which, for most Sicilians, it chiefly represented: taxation and conscription. About taxation there was nothing new; it had always existed, even though in Sicily its avoidance had been developed into an art form. Local taxation was almost entirely under the control of the individual village bosses; friends and relations of the mayor were normally exempt. The peasant's mule was taxed; the landlord's cattle were not. Conscription was more serious. The Bourbons had never dared impose it; when the Piedmontese did, it had nearly caused a revolution on the spot. For Sicily was, almost exclusively, an agricultural society; and it was, furthermore, a society in which women were kept firmly in the home. Never, anywhere on the island, were they to be seen working in the fields; barely even did they venture into the streets. It followed that, if a man were conscripted, there would be one fewer pair of hands to till the soil, to sow the seed, or to reap the harvest. To escape such a fate, desperate measures would be taken: children were kept away from school, boys registered as girls, recruiting officers lynched. Of those unfortunates who despite their efforts were pressed into service, half had disappeared before they reached the barracks.

In short, Sicily – and in particular western Sicily, where there were fewer large estates and where the prevailing poverty was greater – was becoming more lawless than ever she had been. No shame attached to being a shirker, or even a deserter, since no one felt any loyalty to the new state. The fact that the Italian government was more liberal than that of the autocratic Bourbons just made it easier to manipulate, or to ignore altogether. The government had divided the island into six provinces, and had established four police forces, among which the rivalries were intense. Wanted criminals had no difficulty in slipping from one area of jurisdiction to the next. Gang warfare was rife: in Palermo, the British consul was kidnapped; a dozen people were stabbed to death in a single night. In the island as a whole, the murder rate was ten times as high as in Piedmont or Lombardy.

What was to be done? The Italian government took what was effectively the only option open to it – to meet force with force. General Giuseppe Govone had a remarkable military record. He had distinguished himself at the Battle of Magenta and, perhaps rather more surprisingly, in the Crimean War, where at Balaclava he had witnessed the Charge of the Light Brigade.* In 1862, though still under forty, he was appointed to govern Sicily and granted full powers, including that of life and death; effectively, he could do as he liked. There followed something suspiciously like a reign of terror. Men were arrested and held for years without trial; hostages were taken, and often executed; water supplies were cut off; torture was far from unknown. The government became more detested than ever, and Govone himself did not increase his popularity by protesting to the parliament that no other methods would succeed 'in a country which has not yet completed the cycle which leads from barbarism to civilization'. The resulting outcry led to a parliamentary investigation, resignations from the government and a number of duels among the deputies. Govone was cleared of all charges, but it was deemed safer to return him to the mainland. Once again Sicily had proved herself ungovernable.

In 1863 a play was produced, set in the Ucciardone, the main prison of Palermo. It enjoyed enormous success. Its title was *I Mafiusi della Vacaria*, and it gave a new word to the Sicilian – and subsequently to the Italian – language. As previous pages should have made clear, there was nothing new about the Mafia, except possibly the word itself; its nebulous beginnings can be traced back to Spanish colonial times. After 1860, however, it had taken on a new dimension. In those early days it was not in any sense

* The Kingdom of Sardinia's participation in the Crimean War is now largely forgotten. Its army fought in only one small engagement, sustaining 28 casualties.

monolithic: its individual *cosche**** were more often than not at war with one another, as each fought to extend its territory and its sphere of influence. Together, however, they dominated most of the island, particularly in the west. The first parliamentary elections, held in January 1861, saw them already at work. There was little or no counting of votes; the total electorate – which was limited to those able to read and write – amounted to little over one percent of the population; the results were a foregone conclusion.

Five years later, in September 1866, Palermo suffered yet another insurrection – its fourth in half a century. It was clearly organized by the Mafia, which meant that there were no obvious leaders and that nothing was put in writing. (Most Mafia members were illiterate anyway.) But word went round in advance, and the populace was ordered to come out in strength when the shooting began. The primary purpose of the rising was not to overthrow the government; it carried no banners, chanted no slogans. It was there entirely to show its power and to make trouble, and it did so to remarkable effect. Arsenals were emptied, government buildings and law courts looted, criminal records destroyed. Of course it became more uncontrolled as time went on, and the mob saw more and more opportunities to go on the rampage; its beginnings, however – the simultaneous appearance of several hundred men marching down the Monreale road into the city, and their unhesitating concentration on what must have been previously selected targets – showed unmistakable signs of careful planning. One of those targets was the Ucciardone prison; had the insurgents succeeded in breaking into it and releasing some 2,500 convicts, the effects of the rising would have been a lot worse than they were. Fortunately the steam corvette *Tancredi* arrived in the nick of time and bombarded the attackers with grapeshot and grenades. But the fighting continued; some 40,000 troops were mobilized, and a whole week was to pass before the Italian navy shelled Palermo into submission.

The message was clear: the Mafia had shown that it was to be taken seriously. But what exactly was it? Was it just a manifestation of the Sicilian mentality, born of a centuries-old tradition of

---

* The Sicilian word *cosca* refers to any plant, like an artichoke, with tightly folded leaves; they symbolize the closeness of the individual members of the group.

lawlessness, going back, perhaps, even to the Arab invaders of a thousand years before? Was it simply the collective noun for a bunch of criminal gangs, each of them out for what it could get? Or was it an organization, a sworn criminal fraternity, with a chief and a number of lieutenants? This last, certainly, was what it was to become; but it took immense pains to conceal the fact: one of the principal reasons for its long-term success was its ability to make many people believe that it did not actually exist at all.

But not everyone. The mayor of Palermo at the time, the Marquis of Rudinì, was the King's appointee and an honest man. He had fought bravely throughout the insurrection, first from the city hall and then from the royal palace – where he, more than anyone else, had been responsible for saving Palermo's greatest jewel, the Palatine Chapel, from destruction. In May 1867, when a parliamentary commission of inquiry arrived from Rome, he pulled no punches:

The Mafia is powerful – perhaps even more powerful than people believe. Uncovering it and punishing it is very often impossible, because there is no proof, either of the crimes, or of who is to blame . . . We have never been able to gather enough evidence to prepare a trial and bring it to a successful conclusion.

Only those who have Mafia protection can move about freely in the countryside . . . The lack of security has brought about the following situation: anyone who wants to go into the countryside and live there has to become a brigand. There is no alternative. To defend yourself and your property, you have to obtain protection from the criminals, and tie yourself to them in some way.

The Ucciardone – the Palermo prison – is a kind of government. It is from there that rules and orders are issued. In the Ucciardone they know everything – which might lead us to believe that the Mafia has formally recognised bosses. In the countryside around Palermo criminal gangs are very widespread, and there are many different bosses; but they often act in agreement with one another, and look to the Ucciardone for leadership.*

* Quoted in John Dickie, *Blood Brotherhoods*. But it was only in 1992 – 125 years later – that the Court of Cassation (the Supreme Court of Italy) confirmed for the first time that the Mafia was not a variegated collection of local gangs but one single organization, bound by an oath of loyalty until death.

Cosa nostra, in other words, was here to stay.

Perhaps the most far-reaching and disruptive legislation introduced by the Italian government towards the end of the nineteenth century was what can only be called the dissolution of the monasteries. This was not carried out with the same degree of thoroughness as had been shown in England some three hundred and fifty years before; but as the century drew to its close anticlericalism was in the air. In Germany under Bismarck, in France under Gambetta – and indeed in Cavour's Piedmont – the Church was coming under increasingly hostile pressure. Sicily threatened to be a rather tougher nut to crack: first because it was Sicily, secondly because in a land already riddled with superstition the clergy tended to be more popular. The fact remained that a good ten percent of the island belonged to the Church, while the number of cathedrals, churches, monasteries and convents was out of all proportion to the population. Caccamo, for example, boasted a cathedral, twenty-nine churches and nine monasteries; its lay population was 6,000.

Garibaldi had long ago proposed that much of the Church's land should be redistributed among propertyless peasants, thus creating a new class of smallholders who would henceforth have something to live for; but this admirable idea was, it need hardly be said, rejected. Instead it was decided that the land should be auctioned, and sold off in far larger units than Garibaldi had contemplated, for the highest possible prices. Inevitably, the Mafia stepped in; the auctioneers were intimidated or bribed or both, groups of wealthy purchasers formed rings to keep the prices down and dispose of unnecessary competition; the government lost up to ninety percent of the value of the land and the rich got a very great deal richer. Monks and nuns, on the other hand, together with many of the clergy, were rendered homeless; some 15,000 laymen who worked for them found themselves unemployed; meanwhile, the countless charity schools, hospitals, orphanages and soup kitchens which made life bearable for the urban poor were obliged to close their doors. As a final consequence, the government earned itself something it could ill afford: the implacable hostility of the Church – which, as time went on, was to turn increasingly to the Mafia for support.

It had other enemies too: those who dreamed of a return of the Bourbons; those who longed for autonomy within the Kingdom of Italy or even independence without it – there was a sizable group of Sicilian nationalists for whom Italy was 'abroad', and who even refused to speak Italian. The only people hard to find were those who declared themselves in the Kingdom's favour. So much, indeed, was it disliked, disregarded and disobeyed that, according to an eyewitness of the insurrection, any foreign country which might have tried to take Sicily from Italy would now have received the same enthusiastic support in the island that Garibaldi had encountered against the Bourbons.*

Ten years after the Palermo insurrection there appeared a report on the situation in Sicily by two Tuscan barons, Leopoldo Franchetti and the half-Welsh Sidney Sonnino. It is by far the most perceptive and the most thorough of all the accounts of the island in the years following its incorporation into the Italian state; and its conclusions are unhappy indeed. Corruption, it confirmed, was everywhere, in every town hall and government office. Tax money that did not end in somebody's pocket was spent largely on bribes, and what was left tended to go on public buildings, especially theatres. (Palermo had several of the grandest theatres in Europe before it had a proper hospital.) As for the 'Honoured Society' – as the Mafia liked to call itself – it simply filled the gap where government should have been. Crime was the means by which it achieved its ends; and those ends were respect, power and money. Crime, however, was itself respected: many a criminal – even a murderer – was protected by members of high Palermo society. If the landowners in western Sicily really wished it, brigandage could be stopped at once; unfortunately 'there is not a single proprietor living on his estates who does not deal directly with the brigands.' Thus it was that small-time criminals were often linked to powerful barons, in which case they would be virtually immune from arrest or conviction.

So what, if anything, was to be done? Frankly, nothing much.

---

* Giacomo Pagano, *Avvenimenti del 1866: sette giorni d'insurrezione a Palermo*, Palermo: 1867. Quoted in Denis Mack Smith, *Modern Sicily after 1715*.

If honest Sicilians were to be appointed to the leading administrative posts, they would not stand a chance; outsiders, on the other hand, would be constantly deceived, baffled and made to look ridiculous. The problem, in short, had no solution. But Sicily was not standing still. Despite two successive Sicilian Prime Ministers of Italy – Francesco Crispi and Antonio di Rudinì, both of whose names have already appeared in these pages – who with one short intermission held power between 1887 and 1898, life on the island for the farmers and peasants was growing harder all the time. In the words of a British consul, writing in 1891, 'the price of labour has not risen during the last 20 years, while the cost of living has doubled.'

On the other hand, literacy was on the increase, and thanks to military conscription far more young Sicilians than ever before had travelled in Italy – and sometimes further – and had returned with new ideas. It was in 1890 or thereabouts that small groups known as *fasci*, or 'bunches', began to form an embryonic trade union movement, prepared to go on strike for better pay or working conditions. In May 1893 a regional socialist congress was held in Sicily; in July, a meeting of several hundred peasants. These gatherings led inevitably to demonstrations, and the demonstrations led to riots. For the landowners and the civil authorities, the writing was on the wall.

In December 1893 Francesco Crispi was returned to power as Prime Minister. It was some time since he had given much thought to his native island; now, however, he moved fast. A state of emergency was declared throughout Sicily. Without a shred of evidence, he accused the *fasci* of plotting, assisted by France and Russia, to sever it from mainland Italy. The Italian fleet gathered off the coast; meanwhile, 40,000 troops were sent in to restore order, which they did with brutal force, making literally thousands of arrests and occasionally executing their victims on the spot. On 16 June 1894 Crispi himself had a close brush with death when an anarchist tried to assassinate him; a series of anti-anarchist laws followed. Finally he seized the opportunity of staging new elections for his own and his government's advantage, striking hundreds of opponents off the electoral roll – including more than one university professor on grounds of illiteracy – and releasing convicts in return for their support of government candidates. In the words of one recently disenfranchised socialist from Catania, Giuseppe de Felice Giuffrida, Francesco Crispi was the worst mafioso of them all.

In 1896 Crispi was succeeded, for the second time, by his fellow Sicilian the Marquis of Rudinì; and it was Rudinì who made the first experiments in granting the island a degree of autonomy. He trod slowly and carefully – he was certainly not prepared to go as far as to create a local assembly such as Garibaldi had proposed; instead, he appointed a Special Regional Commissioner, a parliamentarian by the name of Giovanni Codronchi. The experiment was not a success – for reasons which were by this time all too familiar. First, Codronchi was a northerner (from Imola), and was consequently baffled by the people, the language and the customs. By basing himself in Palermo, he also instantly antagonized Messina. With all his efforts systematically frustrated and by now feeling totally hamstrung, he tried to beat the Sicilians at their own game, rigging the new elections as blatantly and unscrupulously as Crispi had done before him – even to the point where de Felice Giuffrida, though for years a serving member of parliament, was found to be too young to vote. But it was all to no avail. Sicily won again.

At last, just around the turn of the century, things began to improve in the east of the island. Conditions there had never been so bad as they were in Palermo and the west. Many people attributed the difference to the fact that the west had in the past been largely Arab while the east had been predominantly Greek; or perhaps it was just that Messina and Catania were physically closer to the mainland than Palermo or Trapani. Whatever the reason, the business communities in the east were a good deal less susceptible to Mafia influence than the landed estates of the west, and where brigandage did continue to exist they actively opposed it. In the whole island the most law-abiding province was that of Syracuse, which also boasted the best communications.

The steady improvement of social conditions in the east, however, tended to invite comparison with the west, where they showed a continued deterioration. There, in the provinces of Palermo, Trapani,

Caltanissetta and Girgenti,★ there were far more Mafia crimes in 1910 than there had been forty years before; the murder rate in Caltanissetta was nearly ten times as high as in Messina – one reason being that many mafiosi had spent some years in New York, where crime was considerably more refined and sophisticated. There, the Sicilian underworld was dominated by an organization known as the Black Hand. In 1909 Lieutenant Giuseppe 'Joe' Petrosino, a Salerno-born member of the New York Police Department who in the past four years had arrested or repatriated over six hundred Italian mobsters, was sent over to Palermo to investigate the network of criminal activities between America and Sicily. One March evening while he was standing under the monumental bust of Garibaldi in Piazza Marina awaiting a couple of potential informers, two men approached and shot him dead. The chief suspect was the first *capomafia* in Sicily, Don Vito Cascioferro – a man of immense influence and power in Palermo. Many years before, in New York, he had himself been arrested by Petrosino on a charge of murder; he had been acquitted, but had subsequently judged it best to return to Sicily. It need hardly be said that he possessed a cast-iron alibi: Domenico de Michele, a Sicilian parliamentarian, swore that Cascioferro had been in his house at the time. Nobody seemed to worry that de Michele was the son of 'Baron' Pietro de Michele, a notorious murderer and rapist who had been the Mafia boss of Burgio, near Agrigento; his evidence was accepted without question. (In fact it may well have been true: Don Vito would certainly have used hired killers rather than do the deed himself.)†

Given the hostility between Sicily's two principal cities, it is unlikely that Lieutenant Petrosino found Palermo particularly distressed; but it should have been. Little over a year before his arrival, at 5.20 a.m. on 28 December 1908, Messina had suffered the deadliest natural disaster in European history: an earthquake measuring 7.1 on the Richter scale, followed by a forty-foot

---

★ Which changed its name to Agrigento in 1927.
† According to the subsequent police report, Petrosino 'had stopped to satisfy a personal need'. Typically, his mafiosi killers had deliberately chosen such a moment, to inflict maximum humiliation on their victim.

tsunami along the nearby coasts. More than ninety percent of its buildings were destroyed, between 70,000 and 100,000 people killed. Hundreds more were buried alive, often for a week or more, since all terrestrial lines of communication were shattered; it was several days before the Red Cross and other relief organizations could reach the city. Nearly all the municipal archives were lost – which is why so much of modern Sicilian history has to be told from the frequently misleading point of view of Palermo.

The Messina earthquake resulted in a huge increase in the rate of emigration. Sicilians were already leaving their homeland in greater numbers than any other people in Europe. In the early days many of them had made the relatively short journey to Tunisia, then a French protectorate; but by 1900 – though Argentina and Brazil were also popular – the vast majority were travelling to the United States. By the beginning of the First World War, the number of emigrants totalled not less than a million and a half. Some villages, having lost virtually all their male population, simply disappeared off the map. Here indeed was a terrible indictment of the way the island had for so long been governed; on the other hand, many of those emigrants who prospered made regular remissions to the families they had left behind, and reports of their prosperity gave the younger generation new ambitions towards education and literacy. Moreover, the increasing shortage of labour led to a huge increase in agricultural wages.

The war itself created new problems. Sicily's export markets, on which the island depended, were virtually cut off for its duration. War industries, of the kind which were established elsewhere in Italy, were clearly not indicated in a region in which there was no skilled labour and no efficient transport. The government, desperately needing cheap food, fixed unrealistically low prices for flour; officially declared wheat production consequently declined by about thirty percent over the war years. Black market prices rocketed. As for the Mafia, it had never had it so good. Here the villain was the notorious Don Calogero Vizzini, who somehow escaped military service and made vast sums out of wartime shortages. In 1917 it proved necessary to pass a law against the stealing of animals;

thanks to high prices and government controls, whole flocks would disappear overnight. True, there were occasional compensations: men who went to fight in the north would return with new skills and new aspirations – but also with new political ideas. During the years of war, Sicily moved steadily to the left.

Finally, during the postwar years, more and more emigrants were returning in retirement to their old homes, often with considerable savings, and bringing with them all their experience of the New World. Some, admittedly, also imported the latest techniques of gangsterism, but these were only a small minority; perhaps the most important result of the years spent abroad was a new self-respect, and with it an inability any longer to accept the old cap-in-hand approach to the large landowners. Gradually, the people of Sicily were learning to look their masters in the face.

For obvious geographical reasons, the Sicilians had always felt close to North Africa; and there was rejoicing when in 1911 Italy acquired Libya from the tottering Ottoman Empire, seeing it as the beginning of a great African empire of its own. In fact, the Italian occupation of Libya lasted for only thirty-one years and proved an enormous waste of money, while the war with Turkey that had achieved it was quickly followed by the First World War. This too did Sicily little good, leading to a flourishing black market – conditions ideal for Mafia activity. And, ironically enough, the Prime Minister who saw the country through to the end of the war was a self-proclaimed mafioso – though admittedly he took, or claimed to take, a rather different view of the Honoured Society than that of most of his contemporaries. Born in Palermo and representing nearby Partinico – where he was supported by the boss Frank Coppola, who had been deported back to Italy from the United States – Vittorio Emmanuele Orlando had been connected to the Mafia throughout his life. In 1925 he was to inform the Italian Senate in so many words:

If by the word 'Mafia' we understand a sense of honour pitched in the highest key; a refusal to tolerate anyone's prominence or overbearing behaviour . . . A generosity of spirit which, while it meets strength head-on, is indulgent to the weak and shows loyalty to friends . . . If such feelings and such behaviour are what people mean by 'the Mafia' . . . then we are actually speaking of the special characteristics of the Sicilian soul; and I declare that I am a mafioso, and proud to be one.

This was the man who represented Italy at most of the Paris Peace Conference of 1919, although he was not a signatory to the final treaty, having been forced to resign a few days before its conclusion. Mafioso or not, Orlando got on well enough with everyone at the Conference – except President Wilson – though his lack of English obliged him to leave most of the talking to his dour and charmless Foreign Minister, Sidney Sonnino.* He never bothered to hide his emotions; when he realized that Italy was not going to receive the port of Fiume (now Rijeka) as part of the peace settlement, he burst into tears. Clemenceau called him *Le Pleureur*, 'the Weeper'; the British Cabinet Secretary, Sir Maurice Hankey, remarked that he would have spanked his son for such a disgraceful display.† But there: Orlando was not an English schoolboy but a Sicilian; and, as Hankey may momentarily have forgotten, he had steered his country successfully through a world war.

The coming of Fascism in 1922 and the rise of Benito Mussolini left Sicily unimpressed. The island had always been considered the least Fascist part of Italy; in the elections of 1921 the party won no seats there at all. Only in 1924, when *Il Duce* ('The Leader') – as he liked to be called – was firmly in power, were Sicilian Fascists elected: 38 out of 57. In that year, however, something happened which did immense damage to the Fascist reputation. A courageous young parliamentarian named Giacomo Matteotti had for some time been voicing his opposition to the party and all it stood for; and in the early summer of 1924 he published a book, *The Fascists Exposed: A Year of Fascist Domination*. Then, on 10 June, he was seized by a group of thugs, bundled into a car and stabbed repeatedly

---

* For all his charmlessness, Sonnino was a remarkable man. Born in Egypt to an Italian Jewish businessman and his Welsh wife, he had been brought up in the Church of England, was twice Prime Minister of Italy, wrote passionately about Dante's Beatrice and, in 1909, flew with Wilbur Wright.

† Margaret MacMillan, *Peacemakers*, p. 288.

with a carpenter's file as he fought to escape. The whole country was outraged; perhaps at that moment, if the King and the leading liberal politicians had had the courage to make a determined effort, they could have thrown out Mussolini once and for all. But they hesitated too long; and while they dithered, democracy died.

Matteotti's corpse was recovered only ten weeks later. The Duce's personal involvement was long debated, but was eventually established beyond reasonable doubt, and several distinguished Sicilians – among them old Orlando – broke off relations with him in consequence. The Sicilian* playwright Luigi Pirandello, who was in the process of joining the party at the time the murder occurred, hesitated before going any further, but eventually decided in favour of membership. It was not for another three years that he was furiously to tear his party card to pieces in front of a horrified secretary-general. After that and until his death in 1936 he was kept under close surveillance by Mussolini's secret police.

In Sicily itself, Mussolini achieved surprisingly little. By nature a publicist and a showman, he liked to hit the headlines; compared with the burgeoning Italian overseas empire or the dramatic industrial developments in the north, the island offered little scope for his type of exhibitionism. At one moment he actually boasted that he had solved all Sicilian problems; a magazine entitled *The Problems of Sicily* was obliged to change its name. On the mainland, railways were electrified and the country criss-crossed with a network of *autostrade*, while in Africa road-building also continued apace. Meanwhile, many Sicilian villages remained connected to one another, as they had been for centuries, only by a dry riverbed.

On 3 January 1925, the Duce declared himself dictator. Now at last he was ready to tackle the Mafia. He was not the sort of man who could tolerate any challenge to his own authority, least of all from an organization so mysterious and so powerful. Moreover, he had been conscious, during his two visits to Sicily, that the local bosses were distinctly disinclined to show him the respect to which he was generally accustomed. On one of these visits he took mortal

---

* He was born in 1867 in a village with the somehow prophetic name of Kaos – 'chaos' – a suburb of Agrigento.

offence when the boss of Piana dei Greci, Don Ciccio Cuccia, publicly proclaimed that his visitor needed no police escort – since Cuccia's own presence offered protection enough. By now, too, the Honoured Society had acquired an international reputation. It was plain, in short, that Sicily was not big enough for Mussolini and the Mafia. For the sake of his own self-esteem, one of them would have to go. He summoned Cesare Mori.

Mori was a northerner, born in Pavia, and was already in his middle fifties. He had grown up in an orphanage and had studied at the military academy in Turin. Having joined the police, he could already look back on two periods of service in Sicily, the first in Castelvetrano – where he had distinguished himself by capturing the notorious bandit Paolo Grisalfi – and the second in 1919 when, in Caltabellotta, he had made more than three hundred arrests in a single night. On that occasion he is said to have remarked to a member of his staff:

> These people have not yet understood that brigands and the Mafia are two different things. We have hit the first, who are undoubtedly the most visible aspect of Sicilian criminality, but not the most dangerous one. The truly lethal blow to the Mafia will be given when we are able to make roundups not only among Indian figs, but in prefectures, police headquarters, employers' mansions and – why not? – some ministries.

In 1924 he was appointed Prefect of Trapani; but his power in Sicily really began only on 20 October 1925 when Mussolini transferred him to Palermo, with special powers over the entire island. His job could be simply stated: to eradicate the Mafia. The telegram appointing him made its terms clear enough:

> Your Excellency has *carte blanche*; the authority of the State must absolutely, I repeat absolutely, be re-established in Sicily. If the laws still in force hinder you, this will be no problem: we shall draw up new laws.

Mori started as he meant to go on. In his first two months he made another five hundred arrests, and in January 1926 he moved against the little hill town of Gangi, surrounding it, cutting off its communications with the outside world, making some 450 more arrests and butchering all its cattle in the town square. This was to be the pattern for the next three and a half years, all over western Sicily. 'The Iron Prefect', as he was called, was fighting the Mafia, and he did not hesitate to use Mafia methods. He cheerfully ordered torture when he considered it necessary, and thought nothing of holding women and children hostage until their menfolk surrendered.

The grim work was still in progress when, on Ascension Day, 26 May 1927, Mussolini addressed the Chamber of Deputies to deliver a progress report on five years of Fascist rule. The keynote was, not altogether surprisingly, one of self-congratulation: under his guidance, he claimed, Italy was now greater than it had been at any time since the days of the Roman Empire. Much of his speech was concerned with the Mori operation in Sicily, where murders were down from 675 in 1923 to 299 in 1926. When, he asked oratorically, will the struggle against the Mafia come to an end? 'It will come to an end not just when there are no longer any mafiosi, but when Sicilians can no longer even remember the Mafia.'

It was another two years before Mori was recalled to Rome. After well over 11,000 arrests, he had left the judiciary with a huge task. The subsequent Mafia trials – one of which numbered 450 defendants – were to continue until 1932. Meanwhile, Mori published a book of memoirs in which he declared that the Mafia had been finally destroyed, and that Sicily had won its last battle against organized crime.

He was wrong, of course. He had indeed dealt *Cosa Nostra* a heavy blow, but it was not dead – far, far from it.

In 1937 Mussolini paid his third visit to Sicily. By then Italian troops had invaded and occupied Ethiopia which, together with the already existing colonies of Eritrea and Italian Somaliland and the more recently acquired Libya, constituted a quite considerable African holding; and Sicily, being nearer to Africa than anywhere else in Italy, had thus gained new importance; 'indeed,' declared the Duce, 'it is the geographic centre of the Empire.' He would, he continued, inaugurate one of the happiest epochs in the island's 4,000 years of history. This would involve, first of all, the demolition of the vast shantytown outside Messina inhabited by the thousands rendered homeless by the earthquake. (Many of those affected might have been excused for wondering why twenty-nine years had been allowed to pass before any action was taken at all.) The entire *latifondo* – those vast tracts of land owned by absentee proprietors, still known as 'fiefs' and still being cultivated, if at all, by medieval and feudal methods – would be liquidated; and all Sicilians would henceforth be properly and adequately housed. New villages would be built across the island.

It seemed that Italy would never understand. One of these villages was actually built near Acireale, but the local peasants refused to move from the one-room huts in which they had always lived with their livestock, and a whole company of Tuscan peasantry had to be imported to occupy it. With yet another lesson unlearnt, eight more villages were constructed – and suffered similar fates. Several meetings were held to decide upon their names; none, as far as anybody remembered, to discuss water supplies or electrification.* But by this time the government had other things to think about. The Second World War had begun.

---

* Electricity supplies in Sicily in 1939 were only about ten percent of the average for Italy as a whole.

17

The Second World War

WHEN GERMANY INVADED Poland on 1 September 1939, Mussolini declared his support for Hitler, with whom he had concluded the so-called 'Pact of Steel' four months before. He did not immediately declare war – the Chief of the General Staff, Marshal Pietro Badoglio, having warned him that Italy simply did not have enough tanks, armoured cars and aircraft. To get involved in the European conflict at this point would, said Badoglio, be tantamount to suicide. Nine months later, however, the situation had changed dramatically. Norway, Belgium and Holland had been invaded; France was falling. On 10 June Italy declared war. Mussolini had hoped to help himself to Savoy, Nice, Corsica, Tunisia and Algeria from the French, but to his disgust Germany signed an armistice establishing the collaborationist government under Marshal Pétain at Vichy, which retained control over southern France and all its colonies.

So far as North Africa was concerned, only Egypt was left; and in September 1940 the Duce sent a large Italian force across the Libyan border. The British troops stationed in Egypt were at first hopelessly outnumbered; their counterattack, however, proved far more successful than expected and resulted in massive numbers of prisoners. So decisive was the Italian defeat that Hitler was obliged to send out his Afrikakorps, under the command of General Erwin Rommel. Only then did the British lose the initiative, ultimately to regain it at the Battle of El Alamein in October–November 1942.

The story of the Desert War is not ours, but it exemplifies the several successive humiliations suffered by Italy between 1940 and 1943. Mussolini's invasion of Greece in October 1940 once again forced Hitler to send troops to his rescue; and by the beginning of

1943 disaster threatened him from every side. Half the Italian troops serving in Russia had been annihilated; both his North African and his Balkan adventures had been dismal failures. The Italians had had enough. Then, in July 1943, the Allies launched an operation which, as well as giving them a foothold in Europe, promised to remove Mussolini from the scene for good. They invaded Sicily.

For Sicily, hitherto, the war had been disastrous. As an island, it had suffered even more acutely than the rest of Italy. The ferry boats to the mainland were disrupted; the export market largely disappeared, while imports became irregular and uncertain; sometimes the Sicilians had found themselves with virtually nothing to eat but their own oranges. The rationing system was a bad joke; the black market reigned supreme. For the Mafia, on the other hand, conditions could hardly have been better. With a good deal of help from its branches in New York and Chicago, in the last years of peace it had already begun a swift recovery from the Mori reign of terror; and by 1943, whatever Mussolini might have said or believed, it was flourishing.

American intelligence officers, somewhat better informed than the Duce, understood that for the projected invasion to be successful it was vitally important to have the Mafia firmly on the Allied side. They therefore made careful approaches to the dominant boss of gangland crime in the United States, a Sicilian named Salvatore ('Lucky') Luciano. He had in fact been in prison since 1936 on compulsory prostitution charges, but was still very much in command. In late 1942, after long discussions, the two sides struck a deal. Luciano would have his sentence commuted; in return, he made two promises. The first was that his friend Albert Anastasia, who ran the notorious Murder Inc. and who also controlled the American docks, would protect the waterfront and prevent dockworker strikes for the duration of hostilities. The second was that he, Luciano, would contact other friends in Sicily, who would in turn ensure that the invasion would run as smoothly as possible.

There was, in fact, still a good deal of opposition to the Sicilian plan.* Many American generals strongly advised against any major

---

* For much of the information in the following pages I am indebted to Rick Atkinson's superb account of the Sicilian operation in *Day of Battle*.

initiative in the Mediterranean; all available Allied power should, they argued, be concentrated in Britain and set about preparing for the great cross-Channel invasion that would – in theory at least – lead them straight to Berlin. Others – including the Chief of Naval Operations Admiral Ernest J. King – believed that all available troops were needed in the Far East. The doubters were however eventually won over by Winston Churchill, during talks held in Washington in May 1943. The first objective, he told them, was to get Italy out of the war; possession of Sicily would provide air bases for attacks on the mainland and perhaps on other places in occupied Europe; it was not unlikely that Italy might then be persuaded to denounce the 'Pact of Steel'. The second was to deflect Axis strength from Russia. 'Never forget,' he growled, 'that there are 185 German divisions against the Russians . . . We are not at present in contact with any.'

Operation Husky had been conceived on a grand scale. It amounted to nothing less than the landing of two armies on the southeast coast of Sicily, armies which would reclaim for the Allies the first significant area of land in Europe since the beginning of the war. This involved the mustering of more than 3,000 vessels of every size and shape – in the words of Admiral Henry Kent Hewitt, who commanded the U.S. Eighth Fleet, 'the most gigantic fleet in the world's history'. In the first instance it would carry the American Seventh Army under the celebrated gun-toting General George S. Patton and the British Eighth Army under General (later Field Marshal) Sir Bernard Montgomery. The latter also included the 1st Division of the Canadian army and a Polish corps. Each of the two main armies would number about 80,000, though these figures were soon to be substantially increased. The island was thought to be defended by about 300,000 Axis troops; fortunately, however, the majority of them were Italians, who by now had little stomach for the fight.

Few Allied generals can have hated each other more than Patton and Montgomery. Both of them, in their different ways, loved the limelight; but there the similarity stopped. Patton loved war; Monty loved himself. Patton was a blood-and-guts man, his philosophy best summed up in the celebrated speech to the U.S. Third Army just before the Normandy landings:

We're not just going to shoot the bastards, we're going to rip out their living goddamned guts and use them to grease the treads of our tanks. We're going to murder those lousy Hun cocksuckers by the bushel-fucking-basket . . . The Nazis are the enemy. Wade into them, spill their blood or they will spill yours . . . When shells are hitting all around you and you wipe the dirt from your face and you realize that it's not dirt, it's the blood and gut of what was once your best friend, you'll know what to do . . .

All right, you sons of bitches. You know how I feel. I'll be proud to lead you wonderful guys in battle any time, anywhere. That's all.

Montgomery was very different. Standing just five foot seven, he looked at first glance, according to a Canadian journalist, like 'a rather unsuccessful dry goods shopkeeper'. He preferred to sit alone in the back of his car 'so there won't be any doubt which one is me'. The moment he spoke, on the other hand, there could be no doubt at all. The most revealing story about him tells of when, 'sailing about in a big command car', he stopped to ask a Canadian unit,

Do you know why I never have defeats? Well, I will tell you. My reputation as a great general means too much to me . . . You can't be a great general and have defeats . . . So you can be quite sure, any time I commit you to battle you are bound to win.

There is no doubt that he was a superb leader, beloved – almost worshipped – by his men; occasionally, too, he could display a little touch of genius. But he was bumptious and insufferably arrogant, ever insisting on his own way and, where his fellow generals were concerned, seldom allowing a generous word to pass his lips. 'One must remember,' murmured one of his commanders, 'that he is not quite a gentleman.' More than once, during the Sicilian campaign, he put the whole operation at serious risk.

There was one other Allied commander who deserves a mention here, not only because he detested both Patton – his immediate superior – and Montgomery equally. This was Lieutenant-General Omar Nelson Bradley. Operation Husky had not started well for General Bradley; he had just undergone an emergency operation for haemorrhoids, known in the U.S. Army as 'cavalry tonsils' – and was, he confessed, feeling worse than he had ever felt in his life. Acute seasickness had hardly helped, and the rubber ring on which he was obliged to sit when he came ashore in his jeep had constituted a further blow to his dignity. But unlike his two colleagues, Bradley was sublimely unconscious of his image. He hated Patton's flamboyance as much as Monty's egoism; he had, according to the famous journalist Ernie Pyle, 'no idiosyncrasies, no superstitions, no hobbies'. He was a soldier, and that was enough.

As commander of II Corps, Bradley had an unexpected problem to tackle: the deluge of Italian prisoners. During a single week in Sicily, the number of these prisoners comfortably exceeded the total taken during the whole of the First World War. Many of them were described as being 'in a mood of fiesta . . . filling the air with laughter and song'. Some American units were obliged to post signs saying 'No Prisoners Accepted Here' or advising those wishing to give themselves up to come back another day.

From the first, the planning ran anything but smoothly. Eisenhower's original intention was that the British should invade in the southeast, seizing Augusta and Syracuse, while the Americans landed in the west to occupy Palermo. This predictably failed to appeal to Montgomery, who claimed that to divide the available forces in such a way would result in 'a first-class military disaster'. On the contrary, he continued, the two armies should both attack in the southeast, remaining together for mutual support. It followed that they should ideally be under a single command – his own. 'I,' he wrote in his diary – a good many of his sentences started that way – 'should run Husky.' Monty had a poor opinion of American fighting power; as a result, long before the invasion fleet got under way, he had made himself thoroughly unpopular with the American General Staff. As usual, the dispute ended in another compromise: the armies should remain closer than originally planned, but still a fair distance from each other. The British would land between Cape Passero – the southeastern corner of the island – and Syracuse, with the Canadian 1st Division anchoring their left wing on the Pachino peninsula. Meanwhile, the American debarkation would take place around the Gulf of Gela, some thirty-five miles to the west.

But the gods were angry. Few places in the world can be more certain of calm weather in July than the south coast of Sicily. On Thursday the 8th, however, it became clear that 1943 was to be an exception to the rule. By Friday afternoon a stiff northwest wind had got up and was rapidly approaching gale force, the waves soon rising so high that the smaller ships regularly lost sight of one another altogether. Debarkation was scheduled for early Saturday morning. Fortunately the wind would, the forecasters predicted, drop soon after nightfall; for many of those present, however – hideously seasick and terrified into the bargain – that night of 9 July was the unhappiest of their lives.

By the evening of the first day the Allies had landed 80,000 men on the coast between Licata and Syracuse. The Germans were taken largely by surprise; Operation Mincemeat, when in April the body of a supposed Royal Marine officer had been dropped off the Spanish coast with fabricated plans suggesting that the real invasion would be aimed at Sardinia and Greece, had fooled them all from Hitler down. There were nevertheless two German divisions attached to the Italian Sixth Army, and the fighting was fierce. Whether or not the Mafia was able to make much difference is not easy to judge; resistance to the invaders was certainly greater in the east, where the Honoured Society was a good deal less powerful. But nowhere did the Allies have an easy ride, and the campaign was not helped by the constant bickering between the two commanders in the field.

Bickering, in fact, was putting it mildly. As early as 13 July Montgomery, having already captured Syracuse but meeting with serious resistance south of Catania, had arbitrarily split his force into two, with some of it sticking to the coast but the rest heading off to the west towards Enna. This, as he well knew, was deep in the American sector; in giving such an order he was in fact cutting straight across Patton's line of advance. Only when he had done so did he inform his superior, General Sir Harold Alexander, Eisenhower's deputy. Alexander rather weakly allowed him to continue, ordering Patton to get out of his way. Eisenhower, who always disapproved of any criticism of the British, refused to intervene; but the rest of the American top brass were predictably furious. Bradley later condemned the action as 'the most arrogant, egotistical, selfish and dangerous move in the whole of combined operations in World War II'. Patton himself was virtually speechless with rage.

On Saturday morning, 17 July, he flew over to Tunisia, where Alexander had his headquarters, to complain. Was it really his job, he demanded, prodding the map with a stubby finger, to do nothing but protect the rear of the Eighth Army? If Montgomery were to be protected, then surely by far the best tactic would be to split the island in two by striking off with his own Seventh Army to the northwest and taking Palermo. Alexander hesitated, but finally agreed. Patton, he saw, had suffered enough; it was time to indulge him a little. It was lucky that he did; he had no idea that on the previous day a detachment of the Seventh had marched on Agrigento and captured it with hardly a struggle, taking 6,000 prisoners. The Americans were already well on their way.

The following Thursday they were on the heights above Palermo, but Patton forbade any further advance until his tanks arrived. There was no need to use them, but he knew that they would add considerably to the effect of his triumphal entry into the capital. Not that there was very much left of it; a long month of Allied bombing had taken its toll. Still, the formal entry and official surrender of the city took place that same evening, and the victorious general established himself in the royal palace, built by the Normans on the foundations of its Arabic predecessor some eight centuries before. The operation had been a success, there was no doubt of that: some 2,300 Axis troops had been killed or wounded, and no fewer than 53,000 – nearly all Italians – had been captured. American casualties were a little below 300. Eastern Sicily, however, remained to be taken, and by this time Patton had a new light in his eye: a determination to beat Monty to Messina.

Three days after Patton entered Palermo, on Sunday, 25 July, Benito Mussolini received a summons from King Victor Emmanuel III. The Duce was by now a pale shadow of what he had been the year before. Listless and apathetic, he had scarcely reacted when on 24 July the Fascist Grand Council met in Rome and Count Dino

Grandi – who had until 1939 been Italy's ambassador to Britain – proposed a motion asking the King to resume full constitutional authority, which would effectively remove Mussolini from power. On the following day he was informed by Victor Emmanuel that Marshal Pietro Badoglio would henceforth take over the government. The Duce was now, His Majesty explained, 'the most hated man in Italy'; there was, regrettably, no alternative to his dismissal. He was arrested as he left the palace, bundled unceremoniously into the back of an ambulance and driven to a police barracks in Via Legnano. As the news spread through Rome jubilant crowds gathered, shouting '*Benito è finito!*' There were wild celebrations and dancing in the streets. All signs of Fascism disappeared as if by magic. In the words of Badoglio, 'it fell, as was fitting, like a rotten pear.'

Among the British and American troops, on the other hand, the rejoicing was distinctly muted. They had too many other things to think about. The deaths, the hideous wounds, the sights, sounds and smells inseparable from any field of battle were bad enough; but in Sicily they were only the beginning. They had also to contend with the merciless heat; with dengue, sandfly and Malta fevers; with almost universal diarrhoea; with venereal disease, more widespread in Sicily than in any other theatre of the war; and – perhaps worst of all – with malaria, which claimed some 10,000 victims in the Seventh Army and nearly 12,000 in the Eighth. The military hospitals, it need hardly be said, were worked off their feet.

It was to one of these hospitals – the 15th Evacuation Hospital near Nicosia in Cyprus – that, on Tuesday, 3 August, General George S. Patton arrived on a visit. He stopped before a young private with acute psychoneurosis, combined with malaria and a temperature of over 102 degrees, and asked him where he had been wounded. The boy replied that he hadn't; 'I guess I can't take it,' he added. To the astonishment of those around, Patton slapped him across the face, seized him by the collar and kicked him forcibly out of the tent. 'Don't admit this son of a bitch,' he roared, 'I don't want yellow-bellied bastards like him hiding their lousy cowardice around here, stinking up this place of honour. Send him back to his unit at once.' A week later, at another hospital, there was a similar occurrence. This time Patton drew one of his pistols and brandished it in the face of the young soldier before giving him a heavy clout on the side of the head.

It was not long before detailed reports of these two incidents were on Eisenhower's desk. The Commander-in-Chief was in a dilemma. Striking a subordinate was a court-martial offence. He wrote to Patton, 'I must so seriously question your good judgment and self-discipline as to raise serious doubts in my mind as to your future usefulness . . . No letter that I have been called upon to write in my military career has caused me the mental anguish of this one.' Finally, Patton was ordered to apologize personally to the two men, and to make five separate public statements to various sections of the army expressing his deep regret. His contrition, however, was little more than skin-deep. 'If I had to do it over again,' he wrote to a friend, 'I would not make a single change.'

One can imagine Montgomery's satisfaction at hearing of the disgrace of his rival, but also his frustration as he contemplated Patton's entry into Palermo and imagined him pressing on towards Messina. His right flank was still blocked by heavy German resistance at Catania, while the rest of his army was still floundering through the foothills to the southwest of Mount Etna. Then, during the first days of August, the pendulum swung. The Americans took almost a week to capture Troina; at the same time, the German forces which had been blocking Catania retreated to the north. There was by this time no question that they could hold the island any longer, and they were making for the mainland. At last the Eighth Army swept into Catania – to find that only twenty percent of the buildings were habitable.

It was on 11 August that the German evacuation of Sicily began. Astonishingly, it was allowed to continue. As far as anyone has been able to discover, neither before Operation Husky began nor while it was in progress was there any coordinated plan for blocking the Strait of Messina. The thought seems not to have occurred to Eisenhower, or to Alexander, or indeed to anyone else. As a result, some 40,000 Germans and 70,000 Italians were allowed to escape from the island, together with 10,000 vehicles and 47 tanks. They constituted four whole divisions – divisions which in the months to come were to account for many thousands of Allied lives.

But Patton was not concerned with escaping Germans. He was thinking only of getting to Messina before Montgomery. His men were exhausted, and many by now seriously dehydrated in the heat, which registered some 95 degrees Fahrenheit.* He himself was running a temperature of 103 degrees† from sandfly fever, but he drove them on relentlessly. Montgomery, though now once again pressing forward, could not hope to catch up; and so it was that on the morning of Tuesday, 17 August, Patton drew up his command vehicle on the heights above Messina. A number of his advance troops had in fact entered the city on the previous evening, with orders 'to see that the British did not capture the city from us'; but the General was as always determined on a formal entry. Spasmodic shooting and shelling by the retreating Germans was ignored, while the mayor ceremonially surrendered what remained of his city. Alexander was immediately informed, and cabled Churchill: 'By 10 a.m. this morning, the last German soldier was flung out of Sicily, and the whole island is now in our hands.'

Its conquest had not been cheap – 12,800 British casualties and 8,800 American, as against 29,000 Axis dead and wounded – but it had given the Allies virtual control of the Mediterranean, together with some 10,000 square miles of valuable territory on which in the following months countless new airfields were to spring up like mushrooms. It had brought down Mussolini, and had done much to relieve pressure on the Russian front, since German troops now had to be brought in urgently to defend Italy and the Balkans. Finally, it had taught the Allies a number of valuable lessons. In Africa they had fought on flat desert; in Sicily they had encountered rugged hillsides for the first time, and had discovered that the difficulties of such terrain had been seriously underestimated. There had also been communication problems, several of which had proved disastrous. Infantry, artillery, naval and air forces were all too often left uncertain – and occasionally entirely ignorant – of what the

---

* 35 degrees Celsius.
† 39.5 degrees Celsius.

others were doing; so dangerous was it for Allied aircraft to fly over their own ships that their prescribed altitude of 5,000 feet had to be increased to 10,000. In the course of one particular operation twenty-three U.S. aircraft had been destroyed and another thirty-seven badly damaged, all by friendly fire, resulting in the loss of over four hundred lives – one of the worst such incidents in modern warfare.

The forty days and forty nights of Operation Husky had also been marked by a development that caused Eisenhower – and, one suspects, Winston Churchill himself – deep disquiet: a marked deterioration in Anglo-American relations. For some of this the conduct of Montgomery was unquestionably to blame; most of his American colleagues – who had not seen or heard him among his men – were longing to see the last of him, and could not begin to understand why Eisenhower tolerated him, or how he could have accepted Monty's invitation to lunch in Taormina at the end of August. But the differences ran deeper: on the British side, jealousy of the comparative wealth of their allies, the superiority of their food and cigarettes as well as of their military equipment; on the American, a vague feeling that they were being patronized, and on occasion even secretly mocked. After the invasion of mainland Italy the situation began to show a marked improvement, particularly after Monty's departure in December; but in Sicily it was serious indeed, and boded ill for the future.

Epilogue

THE ALLIED ARMIES were enthusiastically welcomed in Sicily, and for good reason. They brought freedom from dictatorship; more important still, they brought food, together with drugs to help control malaria, which was still taking a huge annual toll of Sicilian lives. The prevailing political confusion also gave the Sicilians opportunities for self-determination. Separatism had been in the air for many years; now it came once again to the fore, and a petition that Sicily should henceforth be an independent republic was actually submitted to the San Francisco Conference.*

The Mafia, meanwhile, had benefited greatly from its collusion with American intelligence. It was, for example, a surprise to quite a few people in 1944 to find Lucky Luciano's friend and fellow mobster Vito Genovese – who was still wanted by the FBI on several charges, including murder – in American uniform, serving as an interpreter. When a few months later Genovese was caught running a major black market operation which involved stealing heavy lorries from the U.S. Army, the investigating officer had to endure months of prevarication from the military authorities before being reluctantly permitted to ship him back to America to face trial – unnecessarily, as it happened, because in June 1946 all charges against him were dismissed for lack of evidence. (This was largely due to the fact that the two principal prosecution witnesses had both been shot dead – one of them in a prison cell where he was being held in protective custody.)

At this time, too, many Mafia bosses were appointed to responsible positions in the administration simply because there was no

* This was held from April to June 1945, to prepare for the establishment of the United Nations in October.

one else. Their Fascist predecessors – several thousand of them – had fled; the Allies had been obliged to find replacements, more often than not acting on the advice of their not always reliable interpreters and liaison officers. Thus it was that such notorious figures as Don Calogero Vizzini – described by the media as 'the boss of bosses' – and Don Genco Russo acquired postwar positions of trust and even distinction.* There is of course always a possibility that the occupying forces never really minded very much; their interest was to keep Sicily quiet while they advanced up the Italian peninsula, and if the Mafia could do this better than anyone else, then the Mafia it would have to be.

In February 1944 the Allies handed Sicily over to the Italian authorities; and such was the strength of separatist feeling that the Italian government at last took the step which many people thought it should have taken the best part of a century before: it granted to the island a remarkably large degree of autonomy – hoping that such a measure would not only assuage the separatists but would also give the Sicilians a new sense of political responsibility. A legislative assembly was established in the royal palace at Palermo, with its own cabinet of ministers, each of its members serving a five-year term. It was given almost complete control over industry, agriculture and mining, as well as very considerable authority over public order and communications. All this was good news indeed for the people of Palermo; their city was once again an administrative capital, and hundreds of new jobs suddenly became available. The Italian government, moreover, finally recognized that Sicily could not continue as the disgrace it had been for so long, and voted it a substantial subsidy. Morale soared, and with it came civic pride, of a kind which had hitherto been noticeably absent. The devolution also ended all talk of separatism; by 1950 the separatist party had virtually ceased to exist.

The Mafia, on the other hand, continued as it always had. Seeing

---

* When Don Calogero died on 10 July 1954, his funeral was attended by several thousand peasants in black, together with politicians, priests and fellow bosses. It was reported in the *New York Times*, and the local Christian Democrat headquarters closed for a week.

the potential threat to its interests from the Communists and Socialists – whose numbers were steadily increasing – its political alignment was now firmly Christian Democrat, which explains why during successive Christian Democrat governments so many trade union leaders came to sticky ends and why, despite repeated representations, no firm action was ever taken against it. The forces of law and order preferred to concentrate their attention on another scourge of Sicily, banditry and brigandage. These bandits and brigands were sometimes mafiosi, sometimes not; but they tended to operate outside the normal Mafia perimeters, largely in their own personal interests. And the greatest of them all – a man who became a legend, and whose name is still remembered far beyond the coasts of Sicily – was Salvatore Giuliano.

It was in September 1943 that Giuliano, then twenty years old, was found by the carabinieri to be carrying two sacks of black market grain. During the discussion that followed, one of the officers drew a gun; Giuliano shot him dead. He then took to the mountains. The following January, he organized the escape from prison of eight of his fellow villagers. Six of them joined him, and with them he began a campaign of banditry, extortion and kidnapping. He was not himself a mafioso, but the Mafia, and in particular the *cosca* of Monreale,* protected him. There was a Robin Hood side to his character: although he certainly robbed the rich of a good deal more than he gave to the poor, he seemed to enjoy administering rough justice – for example, by shooting the postmaster of his home village of Montelepre, who was stealing parcels from America. He was also outstandingly handsome. The picture magazines of Europe and America were enchanted when he broke into the house of the Duchess of Pratameno: he kissed her hand and showed all the proper respect for her rank; but this did not prevent him from demanding all her jewellery and, when she refused, threatening to kidnap her children. Even this, however, was not quite so

---

* Monreale, known to most of us only for its cathedral and superb mosaics, has always been *mafiosissimo*. Lying as it does above Palermo, it can cut off the water flowing down to the *giardini* – the orchards – and can also keep an eye on all goods arriving in Palermo from the interior.

bad as it sounded, at least if we are to believe the Giuliano legend: the children he kidnapped were said to be carefully looked after, fed off the fat of the land and given appropriate medicine when necessary. If they were bored, their captors would, we are told, even read them stories – although, since few Sicilian brigands could read at all, it is not easy to see how this was done.

Such a career could not last for long. Giuliano's life should have ended in a hail of police bullets. It was in fact the Mafia who decided to get rid of him – though just how it did so is, in the highest Mafia tradition, open to doubt. In the course of a mildly ridiculous trial held at Viterbo in 1951, his erstwhile closest friend and fellow bandit Gaspare Pisciotta confessed to drugging him on 5 July 1950 and then shooting him while he slept. This is almost certainly untrue, but we shall never know for sure since some time later Pisciotta, while serving a life sentence in the Ucciardone prison – sharing, incidentally, a cell with his father – was poisoned with 20 centigrams of strychnine: enough, we are told, to kill forty dogs. Astonishingly – at least it would have been astonishing if it had occurred anywhere else – the poisoner was never brought to justice. The Mafia keeps its secrets jealously – so jealously that for twenty years and more after Giuliano's death all those who had been involved were shot down as they emerged from prison.*

The above very brief summary of the life of Sicily's most notorious but – despite his 430-odd victims – best-loved bandit must serve this book as an epilogue. Obviously, the history of Sicily will never be finished until the entire island disappears under the waves; but whereas an account of a specific period can be rounded to an elegant close, one that takes as its subject merely a given region of the world must be brought to an arbitrary end; and this book is long enough already.

In fact, apart from the discovery of oil in 1953, Sicily's recent

* The fullest account in English of the circumstances surrounding Giuliano's death will be found in Gaia Servadio, *Mafioso*.

history has been relatively uneventful; the average reader – if such there be – will, I believe, find in these pages most of what he wishes to know. With any luck, too, they may set him thinking. Why has this ravishingly beautiful island always been so unhappy? I spoke of Sicily's unhappiness in my opening paragraph, and described it as well as I could; but I did not really provide an answer to the question. I come back to it now when my work is done, and am still at a loss. And there are other questions too. Is there in the whole world any other stretch of water, less than two miles across, which has had such an extraordinary effect as has the Strait of Messina? Had Sicily not been an island, how different its history would have been – though few Sicilians, I suspect, would wish the map to be other than it is.★

And yet, for all its troubled history, Sicily remains a jewel. Nowhere else in the world will you find such a wealth of monuments from so wide a variety of civilizations – Greek, Roman, Byzantine, Arab, Norman, German, French, Spanish, Neapolitan – gathered in so small a space and combined with so much that is Sicily's own: the dazzling baroque, for example, of Noto, Ragusa and Modica, the almost unbelievable stucco work of Giacomo Serpotta, even the traditional puppet theatre which, quite apart from its very considerable entertainment value, helps immeasurably in our understanding of the Sicilian people and their past.

For it is they who are the heroes of this story. A few, of course, have always been rich, and have usually managed over the years to acquire a vast plethora of titles reflecting their wealth. Like all European aristocracies, they have looked after themselves to the best of their ability, but we should reread *The Leopard* before we criticize them too much. In any case, they are relatively few. It is, as always, the poor, those who have drawn the shortest straw in

★ Successive Italian governments have long considered plans for a vast suspension road and rail bridge over the Strait. To allow for navigation beneath it, it would be the highest in the world, with each of its two supporting pillars taller than the Empire State Building in New York. There are, however, other serious problems, including Sicily's propensity for severe earthquakes. Preliminary work was begun under the Berlusconi government, but in February 2013 the project was abandoned for lack of funds.

the lottery of life, who constitute the vast majority and whom history – largely for want of evidence and written record – tends to overlook. The Sicilian poor have endured much over the centuries; they have known slavery, and many centuries of grinding poverty. Even the sun, for which we northerners instinctively envy them, is to them as much an enemy as a friend. They have coped as well as they can with the countless difficulties they have had to face, and if in the absence of any effective or remotely sympathetic government they have been obliged to evolve their own solutions – well, we can hardly blame them.

But, in the past century and a half, things have changed immeasurably for the better. Sicily may not be an independent nation – she has not had that distinction since Norman times – but within the republic of Italy she now enjoys her own regional government, her own regional assembly of ninety members and her own president, together with a considerable degree of local autonomy. In consequence, as I mentioned in the introduction to this book, I hope and believe that she is happier now than at any time in the last eight hundred years. Long, long may that happiness continue.

Acknowledgements

GEORGINA LAYCOCK IN London and Mika Kasuga in New York have worn out their fine-tooth combs on the text; my daughter Allegra Huston has copy-edited as only she can; my wife Mollie has made several invaluable suggestions. I am hugely grateful to them all.

Heartiest thanks, too, to Juliet Brightmore for the illustrations, and, as always, to Douglas Matthews, greatest indexer in the world; thanks also to Caroline Westmore.

A very special word, finally, to my agents Felicity Bryan and Michele Topham. They have piloted me through more books than I care to remember, and – who knows? – their work may not be finished yet.

Illustration Credits

～✦～

© akg-images: 4 above right/Alfio Garozzo, 5 above right/Schütze/ Rodemann, 5 below and 7 above/Hervé Champollion, 8 above/ Eric Lessing, 8 below/Album/Joseph Martin, 12 above right, 13 above, 15 below/Mondadori Portfolio. © Alamy: xvi *triskelion*, Sicily/ photo Marka, 2 above/Peter Adams Photography Ltd, 2 below/ Robert Harding World Imagery, 3 below/Visual&Written SL, 4 above left/John Heseltine, 4 below/LOOK Die Bildagentur dur Fotografen GmbH, 6 above/Heritage Image Partnership Ltd, 7 below/David Lyons, 9 and 12 above left/The Art Archive, 11 below/ funkyfood London-Paul Williams, 12 below and 13 below/World History Archive, 14 above left/Everett Collection Historical, 14 below/Classic Image, 16 above/Stock Italia, 16 below/Universal Images Group/DeAgostini. © Bridgeman Images: 6 below/Werner Forman Archive, 10 above left/Ashmolean Museum/University of Oxford UK, 10 above right/Guildhall Art Gallery/City of London, 10 below/Walker Art Gallery/National Museums Liverpool, 11 above/Private Collection. © Getty Images: 1/DEA/A. De Gregorio, 3 above/DEA/G. Dagli Orti, 5 above/DEA Picture Library, 15 above/Popperfoto. Private Collection: 14 above right.

Bibliography

Acton, Sir Harold, *The Bourbons of Naples, 1734–1825*, London, 1956

Al-Edrisi, Abu Abdullah Mohammed, *Géographie d'Edrisi*, trans. A. Jaubert, 2 vols, Paris, 1836

Allsop, K., *The Bootleggers: The Story of Chicago's Prohibition Era*, London, 1961

Amari, M., *History of the War of the Sicilian Vespers*, 3 vols, London, 1850
———, *Storia dei Musulmani di Sicilia*, 3 vols, Florence, 1854–72

Atkinson, R., *The Day of Battle: The War in Sicily and Italy, 1943–1944*, New York, 2007

Beevor, A., *The Second World War*, London, 2012

Blanch, L., *Scritti storici, a cura di Benedetto Croce*, Bari, 1945

Blessington, Countess of, *The Idler in Italy*, Paris, 1839

Cambridge Medieval History, 8 vols, Cambridge, 1911–36

Campolieti, G., *Il Re Bomba*, Milan, 2001

Caven, B., *Dionysius I: War-Lord of Sicily*, New Haven and London, 1990

Chalandon, F., *Histoire de la Domination Normande en Italie et en Sicile*, 2 vols, Paris, 1907

Cicero, *Selected Works*, ed. M. Grant, London, 1960

Collison Morley, L., *Naples Through the Centuries*, London, 1925

Constantine, D., *Fields of Fire: A Life of Sir William Hamilton*, London, 2001

Craven, R. Keppel, *A Tour through the Southern Provinces of the Kingdom of Naples*, London, 1821

Cronin, V., *The Golden Honeycomb*, London, 1954

Damas, Count Roger de, *Mémoires, publiés et annotés par Jacques Rambaud*, Paris, 1912

Davis, J. A., *Naples and Napoleon: Southern Italy and the European Revolutions, 1780–1860*, Oxford, 2006

Dickie, J., *Blood Brotherhoods*, London, 2011

Diodorus Siculus, *Universal History*, trans. C. H. Oldfather, Cambridge, MA, 1935

Eggenberger, D., *A Dictionary of Battles*, London, 1967

Enciclopedia Italiana

Finley, M. I., *A History of Sicily: Ancient Sicily to the Arab Conquest*, London, 1968

Fraser, F., *Beloved Emma: The Life of Emma, Lady Hamilton*, London, 1986

Freeman, E. A., *A History of Sicily*, 4 vols, London, 1891–94

Grady, E., *The Blue Guide to Sicily*, London and New York, 2006

Henderson, N., 'Charles III of Spain', *History Today*, November 1968

Johnston, R. M., *The Napoleonic Empire in Southern Italy*, London, 1904

———, ed., *Mémoire de Marie Caroline reine de Naples, intitulé 'De la Révolution du Royaume de Sicile, par un Témoin Oculaire'*, Cambridge, MA, and London, 1912

Knight, C., *Autobiography*, London, 1861

La Lumia, I., *Studi di storia siciliana*, 2 vols, Palermo, 1870

Livy, *Books 1–22*, trans. B. O. Foster, London and New York, 1919–29

———, *Books 23–30*, trans. Frank Gardner Moore, London and New York, 1940–50

Macchiavelli, N., *The Prince*, trans. G. Bull, London, 1963

Mack Smith, D., *A History of Sicily*, 2 vols, London, 1968

MacMillan, M., *Peacemakers: The Paris Conference of 1919 and its Attempt to End War*, London, 2001

Montet, Baronne du, *Souvenirs, 1785–1866*, Paris, 1914

Mori, C., *The Last Struggle with the Mafia*, London, 1933

Norwich, J. J., *The Normans in the South*, London, 1967

———, *The Kingdom in the Sun*, London, 1970

———, *The Middle Sea*, London, 2006

Oxford Classical Dictionary, The, Oxford, 1949

Pace, B., *Arte e Civiltà della Sicilia antica*, 4 vols, Rome and Naples, 1936–49

———, 'I barbari e i bizantini in Sicilia', *Archivio Storico Siciliano*, vols 35–6, Palermo, 1911

Pagano, G., *Avvenimenti del 1866: sette giorni d'insurrezione a Palermo*, Palermo, 1867

Pepe, Guglielmo, *Memorie intorno alla sua vita*, Paris, 1847

Petrie, Sir Charles, *King Charles III of Spain: An Enlightened Despot*, London, 1971

Plutarch, *Lives*, trans. B. Perrin, London, 1926

Polybius, *The Histories*, trans. W. R. Paton, Cambridge, MA, and London, 2010–12

Riall, L., *Sicily and the Reunification of Italy: Liberal Policy and Local Power, 1859–66*, Oxford, 1998

———, *Garibaldi: Invention of a Hero*, Yale, 2007

———, *Under the Volcano: Revolution in a Sicilian Town*, Oxford, 2013

Romano, S. F., *Breve storia della Sicilia: momenti e problemi della civiltà siciliana*, Turin, 1964

Runciman, S., *The Sicilian Vespers*, Cambridge, 1958

Scirocco, A., *Garibaldi, Citizen of the World*, trans. A. Cameron, Princeton, 2007

Servadio, G., *Mafioso: A History of the Mafia from Its Origins to the Present Day*, New York, 1976

Stefano, A. de, *Federico III d'Aragona, Re di Sicilia, 1296–1337*, Palermo, 1937

Thucydides, *The Peloponnesian War*, trans. Rex Warner, London, 1962

Touring Club Italiano: Sicilia, Milan, 1953

Trevelyan, Raleigh, *Princes Under the Volcano*, London, 1972

———, *The Companion Guide to Sicily*, London, 1996

Wheatcroft, A., *The Habsburgs: Embodying Empire*, London, 1996

Whitehouse, H. R., *The Collapse of the Kingdom of Naples*, New York, 1899

Woodhead, A. G., *The Greeks in the West*, London, 1962

Index